15-
50

HERITAGE

HERITAGE

By

Dr. Robert B. Pamplin, Jr.

COAUTHORS
Gary K. Eisler
Jeff Sengstack
John Domini

PROJECT EDITOR
John Domini

FOREWORD
by
Dr. Norman Vincent Peale

MASTERMEDIA • NEW YORK

In Heritage we have tried to record faithfully, and nowhere to create, a family's history. Reconstruction of events long past entails some speculation. Writing of conversations that no one recorded, we have given the characters words that they might well have spoken.

As we reach the recent past where living memory serves, we have tried to be faithful to the facts as we reliably know them to be. Any inaccuracies are inadvertent; any trespass on the character of any person, living or dead, is absolutely unintended.

Dr. Robert B. Pamplin, Jr.

CONTENTS

ACKNOWLEDGEMENT

The writing of *Heritage* has called upon the learned skills of many experts. The scope and depth of this book would not have been possible without their help. To them a large measure of gratitude is due and given.

FOREWORD

A THOUSAND YEARS is an unimaginably long time. We can almost picture our own lives within the span of a century. At 94 years old as of this writing, certainly I can. But no one has a lifespan of a millennium—no individual person can visualize the beginning of a thousand years from the end.

That is what is so fascinating about this book, coming as it does near the end of the Second Millenium: that it tells the story of the past thousand years through many individual generations of one family, who are "climbing the centuries."

The roots of the family extend back to Viking Scandinavia, to France and Spain and England, then reach to America, the Old South and the Pacific

Northwest. The family is older than the countries where they have lived, than the languages they have spoken, than the religious denominations to which they have belonged, than the economic or political systems under which they have lived.

Those of you who have read my book, *The Power of Positive Thinking,* may recall that I was reluctant to complete its writing. There were so many stories yet to be told of all the wonderful things that had been done for people through the "Higher Power"—that is also called God.

There are so many wonderful stories to tell, God has done so much good in this world, that I wished I could have simply kept going with *The Power of Positive Thinking.* And that is another appeal of *Heritage.*

Here is a single family line receiving help from the Higher Power, generation by generation, with challenges most of us have never dreamed of facing, and overcoming through positive attitudes. This book tells of family members whose lives are affected by some of the greatest events of the past thousand years. These include the Crusades, the signing of the Magna Carta, the Black Plague, the Renaissance and the Reformation, the discovery of America, and the ascendancy of England over Spain.

The positive attitudes of the individuals in this book helped them prevail over their outward circumstances—whether poor or rich, whether at war or at peace, whether ill or well. In that respect, this book is not exactly a sequel to *The Power of Positive Thinking*. I wrote that book as a practical, direct-action, self-improvement manual. But in *Heritage* you will see those principles embodied in the lives of its characters.

In addition to reminding you of *The Power of Positive Thinking*, this book, *Heritage*, may remind you of others as well. It is like *Roots* for its dramatized investigation of ancestors' lives across many generations. As with *Roots*, the authors have started with documented facts about the family members and about the times in which they lived. Using as many authentic quotes as possible from historic figures known to have been acquainted with family members, as well as known circumstances about their lives, the writers then reconstructed and dramatized their life stories. This makes the book especially fascinating at the end of this millenium, when genealogy ranks only behind stamp and coin collecting as the nation's most popular hobby.

Heritage is like James Mitchener's *The Source* in the historic depth and perspective it offers on English and American political, social and economic history. Here one sees the Black Plague reveal how helpless were the prayers and rituals of the early Catholic Church in the face of the relentless pestilence. This exposed weakness undermined the authority of the church, and ultimately led to the Reformation.

It is through the Reformation, *Heritage* illustrates, that widespread personal study of the Bible, made possible by invention of the printing press, created attitudes that aided the triumph of capitalism over feudalism, and England over Spain.

But in Protestantism there were also inherent contradictions that led ultimately to the rise of Oliver Cromwell and the English Civil War. There may be few other books to offer the remarkable insight *Heritage* does into the English roots of the American Civil War.

This book goes even further, showing how the South's humiliating defeat led to this family's determination to succeed. You will read how the family fortunes fell after the War, but how generation by generation they succeeded beyond anyone's dreams. There may be few books other than *Gone With The Wind* to present the Southern view so eloquently—or so convincingly. And there are probably few others that tell so well what makes the South the South, from the heritage of slavery to the tobacco and cotton economy.

As the biography of powerful businessmen, this book may remind you of *Iacocca*. No one has built a company's worth faster than Bob Pamplin built Georgia-Pacific Corp. When he was in charge, that company's stock grew more than any other public corporation. Now that he and his son Bob Pamplin, Jr. have their own company, it is growing even faster than G-P did. Readers interested in how giant corporations are built could learn much by reading this book.

This is also an adventure book. Marching off to the great Crusades is followed by watching the English fleet chase away the Spanish Armada. Later there are tales of hunting and fishing in the now-gone English Fens, in the swamps of the American South, the North Country of Canada and in the African Savannah. There is the adventure of journeying to the New World in the seventeenth century, and to the Pacific Northwest in the twentieth.

This is a romance book unlike any I have seen before. Romance here is not meant to be mere sex, but genuine love and caring. The love portrayed in this book is love bringing spiritual growth for both partners—God's intended outcome of marriage between man and woman.

There is romance remembered, literally of a "knight in shining armor," by his century-old widow, or of a widower for his mystic Scottish wife. There is romance of pastor's daughter and disinherited gentleman during the time of Oliver Cromwell. There is romance of a young man, a newcomer to Colonial Virginia, and a young woman besting the wilderness alone. There is romance in the American Civil War, in the Great Depression, and in the tumultuous 1960s.

Many of these chapters are about women. Women have faced adversities through the centuries, such as being treated as witches, chattel, being excluded from spiritual service, being denied political and property rights. These and other issues come to life in this book. On the other hand, this book also shows women cared for with a tenderness I have seen few other places.

This book is about older people. Many of the characters play out their entire lives in these pages, and many live to a ripe age. Most of them including Bob Pamplin, Sr., who is 81 at this writing—are youngsters by my standard. But none of these people imposed limitations on themselves just because they were growing older.

When Lora de Waldeschef Beville—a woman who in fact lived to be over 100 years old—faced the challenge of listening to the final sighs of those dying of plague and gave them the last rites, she did not let her age stop her. When Amy Butler Beville, in advanced years, had to fight off a greedy new husband trying to grab family property, her age did not diminish her determination. When Bob Pamplin retired from running Georgia-Pacific Corp. at the age of 65, no one bothered to tell him he was too old to start a new company with his son, Bob Pamplin, Jr. If anyone had tried, they would have wasted their breath. The idea that you have to become old and infirm is a self-imposed limitation this book goes a long way toward exposing.

This is a children's book. Young people in these pages learn valuable lessons and find themselves greatly used by God. Teenager Robert Lawrence, for example, in a chapter straight out of King Arthur's court, found himself possessed of a strength and determination he never knew he had when he overcame an injury and became the first to scale the walls of the city of Acre during the Third Crusade.

Bob Pamplin, as a barefoot farmboy in Virginia's Dinwiddie County, in a chapter most like *Huckleberry Finn*, dug the roots of his soul deep into the soil. In his section of the book you see the great value of retaining closeness with the land, and the inner quiet it offers for a lifetime.

As a boy, Bob Pamplin, Jr. followed his family back and forth across the country many times and suffered injuries and illnesses. In his section of the book he grows into a young man with two unquenchable appetites: to achieve and to help others. His achievements are legion, including eight earned college degrees, many honorary ones and appointment to state and Presidential commissions, as well as authoring ten books. His helping others has earned him distinguished awards from Freedoms Foundation, the Caring Institute and other organizations.

It pleases me that the Pamplins have done so well in so many things— including recognition by *Forbes* magazine as one of America's wealthiest families—because their achievement is validation that living by principles is the prescription for success in this world as well as in the next.

Both of them give their work all they have, but they do it in a relaxed and easy manner. There is a Southern graciousness, an English country gentleman's courtesy, a natural way about them that makes them comfortable to be around.

They like to develop the talents of the people around them—they obviously care about people. Their story demonstrates that those who truly love others are inspired to do their best. Those who carefully study the chapters on how the Pamplins built the companies they have run, and follow their examples, have a better chance of becoming more successful in any endeavor.

Merely having accumulated vast amounts of money does not impress me in the least. We read often about wealthy people whose lives crash down around their feet. It's how ethically one got that wealth and what one does with it that is important. The characters in this book have been poor, and they have been rich. When poor they worked hard and eventually became rich—or if they were not rich themselves, then succeeding generations were. When rich, they have often been exceedingly generous.

Being generous is not natural for many people. It is something that can be learned, however, by example, and that is another value of this book. It is a text on creative philanthropy. Who would dream of bequeathing a cow to the village poor in a will, so that they could begin to accumulate capital of their own? That's what a Pamplin ancestor did in Elizabethan England. Few of us have considered writing checks every month to our relatives, but that is something Bob Pamplin does.

Few of us use our creativity to dream up more effective ways to give—to multiply the value of our giving—but that is what Bob Pamplin, Jr. does. He provides food for scores of charities in Portland, by either raising the food on his farms or bargaining with food processors to get even more food for the money. In the end, one of the most valuable things this book brings into the world is an example of generosity that could inspire and challenge us all.

The family standard of integrity is also highly valuable. Few weeks go by without yet another public figure's reputation exploding, splattering us all with disillusionment. Following principle is a key to integrity. It's easy to go with the flow of things—to change with each passing wind. But monuments are built on solid ground, not on sand. In these pages you will find people who have chosen to do the right thing, regardless of the consequences and regardless of what others say. These people listen to the inner voice of right and wrong, not the outer voice of popular opinion.

Many things change in a thousand years, but some things remain. The story of these many generations invites the reader to sift through what is temporary and find what is enduring—the common thread linking them as they climb the centuries. What carried their family through the past thousand years can carry others through the next.

Although I have at this writing yet to meet in person any of the characters in this book, I feel that we are already spiritual friends. We all drink from the same source, and that is the reason for our kinship. None of us has conquered our problems by our unaided strength, but through faith in God. I am convinced the Higher Power can work through people, even people in the pages of a book, and can flow through them and transmit itself to others. Ultimately, that is the reason for *Heritage*.

Dr. Norman Vincent Peale

And we know that God causes all things to work together for good to those who love God, to those who are called according to His purpose.

ROMANS 8:28
NEW AMERICAN STANDARD

Heritage: The Thousand-Year Chronology

	1000 AD	1100	1200	1300	1400
ERA	*Norman Conquest of England*	*The Crusades*	*The Scottish-English Rivalry*	*The Black Plague*	

PAMPLIN FAMILY DESCENDANTS

Geoffrey Paunfilium

Walter Paunfiloun

John Pamphiloun

Andrew Pamphilour

Sir Robert Lawrence

Richard de Beville

Lora de Waldeschef

Idonea de Beville

William de Beville

Richard de (Wells) Bevill

Robert de Be

WORLD EVENTS AND FIGURES

Gütenb Printin Press

Thomas a` Becket

Richard the Lion-Hearted

William the Conqueror

The Magna Carta

Edwards I, II, and III

Prince William of Scotland

Timeline chart — year scale across top: **…00 | 1600 | 1700 | 1800 | 1900 | 2000**

Family genealogy (upper section)

enaissance and eformation	Colonial America	Revolution and Napoleonic Wars	The American Civil War	The Twentieth Century World
aurent Flournoy				
		Mathew Flournoy		
		Thomas Flournoy		
		Sophia Davies		
			Martha Millege Flournoy	
				John William Pamplin
		Robert Pamplin		Claude Alan Pamplin
			John Robert Pamplin, Jr.	
			Pauline Boisseau Beville	
Robert Beville Armiger				
				Robert Boisseau Pamplin, Sr.
	Sir Robert Beville, Sr.	James Boisseau		Mary Katherine Reese
	Sir Robert Beville, Jr.		Ella Athalia Boisseau	Robert Boisseau Pamplin, Jr.
			William James Beville	Marilyn Hooper
		Robert Beville	William Boisseau	Amy Pamplin North
		John Beville	Athalia Keziah Goodwyn	Anne Boisseau Pamplin
		Essex Beville	William Boisseau	
		Amy (Ann) Butler		
	John Beville			
	Mary Clement			
	Robert Beville			
John Beville				

Historical figures (lower section)

enaissance and eformation	Colonial America	Revolution and Napoleonic Wars	The American Civil War	The Twentieth Century World
…nry Elizabeth I	James I		Napoleon	Robert E. Lee
…I Mary, Queen of Scots	Charles I		Andrew Jackson	Ulysses S. Grant
	Louis XIII of France	James Madison		Franklin D. Roosevelt
…omas …ore Phillip II of Spain		The Declaration of Independence	Emancipation Proclamation	
	Jamestown Colony			
…rtin …ther Shakespeare	Oliver Cromwell	Thomas Jefferson		Billy Graham
	John Dryden			
			Woodrow Wilson	

PART 1
PAMPLIN FAMILY HISTORY

CHAPTER 1

Sir Robert Lawrence
and the Third Crusade

E very family begins in mystery. Part of the Pamplin family line, charted at the front of the book, began with some now-unknown Viking out of Europe's north. Like many of his restless, seagoing kinsmen, this "North-man" settled in the area that still bears their name: Normandy, in what is now France.

Some time later came the first of the Pamplin family known to recorded history. A knight named William de Beville, he served in the army of the Norman prince, William the Conqueror; he helped achieve what is still the last successful foreign assault on England, decided at the famed Battle of Hastings in 1066 A.D.

This book's first episode takes up the story about a century later. It concerns a young courtier from Huntingdonshire, Robert Lawrence.

Robert is not a Beville (his descendants will marry into the family some centuries later, as we shall see). And he is not a knight. Rather, he idolizes the current ideal of knightly chivalry, Prince Richard of England, soon to become famous as Richard the Lion-Hearted. And the boy also knows of the trouble in the Holy Land, where Crusader armies are struggling to hold onto the sacred places of Christianity. These three elements combine in a tale of war, faith, and dreams come true.

Trumpets! Robert Lawrence, fourteen years old, had never heard such trumpets. It wasn't only the way they blew the fanfare for the King—like brass voices crying Henry II! King of England!—but how precisely the players moved, jerking their horns to their lips, pumping out their chests to blow, and then dropping the straight, bright instruments to their sides once more.

A courtier to the King, and thus no stranger to Westminster's Great Hall, Robert Lawrence knew this fanfare well by now. It was blown only for visiting dignitaries of the highest stature, but lately the tightly built, almost grown boy had heard it again and again.

Nonetheless, today was different. Today was a day when, indeed, wishes might come true. Everyone in the hall—courtiers, knights, nobility, clergymen, the servants on the fringes of the crowd—everyone realized that today's visitors were something special. They were from the Holy Land.

These were extraordinary times, the last decades of the twelfth century. Since Henry II had ascended to England's throne in *anno domini* 1154, the drama in his kingdom had almost matched what was going on in the besieged Holy Land. In Palestine, the heathen Muhammedans held the sacred sites of Christ's life and teaching, and even the two armed Crusades thus far mounted in Western Europe could not seem to drive the infidels out.

But here in the King's homeland, too, there'd been a struggle over men's souls. Henry's thirty years on the throne were famous throughout the Christian world for his struggle with Thomas à Becket, Archbishop of Canterbury. Though an old friend of Henry's, Becket had eventually been killed by some of Henry's more thuggish guards. So when, in this Year of Our Lord 1185, Henry II received news of a noble delegation from the Christian foothold in the Holy Land, the wheel of fortune had come about: the Church was appealing for help to the very King who had made the

Church's Bishop a martyr. Today's delegation was led by Heraclitus, Patriarch of Jerusalem, and Roger, master of the House of the Knights Hospitaller at Jerusalem. These two represented the religious and military wings of the embattled Christian outpost in the Holy Land.

It might have been that no one in the court anticipated the visit so much as Robert Lawrence. He was the youngest of the regulars in the King's good graces, and small for fourteen. Yet he'd matured quickly, growing sturdy through the chest, the back, the legs. Like all nobles his age, he'd taken part in wrestling matches, imitation sword fights, and climbing contests. In these he'd proved remarkably strong.

Possibly King Henry liked Robert because the enthusiastic young scrapper had something of the royal look himself. Robert's tawny hair was the color of the Plantagenet lions, the symbol of the ruling family emblazoned on banners and tapestries. His blue eyes could have been of either Norman or Saxon extraction, but his elegant frame was clearly the former—Norman, the descendant of Vikings.

Noble in bearing, wiry and agile, the boy had much impressed the veteran knights who'd supervised the courtiers' games. "To watch Robert Lawrence go up a rope," one old soldier had remarked, "is like watching the angel go up Jacob's ladder."

And today Robert was meeting men from the place of angels—from the Holy Land. Like many young Christians, he yearned to know more about the places the Savior had walked, and to make a pilgrimage to those sacred sites himself one day. But then, everyone he'd heard of who'd made that heroic journey was a knight: a warrior in the army of Christ and King. If only he could be a knight! If only! Then nothing would keep him from the paths Jesus had trod. . . .

So Robert's twin dreams unfolded that afternoon, more intensely than ever. The two visitors announced by those incredible trumpets were his desires made flesh: they were Knighthood and the Holy Land, embodied in living men.

The massive oak doors at the far end of the hall now had come creaking open. The first in were a procession of priests. These men came from the Eastern Church; their robes were black, but decorated with stark, geometric icons. Their faces had the sallow darkness of those lands, complexions he'd only seen before on traveling Arab merchants. And they entered swinging incense-burning silver censers, chanting in a Latin more stilted, more imposing even than what Robert had heard at the cathedral in Canterbury—Thomas à Becket's former sanctuary.

Robert was left dizzy as the smoke obscured the high hall's stone columns. He felt as if he already were traveling to distant kingdoms—to impossible places, lands people hadn't even heard of yet.

The priests lined either side of the long arching hall, a gauntlet of strange Eastern robes and faces running from the foot of King Henry's throne to the heavy portals where they'd come in. The throne was bright gold and purple velvet, set high on a platform. The priests kept up their chant, the smoke still curling out of their swinging censers. Then Heraclitus appeared at the open entryway. Black-bearded as well as black-robed, he was crowned with a mitred hat, and he carried a small, gaudy trunk. Like his robes, this little box was scrawled with his Church's symbols, foreign and incomprehensible. Next, beside the high priest, appeared the knight, Sir Roger. A heavy-muscled warrior, he wore chain-mail of bright steel. Even his leather breastplate gleamed, oiled for the audience with royalty. Sir Roger carried no box, but rested both hands on the pommel of his broadsword. The size of his scarred knuckles made clear just how big was the weapon beneath them.

As the Patriarch and the Knight Hospitaller strode towards the English throne, the alien priests at last broke off their murmuring, and in that sudden hush the rustle of clerical robes and the clink of battle armor echoed supernaturally off the surrounding stone. When Heraclitus and Sir Roger had done kneeling before King Henry, the Patriarch gave an ornate greeting, his accent so thick young Robert could hardly understand. As the holy man spoke, his oily black beard rippled, throwing off glimmers as bright as Henry's polished golden throne. Heraclitus also appeared to be doing something with his strangely ornamented box. But Robert concentrated on the old man's face, trying to make sense of his stilted talk.

"In the blesséd last Crusade," Heraclitus was saying, "blesséd by God, we established the Kingdom of Jerusalem. The Kingdom of Jerusalem which has been our protector in the holy places of our faith. Today, O great English sovereign, I make oblation before you as the head of the church in that same ancient and sanctified city. I bring to your liege these few humble tokens."

Then with a priestly flourish the mysterious box was opened, and Robert found himself nearly knocked across the base of his king's throne by the press of the crowd behind him, all struggling to get a look at the Patriarch's miraculous gifts. The crowd's noise was like a beehive at Robert's ear. His first looks were no better than a blur. Nonetheless, in time, the boy understood the magnitude of what Heraclitus had brought: the hefty golden keys to the Tower of David and the keys to the Holy Sepulchre. But the most impressive present was small, unspectacular, even dirty. It was a chunk of wood, dry and cracked, good for nothing but kindling. Yet this, announced the otherworldly visitor, was a piece of the True Cross—the holy cross of Christ.

The crowd's murmur blocked Robert's ears, and the crowd's rocking blurred his vision. Or was it the tang of Eastern incense that left the boy feeling so changed, so new to himself?

He was changed—brought to something he'd never been before by a glimpse of God. Even if the Patriarch's scrap of kindling wasn't in fact a souvenir of the Cross (for this doubt did cross his mind; he was only human), it at least carried the possibility of the Cross. The wood was dark as a seed; it made Robert recall Christ's parable of the seed. With only the faith of a mustard seed, the boy reminded himself in the midst of the blur, in the midst of the buzzing and doubt, a new kingdom could be born.

With faith, a new and better Robert could be born.

After that, the visit passed in a jumble of impressions, a sequence that took the boy a week at least to sort out. He remembered how Henry had trembled, his eyes glistening, as he took the smooth-worn piece. Then there were Robert's impressions of the King's sons, Richard and John. These two flanked the throne left and right, as usual. And Richard was the more demonstrative, also as usual. The strapping, bristling-bearded older prince—almost as warlike in dress as the leader of the Knights Hospitaller—handled the piece of Cross as if it were a juggler's ball. Eagerly Richard weighed it first in one brawny hand, then in the other. But Prince John hung back. A narrow man draped in rich layers of tunic, John kept his thin arms folded. When the King proffered John the wooden relic, the younger prince declined to touch it, keeping his hands out of sight in his gilded cloaks. It seemed to Robert, in his blurred state, that John was looking more at the throne than at the piece of the True Cross.

Blurred, too, were the reports of the Knight Hospitaller and the Patriarch. Sir Roger yanked out his heavy sword and, holding its cross-shaped handle aloft, warned that "Holy Jerusalem itself is threatened by the devil Saladin." Saladin—the name came up often. The Patriarch described this Muhammedan chieftain as a devil, declaring in a shout: "Lord Saladeen possesses cunning and might such as could only have come from the Evil One!" The Knight Hospitaller on the other hand seemed actually, in some part, to admire this new enemy. "I have faced Saladin in battle," Sir Roger said, more level-voiced than his companion. "The man has wisdom, judgment, even mercy. He is the most worthy foe any Christian could find."

But the distinction between the firebrand priest and the combat-hardened knight was swiftly blurred again, in young Robert's memories, because what these two unfamiliar men had to say was swiftly lost under the rousing, hair-raising outcry of a worked-up crowd. Prince Richard was the first Englishman to start shouting. Swaggering down from the throne platform, Henry's older son brought out his own cross-handled broadsword, and waving it overhead began to shout, "Death to the infidel! Death to Saladin!" In no time he was joined by a great clatter, as the English knights pulled out their swords, and the hoarse bellowing was taken up by all: "Death . . . the infidel . . . Saladin . . . death!" The war cries echoed through the redolent smoke, through the oily torch light, more piercing even than the earlier trumpets' fanfare.

Robert understood that many of these eager knights were less moved by love of God than by love of battle. Many times these men had heard their praises sung by troubadours and balladeers: no fighters in Christendom were a match for the Norman English.

"The burning zeal, the blessèd ferocity of your knights," Heraclitus told the King, "is well remembered, in my Kingdom of Jerusalem, from the most recent Crusade." Nonetheless the decision to take up a new Crusade—to win the Holy Land back again—seemed to the young courtier, in retrospect, as if it had happened too fast. Both Sir Roger and Heraclitus appealed for assistance with one Middle Eastern city in particular. Acre—that was the city.

"Acre is the base of our army's supply," the Knight Hospitaller explained. "It is a port renowned in history, much favored by the seagoing Venetians." Sultain Saladin, it was feared, was about to capture Acre; the wily Muhammedan intended to starve into submission the knights he could not defeat on the field.

"Only you, great liege!" the Patriarch cried, with a flourish of his hands. "Only you can provide us sufficient gold as well as indefatigable hearts; only you have in your power all that is necessary to keep secure the blesséd lands where our Savior once walked."

How the old Patriarch talked! Beside stubby Heraclitus, through most of this later speechmaking, stood rawboned Prince Richard. And the big Norman's look, by contrast, showed no indirection, no diplomacy. As over the next few days Robert sorted through his bewildered impressions, nothing struck him so as his memory of Prince Richard's look.

The young courtier at the front of the crowd noticed too his king's canny ways even as he announced his agreement, in principle, to help. Henry II concluded his reply by waving the scepter of William the Conqueror, and by shouting, "Jerusalem must be ours forever!"—so setting off renewed war whoops and cries for Saladin's death. Yet the sly lord of Westminster made no mention of money, or of marching off anywhere himself. Likewise Henry's younger son, John, appeared to have some secret intention. The narrow prince surveyed the Hall's noisy roil of soldiers with a narrow look. A mixture of passion and stealth.

Nonetheless, in the jumble of Robert's impressions, there was ultimately nothing that mattered so much as Prince Richard. Prince Richard's face: troubadour's lips and wolf's eyes, all set off by a florid, spiky beard. Within that beard, the knight kept fighting back a smile. And no, there was no indirection about it. No diplomacy. Anyone could see at once that England's great warrior-prince was spoiling for this Crusade.

Richard was legendary as a fighter. Now his war-making skills had found their calling: their greatest challenge. And there in Westminster's Hall, that evening, that calling became young Robert's as well. And Prince Richard's look took in him.

Later, Robert found it hard to believe how he'd been heartstruck. His eyes had met Richard's, yes—but their shared stare had lasted only a moment. A courtier didn't dare meet a prince's stare for more than a moment. Still that look had moved Robert fundamentally. It had provided the meaning for all the dream-like, jumbled impressions following his glimpse of the True Cross; it had unfolded again the bright, twin banners of his dreams. With that one brief, searing look, Robert knew that he would one day be a knight. And he knew that, somehow, the way to that honor lay through the Holy Land.

Those days of sorting out his feelings took place at Robert's family manor. The delegation from the Holy Land moved on as well, making the pilgrimage to Canterbury Cathedral in the soft April weather. Young Robert Lawrence, left behind, felt himself to be like Holy Mary, Mother of God, left behind after the visit of the shepherds and the wise men: keeping all the things she had seen, and pondering them in her heart.

And while Robert thought things through, it helped to take up again his field work in Huntingdonshire, on the estate his Norman forebears had won from the Saxons. Robert was one courtier who didn't consider himself above laboring alongside his Saxon serfs. In spring he struggled with the plow and seedbags; in autumn he cut the hay and hauled it. With a harvest-load strapped to his back, the blonde youngster would race his Saxon helpers up the barn ladders to the storage lofts. Small wonder he excelled at climbing contests with the other well-born young.

For of course, this season as other seasons, Robert went on learning the skills at which his idol Richard excelled: the sword and the spear, the mace and the bow. At the courtier games, Robert began to ride and even to joust. He took part in his first tourneys, now and again even drawing the attention of Prince Richard himself.

Then, at one of the tourneys, young Robert Lawrence learned of the trial God had in store for him.

A busy, boisterous tourney. Under a pewter sky, hundreds of hoofs and feet had trampled the grass into mud. The air was filled with the sweet smoke of roasting pork. Banners of yellow, blue, and crimson fluttered from the pavilions of the knights. But the shouts of the men and the stampings of the horses weren't loud enough to drown out the news sung by the traveling troubadour.

It was a song of a great calamity in the Holy Land. Accompanying himself with a lyre, the pale artist performed movingly, the group before him getting larger as he went on. Then one line made Robert Lawrence stop short.

"Jerusalem itself," the troubadour sang, "has fallen to the Infidel. Jerusalem it-se-elf."

Sweet faced, sad-voiced, the singer intoned verses about sacred places desecrated. The Dome of the Rock, he sang, was in the hands of the Infidel once again. The Dome of the Rock had become an Eastern Orthodox church after the First Crusade, decades ago now; and before that Crusade the Dome had been a Moslem shrine; and before the Muhammedans had taken over Christ's city, the site had been a major sanctuary to Christ—because before that, it had been Herod's Temple. This then was the Dome of the Rock, where in ancient days the Messiah Himself had wept and prayed.

More of the Holy Land had fallen to Saladin's hordes as well. Acre had fallen—Acre, the crucial port for the Knights Hospitaller. But there was still worse news, bad enough to drain the blood from Robert's face. "In battle a priest did carry the True Cross of Christ," the troubadour sang. Through the wiles of the Devil, the story went on, this precious relic fell into the hands of the Muhammedans, and it was now with the infidel Caliph of Baghdad.

The True Cross! A piece like the one Robert had seen that evening at Westminster! Fallen into the hands of those who had turned their backs on Christ! How was this possible? How could God allow it?

Filled with rage and wonder, there on the muddy tourney grounds Robert fell to his knees and prayed. Seeing the youngster that way, the others who had been listening now also fell and prayed. Even the troubadour broke off his song.

"Father," Robert prayed, "I am filled with horror that the True Cross is in the hands of those who are false to you. But I am also overcome with your mystery, the mystery of how you could ever allow this to happen." Around him, fellow supplicants murmured their assent. "I ask that somehow I can know you better—that I can visit your sacred lands, and experience again the stirring of my soul I felt first at the sight of this same Cross. I ask," the young man concluded his prayer, "to help get back your Cross for your believers."

And perhaps the prayer was heard, for the Crusade drew closer. The Holy Roman Emperor, Frederick Barbarossa, after hearing of the fall of Jerusalem in 1189, left his comfortable palace in Mainz, Germany, to recapture it. And young Robert, who'd heard tales of Barbarossa all his life, shivered with eagerness at the news; Frederick was a great warrior, and all Europe would follow him. The prayers of an English courtier would be heard.

At the next tourneys, the troubadours had a happier song: "Barbarossa will be the second Moses," they sang of the Holy Roman Emperor. "He will lead Christianity to defeat the devil Saladin." But the legendary Barbarossa, for all his battle-hardened prowess, was sixty-seven years old. On his way to the Holy Land, the Emperor drowned while fording a river. Only a small portion of his army made its way to Acre, and these soldiers had little impact on the siege to recapture the crucial port city.

Prince Richard, on the other hand, was then only thirty-one. In 1189—four full years after Henry's promise of help to Heraclitus—he forged an alliance with Philip Augustus of France, then twenty-three. Henry II fell ill and retreated to the grim castle at Chinon, the heart of his Angevin lands. According to the talk round the Lawrence family fireside, the old monarch longed for nothing more than a quiet time in which to die.

Richard was crowned King at Westminster on September 3, 1189. Robert Lawrence, now a man of eighteen, attended with his family. It had been years since the former courtier had seen much of Westminster's pomp and splendor, and he was awed all over again at the procession of bishops, abbots, and other clerics in their robes, and at the many crosses, candles, and censers going before them as they proceeded to the inner chamber. There, the Archbishop placed the crown of England on the head of a man Robert still believed was the embodied spirit of knightly chivalry.

The young man couldn't help thinking of his twin dreams. This new King intended to save the Holy Land. And Robert would be going with him. Perhaps then he could take back the True Cross from the Infidels—perhaps then he could become, at last, a knight.

The summer after Richard's coronation, Robert was back in the fields, managing the serfs. At one point, stopping to wipe the sweat and dirt from his brow, he saw dust kicked up into clouds on the estate roadway. Four knights were on that road.

Soon one of the horsemen spotted him across the field. All four came at a gallop and reigned up abruptly.

"Robert Lawrence!" one of them shouted. "Robert Lawrence, hear your King's command!" At those words alone, the young man's heart leapt.

"Your King," the heavy-breathing knight went on, "Richard the First, greets you and requests you to fulfill your duties to serve your King, your country, and your God. As you know, the infidel Muhammedan hordes have overrun the Holy Land, and are in possession of the True Cross. They desecrate the holy places and shrines and persecute the Church, the believers in God Almighty, the Holy Mother of God, and Jesus Christ. Therefore you are now called to leave your lands, pick up your sword and spear, and join your King and your brother Christians in a Crusade to cleanse the Holy Land."

Robert bowed his head. "I do willingly and joyfully serve," he said, trying to match the knight's formality. But his heart continued to leap and race. As the King's emissaries rode off, Robert stripped off his field apron and flung it high into the blue summer sky. Now there would be no more field work. No more dreams of what lay beyond the fen and the forest. Now, it would be adventure and dreams come true: a pilgrimage to the Holy Land and knightly service to Christ.

Richard spent the first full year of his reign preparing for war. He then placed administration of England into the hands of his brother John. Each brother seemed perfectly suited for the tasks that lay before him: Richard loved to fight, and John loved to collect the tax money to pay for it. Henry II's formerly flourishing lands began to be drained of their wealth, in order to support his son's armies overseas. In Nottingham a small anti-tax rebellion festered for years, led by the son of a dishonored nobleman. A skillful bowman, this fallen scion hid in nearby Sherwood Forest and led raids on the greedy local Sheriff. In the Crusaders' campfire stories, the outlaw went by the name Robin Hood.

Richard of England wanted Philip of France with him on this Crusade. Besides needing all the fighting men he could get, Henry II's son did not trust Philip to keep his hands off the Angevin territories in France. So in June of 1190, both Richard and Philip received a cross from William of Tyre—a renowned old city in the Holy Land—in a moving ceremony at Vezelay in France. Tyre had held out against Saladin's siege two years earlier, and along with Antioch and Tripolis, was the last stronghold of Christianity. Acre, however, remained under the Muhammedan thumb, along with Jerusalem.

Richard the Lion-Hearted—nightly the troubadours sang his praise—then marched his regiments south. At Marseilles they boarded ships for Sicily. Philip and his army rejoined the English there, in September, prepared to spend the winter.

Robert Lawrence was only one soldier among those thousands, and still younger than most. Yet by the time of the voyage to Sicily, the knights who served as King Richard's lieutenants knew of this Norman teenager, small yet tough. The same strength and agility that had placed Robert first in the old children's games, brought him to the attention of the Lion-Heart's closest confidants. Scaling the rigging of the troopship, testing his ever-ready climbing skills against those of the sailors, Robert again enjoyed getting to the top first. He reveled in the cheers of happy countrymen.

In Sicily, the Crusader armies quartered themselves in Messina, around a splendid palace. The castle looked like the Norman strongholds back home, except it had swirling patterns similar to those of the Moors, and it was decorated with golden mosaics such as were favored by the Byzantines of Constantinople.

Here in the Italian sun, Henry II's former courtier made it a point not to go slack. While others lay about on the beaches, Robert practiced the arts of war. When his exercise was finished, he concentrated on what tasks needed to be done about the camp, making arrangements for the daily chores of bivouac. For this too, he won the notice of the King's lieutenants. At last, the busy young Norman was presented to the Lion-Heart as a squire.

Nor did Robert relax then. He attended Richard's every desire, so quick to anticipate and so sensitive about what the handsome king liked that he quickly became a favorite of this testy, tightly coiled sovereign. Often the teenager brought a smile to those troubadours' lips, and a glint of joy to those wolfish eyes. Richard the Lion-Hearted took to keeping Robert Lawrence by his side night and day. Yet loyal as Robert was to his King, he knew enough by now to keep an inward distance.

Once, with young Robert attending, Richard saw a local noble unhood a falcon and send the bird flapping into the sky. Exclaimed Richard: "What a fine bird that is!" And then, after a moment's more watching: "I believe I shall have it." So the King told Robert to summon the owner. No sooner was the Sicilian before him, the horse still snorting from its hard gallop, than Richard had declared the bird would be his. "I want it," the King proclaimed.

The owner hesitated, and at once a shadow passed over the Lion-Heart's face. He yanked out his broadsword and in a moment had it at the poor Italian's throat. "As I am King of England," Richard shouted, "You will give me that falcon." Robert was sure that if he hadn't intervened—he poked fun at the bird; he called it a Sicilian pigeon—the King would have killed the man.

Another time Richard was having a mock joust with William of Barres, merely an amusement, using canes instead of lances. But when Richard was unhorsed in the by-play, he became instantly, insanely angry.

The Lion-Heart was indeed a man to be feared, Robert thought. But was he a leader to follow?

With all that, however, it was hard to remain uneasy through the Sicilian winter. The cool, Eastern-style castle, the fertile rolling land, the palm trees, and the sun were unlike anything Robert had experienced. In the evenings, squire and King often went out among the tents of the Crusaders' encampment, and there they asked the troubadours to remind them of this pleasant winter's greater purpose. They asked for songs of war, and of Infidel atrocities in the Holy Land. Richard and Robert also heard of one Joachim of Fiore, a Cistercian abbot, then living as a hermit at Calabria. This holy ascetic, they heard, had the gift of prophecy. He knew how the Crusade would go, and the King of England's eventual place in Christian history.

One warm night, Richard asked the teenager to bring this Joachim to the Angevin camp. After several days' hot ride, Robert found the holy brother. Joachim passed his days alone in a sod hut, on a stony, windswept, seaside bluff. Robert had dismounted and climbed the last hour on foot—the last fifteen minutes or so, hand over hand. Anyone less able at climbing would never have made it.

At last, at the hut's driftwood door, Robert began his invitation: "My lord Richard I, King of Engl—"

"I know, I know," Joachim replied. "I am ready to go."

There may have been a twinkle of merriment in the old man's eyes, as he gauged the astonishment of his visitor. He had young eyes, Joachim, very young for so parched and grizzled a face. And yet once the two of them were riding back to the Crusaders' camp, the monk's face shadowed by his hood, Joachim began to look frightening. As dark came on, everything but the eyes seemed to disappear beneath that hood. If it hadn't been for those eyes, by nightfall the company of this gnome like, silent, heavy-robed cleric would have been too frightening for Robert to bear.

But at last the squire was home, among more familiar faces. In the Messina throne room, the next morning, the monk bowed low and began. "Man is moving through a succession of ages culminating in the Last Judgment." The monk was so quiet, even the King leaned forward in his throne. "Over the centuries there will be five persecutors of the Church, and one of the worst of those persecutes it today. He has desecrated the holy Sepulchre in Jerusalem, and many other sacred places. His name, Saladin the Saracen."

At this, King Richard's face darkened unmistakably. Robert, however, wasn't so shaken by his sovereign's renewed anger; by now he'd seen it many times.

"But Saladin will soon fall," Joachim was saying. "And you, King Richard I of England—you will be the instrument of his destruction."

The Lion-Heart's face changed again, mottling, rising. His fierce lips set harshly, triumphantly, as he settled back. The instrument of Saladin's destruction!

But the bent-backed old abbot wasn't yet finished with prophecy. Suddenly he turned away from the King, almost dismissively, and pointed at Robert.

"You, Robert Lawrence!" he announced, more loudly. "You who risked the climb to my mountain home!"

Robert didn't dare glance at his King. He concentrated on the old holy man: on those queer, half-merry eyes.

"Robert Lawrence," Joachim went on, "I say to you, remember the words of our Lord. Remember when he said, 'The last shall be first and the first shall be last.' The last shall be first, young Robert, remember."

The monk stopped his pointing. He lifted his hood once more over his face, hid his gnarled hands once more in his robes. Nor did the cleric give any sign of interest one way or the other when, behind him, the English King made a brusque and choked goodbye. And, with teeth still clenched, Richard called for one of his knights to "attend Brother Joachim home"—one of the knights, not Robert.

In the days that followed, the men in the royal circle gossiped like housewives. Had young Robert lost his favored status with the Lion-Heart?

What sort of prophecy singled out a mere squire, as well as a King? What could the old hermit have meant? *

No one in the Crusaders' camp, however, wondered more than Robert.

I n spring the French and English armies traveled from Sicily to Cyprus. They needed this more easterly Mediterranean island as a supply base for the invasion of the Holy Land. And in Cyprus Richard was swiftly victorious, so true to the troubadours' name for him that now his fame began to spread throughout Europe: Richard the Lion-Hearted, roaring and powerful, so perfect a warrior not even Saladin would withstand him.

But there was no such glory for Richard's squire Robert. Before he got to see much of the fighting on Cyprus, the wiry teenager was bucked off his horse. He landed hard on his hip and lay helpless for hours. His groans were the feeblest echo of the true heroes' cheers and outcries, coming to him from across the battlefield. For weeks afterward, he was unable to walk. And that was all it took for the Lion-Heart to abandon his one-time favorite. In no time, Robert was shuttled from one of Richard's royal litters to the grim supply-carts that followed the army. Coldly, the same lieutenants who'd brought him into the King's circle now ushered him out.

In the lonesome days that followed, racked by the painful jouncing of the wooden-wheeled carts, young Robert Lawrence lay useless, trying now and then to stay strong by means of small exercises between the low walls of his cart. He seemed likely to miss the very action that had brought him all this way. Despite his hard work earlier, he would never become a knight. Despite his thousand fervent prayers, he would never serve his God in battle.

His love for his monarch was now tinged, inevitably, with bitterness. When the Crusaders hit the beaches near Jaffa (striking there first in order to relieve a garrison under siege) King Richard called back to those in the boat, "Shame on him who lags behind!" And these words were the first blow the King's former squire received in the Holy Land; because of his ruined hip, it was Robert Lawrence who was last off the boat.

Ruefully he recalled the words of Joachim, the Sicilian holy man: The last shall be first. Hollow, hurtful words, they seemed to Robert now.

After reinforcing the Jaffa garrison, Richard I headed north. North, towards Acre. This remained the best potential port for the Crusaders, as Sir Roger had declared it to be that long-ago night in King Henry's Hall. Now it was three years since Saladin had captured the city his infidel troops called Akko. It was nineteen months since a small band of the faithful, under the Christian King of Jerusalem, had laid a hopeless siege to the Muhammedan interlopers. Thousands on both sides had perished. When Richard's army arrived at the front, Robert had to hobble off his ox cart so it could be used to retrieve the dead.

The Lion-Heart established a headquarters on a hill overlooking the city and its bay. Flag bearers held high the three-lion banners of the Angevins, and there was more trumpeting, more cheering. How galling those happy noises seemed to Robert Lawrence! How far from the promise of that evening in Richard's father's court!

But a fallen soldier must be a soldier nonetheless, and he made it his business to assess the military situation. The new Crusaders, Robert learned, had come almost too late. The army from Jerusalem was inexperienced, and more than once they'd been soundly beaten by Saladin's troops. Now the two sides were arrayed in trenches facing each other—a strange, slow, unchivalric way to make war. Worse, the Christian lines lay far from the city gates, too far to effectively cut off the Muhammedans' supplies. Still, these troops, which included a few real soldiers like the Knights Hospitaller, continued to pester the Infidel as best they could. Now with the arrival of Richard and his Angevin warriors, who was to say that God wouldn't heed their prayers after all?

Every evening the sun cast an eerie light over the city walls: part gold, part blood. The darker hue was due in part to the smoke from burning Saracen ships in the harbor. And when Robert stood up in his cart—when he began testing his leg and hip, hoping against hope—from the Crusaders' hillside encampment he could make out a few landmarks within the walls. He could see church steeples, bell towers. Though silent for three years now, the bells still caught the receding sun. And though oppressed by the Infidel, within those city walls Christians still lived and prayed.

These walls had been built by Crusaders a hundred years before, and so they had the standard crenelated battlements of the time, with slits for archers and spearmen. Below those crenellations stretched the outward-sloping glacis, impossible to climb without ladders, exposed to all manner of death from above. Only now, instead of Christians fending off the Infidel, the battlements harbored the enemy. Robert could see shadowy figures scurrying between the slits, spears waving like the antennae of roaches.

Richard the Lion-Hearted, for all his youthful impulsiveness, knew the importance of being prepared for battle. He ordered fortifications extending the Christian lines, truly surrounding the city for the first time. He likewise took time to arrange the catapults and ballistas, the artillery bows and fire arrows, and the battering ram. He was especially careful about the tools for those first crucial breechings of the enemy walls: the scaling ladders for the initial assault, and the pulleys to pull up reinforcements quickly.

Soon there came the morning when Richard I of England and Normandy sat astride his horse before phalanx after phalanx of knights and foot soldiers, his battle-armor glinting its challenge to them all. Spears pointed skyward, forming a forest of killing barbs, and the Crusaders' shields burned their blood-color crosses into the air. The King's speech was borrowed from the poetry of the troubadours—for this strange, warlike man was a balladeer himself. He allowed no doubt concerning the day's outcome: "This ancient city will be Christ's again!" He declared that his listeners, too, had but one choice before them: "Today you find glory, or you find death!"

And the speech ended with the same cry Robert Lawrence had heard what seemed like a lifetime ago, in a land that felt too far-off to believe in:

"Death to the Infidel! Death to Saladin!"

Had the walls of Acre been the walls of Jericho, they would surely have fallen down under the outcry of the horsemen and infantry. Robert took part, cheering till his throat was raw, trying to shout down his disappointment. His job now was administering the flow of supplies to the front. Today he was to drive an ox cart. He had to keep the crossbow battery freshly supplied with artillery arrows—long and devastating as spears. There goes my contribution, he told himself, as the first one whistled away above the bellowing Crusader attack. At least the thing made it over the · city walls.

"The next load," he told the archers as cheerfully as he could, "I'll write Saladin's name on every arrow."

By the time the hobbling Norman returned with that second load, the sky was filled with arrows. They came not only from the crossbows and longbows of the Christians, but also from the Saracen soldiers in their crenelated battlements atop the city walls. Also the sky was occasionally streaked by the catapults' burning balls of pitch: comets trailing black smoke. The Muhammedans responded by pouring boiling oil down on the ladder-bearers and the Crusaders who tried to climb. The stinking, mucilaginous stuff flowed back as far as Robert's supply depot. It reached the young Norman even before the stretcher-bearers arrived with their screaming wounded: the men scalded and knocked off their ladders by the same foul liquor.

All day the battle raged. So long as there was fighting to be done outside the city walls, Richard the Lion-Hearted led the charge. From time to time the slow-moving Robert got a glimpse of his former friend's Danish ax, dripping darkly as the King raised it over another enemy trench line. But after several hours the remaining Infidel hordes had retreated within Acre's vast, Crusader-built walls. Then Richard was at a loss. He couldn't lead a charge up a scaling ladder; on those every man, no matter his rank, was alone with his prayers.

Eventually the Lion-Heart withdrew to a pavilion on a hill, where he could confer with his generals. At least he had Saladin trapped, and could force him to sue for peace. The King drew up terms of surrender, including 200,000 gold pieces to help defray the battle's costs. And the Crusaders' terms included something more important than money, namely, the True Cross. There over the call for surrender, the King brandished his axe and declared he'd kill every Muhammedan in town if the Cross wasn't returned at once.

But this obstreperous carrying on only confirmed, among the nobles in his war-tent, the King's deeper disappointment. Yes, Richard put his seal on the documents. Yes, he had them taken to the nearest artillery crossbow, where the scroll was tied to an arrow and shot over the walls. But the Lion-Heart's bristly scowl was easy to read, as he watched the weapon fly where he'd been unable to go.

A victory that didn't include actual capture of the city was hardly the stuff of legend. It was as if he'd challenged the great Saladin to a duel, and then only defeated him on paper.

And yet it was at this same time—after the news of the King's call for surrender had spread through the Crusader rear guard—that the supply-driver Robert Lawrence noticed one ladder standing unattended, against the Acre walls.

A ladder, unattended. Its climbers must have been knocked off some time ago, but still it stood, against a tower, out of sight of Saladin's archers.

A ladder, unattended, out of sight.

Most of the fighting was around the main gate now. The Saracens had massed their archers and vats of oil overhead. Robert Lawrence—unlikely as it seemed even to him—appeared to be the only man on the battlefield aware of this one exposed vulnerable spot, on the city's flank. A dead Muhammedan lay hooked on one of the crenellations at the ladder's top, but otherwise the battlements there were empty. Staring, starting to make for the ladder already, the young Norman found himself calling on God. "Could this be Your sign?" he asked aloud? "Could I have a place in this glorious struggle after all?'

Smoke rose around Robert Lawrence, the stinking smoke of burned men and the Infidel oil that had hurt them. The wounded littering the rear cried out to him: "Go back! Where's your armor? You'll be killed!" But he was making for the ladder already, shrugging off his last bundle of arrows, limping in a supply-officer's tunic down from the safety of the staging grounds.

An oxcart of wounded struggled uphill, past him. On its open tailgate sat a man with one arm and a Saxon beard: a red, red beard, almost as red as his blood. "Take me sword," the Saxon croaked, his accent clearly lower-class. "Take-ee, take . . ." Then no sooner was Robert armed than another soldier, his shield up to protect against a fresh flight of Saracen arrows, pointed out an unclaimed shield on the ground nearby. When Robert took up the protection, he found its handle slippery with gore.

Still the injured teenager descended into the battle, toward the over-looked ladder. Here and there he pulled his bad leg over corpses. And there were arrows to fend off, clattering so loudly against his shield that his head rang. By the time he reached the outward-sloping glacis—littered with armor and weaponry, with bloodstains and oilslicks—Robert could at least come up with a half-sensible explanation for no one noticing this one ladder. In this chaos, a man could overlook a lot more than a ladder. In this stench and pandemonium, a man could overlook Christ Himself.

So Robert Lawrence began to call on Christ, as he sidled along the base of the glacis. "Jesus, help me," he murmured. "Let me not forget You, in this chaos. Let me not falter." Once or twice he had to crawl, his calloused laborer's hands (indeed, wasn't he only a supply officer?) holding up well against the hot oil, the scarred stone. And this made him realize how harmless he must have looked: only another mortally wounded Crusader, crawling to his death. His very injury was helping him, here.

"Jesus," he gasped, "Now I see just how mysterious are Your Miracles."

Did it take him ten minutes? Ten years? Finally Robert was at the forgotten ladder. His heart seemed to hammer up and down between neckline and stomach, and he tried to calm himself with reminders of similar trials from his past. When he hung his sword and shield on the strap across his back, he recalled the haybundles he used to carry up the lofts in his Huntingdonshire barns. When he began to climb, hand over hand, he recalled the stony, uppermost approaches to the hut of Joachim the holy man.

And what enigmatic prophecy might he be moving towards now? He watched the crenellations for the sign of an archer, and saw again the dead Muhammedan hanging in one crook of the stone. Was he climbing to such an end? To end up like a piece of meat on a stone counter? Or was he climbing towards Christ?

"Jesus," he whispered, "help me. Lead me."

Yet while he was alone with his prayers, by the time he neared the top Robert Lawrence was no longer alone on the scaling ladder. First, among the attackers at the city's main gate, a group had fallen back far enough from the impregnable glacis to notice this lone, unarmored soldier, hauling himself stiff-legged up this previously abandoned corner ladder.

Knights and foot soldiers, a score or so, had moved this way. At the city gate, meanwhile, the main assault continued. Dozens of Crusader Knights lay dead around the battering ram, and over the gate the Saracen archers clogged the battlements. So it was that the King never noticed Robert's climb—joined now by a smattering of other brave souls—till a lieutenant called him from the far side of the war tent.

"My liege!" this breathless knight exclaimed. "My liege! Look! It's, it's Robert, sire. It's the boy Robert!"

Richard's wolfish eyes narrowed. His former squire—couldn't be any-one else, not that small, and not dragging one leg—was nearly up to the Infidel walls already. Now the wiry young pup had one-handed his sword off his back; now he silently signaled the group that, when he'd turned to retrieve his sword, he'd seen beneath him on the ladder.

"Isn't, isn't his name Lawrence, sire?" the lieutenant beside Richard asked.

"Robert Lawrence," the King replied quietly.

"Well, well God be praised, sire! Robert Lawrence is the first to scale the walls of Acre. The first!"

But then, like a wasp at a window, the dark, thin figure of a Saracen archer appeared behind the crenellations. Darting along the path atop the wall, his short bow out and armed already, the foe closed in on the top of the ladder. On the ladder Robert's hobbled figure both curled closer to the rungs and at the same time climbed still faster. Nonetheless he couldn't match the speed of a two-legged man on the run, and now the Muhammedan was at the ladder. For a moment the infidel tried to finish off all the attacking Crusader at once, shoving at the ladder's top, his pointed helmet bobbing back and forth as he strove to topple it over backwards. But the thing was too heavy, with so many soldiers on it. So the Saracen stepped back and drew his bow. The Lion-Heart, watching, smelled the day's blood on him; he felt the ache in his axe-arm.

"Watch it, boy," the King found himself saying.

The sun glanced off Robert Lawrence's sword; perhaps the glare reached the archer's eyes. The arrow struck the lifted sword; perhaps Robert had fended it off. In any case, in another moment he was over the top before the archer had time to reload. He lifted his sword again, again, its glint growing darker each time as the last obstacle to the Crusader assault crumpled before him.

"Go!" Richard the Lion-Hearted shouted, striding out to the edge of his generals' hilltop. "Go!"

None in the rippling war-tent needed the order explained. Right and left, lieutenants swung up onto their mounts, taking off to rally whatever reserves remained. And from where he stood, the King could see that the small band who'd come after Robert Lawrence had grown to hundreds. He could hear renewed Christian cheering rise from the battlefield, even from the tired regiments at the main gate. Once more their raised weaponry glittered fiercely, caught this time in the low slant of westerly sun.

"The last shall be first," Richard said quietly. "All day long we fought, and yet—the last shall be first."

But the King had one more surprise in store, that day. After Robert Lawrence and the other assault troops had reached the tower that held the controls for the main gate, after the city had been opened to the Crusaders for good, Richard the Lion-Hearted rode into Acre seeking not a treasure, nor even a Cross, but a man. In the crowded, smoking streets, amid the happy outstretched arms of liberated Christians, the King asked officer after officer if they'd found "that devil Saladin." He wasn't going to be outwitted again by that shrunken Sicilian hermit! Hadn't the old coot said that Richard would be the instrument of Saladin's destruction?

But perhaps that general was, in fact, the devil. Today again he'd given the Christians the slip. After a city-wide search Richard found nothing more of his legendary opponent than a slip of paper. On it, beneath a Saracen seal, the infidel warlord agreed to the English King's terms and approved safekeeping for the True Cross. The relic would soon be on its way from Mecca, the document declared, via emissaries of the Eastern Church.

I dub thee Sir Robert Lawrence, knight of the realm."

It was morning again, morning in Acre, and young Robert's injured hip was killing him. He couldn't remain down on his knees like this for long, not on the sticky, still-bloody stones of the city's waterfront square. Even the weight of his King's sword on his shoulder was too much for the young man, after yesterday's climbing and fighting.

And yet Robert's chest seemed to be filled with a swarm of happy, stingless bees, he was so overwhelmed at his dream coming true. As the Lion-Heart spoke, Robert kept blinking back tears of joy.

"In recognition of your courage and the service you have performed . . ." the monarch was saying, . . . and by this you have reclaimed for Christendom not only the city of Acre but the True Cross of Christ. . . ." The nineteen-year-old didn't bother to follow the words. The memories of a past suddenly understood differently, the glimpses of a future that would never be the same—these were what he had to concentrate on. As for today, what struck him most deeply wasn't anything the King said, but rather the look in his eye, before he'd ordered Robert to kneel. The monarch's gaze had been almost as soft as his father Henry's, at that moment; he'd even shown a trace of the hermit Joachim's aged merriment. Down on his knees, fighting back tears, Robert still couldn't resist a smile at the memory of that look. Had the Lion-Heart for once been humbled? Had the King too been forced to recognize his smallness before God's never-ending complexity?

"Rise, Sir Robert Lawrence, knight of the realm."

The young man rose into dreams come true. He'd come to the Holy Land and fought for Christ; he'd been made a knight. The King resheathed his sword, then swept off decisively, for a moment filling the square with the echo of his boots on the stones. The ceremony was over. Regardless of whatever ironies destiny might have in store for him next, the ruler of the Angevins wasn't about to sink into mere philosophy. There were the spoils of Acre to divide; there was an assault on Jerusalem to plan. But as Robert Lawrence hobbled after his sovereign, wincing against the pain, he felt less like the proud, erect figures he'd seen when he was young, and more like the hunchbacked old holy man who just this year had helped him understand the unpredictable justice of God.

The last shall be first, Sir Robert was thinking, and the first shall be last. And then, drowning out even the King's bootsteps, there erupted a fanfare of trumpets.

CHAPTER 2
Geoffrey Pamplin and the Hanging

S*ir Robert Lawrence returned soon to Huntingdonshire. There he spent the rest of his days managing his family estates.*

Staying at home, all in all, made for a better life than that of Robert's old commander, Richard. "The Lion-Heart" served only a few months of his reign in England; he endured captivity in Bavaria and war with his former ally Philip. And Richard's brother John, de facto ruler for the many years of Richard's absence, finally so angered his overtaxed barons that they forced him to sign the Magna Carta in 1215, that limited royal powers and established a precedent for future constitutional protection of freedom.

Robert's descendants eventually married into the De Beville family line, that later joined the Pamplin family. But those marriages occur later.

Although Robert Lawrence's effort at Acre was heroic, the Crusaders were unable to hold onto the Holy Land for many more years. The Crusades were, however, a major turning point in the past millennium and ushered in the beginning of the end of "the Dark Ages."

Robert and other Crusaders developed a taste for the luxuries of the Orient—such as spice, silk and perfume—that they encountered in their travels. They also told tales of far-away places that set imaginations on fire. At the same time, the Crusades so antagonized the Muhammedan world that land routes to Asia were now forbidden to Christendom. These results of the Crusades set the stage for the "Age of Exploration," when men set out in ships to find a sea route to Asia.

It was this movement of people that brought the first family to bear the present name to England. The next chapter tells the story of this branch of the family—a branch that was almost cut off.

A t first, those who lived there took the spring for granted. Tucked at the edge of a forest, at the base of a hillside, it seemed only another of the small gifts of nature that abounded in England's farm country. Year round, it provided so much good clear water that by the middle of the thirteenth century an entire village depended on this spring. It was an essential resource for Thaxted, Essex, a settlement near the coast north and east of London.

The spring gave life, created community. So, too, it gave rise to envy and greed. Water was what made a landowner; water was wealth.

But during the reign of Henry III, Thaxted was enjoying a relatively stable era of improving farm life and increasing profit. The spring at woods' edge remained likewise tranquil and uncontested. One man had his eye on it. This was Ferdinand De Berlada, a trader from the state of Navarre, in that northern strip of the Spanish peninsula still unconquered by the infidel Moors. Though used to Spain and the sea, De Berlada had developed a special feeling for woodsy Thaxted. He'd made good as one of the merchants with a trade grant from the business-minded King Henry. His specialty was Spanish iron, more finely edged and durable than any in England; he shipped between Navarre and Colchester, a fine protected port. After unloading, De Berlada often turned traveling salesman, venturing inland with his swords and cutlery. Thirty miles off the ocean, he discovered Thaxted.

Henry III had foreseen that ironwork would provide an exceptionally strong economic base for the Essex area, so easily reached from Spain. And Ferdinand De Berlada, encouraged by a government so friendly to business, could see his future in the region. Establishing a home in Colchester, he became one of the great immigrant success stories of his day.

De Berlada enjoyed riding the Essex countryside, exploring his adopted land. Of course, this was only after the last goods of the season were sold, and the money was safe in his Colchester safe boxes. De Berlada hadn't made his fortune by leaving himself easy prey to forest brigands. Nonetheless he liked to ride alone when he felt he could risk it, and he was alone when he discovered the burbling stream at the border of meadow and wilderness.

The stream's source was obvious. Even without dismounting, De Berlada could spot the bubbles of uprushing water, breaking the surface at the center of a pool just beyond the first rank of woods growth. And his horse began neighing, thirsty after the long ride; and the stream kept on whispering, calling to man and rider both.

So the hard-driving businessman came to spend many an afternoon in this soft-speaking, peaceful place. No longer a Spaniard, no longer a seaman, he grew to middle age and beyond, passing as many solitary hours as he could among the colorful crocuses, lilies, ferns, and sweet-smelling long English grasses. His companions were butterflies and jaybirds, salamanders, squirrels, forest pigs—and the occasional local villager, people he thought of more and more as his countrymen. The place was his refuge, his oasis.

For despite his successes, the transplanted Navarran needed a refuge. Storms took their toll on ships and cargo, while overland shipping lanes were beset by outlaws and the hazards of neglected roads. The last thing a businessman needed, on top of all that, was the stigma of being a foreigner. Nothing would make him an Englishman so much as owning English water. The spring was De Berlada's oasis, in other words, because it was also his hope. If he owned the land, then finally he would belong.

Owning land, in feudal Western Europe, was primarily a privilege of royalty and its appointees, and in England nearly all the best estates were held by old Norman nobility. Some of these, however, were open-minded and fair-dealing. De Berlada himself did business with one such clan, descendants of a Crusader famed for being first over the wall at the battle of Acre. This family owned a considerable spread farther inland at Huntingdon; they urged De Berlada to petition for the property he wanted.

De Berlada went to work with an immigrant's persistence. In 1260 he succeeded in purchasing the spring and the land around it, thirty-five acres in all. The beauty and significance of the place were lost on its former owner, an all-too-typical Lord of the Manor eager to convert whatever he could to ready cash. Indeed, his name was de Wanton. Despite this lord's spendthrift way, he and his family would retain their high local rank for decades to come—and prove themselves, when it came to this spring, wanton indeed.

Though now an Essex landowner, De Berlada retained a fondness for the place he'd come from. Some years after he was able to buy his beloved Thaxted spring the tradesman began to groom a young man from Navarre as his successor. This was one Geoffrey, from the Spanish kingdom's capital city, Pamplona. Like many ambitious up-and-comers, Geoffrey was a bit vague about his background; for a last name, he simply borrowed that of his native town—Pamplin.

Pamplin had first worked for the cutlery merchant as a deck hand. Shipping wrought iron, between Navarre and Colchester, required slow, stout vessels, difficult to maneuver. Only the most seaworthy crewmen could insure a safe voyage, and Geoffrey proved to be more than up to the task. Dark and energetic, he was the sort of ever-ready youngster seamen call, with respect, a "tough monkey." He had black Catalan eyes that always glittered, somehow, with a touch of fun. Dock workers and ship captains alike quickly came to respect his good will, his drive, and the deck hand found himself assigned extra authority. So De Berlada first noticed him, on the piers of Colchester, a bustling youngster with glittering eyes.

Geoffrey's service to the transplanted iron-merchant continued for twenty years. He captained De Berlada's ships and hired their crews. Like his boss, he took up residence in affluent Colchester; his ties with the older immigrant deepened into friendship.

Early on in his tenure with De Berlada, Geoffrey often traveled up England's east coast, and on one such trip he met a Scot named Mary—a woman who stirred feelings he'd never known before. Pamplin found himself requesting additional assignments to those cold and rock-bound lochs, and every time another sojourn with his Scotch Mary ended, he felt worse about leaving her. She was an unusual woman for the times.

In general, women of feudal Western Europe had a considerably lower status than men. But the women of high society were required to be that much more subservient to their noble husbands, brothers, or fathers, in order to keep up social appearances. But Mary would not accept her assigned station in life. Independent, confident, forthright, she set herself apart.

Geoffrey Pamplin, the immigrant with a borrowed last name, fell in love with a woman who took pride in tracing her own family back to the Celts.

While a Catholic in name and a Christian at heart, she retained many proud vestiges of her Celtic past. She had the looks of her tribe, its eruptive red hair and fine, bright skin—a very different appearance from dark Pamplin's. Besides that, Mary's religious icons and household decorations incorporated designs from the ancient Druid forest-worship; she liked the geometric symbols of her pagan forebears, the surreal animal statuettes. Nor was Mary alone, in her region, in honoring the old mythology. The very flag of Scotland retained some of the same Celtic arcana, such as the two-faced monster sometimes called a hippogriff.

These ties to her ancient past created in Mary, as in many true Scots, a strong will. She had the depth of character necessary to fall in love, and the gumption to go wherever that love required her to go. When Geoffrey proposed marriage, it meant that his proud Mary—his "sweet witch," with her figurines and fairy tales—had to move several hundred miles south. Worse, though of course she'd heard of Essex and Colchester, she'd grown up considering such places the home of the enemy. The England of the Normans and their so-called "Angevin Empire" was constantly bickering over borders with its northern neighbor Scotland. More than once, even under the business-minded Henry III, that bickering had erupted into war.

Yet when Geoffrey Pamplin asked her to go, Mary tossed back her rich red hair and, squeezing her lover's hands, agreed at once.

Over the next fifteen years in Colchester, Geoffrey and Mary raised a family. This was no small feat for two immigrants in a cluttered, changing medieval town. It was well that Mary had been made hardy by her rearing in stern northern climes; she survived five birthings, and nursed five sons to full-grown health. Also the new family had to prove strong in soul, as well as in body. The husband spent much of his time at sea—hardly an easy situation for a woman whom many in the boom town port considered, at the least, suspicious. For wasn't she a Scot? And didn't she have primitive, witch-like ways? The woodsy Celtic fables Mary told her boys leaked out, inevitably, to other children running the Colchester streets and fields.

But what really galled the locals—at least, those who didn't trust outsiders—was the Pamplins' luck with money. Hard-working Geoffrey continued to earn good wages and commissions from his aging countryman De Berlada. True, the one-time deck hand wasn't alone in his success. As the area's economy grew, there emerged an entire new class of such mercantile success stories, not just ironmongers but people in related businesses, like blacksmiths and cartwrights. These linked successes had created a whole new social element, one that ranked somewhere between the old nobility on the one hand and the subsistence poor on the other. Clearly Pamplin was among the foremost of this emerging group. So while jealous neighbors groused about Pamplin's friendship with old De Berlada, or even whispered about Celtic spells cast by his handsome wife, the more tolerant citizens understood that merchants like these enterprising Spaniards had merely made good use of a thriving economy.

But no era of general well-being can survive chronic warfare. And in the last years of the century, hostilities were breaking out on all sides. These wars all were rooted in ancient conflicts. England and France had squabbled over territory ever since William the Conqueror had claimed both countries as his own. Indeed, the legendary Richard the Lion-Hearted had died during a siege in continental France. As for England and Scotland, they'd been quarreling even longer. Often these two enemies of the English Crown linked up in their struggle. More than once both Henry III and his son Edward I found themselves up against such an alliance. Worse still, in the last decade of the thirteenth century, the first Edward found himself fighting with all three of his neighbors: not only with Scotland and France, but also with Wales.

Pamplin and De Berlada, sophisticated leaders of the new middle class, kept up on these events. More than that, they understood what their country's quarrelsomeness would mean for business. Yes, war meant a greater demand for swords and lances; that was a short-term gain. But long-term, even the strongest Spanish iron wouldn't stand up to the extra taxes, the hampered shipping conditions—or, especially, the renewed hostility towards foreigners.

De Berlada was nearly seventy. He'd stored away enough of his earnings, by then, to sustain him until his death. But he could see that his good friend Geoffrey Pamplin, a man like a son to him, had no such security should the iron trade collapse. Yes, Pamplin was like a son to him, and Pamplin's family was like his own . . . so De Berlada came up with a way to help.

The old man made his proposal after dinner at his house. De Berlada relished such evenings, under the sturdy oak beams of the home he'd earned with his own wit and labor. Geoffrey and Mary were always fine company, and their five miraculously healthy boys were if anything even more fun for the old man. Wonderful it was to see how Santa Maria, the Queen of Heaven, had smiled on these brave, hard-working newcomers.

When the roast and fruit were gone, when they all were lingering over the best wine in the house, De Berlada spoke, with his eyes on the boys.

"A ship may go down," he said, "and iron may rust. But a farm lasts as long as the earth itself. So long as there is water, it lasts."

Geoffrey had seen the spring, out in Thaxted, at the edge of meadow and wood.

"Would you boys like to own a farm?" the old man asked. "Would you like to have land and water of your own, forever?"

"Dear friend Ferdinand" Geoffrey exploded. "I owe you so much already—"

"Not half what I owe you," Ferdinand De Berlada declared. "You owe me nothing that's worth a family's love. Nothing that matters so much as five boys to bring joy to my old age."

So the merchant made his offer, a bit brusquely. He found himself so near tears, at that moment, he needed to be businesslike just to get through what he had to say. He'd drawn up documents, he explained, naming them stewards of his little spring, his oasis. He pointed out that his health and frailty had kept him from making the seventy-mile round trip to Thaxted and back for several years now. "I know that before long I will go join our Lord Jesus and his saints." The merchant crossed himself, and even the boys could see how his spotted old hand shook. "And so I have made certain under the law that this land will always be yours."

Before the evening was over, De Berlada presented his Colchester family the parchment deed. Both Geoffrey and Mary looked it over—for the wife could read, in this unusual family. And both were still so thunder-struck at the new life opening before them that they never much noticed, in the sentences defining the property's boundaries, the name of the Lord of the Manor: de Wanton.

T he decision to move was by no means an easy one. Geoffrey was no farmer, but rather a sailor and tradesman. His wife had more the landowner's perspective, given her upbringing, but she too had ridden out to Thaxted; she'd seen just how small the village was—and how hard the life.

In those years, farmers lived closer to subsistence poverty than to the new, middle-class comforts the Pamplins had come to know. Weather, pests, and the whims of the Lord of the Manor could all undo years of hard work at a stroke. In the best of years farmers produced barely enough income to pay for the few household items they didn't make themselves, and in years of drought or cold they could be starved off their land.

But Mary Pamplin also saw an independent spirit in these English farmers, the same spirit she'd always felt in herself and knew was in her husband. And for the Pamplins there would be an essential difference between them and most other farmers at the turn of the fourteenth century. The Pamplins would own their own property.

The Pamplin spring turned out to be just one of the water sources in town. Locals drew not only from that woodside stream, but also from another alongside one of the village's two roads. For this was a crossroads, where the Pamplins found themselves, a former travelers' rest.

At first the family shared a one-room hut, a place patched together of wood and sod. The windows were mere holes in the sod, covered with sackcloth. They slept on rough straw mattresses, and the boys used logs for pillows. A small collection of flat stones in the center of the dirt floor served as both fireplace and stove. Kettles were hung over the fire on an iron bar, and bread was baked in a small clay oven—all vented through an opening in the grass-thatched roof. When winter closed in, smoke permeated their clothes and skin. And nonetheless the family was cold, since snow and rain fell through the vent and wind found its way through chinks in the walls and doorway. The first winter, pigs and poultry joined the family inside. It was dreary, damp, desolate living. Yet on the whole, it wasn't much unlike the way nearly everyone else passed the winter in Thaxted.

In sunnier seasons, their labor proved back-breaking. The Pamplins farmed their land cooperatively with their neighbors, staying with the feudal open-field system. Already Geoffrey and Mary had a great advantage over nearly everyone in town, owning their land. Already their sons heard the same dark talk they'd heard in Colchester, the old slurs: Spanish, Scot, witch. The family didn't want to stir up additional resentment; they took care to do their farming the same way as everyone else.

Thaxted was surrounded by three large fields, several hundred acres each. Each farm family had responsibility for particular strips of land, but all farmers worked together, ensuring that all the crops matured at the same time. Each family owned a pair of oxen, and teamed them with others during the twice-yearly tilling. At this time, women would follow the plows, dropping seeds into the freshly turned earth. Then came the daily hoeing, right through growing season, the heavy work that kept down weeds and chased off vermin. Come harvest time, medieval farmers worked as a team again. Four cutters went after the stalks with long-handled scythes, and a fifth bound them into sheaves.

As for the crop rotation, that was set down by the Lord of the Manor—in Thaxted, William de Wanton. De Wanton stipulated that one field grow wheat or rye and another oats or barley, while the third field lay fallow, unplanted.

To the Pamplins, de Wanton's rotation at first seemed sensible enough. It gave the land time to recover, after two growing seasons. But as the seasons progressed and the Pamplins' neighbors opened up to the newcomers, Geoffrey and Mary learned that, in fact, the Lord's system had every farmer in town worried about the future.

William de Wanton, Geoffrey and Mary learned, was new to the land's stewardship. Only a year before they'd arrived had young Lord William taken over from his father—the estate-holder who'd originally sold the spring-land to De Berlada. And for more than two centuries before William, locals had left half the land fallow each season, not one-third. Half fallow had meant less total production each harvest, but had insured fertile soil for a good eight or ten generations of Thaxted farmers. But Lord William wanted his lands to produce more. He wanted more ash on hand, and fast. More ash meant more influence with his beleaguered King, Edward I, who himself remained desperate for funds, for his campaigns against France, against Scotland, and now against Wales.

Lord William was a husky, tall blonde, the very picture of a hale Norman prince. He did, however, have an odd habit of looking at things with his head slightly cocked.

The de Wantons' was a town within a town. Two protective embankments, studded by spiked wooden poles, surrounded William's compound. A deep ditch lay between these walls, traversable only by two crude drawbridges. The inner compound contained William's house, stable, and barn, plus a family chapel and a few workshops. The Lord of the Manor oversaw a kind of family hive, in which workers, farm animals, clerics, and his own relatives milled about busily.

The largest space in the Lord's house was the dining hall, and evening meals there gave de Wanton an opportunity to show off his new stature in the world. More than a dozen relatives and friends might feast at a single sitting, making short work of such delicacies as roast venison or mutton stuffed with herbs. There was always more than enough, with plenty left over for the house pets, and nearly every meal was accompanied by musical or theatrical entertainment. This was the life of feudal lords all across western Europe, an easy excess they claimed by right of inheritance alone.

Each year the Pamplins worked the town's shared open fields, more of their harvest went to providing for William. Villagers had to pay rent by working on William's land two or three days a week, plus providing occasional in-kind provisions: eggs, vegetables, smoked meat. In the fall, William's crops were harvested first. De Wanton even owned the mill, where the wheat was ground to flour; he charged for every load.

Geoffrey and Mary, by working their own acreage diligently, could at least protect a few family resources from this greedy overseer. They maintained a large vegetable garden, and along the spring-stream grew greens and onions, berries and apples. The Pamplins even raised a few livestock, but since they had little food to spare, the farm animals foraged for themselves. Pigs found acorns in the forest, chickens scratched around the yard.

In the Pamplins' first few years, they were wracked by famine twice. The tradesmen in the Thaxted aileyways nodded their heads, as knowledgeable about lean years as their farmer friends. It was Lord William's doing; it was the crook-necked Lord who'd bled the good land dry. Granted, the de Wantons had no control over rainfall levels or plant disease or insect infestation. But throughout those mean times, the pretty Lord William and his friends always had more than enough to eat. Worse, they flaunted their excess. The de Wantons' feasts became more lavish than ever. The hungry Pamplins, in their hut, fell asleep to the sounds of singing and laughter in the manor house, a raucous noise carrying across peaceful fields.

During the second of these famines, in 1301, more than a few farmers began to steal. Starving fathers needed to feed their starving families, and Thaxted remained a crossroads for travelers—travelers who could never identify their assailants. There were days Geoffrey Pamplin would spot an unexplained bit of jewelry or a fine pair of boots in the hut of one of his hungry friends. The Pamplins' friends often brought up the old tales about Robin Hood, robbing the rich to feed the poor, their voices alive with a quiet bitterness. Geoffrey and Mary understood full well what those tales were actually about. And yet, just as the couple couldn't condemn their friends, they couldn't take the law into their own hands themselves. They wouldn't steal, and they forbade the boys to do so either. Pilfering simply wasn't an option for a family that had come so far with hard work and integrity.

Mary again revealed the strength at her Celtic core, praying to Jesus for her friends' souls, praying to Mary for some miracle to help them all. And she touched a few old Druid figurines as she prayed, taking comfort in these reminders of her childhood. As for Geoffrey, he fell back on his old deck-hand's resourcefulness. The Pamplin men supplemented what came from their garden with wild game from their private patch of forest. The grown boys shot deer, while the younger dug out rabbits and snared squirrels.

But the family also had practical reasons for leading a righteous life. In medieval England, the punishment of criminals was nothing short of draconian. More than that, the two canny immigrants had recognized by then their local Lord's desire for the water-source his father had so thoughtlessly sold away. Young de Wanton seemed to be forever taking riding parties past the Pamplin property, and Geoffrey and Mary had noted the greedy way the Lord looked over stream and meadow and woodlands as he rode by. Even with his pretty head cocked to one side, William couldn't hide his yearning. Less than a hundred years before, Geoffrey knew, his Lord could simply have taken the land by ordering the owner to give him title. But a former international tradesman like Pamplin also knew the impact of the Magna Carta, reluctantly signed into law by the hated King John in 1215. The Carta guaranteed the rights of landowners—against local nobility as much as against the King. So, floundering for ideas, de Wanton's thoughts turned to catching Pamplin somehow outside the law. If a man was convicted of a felony, he'd lose all title to whatever land he might own. A felony, however, was a serious crime: either murder or treason.

Proving that Pamplin had committed a murder was of course out of the question. The new farmer's reputation was impeccable, right through the two recent famines. But a charge of treason—when dealing with black-eyed immigrants like Pamplin—treason might be made to stick.

N ext winter was better than the last. Thaxted's farmers had enjoyed a good harvest, and Geoffrey could see that, among his friends, pilfering had gone down considerably. Perhaps his family's upright example had made a difference. If so, then the example that mattered most had been set not by Geoffrey, but by his oldest son, John. Twenty-seven years old, married to a local girl and the father of a six-year-old boy of his own, John was a true townsman. His hair was strawberry-blonde, British blonde; he spoke without an accent. The oldest son had his parents' resourcefulness as well as their integrity and Christian faith.

So it was John who Lord William went after first, in his campaign against the Pamplins. His accomplice was Edmund Beaufort. Some payment changed hands, and early in 1302 the Pamplins were shocked to hear their virtuous John accused of robbery.

The crime was said to have taken place in the forest near the neighboring village of Widdington. The story ran that John Pamplin, accompanied by other forest roughs, had taken this nobleman's purse—though the strapping son of Mary and Geoffrey, everyone could quickly see, would have needed no help subduing a fop like his accuser.

Lord William had waited until John was out of town, two days' journey distant, visiting his wife's ailing father. He made sure Beaufort brought his accusations over in that town—in Widdington—so that John

Pamplins' salutary Thaxted reputation wouldn't carry any weight with the local judge.

But the scheming Lord of the Manor hadn't counted on the depth of Pamplin's support. Several of the young man's family and friends took time from their subsistence living in order to make the trip to Widdington. They testified to his character, and to the absurdity of the evidence. The oily Edmund Beaufort, on the other hand, had no one to stand with him. Under cross-examination by the Widdington judge, his story stumbled into one inconsistency after another. When the judge declared him not guilty, young John Pamplin returned to Thaxted more highly esteemed than ever.

William de Wanton, now hurt in his pride as well as his pocketbook, was left all the more resolved to bring down these proud small landowners. How dare they outwit a Lord of the realm! And the aging Geoffrey and Mary, though happy for their son, likewise understood that the family's struggle was far from over.

William recognized he needed something big, something dramatic, in order to bring down the Pamplins. Once more he considered the larger stage: the situation of his country and his King. Throughout 1302 and into 1303, Edward I continued his effort to claim the throne of Scotland. He had by now achieved his initial goal of assuming control of Scottish government. But the northern clans still resisted all efforts at royal control. Thus, by 1303, Edward needed still more war financing, and he was desperate to capture the Scottish warriors' refugee leader, Prince William Wallace. If Edward I ever got his hands on the runaway Prince, he'd make an example of the man!

So the anti-Scot sentiment blew hot once more, south of the old Roman wall, Emperor Hadrian's Wall—the traditional border between the island's two kingdoms. And in Thaxted, a cruel summer had taken its toll. Rains had continued unabated through July. Plants drowned in their fields. Then when the skies cleared, the wind turned hot; it parched nearly all that was left of the wheat and barley. Without forage, the cattle withered. Given such a bleak outlook for winter, many townspeople turned to superstition and finger-pointing. The time was ripe for finding a scapegoat.

One early victim of this bad luck was John Pamplin's father-in-law. He had no chance to recover from the illness that had led to John's visit the summer before. In the summer of 1303, the sick old man could see that his wife and daughter would be his only survivors, and under feudal law, a widow lost her husband's allotment of land if there was no male heir to continue working it. So in this case, the right was willed to the man's son-in-law, John.

The oldest Pamplin son—the sturdiest branch of the family tree—didn't want to leave Thaxted. These trying times had also taken their toll on his mother Mary, whose fine Celtic skin was by now seamed and dry with age. But then again, if John took his wife and boy to Widdington, there would be three fewer mouths to feed in Thaxted. The young man packed once more for the two-days' journey to his wife's father's farm.

That same summer another son had left. This was the fifth, the youngest: Walter. Walter Pamplin was the philosopher among the siblings. He put as much effort into farm work as the rest of the boys; but his mind was always elsewhere. He took his father's and mother's Christian faith further than either of them. He would talk for hours with those few Thaxted travelers who had religious training. Now, in this same hard summer of 1303, at the age of sixteen, the youngest Pamplin had made his goodbyes to the rest of his family. Walter had set off for the nearest monastery that took in novices; he was determined to become a priest himself.

So it was a smaller Pamplin household that labored to withstand the winter. The bone-chilling damp tested old Geoffrey as few winters had, but Mary, now fifty-three, had the worst of it. There came a day when she couldn't rise from her bed. When Geoffrey stroked the red hair he'd adored for more than thirty years, a clump came out beneath his loving palm.

"My little witch," he murmured.

Mary smiled. In her weakness she'd asked for her old Druid figurines; a couple of the worn wooden dragons rested in her trembling hands.

"Little witch . . ." Geoffrey heard himself repeating.

"Jesus knows my heart," the woman whispered. "He knows this is one witch who'll be happy to see him."

In her last hours, Mary asked for all the arcana out of her past: the sculpture of the two-headed hippogriff, the bright pennants with the winding Celtic geometry. The old woman then began to sing in old Scottish—in Gaelic. Between songs she spoke with her statue. Her childhood had risen again round her, taking over the thatch-roofed home far south of her homeland.

By then the Pamplin Thaxted house had become a sturdier, roomier affair than the one with which the family had started. There was even a chimney. And the men who attended the sinking old woman were no country bumpkins. Geoffrey and his remaining three boys knew well the danger of waving around Scottish flags, in this tempestuous time of constant wars. Scotland's Prince, William Wallace, remained at large. Supporting him meant treason, and treason meant hanging—at the least. All this the Pamplin men knew, that winter, as there before them Mary slipped deeper and deeper into her Scottish past. But they knew too that this sweet-voiced old grandmother was no enemy of the Crown, nor of Christ. They knew they had the support of nearly everyone in the community in honoring the last wishes of the most important woman in their lives.

Nearly everyone supported them. Nearly everyone.

D espite the bitterness of that year's winter, Mary Pamplin's funeral was well-attended. Even those villagers who'd remained suspicious of the Northerner in their midst had come to grant her a grudging respect. They came in the name of goodwill, and in the name of Jesus.

The service had ended, friends had led old Geoffrey from the open grave, and most mourners had turned for their homes. But the three remaining Thaxted sons—Richard, Roger, and Thomas—lingered over their mother's coffin. Then suddenly, the emotions of the moment clouding their judgment, all three pulled out a few small items they'd concealed under their coats.

The youngest, Thomas, withdrew a statue: his mother's two-headed pagan sculpture. Dropping to his knees, the boy gently placed the thing in the woman's grave, on her coffin. Next, Roger pulled out a rolled-up canvas. It opened to reveal the ancient geometry, in orange and black, that to Mary represented the magic of her ancestors. Roger kissed the scroll, then reverently laid it beside the statuette on her coffin. Finally, Richard (at twenty-six, he was the oldest son still at home) unfurled a colorful pennant.

To those few onlookers nearby, the boys' first two offerings had seemed merely odd. They weren't Christian, the little monster and the colorful scroll, but they weren't dangerous either. But this last memento drew gasps from everyone who remained. The flag of the Scots! The monster! Prince William's monster!

Among the gossips of Essex county, it was known as "the Pamplin blasphemy." Lord William de Wanton wasted no time convening a court.

To Lord William, what the Pamplin boys had done wasn't blasphemy. No, far better; the sons' display of the Scottish flag, however briefly, was treason. No sooner had the court convened, it seemed, than the boys were convicted and sentenced. This time, unlike when he'd gone after John Pamplin, Lord William was able to pick the judge. Even those one or two vassals who dared say a word on behalf of the boys' character were forced to admit that they'd heard rumors of the mother's pagan ways and Scottish sympathies. And—the judge asked—hadn't the incident occurred during a Christian service? On consecrated ground? Those infernal foreign idols have desecrated a holy rite!

The boys were convicted and sentenced to death by hanging.

February 9, 1304, was more of the same for that terrible winter. The sun came up as dark and cold, but Lord William de Wanton, looking out over his Manor House courtyard from his bedchamber, found the morning splendid. He'd opened the grounds to anyone who wanted to see the show: virtually an entire family on the gallows. Already there were a dozen or so on the grounds, trying to find a dry spot before the grotesque, skeletal platform. Hangings always drew a sizeable audience, even when, like today, there weren't many around who agreed with the sentence. If someone was to make a public show of their disagreement, after all, they might soon find themselves mounting those slapdash platform stairs, towards that swinging double-thick noose.

It especially pleased William that hanging was a slow death. The platform was merely to provide a better view; the victims were pushed off a stool. They lost consciousness only after long minutes of choking and struggling before the fascinated eyes of the onlookers. De Wanton had instructed his guards to keep an eye out for any spectators who might try to rush the platform. He wanted no one to grab the boys, no one to yank on their legs and break their necks. That would be far too quick and gentle a passing.

So too, he was pleased that the patriarch, Geoffrey, would be there. Front row center, at a hanging, was usually reserved for the victims' families.

The practice was in part a mercy. It allowed the dying the comfort of their loved ones. But it was also in part a message; it made clear that the King's words was final. Too bad, then—Lord William mused further—that the news didn't appear to have reached the two surviving sons. One would think that even the teenaged Walter, shut off in a monastery though he was, would have learned that his mother had died and his brothers were to be hanged. And that big, well-respected John, only two days' walk from here, must certainly have heard by now.

But the Lord of the Manor wouldn't let anything spoil his happy morning for long. He concentrated instead on a mental picture of Geoffrey Pamplin struggling to work his land alone, without his sons. If a man couldn't properly farm his property, by law he'd have to give it up. And the Lord of the Manor imagined riding up the Pamplin stream, wetting his pretty lips at last at its spring.

Some long minutes later William de Wanton stood finally on the hanging platform, above the crowd. He found himself a bit chilled; the finery for a state occasion was not usually intended to be worn outdoors. Also the three Pamplin boys behind him stank pretty badly after their days in his underground cell. But as he declaimed the high-flown words of his King's proclamation, William was buoyed up anew. He wasn't even bothered by not seeing the patriarch Geoffrey, in the crowd below him. While he didn't see the old man's face—that foreign, black-eyed face—he did see a number of men with hoods. Often the families of the victims wore hoods at these hangings; they wanted to hide from prying eyes. Perhaps, the Lord thought, Geoffrey Pamplin was that one with a brown rag swaddling his head. Or perhaps he was that other man in a black scarf. A few of the men with hoods, William noticed, also held places in the front.

The proclamation was finished, the victims readied. To the Lord of the Manor, the boys' obvious courage was an irritant. Did they have to lift their heads so bravely for the noose? Did they have to keep up that low, unbroken prayer?

All three of them appeared to be staring intently, as if with some meaning, towards the front of the crowd—towards the men there with hoods.

But then, Lord William also had his own man in a hood: the executioner, now testing each rope with one final tug, now tightening the loops over the young men's heads. In the crowd, shouts and taunts began to rise—some not quite sincere, it sounded to the Lord of the Manor, but never mind. He relished the moment nonetheless, his vicious eyes scanning the mob once more for old Geoffrey. He still couldn't find the man, but he wasn't going to waste any more time. William de Wanton nodded.

At first all the Lord noticed was some disruption at the front of the mob. A blur of movement; an awful grunt in the sudden hush. But then he saw: three of the men with hoods had leapt forward and taken the dangling legs of Geoffrey Pamplin's sons. Before he could speak—before the executioner had stepped back from kicking away the last chair—these unknown friends of the family pulled down hard. In the sudden hush, the crowd silenced at the moment of truth, everyone heard the boys' vertebrae crack.

The sons' death was swift and painless. Their accomplices melted back into the crowd in a moment.

Lord William simply couldn't comprehend the affection felt by his villagers for Geoffrey and the boys. Such affection was altogether beyond his ken.

T he unselfish love extended to the three Pamplin brothers on the gallows proved to be the first of many such acts over the next months. Geoffrey was now alone, and plainly devastated: his hair a solid white, his face a web of lines. Nonetheless, under feudal law he was required to work. Not only did he have to demonstrate that he could still cultivate his own private gardens, but also he still had to put in his share on the Manor farms.

Thaxted farmers knew well the law they lived under, and as March softened the ground enough to take seeds, they began to pitch in for the grieving father. They worked even longer days than usual, taking over the Pamplin portion of the feudal open fields. Geoffrey meantime tended to his fruits and vegetables. As spring turned to summer—driven by a burning need to save something, to redeem this murder somehow—the property's lone survivor earned the right to live beside his shimmering stream a while longer.

News of the man's quiet heroism abetted by friendship and proof of his long-standing integrity, began to reach beyond Thaxted. A triple hanging connected to the Scottish resistance was a sensational story. Inevitably the tale made its way northward, and crossed Hadrian's Wall.

By this time the leader of the Celtic struggle, Scotland's Prince William Wallace, had been in hiding for four years. The merest whisper of his appearance anywhere on the British Isles would stir up fresh uprisings among those opposed to English rule. Not only the Scots were inspired by the outlaw Prince William, but the Irish and Welsh as well. Thus for Edward I of England, there was no greater enemy than this half-legendary prince. He established a hefty cash reward for any news leading to Prince William's capture.

In any real sense, Scotland's Wallace was a defeated man. His country lacked the resources of forward-looking, ever-growing England. And the runaway Prince was himself drained, emotionally and physically. He had spent most of his exile in France, and now wanted nothing so much as to return home in peace. In 1304, weary and desperate, the refugee prince risked a return.

He sailed to Colchester, planning to sail up the coast next, passing himself off as a French nobleman. In Colchester, many of the tradesmen remembered the young and energetic Geoffrey Pamplin, and it wasn't long before the incognito Prince heard the entire story.

So as the year turned to summer, there arrived another solitary traveler on the Thaxted crossroads.

Anyone who watched the rider trot by, however, could see he was no ordinary Colchester tradesman. He was noble-born, plainly; his horsemanship was superb, his manner refined. When the traveler needed directions, he approached a woman of his own class. And this woman, finely veiled and athwart a gilded saddle, couldn't help noticing the man's aristocratic demeanor. Besides that, he had an accent she'd never heard before. But the most startling thing about him was where he was going. The mysterious horseman asked directions to "the property of Geoffrey Pamplin."

The woman watched the stranger as he rode off. She was Lady Beaufort—wife to Edmund Beaufort.

Geoffrey Pamplin had just completed a day in his vegetable garden when the stranger rode up. Silently he leaned on his hoe, as silently he'd spent almost every waking moment since his last farewell to his boys.

Prince William Wallace—for the rider was he—saw no rudeness in this. Long exiled and downtrodden himself, he understood. He asked if he could water his horse and rest for a bit.

Geoffrey hadn't lost his Christian charity. As warmly as he could, he told the man he was welcome. But this was also more than charity, to Geoffrey: the stranger's accent had at once recalled the Celtic burr of his own dear Mary.

But then who was he, this red-haired Scotsman in enemy territory? And why had he come to Geoffrey?

"You know," the patriarch ventured, "I've worked up a powerful thirst here in my garden. I believe I'll join you by the water myself."

Soon the Prince and the immigrant settled together at the water's edge.

"Where did you say you came from?" Geoffrey put in finally.

"From France," Wallace replied, straight-faced.

All his youth Geoffrey had sailed with men from France. Not one of them had sounded so like a Scot. Well, he thought. It looked as if it was up to him to bring them both round to serious matters.

"Myself," he said, "I intend to end my days right here. I have two sons still living, and"—he gestured at the stream before their feet—"I'd like them to inherit this good water."

"Two sons still living?" the Prince said sharply. "Two sons, besides the three who were hanged?"

Geoffrey narrowed his eyes, waiting.

"You had three strong young boys hanged," William Wallace went on, "simply because they honored a fine brave Scotswoman."

When his seamy, staring ghost still wouldn't answer, the Prince added, in a voice barely above a whisper, "Isn't that so, Geoffrey Pamplin?"

Finally the old man's peering softened. A smile played at the corners of his mouth. "So-o-o," he said, "you say you're from France?"

Both men laughed, forgetting themselves. Defeated and heartsore and without much hope for the future, the two laughed and laughed some more, seizing the happy moment.

It was the older of the two who came back to his senses first. Geoffrey bent and cupped spring-water onto his teary face. Then he sat up straight once more. "Tell me," he said. "Tell me who you are. If you were the Prince of Scotland himself, I swear by the shrine of the Virgin in old Navarre. . . . "

"I am that Prince," William Wallace declared. "Heir to the throne of mighty Duncan and fearsome Macbeth, now these many years in lonesome exile."

"You say you're lonesome?" Geoffrey parried, smiling more soberly.

"Oh yes. Very lonesome, and in need of every last friend I can find."

"Well." The farmer put out his hand. "I know how that can be."

The two shook hands—first two, then all four—warmly in the gathering woodland dusk.

"I came to tell you," the Prince began, "how sorry I am for your loss." Then Wallace went on to describe the family's sudden fame throughout the kingdoms of greater Britain. Geoffrey learned how his sons were martyrs, his wife was a heroine. Clansmen hundreds of miles away, and without a drop of his own Latin blood, honored him as a brave compatriot. But rather than hearing himself praised, Geoffrey asked to be told more about the lochs and heaths where he'd once courted his young Mary. The two men talked long into the night, first there beside the stream and then in the Pamplin home. How wonderful it felt to Geoffrey, having someone share his little hearth once more!

But in the Manor House compound, meantime, Lord William had company as well. There Lady Beaufort and her husband Edmund had just finished the evening repast. Now while the men sat back stroking their well-fed stomachs, she entertained them with the story of her strange encounter on the Thaxted crossroads. She dwelt on the mysterious traveler's apparent high standing; she tried to mimic his accent. Before she was through, William de Wanton had swung forward in his big chair at the table's end. His head cocked, he peered at her closely.

"Lady Beaufort," he asked evenly, "might we hear that accent once again?"

Rumors about the outlaw Prince William Wallace were of course rife throughout England. If the refugee Prince was in Colchester, chances were good that he'd heard about the Scot sympathizers in Thaxted.

Lady Beaufort completed her imitation of the mysterious rider. In a moment, her husband Edmund redeemed himself for his miserable performance presenting the case against John Pamplin in Widdington. "'Tis William Wallace! The renegade himself!" Edmund declared. "My Lord, the reward is yours!"

Swiftly the Manor guards were gathered. De Wanton and his friend took a while longer; they had to gird themselves for hard riding and swordplay. During those busy minutes, the Manor servants once again showed Geoffrey Pamplin the depth of the affection felt for him among Thaxted's common people. They sent a runner, a friend named Robert Coyne, to the house by the stream.

With the breathless Coyne still out in the dark beyond Pamplin's doorway, Geoffrey and Wallace were forced to make hasty good-byes. The night was moonless and cool, good weather for outlaws; the late-summer wind in the forest should hide the sounds of the Prince's riding. But the nobleborn renegade lingered a moment more before going for his horse.

With a swordsman's quickness, he suddenly reached under his cloak and took a good medallion from around his neck. "You and your sons have done more than you know," he said. "You have rekindled the spirit of independence in my land—in your wife's native land. We can never repay you for your family, but I hope that this will remind you of our gratitude."

Bending in by his doorway, Geoffrey squinted at the medallion, the gold.

"I can't accept it," he said. He knew better than most the risk of keeping a Scottish emblem around the house. Moreover, he knew that Prince William Wallace knew. Thaxted had no need of another martyr to the Scottish cause. No patriotic token was worth a good man's life.

"I can't take it," the old man repeated. Wallace, nodding, understanding, hastily slipped the medallion into his saddle bag.

The trio could hear the baying of Lord William's dogs. Besides tracking wild game, they knew how to pick up the scent of escaped prisoners.

"Ride your horse up the stream, into the woods," old Geoffrey whispered hoarsely. "The dogs can't track you through the spring."

"Farewell, good friend Pamplin," Wallace said.

"Godspeed," Geoffrey said. "God-speed."

Using the stream gave the exiled Prince the head start he needed, and he slipped out of Thaxted undetected, denying Lord William the reward he'd lusted for. Nonetheless, the outlaw's freedom would be short-lived. Soldiers of King Edward would capture William Wallace a scant two weeks later. Back in the domain of William de Wanton, this news made dealing with Geoffrey Pamplin's transgression all the easier.

The night William Wallace escaped Thaxted, de Wanton's soldiers quickly noted the stranger's hoofprints in the dirt. De Wanton and one group then took the hounds into the woods, towards Geoffrey's spring. So they found the medallion. It lay shining in the clear water; it had come out of the hard-riding Prince's bag. In a single flashing moment the gold had been jarred free.

The ornament was all the evidence de Wanton needed to prove Geoffrey Pamplin was a traitor. Circumstantial evidence, yes. But the Lord of the Manor once again turned to the judge who'd helped him convict the three brothers—and at the same time, a mere forty miles away, Prince William Wallace was standing trial in London.

Both Pamplin and Wallace were scheduled for the gallows the same day: August 17, 1305. In de Wanton's filthy cellar, Geoffrey now and again shivered at the thought of how much worse it would be for his momentary friend. Scotland's William Wallace was the rebel devil, the focus of countrywide hate; word was that the King would have him disemboweled, then drawn and quartered.

Geoffrey took a real comfort in knowing that his own death would be more gentle. It would prove that, even in a land sick with intolerance, there remained a few who respected humanity. For de Wanton's prison-keeper was the same servant who'd looked the other way while Geoffrey had arranged to help young Richard, Roger, and Thomas, and he assured their father that Roger Coyne and another of his friends would perform the same merciful service for him.

On his last evening, Geoffrey was allowed to say good-bye to one of his two remaining sons. The news of his trial had of course reached his eldest, John, and this time not even his father's warnings to stay away could keep the young man from his side. John was the one son who could still carry on the Pamplin family name; Walter, after all, seemed likely to die a priest, celibate and childless. So the Widdington farmer came to the de

Wanton cellars. The Lord didn't object, since the treason conviction had stripped Geoffrey's children of any Thaxted inheritance.

John Pamplin found a spidery, white-haired patriarch who, even languishing in a dungeon, retained a stubborn Spanish glitter in his eyes. Geoffrey spent his final visit trying to provide a meaning for their tragedies.

"My son, we are farmers," he said. "Farmers. And now I ask you, as a farmer—do you recall the mustard seed? That tiny brown seed?"

Big John had been weeping. "Father," he said wearily, "I remember the parable, yes. Christ said that all we require is the faith of a mustard seed. But don't speak to me of Gospel now. We've hardly anything to show for our entire hard-working lives. You too will soon die on the gallows, and everyone knows—" he raised his voice for the prison-keeper to hear—"it is only as a ploy to give the fat Lord William more land and money!"

The farmer hushed his son, reaching through the bars. He and John knew they could count on the gaoler's silence, but there was no point tempting trouble.

"Son, we've lived well enough, haven't we?"

The strapping young man groaned.

"We've lived well enough boy," Geoffrey insisted. "We have many friends and have touched the lives of all of them. I daresay even your own son Andrew has learned much from his years with me and your three dead brothers."

John bit his lip. "He is seven now, father. He'll never forget what he learned at your knee."

"He is the mustard seed, my son. One tiny seed may travel far, very far. It may grow in strange places. But all it needs is to find water, good water. Then, Maria, it blooms. It lives."

Again the big visitor began to weep, ducking his bearded face into his arm. " Oh, father, I'll miss you."

"I am in the mustard seed," Geoffrey said gently, stroking John's muscular neck. "I've traveled far to bloom like this. And I will bloom again, and your brothers as well, and also your lovely freckled mother Mary."

The next morning as Geoffrey's friends rushed the gallows after the stool was kicked way—when they yanked at his legs as they'd yanked at his sons'—it may have been the Scotswoman's name they heard the old immigrant murmur, before the echoing snap of his neckbones.

This time Lord William de Wanton hadn't bothered to try and stop Geoffrey Pamplin's friends. If they wanted to give the pesky small land-owner a painless death, let them.

For all his rapacity about extending his borders, Edward I remained a skillful and conscientious monarch regarding issues closer to home. Till now, consumed with the trial and execution of the outlaw Scottish Prince, William Wallace, the King had paid no special attention to the Pamplin trials northeast of London. There'd been a lot of hangings, over these war-torn years. But now the King's suspicions were aroused. Was one of his subjects slaughtering others just for personal gain?

Edward ordered an investigation. With that, events began to move swiftly. As soon as the full pressure of the Crown was applied, William de Wanton's network of influential friends proved to be no more solid than a house of cards. Scant months after the proud Lord had thought he'd proven he was born for victory, he was found guilty of improperly charging Geoffrey Pamplin with treason. At the King's order, the immigrant farmer was pardoned posthumously and the Lord of the Manor was hanged. Up on the gallows, the bulky William de Wanton was so bewildered by how quickly his fortunes had fallen that, for once, he didn't smugly cock his head as he looked out over the common crowd. They were much the same as had greeted Geoffrey and his boys. But there was no one among them to do him any last act of mercy.

As for the Pamplin farm, it was returned to the oldest son John. The next spring the big man found himself once more walking the banks of his childhood. He walked those banks wondering, stumbling, still barely able to believe. God's justice had come round in no time at all. It had come round at great cost, John reminded himself, at terrible cost. But when justice at last found its way, it took up no more space, in the larger scheme of things, than a mustard seed. In a bad moment by his mother's grave, his brothers had been doomed; and in a moment by his father's doorway, the old man's fate too had been sealed. Then in one mysterious moment more, the essence of all his lost family had been finally, irrevocably restored.

The young farmer walked, trying to understand. At his feet he heard, once more, the spring's murmuring. It was like the chuckle of a much-trav-eled old man.

CHAPTER 3

Lora de Waldeschef Beville and the Black Plague

T he next two generations of Pamplins worked Geoffrey's and Mary's farm; the two after that turned to cutlery. But throughout these generations, hardships continued. In each, only one son survived to carry on the name.

In the meantime, Edward I was succeeded by Edward II, and then by Edward III. These kings and their French counterparts continued their bickering over territory, and finally drew both nations into the bloody Hundred Years' War.

Through all this and more, the Pamplins endured. Some raised sheep; some made violins. It was fourteen generations after the hangings that one of Geoffrey's descendants sailed to America.

In this volume, there isn't room for all those fourteen generations. Our story concentrates instead on the de Beville family line. For the next episode we return to a time only decades after the executions of Geoffrey Pamplin and three of his boys—a time when Walter, his other surviving son, has returned to Thaxted. An esteemed clergyman, from 1340 to 1348 Walter served as a vicar of the town's first church. His tenure ended in tragedy, however, though a different sort from his father's.

Vicar Pamplin was cut down by the bubonic plague. This "Black Death," as it was known, devastated Europe. Carried by the rats that ran amok in those unsanitary times, the disease killed one-third of the known world's population in a few short years.

Our next chapter concerns the plague. The fever carries off many of the young and strong—and yet spares one remarkable old woman.

At night the fears would come. She was old and long familiar with death's ravages, and nonetheless Lora would suffer the fears. First she'd picture again the particular horrors of that day. She'd see, for instance, the sore-encrusted lips of a dying young man, lips that whispered some final desire which might sound simple but always proved impossible. The youngster might hope for a last kiss—yet who would kiss the plagued? Who would risk the Black Death, in this terrible Year of Our Lord 1348?

Dear God, the horrors of the day: the carts heaped with limp, filthy corpses, blood-blackened, blotch-bruised; and the wheels of those carts creaked more fiercely, more piercingly, as their load grew heavier; and they were driven by men, their faces wrapped in rags to ward off the stench.

But this was only the first wave of horrors in Lora de Beville's nights. After it came the personal fear: the imaginings of her own death.

It shamed her, this second fear. It was silly, that she should still be afraid of dying. Lora de Waldeschef Beville had by then reached an age well-nigh impossible to credit, an age doubted even by clergymen she worked with.

"One hundred?" the normally placid Brother Thomas had asked, when he'd first heard. "Can a woman actually live to one hundred?"

But she'd done it, yes. She had outlived husband, children, even most of her grandchildren. Then how could the inevitable business of her own, no doubt swift death leave her so afraid? Oh truly, there was horror in the buboes, the boils in groin or armpit as big as eggs, stinking worse than the rottenest egg, the ugly bruises that multiplied over body and face, racking the body with agony. These bruises gave the Black Death its name. And the pain they caused drove its sufferers to mad, final humiliations.

Between the waves of fear, the old woman tried to distract herself with memories. It was hardly as if the last century had been so easy on humanity. Though her home was in peaceable Warwickshire, more or less at the center of prosperous England, Lora looked back on a lifetime during which the nation had been beset by foes without and within. Indeed, her century on this earth had been calamitous and unchristian. Nonetheless she'd outlasted its wickedness, her small body erect, her cheeks rosy, her smile kind. And still, still she found herself afraid.

The Death and its stink had arrived in Warwickshire in the spring of that year, 1348, and in the few months since, Lora had seen so much death that she feared all humankind would never see another year. She feared there would be no Warwickshire, no world at all, for her great- and great-great-grandchildren. And if so—then why, oh why, did Lora have to be the last one left? If this pox was God's judgment on a sinful world, what did He want with this old woman?

To calm this last, most sweeping fear, Lora would strain her ears for the familiar sounds of the Warwick night. Was William's dog still barking out there? Were there peasant voices in the village below? She wanted at least to hear the lowing of cattle, the bleating of goats. But lately, the nights had been hushed. There'd been no comfort in the familiar. The world had been turned upside down—like a bag being shaken out before it was thrown away.

Mornings, Lora reached first for her cane. The well-worn, fine-carved length of oak made it easier to rise, and the dry rushes scattered on her stone floors made it comfortable to stand. Every week for years, Lora's man Theorick had cut the rushes at the edge of the fen, dried them at the hearth, then scattered them across the Manor paving-stones.

But Theorick, too, had died, just ten days past. When these rushes were worn through, who would replace them?

Lora busied herself with her hair and washing, always useful distractions. Pinned up, her crown of white braids enhanced the faint rosiness of her cheeks. Those cheeks remained remarkably smooth. And her eyes still had their old intensity, in the mirror over the washbowl. She was always a small woman, but stooped over as she was now she seemed rather too small for her tastes, too much like a child. Irritated by the thought, she took up the washbasin herself and hauled it back to the kitchen. One of the women there had taken over the job of replenishing it, after Theorick had passed on.

The kitchen help of course made a terrific fuss at seeing her labor in with the basin. Flour billowed from their hands and aprons as they rushed to take it, but chores such as these were just the thing, for an old woman who needed to keep up a good front.

Lora was looked to as the matriarch, not just within the family but across the shire countryside. Anyone who knew ancient Warwick Castle—a stronghold dating back before the days of William the Conqueror—knew Grandma Lora. She was the oldest person anyone had ever seen. That a woman should live so long was itself a miracle; that it should be one of the manor gentry, to boot, won her a grudging respect even among those less generous titled elite who questioned the way she opened her home and chapel to the peasants. But among the more broad-minded (and big-hearted) local lords, among the tradesmen and artisans who had their shops in the alleys surrounding the castle, and especially among the hard-pressed men and women who worked the fields, Lora de Waldeschef Beville was honored as an extraordinary spirit, a blessing on the community. As the oldest in the shire, she was entitled to courtesy. As the grandmotherly soul of kindness and godly giving, she'd earned a great deal more.

And today as everyday since the Death had come to Warwick, Lora was going out to do what she could for the people who so revered her. She was meeting Brother Thomas again, to visit the homes of the infected. So she wasn't about to fret over "straining herself," as the kitchen help cried she would, while carrying a washbasin. She wasn't going to forgo any chore that might keep her spidery hands from trembling—that might distract her from her night's doubts. Others might wail and cover their heads; Grandma Lora felt she had to carry on, apparently unconcerned. Unconcerned, and practical. She had to look as if the Apocalypse wasn't just around the corner.

Over the fruit and bread her kitchen-women laid out for her, Lora recalled Brother Broderick, who'd succumbed to the plague two months earlier. He was an older man—he had no need to shave his tonsure spot, on the back of his head. But despite his years and the hundreds of deaths he'd ministered to, Broderick had never come across something like this pox of boils and bruises. The people learned early in the plague's assault on the shire which of the dying it was safe to approach and which not. Those with "the shilling in the armpit" as it was called could be given final rites face to face. But those who coughed—sweet Jesus, they coughed like the drowning, coughed blood and the stench of offal—could pass the Death along, and swiftly. The coughing, yes, that was the worst. There were stories of doctors or parsons who'd come to help and ended up dying before the patient.

Such had been the fate of poor Broderick. He'd gone to hear the confession of James Cooper, one of the freeholding tenants on the de Beville's manor lands. James, his eyes more red than white, had coughed wetly into Broderick's face. And before the hard-working freeholder breathed his last, Broderick had begun coughing himself. After perhaps an hour of heaving and spitting before the terrified Cooper widow and her children, an hour in which the priest's face and neck mottled more and more black, Brother Broderick summoned up a last show of fortitude. He rose and made it out the door, even a dozen yards or so down the path, though at the end he staggered as though drunk. Lora herself had seen him in the bushes not far from the Coopers: another stinking, bruise-gray corpse.

Worse, Brother Broderick wasn't the only local clergyman who'd made this final sacrifice. Lora didn't even know exactly how many others like him had gone down, dying in their priestly robes. Was it a half-dozen? Was it ten? So far, Brother Thomas—thin as a skeleton, these days—had survived, but after him, there would be no one. "I'm the last," the hawknosed Brother had told her. "The Bishop can spare no more priests, no more parsons, no brothers or even friars." Soon people might be dying without last rites. And who knew what would happen to their souls then? Lora had kept the Brother's bad news from her family and her help.

But there in the kitchen, among women she'd come to look on as friends, her prayer for the Brother's health was followed by all-too-familiar nightmare shivers. That it should come to this! That the Lord should wreak so much damage on the innocent and the godly, in his mighty move towards final Judgment!

One of the older kitchen-women noticed how Grandma Lora lingered at table, though her bread and apple were long since done. This woman laid a hand on Lora's shoulder, a rare gesture of kinship between servant and mistress. And the woman asked if "her Lady" would be going out today. Did she really have to make the rounds with Brother Thomas?

Lora took a deep breath and put on her best smile.

Outside a well-kept manor compound like Lora's, towns like War-wick were a mire of unhealthy leavings and offal. Farm animals wandered in and out of their keepers' cottages, and on cold nights the beasts slept on the dirt floor beside the families, adding what heat they could to the home. Garbage and feces trickled sluggishly down gutters in the center of the roads. Over all this exposed filth roamed black rats. These bristling scaven-gers lived in the mud and wood and thatch of people's homes. In broad daylight, they scurried from houses to garbage piles and back. Even the cats couldn't keep down the creatures' numbers.

As Lora's hay-cart emerged from the manor compound that morn-ing—she didn't take anything so pretentious as a lady's carriage on these errands of mercy—she spied a few rats scrabbling over something in the road's gutter. The grandmother had her driver, a luckier man than Theo-rick, go after them with her sturdy walking-stick; he chased the ugly animals into the underbrush. More than once in these last terrible months she'd seen a rat gnawing on an abandoned corpse. The vicious rodent, looking up at her from its despicable meal, had shown its bloody teeth in what seemed terribly like a smile of triumph.

They were wheeling now into one of the worst-hit alleyways of town, where Brother Thomas was waiting for her. Huts here no longer had any vestige of doors, and the battered ground before each was littered with the scraps left behind by those desperate passer-by who'd ransacked the homes after their inhabitants were dead. In roof after roof, smoke-holes gaped cold and unused.

Brother Thomas stood waiting for her by the hut at the end of the lane. The town's lone surviving priest was so starved and sleepless these days that he at first seemed barely more than a shadow within the death-house door. The cabin belonged to one Frederick. Frederick had one re-maining son; his wife and other two boys had been taken this year. When Brother Thomas waved from Frederick's doorway, his bony hand resembled a scythe.

The tiny old woman had a hard time hobbling down from the cart; she needed her stick and her driver. But her first words were crisp and full of authority. "Is he—" she indicated the door—"one of those who cough?"

Brother Thomas rolled his weary eyes. "Oh Lord. Stop worrying about me, Grandma Lora."

"Brother, neither man nor woman should go close to those who cough."

"This one doesn't cough, Grandma. Listen for yourself."

Putting her head into the dark house, smelling the bilious stench, Lora heard only a wet occasional choking. Now and again poor Frederick groaned the name of his dead wife, and as Lora's eyes accustomed to the lack of light, she saw that the man's surviving boy didn't appear to be anywhere nearby. The shame! Was this terrible illness now severing son from father? But the father himself, desperate to save his family, might have told the son to flee.

With one last breath of the relatively fresh air outside, they stepped through the door. Bending over a blotched and hardly recognizable face, over bedclothes stained with blood and pus, over eyes maddened by pain to the point of hallucinating—once more the old woman and the young cleric tried to provide some hope of God's mercy. Brother Thomas swiftly checked under the man's arms. There they were, bulging, the buboes: the grease-gray color of a dirty shilling.

"Frederick," the cleric asked, "do you believe that Jesus Christ is your Savior?"

The farmer's look showed no understanding. Once again he groaned the name of his wife.

"Frederick, you—" Lora began. But then one of the dying man's arms shot out to cup her small head. Hotly his rough hand palmed the back of her skull. After a moment's bent-necked struggle, she realized the man was trying to pull her into a lover's kiss.

Brother Thomas got his hands on the man's outflung arm. "Is there anything you wish to confess?" he cried, finally wrestling Lora's head free. "Anything to confess before you go to God?"

"Sweet Jesus," Lora murmured, stumbling back, "sweet Jesus, why have you done this?"

Over Frederick's rolling, tormented face, Brother Thomas was making the gestures of absolution. In a sober monotone he recited the deathbed Latin.

"Why, Jesus, why?" Lora tried to shake off the dizziness of her struggle with the poor man. "Why must the innocent suffer so?"

The farmer could no longer even call on his wife. He was spitting up gummy blood, spattering the priest's hands.

B ack outside in the street, Lora still felt dizzy. The sun was no help. A tarnished disk behind the clouds, it was like the Earth's own "shilling of the armpit." Her driver noticed her problem at once, and actually took her into his arms like a sleeping child. He tried to lay her in the hayrick.

Blinking, waving her stick, she told the man to stop. "I'm not ready to be planted in the far meadow yet," she snapped. For this was where she and Brother Thomas had established the town's new cemetery—out in a far meadow beyond the city wall. The old graveyard, near the church, had filled quickly this spring. After that it had been Lora who helped the tired cleric see other possibilities.

"But we can't bury the dead beyond the walls of the church," Brother Thomas had protested. "It's not consecrated ground. You don't expect the Bishop to come here and do it, do you?"

She'd reached for her gospel. "When the Savior and his disciples were hungry, did they harvest grain on the Sabbath?"

"Lord, my Lord." Brother Thomas had shaken his head. "That I should be learning Scripture from a woman!"

"Neither man nor woman," Lora had said, "deserves to be heaped like so much garbage and burned."

So the bonfires of plague victims, a common sight in other parishes, hadn't yet darkened the skies over Warwick. But now outside the house of poor, mad, dying Frederick, she wondered what such small mercies were worth in the time of the plague. If all the world were to be destroyed—if so many of God's fallen children were to be burning soon in hellfire any-way—then what did it matter if their carcasses burned first? Lora told her worried driver to set her up in the cart's seat. There she steadied herself with her chin on her cane, squinting up at the dark, inscrutable sun.

"Parson, come quickly!"

The shout had come from behind her. Brother Thomas was already looking back up the fetid alleyway, towards the noise. He'd come out of dead Frederick's house, wiping his bloody hands clumsily, stiff-armed, using a rag he must have found at the latest victim's bedside. He blinked as he tried to spot whoever was in need. Poor tired Thomas, Lora thought. Tired and underfed.

"Parson, please!" the call came again. "It's Rodwyna! Rodwyna! She's going fast."

Rodwyna was a particularly hard one for the community to lose, a midwife and herb-doctor. When Lora came round on her cart seat, her vision swam. Sweet Jesus, these old eyes. But something in the shout from up the street combined with something in the blur before her. Lora understood it was Maria, a woodworker's wife, a Spanish woman with a trace of an accent still. She waved, she called on tiptoe. Yes, Lora could see the woman now, through the headache Frederick's hot grip had left her with. Brother Thomas dropped his rag and moved off at a bent trot fishing in his robes for his crucifix and rosary.

"Thomas!" Lora called. "Be sure she isn't one of those who cough!"

But already the black robe was out of sight, in the blurry swarm of close-set shops and houses along the alley. Then Lora's driver swung up beside her, causing the cart to sway, and her vision swam even worse. Another squabble ensued, the driver urging "my Lady" to return to the Manor House now, to rest, and Lora insisting she was all right. The horse crooked back its head, looking their way, as if wondering at a servant and mistress conversing as equals. Finally, the driver set his mouth, his beard folding in. Slowly he gee'd up the horse and they began to come round.

They rattled back up the alley, then climbed cumbersomely down, first the driver, then Lora. She needed a moment beside the cartwheels to steady her reeling head, then she entered the cottage. Rodwyna lay in a heap at the center of the floor, and beside her lay Brother Thomas. Rodwyna's eyes were sunken and bloodshot, and Thomas's were if anything worse: his lack of weight gave him skull-eyes. Spiderwebbing up both agonized faces came the black hemorrhaging that marked the Death. At the corners of both mouths dribbled the ooze of its infection.

At least the air in here wasn't quite so rank as in other death-houses, because this morning before the pain had become too much for Rodwyna she'd gotten a flower-scented pot going on the fire.

Unlike Frederick, these two remained sensible to the end. Lora helped them settle more comfortably across Rodwyna's straw. She brought water and spoke soothingly. Neither of them coughed. Brother Thomas in fact had no idea just who or what had sent him to this pain-racked death; he could only smile faintly and say, "I do not give as the world gives."

"Oh there, Brother," Lora gently chided him, "we're not going to haggle over God's justice now, are we?"

"You'll have to do that for yourself," Thomas said. "From now on you'll be the—" and he choked, coughing shallowly. He'd put his hand over his mouth and bile seeped between the fingers.

"Oh no." Lora shook her head firmly. "No, I'm not right for it, I'm not worthy."

The dying cleric nodded hard, swallowing and pointing a slimy finger at her.

"Sweet Jesus. How can I be priest to these people? I am a woman. . ."

"Nonsense, Grandma Lora," said Rodwyna. The thickset midwife, despite the pain it plainly cost her, heaved up on one elbow. "Don't say that. A woman. You're Grandma Lora. Godly Grandma. Sister."

Brother Thomas fished again in his robe, bringing out his rosary. Trembling, he held it towards her. "Did not the Savior," he gasped, "gather food on the Sabbath?"

Lora took the beads and crucifix. She found them heavier than expected: a load you could never forget, around the neck or in the pocket.

"This is God's doing," she told her two dying friends, "not mine or yours."

Rodwyna lingered the longer. The midwife helped with the final prayers and confession of Brother Thomas, enunciating plainly a few words the skinny, stubborn, still-young believer garbled as his mouth filled with blood. Rodwyna eased him into the next world, Lora thought, just as she had eased so many into this one. Then her gaze too became blank.

Lora emerged from the cottage weighed down by the Brother's beads. She'd had nowhere to put them except around her neck. She had to blink to see clearly. There was a lot of activity for a street so hard-hit. Maria had come out again, dumping a bucket of carrot-butts in the alley's central gutter. A boy across the way was trying to do a man's work, refitting the iron head of a blacksmith's mallet, and Lora's cart-driver squatted beside the youngster, lending some middle-aged muscle to the task. A very old man came down the street. In his free hand the grandfather toted a boot that needed repair, and his naked foot had a ludicrous big toe, red and hairy and swollen.

Sweet Jesus, Lora thought, it's a weekday. It's a weekday, and they're all just going on.

Then, like a girl, she put her face in her hands and wept.

Beginning the next Sunday, Warwick's services were no longer held in the town church. Not only was there no longer a parson, but also the building itself had fallen into disrepair. For a time it became yet another home to rats. Instead, survivors of the Black Death came together in the Great Hall of the Manor House. Once more Grandma Lora threw her home open to the needy and lowly. Now practiced in administering last rites, she would venture to the head of this exhausted but still-searching crowd; she'd share her new sense of the Holy Spirit.

"I don't pretend to explain God," she might say. "I've lived a long time, but I wasn't there at the beginning."

In general, Lora didn't preach like a priest, out of Scripture. Rather she spoke from her experience. "Even before this plague," she declared one Sunday, "many times I saw the righteous suffer."

This was a day of welcome sunshine, gentle sunshine, gracing them now in the middle of autumn. "Many times I saw it," Lora continued. "My son, Sir Richard—how hard it was to accept, once God took him! And my husband before him. Over seventy years now, at least seventy times every year, I've asked God why my Richard had to die and leave me alone for so long."

And who, Lora asked, was truly being punished? "Was it Richard who died," she asked, "or me who did not? I ask because it's likewise with the Black Death. Is it the loved ones you've lost who suffered worst? Or is it we who suffer, struggling on without their help?"

The small crowd murmured, assenting. To Lora, whose old eyes couldn't handle the day's sun, they seemed like visitors made of light, weightless and floating. "We must struggle on without help," she said, "and yet with the pain of remembering."

By this Sunday, in the middle of harvest season, struggling on appeared to be the order of the day. The plague's virulence had begun to ease only a month or so after the passing of Rodwyna and Brother Thomas. By the end of August the worst was clearly past. A central alleyway or two in the ancient town center still bred the occasional case, but apparently the world-blackening Death was, in the end, a disease like any other: it had its epidemic and then subsided.

And who were those spared? And why? But this was no time for philosophy, among the town's working rank and file. There was too much to do for that. Even highborn overseers like the de Bevilles had to scramble, that season. Virtually all Lora's tenants had died; if it hadn't been for the assistance of the same common people she'd always tried to help, Lora would never have seen her grains and vegetables brought in that year.

"We survivors are left," Lora repeated now, at the head of her Great Hall on this sunny autumn Sunday, "without the help we've grown used to. And yet," she whispered with sudden ferocity, "death is part of His Kingdom. All, all, even death—all is a part of it, the kingdom without end."

The weightless sunlit creatures before her appeared to nod, murmuring again. This had become Lora's great theme over the last few Sundays.

"In His kingdom," she went on, "all has value: man and woman both. Also Jew and Christian, animal and herb, the sun and the darkness—they all have a part in His justice."

Lora raised her braided crown of white hair, gesturing with her broad face and her raised cane towards the crucifix between the room's iron-laced windows.

"This man asked 'Why?' didn't he?" Lora asked. "Didn't the Savior Himself have his night of fear in the garden? And yet I tell you that God the Father was also pained and grieving that night, knowing that He had to hurt our sweet Jesus, His only Son. In the same way, of course—of course—He is grieved every time we hurt the ones we ourselves have known and loved."

She jabbed her cane once more at the crucifix. "But death," she went on, still fiercely, "is part of what God gives us. It is ours to share and love even if we cannot understand it. Death is a part of the kingdom—it is not the end of the kingdom."

She lowered her cane, clumsily, showing her age. "I'm old, yes. And yet still I have no idea how I'll die. No idea at all, you know."

Wondering for a moment, she rubbed the spot where poor dying Frederick had hurt her neck.

"We die, my brothers, my sisters, of the most baffling afflictions. We die of illnesses we never knew were in His universe. And yet in our dying we surmount trials we never knew we could dare." Once more Lora raised her head. "We die because we are in His kingdom, in His hand. We are never outside that kingdom, never abandoned by Him. And that is how we must treat each other and this world, even the least drop of sick, black blood in it. All, all, is cherished. All is sacred. All will live in His hand forever."

She felt again her neck's sore spot. Then the little woman began to move, slowly, back down through her townspeople to her seat.

After the sermon, this sun-struck weekend, Grandma Lora took time as usual over her day's meats and vegetables. These too she shared with those less fortunate. She heard their concerns, shaking her head over the bad news, lifting her wide face happily over the good. She was driven out over the grounds, where she delighted in the sweet smell of the grains in the storehouses. But as sundown came on, the western sky fingered by odd, dark, bloody patches—odd blotches, yet quite beautiful—the old woman declined all offers of company. She liked to spend the day's last hours alone, Lora said. There was nothing to fear in the night.

CHAPTER 4
Robert Beville and the Spanish Armada

L ora de Waldeschef Beville outlived the Black Death. She survived for another three years, and all of Warwickshire came to her funeral.

One of the few remaining clerics from the decimated priesthood was found to give prayers and rituals at her funeral, but they rang empty. The innocent trust people felt in the Roman Catholic Church—so ineffective in warding off diseases—had also died.

Thus Lora's descendants then saw Europe plummet into religious wars that piled corpses on top of the graves from the Plague. At the same time a New World was discovered, and nation states struggled over its wealth.

In the middle of these great conflicts was the de Beville family. They remained large landowners for a long time.

Their stature is illustrated in St. Michael's, a small, stone church in the countryside of Huntingdonshire, where one wall bears a bas-relief of two later generations of de Bevilles. Altogether these generations spanned more than a century, from the time of King Henry VIII, who ruled in the early 1500s, to the short-lived Cromwell Commonwealth of the mid-1600s. During this period, too, the family made the move to America.

One side of the bas-relief depicts Robert Beville Armiger, born in 1536, along with his wife and nine children. The other depicts a full-grown man who, on Armiger's side of the sculpture, is shown as a child: Sir Robert Beville, knighted by King James I in 1603. With Sir Robert are his wife and eight children.

Our next episode follows this generational transition—a trial for father and son, as well as for country.

R obert Beville Armiger tried not to let the clouds distract him from his duty. An inland farmer like himself wasn't used to the beauty of the North Sea's horizons: sudden clouds and unpredictable clearings, all stippling hypnotically as day turned to night.

It was a stained-glass landscape. Beville Armiger would've believed himself too old to fall under its spell. He was fifty-two, a widower, a High Sheriff, and many times a father. Yet all the sensations of the seashore seemed to conspire to take his mind off the job at hand. He had a post in a sturdy tower of tone and mortar, on a bluff that rose out of coastal wetlands against the crashing of the waves. The day's air came off the land, out of the west, carrying the ripeness of the growing season and of livestock slowed by the heat. The sea before him, he knew, reached to the ancient rockbound harbors of the Vikings. And this had him thinking of his son again, latest heir to the venturesome Viking character on which his family had been built.

Eventually clouds and sea darkened to black. The man on sea watch drew his cloak more firmly round him, straightening up shoulders and head. He touched his helmet, his sword. Watchman, he asked himself, what of the night? It was an Old Testament passage that often helped keep him on his toes.

Watchman, what of the night? A midsummer night, early July. The year? 1588: more than fifty years since Henry VIII had broken from the Roman Church and set England against all of Catholic Europe; more than eighteen years since the Pope had excommunicated Henry's daughter Elizabeth I over the matter of Mary Queen of Scots; and only sixteen months since that same Mary's execution had triggered the King of Spain's decision to attack.

Thus Robert Beville Armiger, High Sheriff of Huntingdon and Cambridge Counties, stood on duty at the North Sea coast. He was a leader in the rapidly mustered English militia. His "trained band" was a cavalry troop. They were mostly estate-holders like himself, the experienced horsemen of the middle and upper classes; they had some small military education at least. But by far the majority of the Englishmen rallying to their country's defense were rank-and-file farmers, artisans, merchants. Into the eastern ports of Elizabeth's Britain they'd swarmed, well-nigh every available man between sixteen and sixty, carrying pikestaffs and crossbows, muskets and pitchforks. They'd sworn to fight off Lord Parma and his Spanish legions: the mighty Catholic invasion force called the Armada.

A committed churchgoer, honored throughout his shire for charity and good works, Robert Beville was built small but thick. He was only one step shy of becoming a fully titled knight of the English nobility. Thus the honorific Armiger, from the Latin for armor-bearer; it signified a gentleman qualified to carry his own heraldic insignia.

Indeed, Beville would long since have earned his knighthood had he taken the time to court the Queen's favor, down in London. But he was one Armiger with no taste for courtier's flattery. Of course, there'd been knights in the family before. There'd been heroes, in fact, like one of his wife's ancestors, a Crusader who'd been first over the wall at the battle of Acre—a favorite of King Richard the Lion-Heart, so the story went.

In his watchman's tower, Robert kept his eyes peeled for the hefty galleon sails of Lord Parma and King Philip. Every night he stood first watch, sundown till midnight. It was a time of day when less diligent men would be thinking of dinner—or, perhaps, romance. Yet Beville stood and watched the cloud-ornamented sea. Besides that, he'd spend several minutes every hour staring south along the coastline, making sure there wasn't a light down that way. A light meant a bonfire at the next fortress tower. A bonfire meant the arrival of the Armada, the galleon sails at last heaving into view.

Robert Beville knew well the grim facts concerning the invasion force. Philip II, lord of the ever-spreading Spanish Empire, had gone deep into his stores of booty from the savage New World across the Atlantic. He'd mustered a force as large as the storied armies of the Crusades. To Philip after all this was a Crusade: a battle for the newly unchurched souls of northern Europe—the souls misled by heretics like Martin Luther and John Calvin.

The *Armada Invincible* had sailed from Lisbon (for Portugal too was part of the Empire) and numbered no fewer than 130 warships, carrying some 8,000 sailors and nearly three times as many infantry. Just across the Channel, in the Spanish Netherlands, there waited still more thousands of Spain's finest. And these troops were battle-hardened. Under the able leadership of the Duke of Parma they'd suppressed every movement towards Dutch independence—as violently as their conquistadors had subdued the innocent natives in New World colonies like Hispaniola and Mexico. If even half the rumors Beville had heard about the conquests of the so-called Indians were true, it made him shudder to think what might happen to the good reformed Anglicans in his own country.

"Anything tonight, Sheriff Beville?"

Beville made certain he'd mastered his shuddering, pulling his night-cloak tight once more, before he turned. His visitor—his replacement for second watch—was of course Charles Bickells. Beville had appointed this angular Norman neighbor from Huntingdonshire his lieutenant.

"Anything?" the taller newcomer repeated. Some anxiety came into his voice, just audible over the surf beneath them.

"Nothing, nothing," Beville hastened to reply. "The sea's been empty."

Charles Bickells relaxed visibly, his smile returning.

"I only needed a moment," Beville went on, "to get used to you calling me 'Sheriff.'"

His good-looking companion laughed, and for a few moments they exchanged notes on the July heat, the seaside sunsets. But as Bickells chatted he kept his gaze moving, upcoast and down, and out over the water.

"If they come," he began, after a silence, "if they take over. . . ."

"Impossible, impossible," Beville cut in. "There hasn't been a successful invasion since William the Conqueror."

Bickells nodded, but without much conviction. He gestured toward the sea. "You know as well as I do that if the Spanish come, they'll take my estate and every acre you own from Northhampton to Eleton."

Beville could only nod. Part of what he liked about this man was his honesty.

"The Spanish," Bickells repeated bitterly.

"Charlie, Charlie. It's not 'the Spanish' who are doing this—not the whole people. Why, we've Spanish blood in our own troop. You know that back in Thaxted, on our way here, I heard of a family from Pamplona who'd been living in that town for over 200 years?"

Bickells sighed. "The family founder was hanged with his three boys, yes. Isn't that how the story goes?"

"Unfairly hanged, Charlie. As foreigners, they were unjustly accused of treason."

Bickells looked over his shoulder at the foursquare man in cloak and helmet. This was one Armiger, plainly, who didn't quit his watch ready for sleep.

"You talk like such a Christian," Bickells said. "But, friend—if they come, they'll take our Bibles too."

Beville pursed his lips, thinking, untired. "I remember the years when Bloody Mary held the throne. I had to meet with our pastor in secret."

"If they come, Robert, you may be meeting with him on the gallows."

Beville winced. Friend Charlie didn't varnish things, did he? The Bevilles might be the most prominent Protestants in two counties; the Armiger himself had appointed, thanks to his family's long-standing right of advowson, the new Rector of St. Michael's Church in Huntingdonshire—a highly Protestant thinker named William Acrode. Thus any Catholic conquerors would view Beville as a heretic, he and all his remaining children. Perhaps they'd spare his girls, but never his son. Young Rob, the last-born of the Armiger's brood, was the only male heir who'd survived.

"Your boy, Rob, too," Bickells went on, as if reading Beville's thoughts. "He'd probably join you and your good Rector up there beneath the noose."

Quickly, surprising Beville, out of his fear erupted annoyance. "What are you doing?" he snapped. "Why even bring up such things?"

The taller man came upright off the watchtower wall, focused now entirely on his friend. "I saw you shudder," Bickells said quietly.

Beville blinked up at him, still angry.

"Robert, friend—I saw it." The handsome Norman features were soft with sympathy. "You tried to hide it, yes," Bickells said. "You pulled that big cloak of yours tight. But I saw that you shuddered; I knew you were frightened."

St. Michael's Church, Hutingdonshire, England.

Beville, startled, warmed, fell back on his humor. "And you decided to frighten me even worse?"

"I decided," Bickells went on with a smile, "that you would never open up your heart on your own."

"Oh, you know my heart, now?"

"I knew you'd keep that cloak around your neck and never admit you could use someone to share your fears."

Beville Armiger touched his cloak, his helmet. Blinking, he saw again the clouds at sundown: trembling, waterlogged. Finally, with a rueful smile that made clear his rangy friend had been right, he fell into a soldierly embrace. We'll be brave together, Beville Armiger either said or thought to say. We'll try to be brave together. But as they pounded each other's backs, encouragingly, bracingly, Beville faced the sea. The waters were black.

Robert Beville Armiger mulled over the incident for a long time afterwards. Not that he didn't have his fill of distractions—an encampment of this size had much to keep a High Sheriff busy. In the worst heat of the day he'd usually try to find refreshment in his Bible—for he was one of those who carried the Book—in a spot of shade by one of the wetland's creeks. His mount would graze beside him, whickering occasionally in echo of the brook's babble.

As Beville perused his Bible, the very feel of the Holy Book cheered him. A reader like him could decipher the large letters at the start of each book by touch alone, eyes closed and dreaming of less uncertain days. He often thought back to that fearful evening on the watchtower when his neighbor had taken time to reassure him. Eventually he came to realize that his surviving male heir had been behind a lot of his turbulent emotion that night.

Rob was the youngest of his nine children. As a boy he'd been indulged, possibly even spoiled. He'd been the second son after all:; not the primogenitor, the male heir. He'd been allowed to caper, young Rob.

But then had come the hard years. There was a stretch in the 1570s that Beville Armiger saw now as the most terrible time in his life, when both his wife and his oldest boy had died. His own dear Joan Lawrence of St. Ives was devout, cheery, tough; in her survived more than a little of her heroic ancestor Sir Robert Lawrence, the same Crusader knight who'd been first over the walls at Acre. But after surviving so many childbirths, in 1574 Joan succumbed suddenly to fever. Like that, she was gone, and two years later their oldest son—named William, after his grandfather—passed on too. Worse, William left no heirs. He'd been a scholarly young man, one with whom Beville Armiger could discuss religion or the Renaissance with equal pleasure.

During those battered years, his friend Bickells tried to cheer him up with reminders of his surviving sons. Rob had found a wife worthy of the Armigers' heraldic seal, the Swanny Mark. Lady Mary Coles was every inch the swan, refined and lovely. Better yet, Lady Mary and young Rob began to produce Beville heirs even as the unhappy 1570s came to a close; there was very soon a baby Robert.

In the shade of a seaside oak, in this hot later time of wondering whether his world would end, Robert Beville would caress his signet ring, his engraved family seal. Not long ago only the gentry had been allowed to own swans. Every family had had a Swanny Mark of some kind, used to stamp an identifying symbol on the birds' bills.

Beville Armiger's particular Swanny Mark was now only a keepsake, a sentimental item he'd once joked about with his wife. Yet now as he touched it he felt again the unsummery chill he'd suffered on the North Sea watchtower that recent night when Bickells had noticed his shuddering. Would his son Rob be up to the challenge of the swan's beauty and freedom? For even if the Armada was defeated, there were bound to be new challenges to humanity's growth. Even the New World, the father guessed, would one day struggle with oppression and blind hate.

Yes, his thoughts ranged far, as the leader of a troop so hastily assembled, so desperately frightened. In his few quiet moments, Beville Armiger also pondered his odd lifelong correlation with his Queen. The correlation was entirely accidental, he realized. It happened that he'd taken over his estates from his mother Joan the year after "Bess" took over the throne from her step-sister Mary. Her administration was the most efficient in Europe, the envy of bureaucracy-bound older kingdoms like Spain's. She was no remote monarch, listening only to the flattery of self-interested courtiers, but "Queen in Parliament," depending on the counsel of her countrymen as much as they depended on hers. Beyond that, she required only a trained and observant circle of civil servants and justices of the peace. As Beville reached out to the indentured servants and small farmers throughout his shire, offering them livestock and whatever tools might allow them to better their position in life, so Elizabeth had swiftly ameliorated suffering among the nation's underprivileged. She'd even passed an ordinance (the Statue of Apprentices, in 1563) insuring everyone the right to work.

The times were extraordinary. Beville never finished his sessions alone without a sense of wonder at all he'd seen over the years. But would his young Rob recognize England's new spirit of growth and challenge? Would Rob take part?

T he beacon, Robert! Southerly! The fire!"

Charlie Bickells stood at full height, pointing along the darkening coast. Beville propped his hands on the granite watchtower wall, leaning forward to squint beneath his friend's extended arm. There it was. The bonfire at the next tower south.

"I see it," he said, as evenly as he could. "Time for the light."

In the center of the tower-top, brush and timber had been piled head-high. The men touched it here and there with torches, working round the stony circle of wall. The tinder, daubed with pitch, caught instantly. The flaming heap crackled so loudly the two militiamen had to shout.

"Watch the north, watch the north!"

"They've seen us, Robert! There's the flame!"

The initial sighting had come off Cornwall, at the far tip of England's southwestern peninsula. Beville had made it his business to know the names and basic tactics of his country's naval commanders. The Queen had other men besides the world-girdling—and profit-skimming—Sir Francis Drake. There was also Sir John Hawkins, superbly adept according to all reports. Yet it was no knight like Sir Francis or Sir John who commanded Elizabeth's fleet, but rather Charles Howard, an unpretentious and hard-working lord like Beville himself. It was Howard who'd come up with the strategy of attacking the Spanish array in parallel lines. Philip's admirals still favored the old-fashioned crescent spread that had helped them suc-ceed in Mediterranean wars.

So too, the High Sheriff had taken time to understand something about the English boats. They were far swifter than Philip's galleons, he'd learned. Lying lower in the water, their very smallness worked in their favor, allowing them to maneuver quickly and concentrate fire blisteringly. Their guns had a greater range than the Spaniard's, too. Culverins, these guns were called. Longer than cannon, they fired a smaller ball; they could do damage from beyond the galleons's reach.

As Beville saw it, the conflict came down to shaky unknowns, to unlikely ifs. If Lord Howard's squadrons could mount a pursuit that pre-vented Philip's mammoth warships from getting in close. . . . If the British could keep the Empire on the run. . . .

"Why then," Beville Armiger declared as loudly as he could muster, "They won't get our Bibles after all!"

The Armada moved closer every day. On the morning the Spanish sails hove into view, clustered on the deep-summer cerulean waters like a crescent of white wingtips on an blue jay, Beville surveyed them from the tower, using a Dutch spyglass. A glass made under the iron Spanish fist, in their subject nation across the Channel.

He made out fluttering lance-pennants, glittering helmets, the gape of the big unwieldy cannons. There were the scowling faces of the infantry-men on board. The very sails of the warships bore Catholic crosses: barbed, blood-red crosses that seemed to billow in his face.

"Take your eye from the glass, Robert," Charlie Bickells said, beside him.

"What, what?" Beville asked, still glued to the telescope. He'd almost forgotten his friend was there. "Don't you see them, don't you see?"

"Take your eye from the glass, friend," Bickells repeated. His voice was as gentle as the inland breezes. "Take a look at our good English boats."

Lord Howard's fleet came low and swift across the water. One look with the naked eye and it was obvious the English were faster. In strict lines they cut broadside past knots of lumbering Spanish vessels. They snipped odd curves off the Armada's crescent, moving too quickly to sink any of the enemy, but at the same time keeping Philip's mighty boats from massing and doing real damage. Beville had all he could do to keep from dropping his spyglass. Ye gods, the change in perspective! And the shift in fortunes!

The lead British boat was perhaps the *Disdain* of Sir John Hawkins. It was Hawkins who'd designed such quick and easy-handling warships. It was Hawkins and Drake together who'd made certain the English fleet was manned with veteran, seaworthy crews. At a single pass, this front-runner and the squadron that trailed it left cracked masts and billowing fires across the decks of several galleons—all without a single Spanish return salvo coming anywhere near. Beville checked his tall friend's face, making certain his own rising joy wasn't out of line. Yes, Bickells was grinning ear to ear. The *Armada Invincible* couldn't even get close.

Around Beville, around the foot of the tower, the men began to roar. They waved their hats, their swords, their muskets. The happy bellowing filled the air, swelling hotly, dinning off the charcoal-blackened stone of the parapet.

Once more the Armiger tried the spyglass. He and his men had expected a battle for the ages, an Armageddon. Instead they'd gotten a game of Run, Goose, Run. With the help of the Dutch glass, he saw the Queen's seamen hustling up and down their ship's decks with the same unruffled efficiency as her councilors resolved problems of government. And he saw that this was, in fact, a victory of that entire government: a victory won by speed, responsiveness, and close give and take between every working part. It was the streamlined new way running circles round the top-heavy old way. It was the humane design of the Renaissance proving better than the hidebound system of old feudal Europe.

So at last he and Bickells joined in the cheers. The High Sheriff waved round his spyglass like a boy waving round a winner's baton. And when he came down the tower stairs, this same sober churchgoer—this commander who'd made clear that he liked his time alone, his officer's distance—this Armiger yielded carelessly to his men's desire to hoist him on their shoulders.

As they jounced him round the encampment, the roars of victory surrounded him like a cloud. Charlie, friend: my son Rob should see this, he shouted to the friend behind him, or meant to shout. My son, my young Rob—he needs to feel this. Yes, it was a cloud, astonishing. It was as if he'd entered one of those upswept parti-colored vapors that gathered along this same seascape every sundown.

And this time, the party would last long after sundown. This time he didn't have to guard against falling under the spell of the beauty.

An ex-soldier is hardly a has-been. Back in his Chesterton manor, Robert Beville found a number of tasks to occupy his remaining years. His experience as High Sheriff got him appointed commissioner for draining the local fens, and he found himself spending afternoons by wetlands again, as he had in his seaside encampment. Likewise he spent a lot of time tending to the needs of family and community. He often thought of inventive ways to help the townspeople, who shared his estates. Sometimes his gifts went through Pastor Acrode at St. Michael's. Other times the old Armiger himself would show up with advice, a needed tool, or even cash in hand.

He died in 1602, quietly, at home. Elizabeth Regina, the noble standard against which he'd measured his own accomplishment, was less than a year in the grave herself.

Yet despite everything that seemed just and balanced about Robert Beville's passing, the reading of his will after the funeral caused more than a little consternation. The man himself was in that paper: his special sense of a world remade.

Pastor Acrode read the will, there in St. Michael's, after the hundreds of well-wishers at the funeral had at last gone home. Small as it was, the church felt suddenly quite spacious as Acrode opened the document; the service had filled both building and yard to overflowing. The Reverend cleared his throat, a bit hoarse from having to deliver a eulogy over such a murmur.

But the will didn't tax him much at first, running through the customary provisions for family, friends, servants. Charlie Bickells was remembered. Then the document went on to the usual specification that the property was to be passed along to male heirs.

But then Parson Acrode paused. He looked over the inscribed heavy paper carefully, squinting, mouth pursed, then cleared his throat again. The only surviving Robert Beville straightened up in his pew, wondering.

Little more than a year later, "young Rob" was referred to in shire documents as "Sir Robert Beville, Senior"—a knight of the realm and the father of his own baby Robert. He'd enjoyed the congratulations of his king, the former Scot monarch James I. He'd fulfilled his father's dream, bringing knighthood back into the family. But on this summer evening some months after his father's will had been proclaimed, Sir Robert Beville, Senior, rode a back way out of his estates, leading a cow. He was delivering this animal to the owner of a tiny local farm.

Rob was on his favorite mount, the chestnut gelding Vigor. He led along Bea, one of the best out of the Beville herds, her bell clanging as they went. He and Vigor would have preferred a more spirited pace, all in all, but he tried to take pleasure in the slow errand. There was sweetness in the face of a Jersey cow, consolation in the peaceable greenery surrounding him, pleasant remembrance in the sun-warmed Swanny Mark on his finger. He even found a moment or two for a daydream, eyeing the puffy summer clouds. It actually surprised Rob when, looking round after such a heedless moment, he found a small knot of children and townsfolk trailing behind him.

His gift was for Tom Cooper, a farmer with a cottage hardly the size of Rob's study. Bea would be the best milker Cooper had ever owned; more than once she'd outproduced every other cow the Bevilles had. And she was only the first of two cows "going on tour," as Rob liked to call today's duty. Yes, he'd learned to joke about the obligation, in the year since his father's will had sprung it on him.

Indeed, Rob had learned to enjoy it. When Rector Acrode trotted up to join the small procession, the two of them exchanged the chuckling banter of men on a fishing trip. Though Tom Cooper's place, when it came into view, was hardly a cheering prospect. With its thatched roof and sloppy chimney, Cooper's cottage looked like something from the harsh days of the Black Death.

But now Rob was helping out, as he'd heard a long-ago grandmother had helped during the Death. His father had stipulated that Rob had to, in that strange last will and testament—but by this time the aging son's heart had told him that he wanted to. Today he found himself grinning hugely as he swung down from Vigor, before the farmer's door.

"Well, Tom!" he began. "Here's Bea, and may I say, best of luck to the both of you."

He patted the tawny milker, and the children who'd followed him gathered close, giggling, getting a hand on the animal themselves. The few adults who'd made the trip briefly applauded, led by the nodding Rector. This always embarrassed Rob. The new knight sheepishly lowered his head. Meantime Cooper himself, stooped and nearly toothless, managed a grateful smile.

Among the poorest of the villagers, this man could never have accumulated enough without help to buy anything of lasting value—like a good milk cow. And there were many like Cooper. Hard as they might labor, such people lacked the essentials needed for true gain, true security.

Rob returned to these ideas a short while later, while he accompanied Rector Acrode on the way back to St. Michael's. "Wasn't it just like father," the knight said, "to come up with this way of giving to the poor?"

His companion in the black robe nodded. "It wasn't enough for him," Acrode said, "to have had a gift for just about everyone in sight. But this idea of giving the poor the opportunity to share a cow—why, I can almost see your old father grinning now."

Rob recalled the day of the funeral and the reading, the way Acrode had cleared his throat before going on. Apparently the parson himself hadn't known about this codicil.

"The old Armiger told me there'd be a surprise in the will," Acrode had admitted, after the reading was over. "But I never imagined anything like this."

The shared cows were the outstanding stipulation of Robert Beville's will. "I give and bequeath two milk cows," the old philanthropist had written, "to be to the use of the poor people of Chesterton, yearly to be let out to the poorest sort of the inhabitants of the town. . . . The poor are to have the whole profit of them without paying any money or other consideration for them. . . . And when the first two of the said inhabitants have had them a full year, then two other of the poorer sort of the inhabitants are to have them another year, and so from two unto two. . . ."

Under this plan, the town's have-nots could become haves. It gave the poor an opportunity to join the brave new world Robert Armiger had glimpsed from the watchtower by the North Sea. It let them take part in the smartly managed, communally shared prosperity of a growing Renaissance kingdom—in a system where wealth produced wealth. Now, as Chesterton's parson and newest knight trotted away from Tom Cooper's, Acrode spoke again of these notions, of the former High Sheriff's vision of his times. And the son concurred with the cleric. Rob remembered what the old man had said after the Armada's defeat.

"My father told me," Rob said, "that the Spanish looked terrifying through the spyglass. But when he put down the glass and saw the larger scene, the longer view—then he could see that the enemy was nothing."

CHAPTER 5

Sir Robert Beville Junior, the Cromwell Revolution, and the Move to America

T he family bas-relief in St. Michael's church, described at the beginning of the previous chapter, presents what may be the high point of the Bevilles in England. It depicts three Robert Bevilles, each much-honored.

There's Robert Beville Armiger, his son Sir Robert Beville, Senior, and (among Sir Robert's eight children) his namesake first boy, also eventually knighted: Sir Robert Beville, Junior.

In the early seventeenth century, the family sent members to Parliament and added thousands of acres to their holdings. Their monarch, James I, headed an England that was colonizing the New World—and revitalizing its library. The famed King James Bible appeared in 1611, the first Shakespeare folio in 1623.

But less than a hundred years after Beville Armiger's stand against the Armada, his descendants had lost their vast farms and left the country. They'd emigrated to the struggling new settlements in America. In effect, they'd started over.

This remarkable change of fortunes took place in a similarly changing land, during one of the most turbulent eras in European history.

B y the closing days of 1625, it seemed as if the only place Robert Beville Junior and his friend Oliver Cromwell could be happy together was the Huntingdonshire fens. Every other landscape in England, it seemed, was marred by some unhappy association for either the ambitious Beville or the embittered Cromwell. Both were educated enough to see the dangers in the tendencies of the young King Charles I. And both were still young themselves, in their mid-twenties, like the century; they hadn't yet learned acceptance and compromise. Only in the muck of the fens could both men forget how their futures appeared to be going from bad to worse.

In the fens the future didn't exist. Nor did the past. The two huntsmen would lose all track of time in the algae-tasting mists off those wetlands, in the bleat and plash of reptile and bird. They whooshed through saw grass, they slogged belly-deep in an ooze as ripe as manure-rich farm fields.

When Beville Junior and Oliver Cromwell emerged from their happy swamp hunting, they generally repaired to an unprepossessing roadhouse inn called the Lamb & Flag.

Even as they settled onto their usual bench in the Lamb & Flag, on this late-autumn day in 1625, they came back to a source of discord—increasing discord, outside the timeless fens.

"You will become a knight, then?" Cromwell asked. He hadn't yet sat down; on extended arms he leaned into his friend's face, over the table.

"I believe I will."

As soon as Beville said these words, he reddened at their weakness. Only Cromwell could make him feel so sheepish. The twenty-two-year-old Beville Junior was up for knighthood. The new King, Charles I, eager to increase revenues, was creating more taxable nobility. The looming honor was another vivid proof of the difference between Beville and his common-born friend Cromwell.

"So it's Sir Robert Beville, is it?" his friend jeered. "Sir Robert Beville, Junior."

Only the Saxon Oliver Cromwell, among Beville's acquaintances, could draw out that last word so coarsely. Beville had the high forehead and long, straight nose of the Norman English—still a distinct type, nearly six centuries after the invasion by William the Conqueror. But Cromwell was of older and grainier stock. He looked every inch a man of the common herd, with homely features and a mole on his chin. Today his rude woolens had served him better in the fens than Beville's aristocratic silks and leathers. The knight-to-be, moreover, had an air of urbanity; he was on holiday after his first year of law at Gray's Inn, down in London. Nonetheless Beville Junior wasn't to be trifled with. Though small, he had his ancestors' power through the hips and chest.

"Zounds, Cromwell," he growled. "Would you badger me with reminders of my father?"

"Won't you be Sir Robert Junior," Cromwell asked more gently, "as he is Sir Robert Senior?"

To Beville Junior his father seemed a pale imitation of the monumental Armiger who'd sired him. God's wounds, Beville Senior was best known for leading around cows! Like a common milkmaid, leading around cows!

"Never as him, friend. Never as him."

The commoner lowered his large body onto the tavern bench, across from his glaring fellow huntsman.

"I'm not doing this," Beville went on, "just to avoid the King's fine. Sixteen pounds, do you think I care about that?" Friend Cromwell wasn't going to get a rise out of him on this point. Not here at the Lamb & Flag, after a cold and happy day in the fens. "Sixteen pounds, twenty pounds," he said, "do you think I care? I'll take the knighthood, Cromwell; I will. I have my reasons."

"Well what in God's name might they be?" his older friend snapped. "Why should a man cheapen himself to pay for pretty paintings on the stinkin' palace ceiling?"

Sixteen hundred twenty-five was the year Charles had succeeded James I to the throne. Such a moment is dangerous for any ruler, since he hasn't yet proven his power. In the case of Charles I, his father had done much to smooth the way; his reign's greatest accomplishment may have been the magnificent King James Bible, many passages of which Parson

Acrode had insisted young Beville Junior commit to memory. Nonetheless, nothing could hide the fact that Charles I was very young—a year younger, for instance, than the sneering Cromwell. And nothing could hide the way he'd spent government money on frills. Already the young monarch was notorious for bringing the renowned Dutch painter Rubens across the Channel simply to redo the ceiling of the Whitehall banqueting house.

"The whelp," Cromwell went on, outspoken as always. "Our King cares for nothing but fripperies. You know he's in the pocket of that fop Buckingham. His father's old sweetheart the Duke of Buckingham."

"Spare me, gentle Oliver."

"Do you deny that our King listens only to Buckingham? Buckingham and not Parliament, Buckingham and not you or I?"

"I don't deny that Buckingham appears to be determined to plunge England into some spectacularly idiotic wars," Beville said, once again astonished at his friend's boldness. Of course many in the country held the same opinions. Many hated the long-time councilor Buckingham.

But Beville Junior knew no one who'd express what he thought so openly, or with such guttural fervor. "This king," Cromwell went on, "he doesn't care about what's best for our country."

"He's as young as we are," Beville Junior tried—though he himself was actually a bit younger, twenty-two. "Charles may yet learn."

"And how many times must we pay in gold and in blood—in blood, I tell you—while some king learns?" Cromwell tossed back his unkempt black hair.

"Gentle Oliver. Do you mean to say that England should have no king?"

"I mean to say," Cromwell quietly declared, "that Englishmen will remain little better than slaves so long as they honor the so-called divine right of foreign-born boys and the fops they trust."

Beville Junior held his peace. With a significant look at his radical friend, he noted the approach of the innkeeper carrying two tankards of ale and one of the day's game-fowl on a spit. The young nobleman took them with a smile; like most of his class, he wasn't required to pay on the spot.

The innkeeper smiled back at the young scion; he knew the Bevilles were still good for their debts. Nonetheless, Beville reflected as he got his first foamy mouthful, the economy was the worst of the country's problems just now—the worst strike against the King.

The state of the economy was one of the few subjects concerning which young Beville would listen to his father. Charles I had inherited a steeply spiralling inflation, bald old Beville Senior had explained—inflation, meaning a loss of value in the currency. This was happening in part because of Buckingham's wars, since they affected the trade value of British pounds and shillings, and yet the foppish Duke appeared determined to wage additional wars, this time with France.

All the while, the real need was at home. The collapse of the wool trade had left the country with a growing class of urban poor, people who'd come in from their farms in desperate need of work. And then there were the expenses of the Virginia Colony. The tobacco and potato crops from that colony appeared promising, but without real investment from London, the level of production would remain too puny to matter.

And what had Charles I done, with his kingdom on the verge of collapse? A kingdom that under the great Elizabeth had been the envy of Europe, all sound finances and swift administration? Like his father before him, Charles had begun selling knighthoods.

"Either way, Charles wins," Cromwell complained between bites of fowl. "If you won land, you pay a fee for 'the honor of knighthood.' If you refuse, you're fined!"

"Nonetheless," Beville said, "I'll accept the title." He tried to put some strength into the assertion this time—tried to match his older friend's fire.

"You feel you owe it to your king and master?" Cromwell asked sardonically.

"I owe it," Beville declared, "to my son."

On this point at least, Oliver Cromwell had no barbed comeback. He shrugged, his homely face falling into an uncharacteristic passivity. The two ate and drank in silence a while. Many times Beville Junior had made it plain that he wanted to be a father unlike his own, wanted to be someone who "left his mark on the family." And becoming a knight, for better or for worse, would help him in that aim.

"The real question is," the older man said, "who is to govern? What sort of rule is the best rule? That's the question of the age."

Robert Beville Junior fell into silent speculation on the vast differences between king and commoner. The contrast was especially vivid to

him, since he'd just come from out of the Inns of Court, and the company
of the young Charles.

Charles I was handsome enough to be a favorite subject of Rubens and
other portraitists. He was built small but tight, like Beville himself. Many
took the monarch to be cold, aloof; in fact, England's latest ruler was shy.
The distinguished Charles had a stammer—apparently a holdover from
longstanding conflicts with his father James.

Oliver Cromwell, on the other hand, had a rather sizable chip on his
shoulder about his commoner's bloodlines. He wasn't peasant-poor, of
course. The Cromwells went back centuries, in Huntingdon and Cambridge Counties, and the man had relations almost as rich as the Bevilles.
Nonetheless young Oliver hadn't had family resources enough to finish his
law studies in Cambridge. His father had died and he'd been needed at
home. Cromwell had married shortly thereafter, at twenty-one, and he'd
chosen a woman two years his senior, whose maturity he could rely on.

Perhaps the most embittering experience in his life had been the loss
of his career as a Cambridge scholar. As good a horseman and marksman as
he was (good enough to have considered a career in the military), Oliver
Cromwell appeared most at home with books and ideas. Nothing so infuriated his easily angered friend, Beville Junior realized now, as the way the
messy, changing world never quite came up to his clean, perfect notions.

The knighting took place within the year. Now there were two Sir
Robert Bevilles—and the new one, Beville Junior, remained determined to leave his mark on the clan. A mark to rank with that of the
Crusader hero Sir Robert Lawrence. Beville Junior wasn't about to be
distracted by matters like his new step-family, either.

His father's remarriage had occurred back in 1617—too few years
after his beloved mother Mary had died, to Robert's way of thinking.
Worse, he didn't like his new kin. Parson Acrode had tried to soothe his
hurt feelings, but Robert wouldn't hear of it. Just look, he complained to
the old rector, at the sort of fops his father embraced! His stepmother
Elizabeth had a fawning fascination with London's high society; her sons,
Robert's stepbrothers, felt the same. Far from the sort of men who liked to

spend a day slogging through the fens, these young noblemen actually admired the snooty Duke of Buckingham.

Beville Junior's best recourse, he decided, was simply to keep his peace. And the year after the remarriage, 1618, he'd kept his peace when unexpectedly confronted with his fortunate little cousin John. John had come into young Robert's life at the death of Robert's great-uncle. This great-uncle had lost his own son in 1611, the same year his grandson was born. So in 1618, the seven-year-old John was practically an orphan, without a male forebear to manage his holdings. Old great-uncle John therefore had entrusted him and his properties to Beville Senior, Robert's father. Beville Senior was to turn over both the property and the income off it when the boy turned twenty-one. Little John was going to wake up a very rich man, the morning he turned twenty-one. He was going to be just the sort of pampered fellow, born with a silver spoon in his mouth, that set Oliver Cromwell's teeth on edge.

But in the years immediately following 1618, Beville Junior had been less concerned about John than about his own father. In those years, he'd seen just how venal the fat Beville Senior could be. Robert's father used John's income for himself. Beville Junior had seen the books: the funds going from John's account into Beville Senior's.

In vain did Parson Acrode, in session after session at St. Michael's, try to reason with Beville Junior about his father's motives. Didn't the expenses of putting up the child at the Chesterton mansion count for anything? the rector asked. And didn't the fact that Beville Senior had allowed Beville Junior to look over his account-books make it obvious that the father didn't believe he'd done anything wrong?

As ever, the headstrong Robert wouldn't listen. There under the bare wall at one end of the church, he gave the rector back argument for argument.

"If my father believes he's done nothing wrong," he declared, "then I've all the less reason to respect him."

Yet outside of St. Michael's he kept his peace—kept his peace and played the smiling, if silent, son and heir. And the strangest element was that Beville Junior actually liked little John's company. Lucky as the young scion was, John had a toughness, a quiet, a practicality, a wit that transcended the accidents of his birthright and inheritance. And finally, perhaps the reason Beville Junior came to like John was simply that he was another young man with a yen for the outdoors. Though eight years younger than Robert, John was willing from the first to hunt, fish, and explore, no matter how messy it made him.

Even before Beville Junior was knighted, the teenaged John was joining him and Cromwell in the swampy fens. Sometimes young Robert would stop and watch his two companions slogging through the steaming landscape—one five years older, common born and outspoken, the other seven years younger, noble born and restrained. Now how, Beville Junior wondered, were this odd pair to help define his destiny within his family line?

One day in the spring of 1628, as the three young men and their dogs slogged through the sun-softened muck, Cromwell with a full sack of game already and the others doing pretty well themselves, all three huntsmen getting thoroughly filthy and enjoying every minute of it—one day, in those edge-of-summer mists, Beville Junior's destiny felt closer.

"You know, I'll be going to London soon," Cromwell suddenly remarked. "I'm to be in the Parliament representing the shire."

He'd been uncharacteristically quiet all day: hunch-shouldered and squint-eyed about the hunt, chillier even than usual towards young John.

"Oh la, Oliver!" Sir Robert Junior clapped his friend on the back, so loudly he startled a quail. The bird flew off untouched; no one had been ready for him.

But Cromwell, his pack full, only laughed to see the quail escape. As for the laconic John, he tracked the bird with his musket before offering congratulations of his own—tame and businesslike congratulations. The seventeen-year-old cousin had long since gotten used to Cromwell's disapproval, and today as earlier John had carried on unfazed.

Cromwell, however, didn't appear to notice. The new Member of Parliament fell into an earnest monologue of the how sand whys of his position—he'd have his work cut out for him, if he were to get through any legislation on behalf of the county. He'd been chosen along with a member of a rival family, a Montague. And then, like every other man in the House of Commons, he'd have to struggle against King Charles' disapproval.

Two years earlier, Charles had dissolved Parliament when it refused to approve a new tax to support his and Buckingham's assault on a French stronghold. The King had then ordered the nobility to give him a loan. An astonishing number had meekly gone along with the demand, including Beville Junior's ever-malleable father.

"If we'd just had a hundred estate-holders with the necessary backbone!" Cromwell growled, this spring afternoon in the fens. "Aye, then we'd've seen some changes. 'Twould've been like old King John and the Magna Carta all over again. Somebody has to stop those madmen, and soon."

"God willing, friend Cromwell, it will be you."

"God willing, it will."

Decisively the big Saxon turned his back, slogging determinedly back towards the roads. Once again Beville Junior was left staring at the back of the driven man now emerging as his idol. This time he thought: you and me together, Oliver. Together we'll make a mark such as England's never seen.

And yet over the next few years, whatever great work was in store for Beville Junior remained hidden. Wandering his father's grand new brick mansion without much to do, he sometimes felt as if he were wandering through history with similar aimlessness. Zounds, if only his time had some great, clearly defined cause! Something like the Crusades, or the Armada!

Others of his generation appeared to be finding themselves satisfying places in life. His older sister Honor had married, and her husband was no inconsequential figure himself: a cousin to the renowned poet John Dryden. And Robert's younger brother William seemed well on his way to becoming a major English attorney. But what was to be Robert's calling, Robert's achievement?

Parson Acrode had tried to help him with the question. In one of their last conversations, the old rector had warned Beville Junior that he was in danger of growing up a tragic figure. He was full of dreams, the parson said, of rich visions he'd inherited from his grandfather. But so long as he refused to accept as well his father's humble practicality he'd never realize those dreams. Sir Robert Junior, a knight or no, seemed too easily bruised to do the work a dream required.

"Easily bruised?" Beville asked, bristling. "You should see me in the fens, parson. I can hike those swamps all day with nary a whisper of complaint."

"Really," the clergyman replied. "And do you find any talents out there, buried in the wet ground?"

His compact young questioner frowned, puzzled.

"Oh come, master Robert, you remember the talents." The parson's ancient, wrinkled smile gently reproved him. "The good coin of Christ, buried uselessly in the ground?"

The nobleman recalled the parable from St. Matthew. Still frowning, he tried to apply the moral to himself.

"Don't simply bury your talents out at the fens, master Robert. Don't."

Robert meditated on these words for weeks—for months. Of course, in one sense old Acrode was suggesting something simple, namely, that the indecisive nobleman try his hand at good works. Certainly, there was plenty of opportunity for philanthropy. England had plenty of unfortunates.

Beville Junior had been raised with the English Puritan ethic—and in 1629, left bereft by the passing of his lone family confidant, Parson Acrode, the confused and heartsore nobleman tried returning to the basic issues of faith, works, and salvation. Was a man's soul saved because of what he did in this world? Was there some one deed or accomplishment that would give his life meaning? Not according to most Puritans. Their creed argued that men and women had a destiny that was entirely a matter of God's grace. They were predestined for Heaven or Hell, regardless of what they did.

So Beville Junior found himself without a clear direction in the lonely days after the death of Parson Acrode. In his heart, he felt a yen for doing good works. Such works were, indeed, already part of his responsibilities around the estate—what few responsibilities he'd taken on. He kept up the public services his father and grandfather had established. His father wasn't around to take care of them anyway. Like Cromwell, old Sir Robert Senior was in London just now, trying to do what he could to save England's government. King Charles had once again dissolved the Parliament. The high-strung, coltish monarch instead asserted what he called "personal rule," relying on a small and largely arbitrary circle of councilors. And in the midst of this turmoil was Beville Junior's father—that mumbler! The old man was there as much to appease his new society-minded wife as to provide some benefit for his country. It was a perfect example of how all the engines of civilization seemed to have stalled: crown, church, state. And Sir Robert Senior had the gall to appoint, from that distance, a new parson.

The choice was the Reverend John Clement, a lean, tall, easy-smiling man, by reputation a brilliant scholar. When Beville Junior came to him, still seeking clarity and comfort for his rattled soul, Clement explored new ways in religious thought. He pointed out that his young Lord of the Manor—and his distinguished friend Oliver Cromwell—weren't alone in fearing that Charles was leaning too much toward Rome. Other good Puritans, such as the Presbyterians of Scotland and the Pilgrims in distant Plymouth Colony, actually voiced such fears from their pulpits. Instead these sects embraced the rigorous theology of John Calvin of Geneva, who'd first outlined the notions of predestination, about a hundred years before.

And there were more radical groups, Clement pointed out, who believed in a wider freedom to interpret the Scriptures. They felt individuals had the right to choose their own preacher, regardless even of ordination; they developed their own congregations of like-minded men.

"Separatist congregations," Clement told Beville Junior, "are like the New World of America brought into the churches of England. They're whole new communities hacked out of the wilderness of contemporary faith."

To anyone listening, it was obvious the new parson was intrigued by such ideas. And Clement soon set up small parish study groups, to work out their own interpretations of Bible wisdom. One morning he initiated a class in Latin and Bible-study, including a dozen children from the manor house and other families. Young John Beville was among the group; with typical lack of presumption, he'd thought he could stand a bit of self-improvement. After the preliminaries, the tall reverend called to the front of the room a pretty young woman with flowing dark hair and glittering blue eyes.

"I'd like to introduce you to my daughter, Mary," Clement told the class.

Mary Clement was then sixteen, John Beville eighteen. After a single class of watching their shared smiles the Reverend Clement—he kept

catching glimpses over his spectacles—could tell that both were capti-
vated.

John and Mary at once took to studying the Bible together, walking
to all corners of the vast Beville estates together. To those who spotted the
couple out wandering, they seemed to give those meadows a new vitality.
Loose-limbed and pure-hearted, they opened their souls about every least
issue that concerned them.

Mary began to join in social occasions at the great house at Chesterton. She came with her father, as propriety demanded. The gossip at these
affairs ran quickly to marriage—and to all that the lucky girl stood to
inherit, once her soft-spoken young man turned twenty-one.

To Beville Junior, however, these were hardly happy occasions. His
cousin's finding a partner for life seemed to mock the unattended Robert,
now nearly thirty. At family celebrations he fell back into the baleful
silence that he'd adopted ever since his father's remarriage. It was a silence,
the partygoers complained, so different from the polite restraint of his
cousin. Yet as Beville Junior watched from the corners of the hall, he wasn't
thinking of becoming more like his cousin. Rather he continued to ponder
the declining fortunes of his friend and idol Cromwell.

Cromwell had been named after a highly successful uncle, a man with
a large estate in Hinchinbrooke. This older Oliver Cromwell also loved to
entertain. Indeed in recent years he'd often held great banquets for Charles
I, to which he'd invited every nobleman in the surrounding countryside.
He had kept up the merry making, hoping to gain some benefit from the
King. But in the end his extravagance had left him devastatingly in debt.

Beville's friend's uncle had been forced to sell the estate. He'd humiliated the family, in fact, turning it over to their longstanding rivals the
Montagues. And young Oliver, his inheritance seemingly gone for good,
once more had no one to blame so much as Charles. The next year, he was
forced to sell his own small property. The price agreed upon was 1800
pounds, barely enough to move his now-completed family—he'd had six
children before 1629—to St. Ives. There his only choice was to rent. The
former Cambridge standout and Member of Parliament had become a
tenant farmer.

Sir Robert Beville Senior died in 1634, passing on the home of his daughter Honor—the wife of Sir Robert Dryden, cousin to the poet John. His namesake son received the usual compensation as the first male heir.

Beville Junior enjoyed his prosperity. Yes, he still struggled with the fact that his idol Cromwell had fallen, and that greatness seemed to be passing him by. But as the Lord of the Manor at last, he could explore other means of making a mark on the world. He began to spend time at the court of Cromwell's old foe Charles, hoping at least to understand the enemy better. And beyond that, Robert told himself—beyond that, who could say? He was only thirty-three after all; he wasn't too old to learn.

As if to prove that destiny might yet be kind, at court Robert met Lady Essex Cheeke, the granddaughter of Lord Rich, Earl of Warwick. Witty yet kindly, plain-spoken yet refined, Lady Essex had berry-brown eyes that showed more spunk than those of the fawning country noble-women Beville Junior was used to. In no time, he was laying his title and his lands at her feet—all that he had, he declared, was hers. The Lady Essex, with character enough to see the lonesome boy within the ambitious court-ier, accepted. Soon she was hosting the balls and banquets at the Beville Chesterton mansion, events that nearly always included Robert's cousin John and Mary Clement.

And in the Bevilles' home county, at the same time, there was other big news. Oliver Cromwell was returning with his wife and six children: a changed man and now a rich one to boot. Cromwell had found Christ. The formerly atheistic young radical described his conversion as a movement from darkness into light. When asked about his days of disbelief, Cromwell would insist that he'd been nothing less than "the chiefest of sinners." And (the new convert would go on) wasn't this proof of God's grace? That it had saved a wretch such as he? Indeed, friends like Beville could see that Cromwell's new Puritan fire had much in common with his old outspoken rage.

Whether by grace or good fortune, it was during this same time that yet another rich relative came into Cromwell's life. The relative left the

King's longtime antagonist lands near Ely, and a comfortable income. In 1636, the ostracized tenant farmer returned to his home county in glory.

John Beville and Mary Clement hadn't yet married. Though they were always welcome at the manor house in Chesterton, and though Lady Essex Beville had become like a sister to them both, at present the young couple had practically no source of income other than whatever allowance Sir Robert Beville Junior saw fit to give.

John's inheritance had proven a terrible disappointment when he

The bas-relief monument to the Beville Family in St. Michael's Church. The sculpture depicts Robert Beville Armiger and his family on one side and Sir Robert Beville Senior and his family on the other.

turned twenty-one earlier in the decade. Everyone knew that his grandfather had entrusted the management of his estate to old Sir Robert. Yet when John came of age Beville Junior kept dragging his feet about giving the will a proper reading, and when at last the will was read—in St. Michael's, with the financial counselors present—everyone understood why. John's grandfather's estate, over the years when it had been managed by the old Sir Robert, had been frittered away. The money was gone.

"I saw his account-books," Beville Junior said in a harsh whisper, in the silence that followed the reading. "I saw the old mumbler throwing it all away. But what could I do? He was my father and Lord of the Manor."

The family's trouble was then aggravated by tragedy. Lady Essex continued to try to repair the damage, suggesting to her husband that John and Mary be provided for in Robert's will. But Sir Robert never gave any response one way or the other, not even during those happy months in 1637 when his daughter Essex was alive. A beautiful baby girl, Essex Beville damaged her father's heart worse than any battering so far when she died during her first year. When Sir Robert and Essex were blessed with a son the next year—another Robert, the fulfillment of lifelong dreams, the sole reason Beville Junior had submitted to the indignity of a knighthood-for-money—the boy also died in infancy.

In infancy, in the blink of an eye, the male heir was gone. The last diseased look his tiny son gave Robert seemed a mirror of the hurt and accusatory silence he himself had worn for nearly his entire life in his vast stony home.

By the time John and Mary were married, Sir Robert Beville Junior had fallen back into his old habits of acting like a stranger in his own house. The saintly Lady Essex occasionally could get a smile out of him, and the Lord of the Manor never overrode his wife's standing invitation to John and Mary—not even after it became clear their son would survive his first months, unlike his doomed babies.

The boy was baptized early in 1639: Christian name, Essex. John and Mary wanted to honor their ever-generous hostess, they said. But Beville Junior said nothing. Coldly he stared at the child in his cousin's arms.

No, no one could reach the man. Robert withdrew further and further into a heavy-faced wordlessness, lurking in his mansion's shadows. Sometimes not even his wife would notice him until he broke into a coughing fit. And these spasms came on often, each time more phlegmy and more disturbing, as the troubled lord began to near forty.

If Beville Junior had one friend at the close of this hard decade, it was his first friend—Oliver Cromwell. More and more the richest man in Chesterton was seen huddling with the common-born Puritan zealot with the radical notions.

"I tell you," Cromwell would insist, "Charles's gone too far, tellin' the Scots they need the Book of Common Prayer!" And hours later—more often than not, over a tankard at the Lamb & Flag roadhouse—Beville Junior would be raising the battle cry himself. "The Scots aren't Church of

England," he would shout, "they're Presbyterian. No wonder they rose in revolt in Edinburgh."

When the embattled King Charles relented to the demand for a new Parliament in 1640, the table-pounding Oliver Cromwell was once more appointed to represent Cambridge County. The Scottish objection against the Anglican prayer-book had turned swiftly into a full-scale war, a war Englishmen in general despised. The whole issue was one more proof that the Church of England would do everything in its power to oppress all other faiths. Not just Presbyterians were in danger, but also Baptists, Quakers, Congregationalists—and of course the Separatists. A man like Cromwell, remade in Christ but harsh as ever, believed it was time for revolution.

The Scots actually succeeded in occupying northern England; they refused to leave until England paid damages and back pay for their soldiers. Charles I had no choice but to reconvene Parliament.

Sir Robert Beville Junior, during these same turbulent weeks, had spent most of his time in London. He'd acted as an important go-between for his old companion the King and his fellow huntsman Oliver Cromwell. Was this role finally the great destiny he'd imagined all his life? Was this his chance to leave a mark of his own on the land? Certainly Sir Robert appeared inspired, a strange and almost feverish new light shining in his eyes as his carriage rushed back and forth across the noisy city.

During Beville Junior's lifetime thousands had poured into the town. The poor had been forced into every nook and cranny. Sewage ran down the streets and garbage was heaped on every open lot and corner. Outbreaks of typhus and plague had raged through London several times since the latest influx had begun.

Nonetheless Sir Robert never expected to die in that city, in that dissension-torn year. He was only thirty-nine! Still young enough to run from Cromwell to Charles and back again, still in far better health than he could ever recall his father being. But Sir Robert Beville Junior, already weakened by the frustration inherent in his impossible longings—and by his many long, unprotected days in the cold muck of the fens—succumbed swiftly to the latest wave of disease to infect London.

Loyal Lady Essex rushed to his side at the last, to his shadowy and stinking city bedchamber. There she found, while she nursed her unhappy husband's final delirium, that she had to play the role of a dead man. She had to be Parson Acrode.

"Parson, Parson," Beville Junior would moan. "I didn't bury my talents in the ground. I didn't, believe me."

"Of course I believe you, dear," Lady Essex would say. "St. Matthew warns us not to bury them."

"I didn't, Parson. Truly."

"I know you didn't. You've always followed the Gospel."

"But I couldn't bury them, Parson." Beville Junior's look revealed a terrible shame. "I couldn't because I never found them. I never found my talents."

Sir Robert's will was thorough, and entirely in keeping with the regulations. It bore his family seal, the Swanny Mark. In the document he remembered his persevering wife, and all of her family. These all received generous gifts of lands and money, as did many of his servants and neighbors. Even each of John Beville's sisters got something. But the document left out any mention of John Beville. The lord's closest male heir received nothing.

Ultimately the principal Beville properties were awarded to Sir Robert's sister, Honor. In the end, cousin John and his wife Mary, along with little Essex and the "Reverend Grandfather," abandoned not only the brick Chesterton mansion but the town itself. The aging clergyman said goodbye to his local study groups and returned to St. Augustine in Canterbury, where he'd begun. As for John and his small family, they moved into a cottage owned by Mary's brother on the main street of Stanground, overlooking the Nene River, not far south of the tragic Sir Robert's favorite fens haunts. It was a sturdy middle-class Anglian home, with thatched roof, wood-beam frame, clean whitewashed plaster walls. To be sure, the rooms were small by Chesterton standards, but they were clean and snug, their furniture modest but comfortable. Under the windows hung boxes of yellow and orange marigolds, and the path to the front door wound its way through a pungent herb garden.

Throughout that bright, promising autumn of 1640, Mary would open her segmented windows to a view of the Nene. Upriver fluttered the white sails of merchant ships, arriving with cargo from all over the world. And as the weeks passed the young mother discovered the usefulness and comfort in having her brother and other family members nearby.

"I'm perfectly content," she declared to John on more than one occasion, as fall turned to winter. "Little Essex and I don't miss Chesterton at all."

John would smile, feeding the crackling hearth-fire, but his lean face never quite lost a deeper element of concern. This was a man, Mary reminded herself, who'd twice lost his rightful inheritance. Twice, without his being able to lift a finger against it.

"I'm content as well," John would assure her, those winter evenings by the hearth. But when he looked back into the flames, Mary could see the unspoken concern in his eyes.

I n 1645 Cromwell decimated Charles' forces at Naseby. Defeated and cut off, Charles I ran north from Oxford, wearing a disguise. He threw himself on the mercy of the Scots, but in early 1646 they turned him over to the gray-clad Puritans. The Civil War was over, and the fire-eyed and unforgiving Oliver Cromwell had taken charge. He called himself Lord Protector.

John Beville was by then thirty-five. The limber towhead who'd stood to inherit one of the biggest estates in East Anglia had, by now, settled happily into a life as a prosperous international tradesman. Beville imported everything from Far Eastern spices to Virginia tobacco, and he sold the goods inland. There he bought the Thaxted-area ironware and cutlery, as well as good East Anglian woolens. All these he sent overseas.

Beville generally turned his best profit on tobacco—better known as "sot-weed," for both its softness to the touch and the intriguing soggy-headedness that smoking it seemed to induce. But his older son Essex also enjoyed the New World herb, in his own seven-year-old's way. Whenever the boy came to his father's warehouse, he liked to stand by the tobacco bales, drinking in the rich aroma.

Essex had, as well, a deeper reason for frequenting his father's shop. There was by now a second son, John, baptized by the "Reverend Grandfather." And Essex, as the older brother, grappled to achieve a more adult understanding of his Da's awesome personal trials. Essex had to rely on his mother for the story of the lost property; John Beville himself never spoke of the matter. On trips inland, too, the boy had seen the great brick

Chesterton house of the Bevilles—now moving inexorably, with all its vast former holdings, into other hands. More than that, Essex had seen his father hard at work, building a successful business despite the terrible hazards of civil war.

What the boy respected most was that his father had done it out on his own—and kept his kindness, his family man's humanity, in the process. The boy Essex couldn't put these ideas into words. But he could feel how his father, despite his misfortunes, had carved out a liveable middle ground for himself. John Beville had avoided the bewilderment of too much birthright, on the one hand, and the bitterness of gifts denied on the other.

But while Essex had a remarkably mature sense of what his father had accomplished, he couldn't hope to understand what his country was up to. England had officially become a Puritan Republic. Under Lord Protector Cromwell, by the end of the decade, businesses like John Beville's were taxed at three times the level King Charles had charged fifteen years earlier. And they were paying for a dishearteningly familiar reason: Cromwell kept going to war.

In 1649 he marched into Ireland and, when a garrison like Drogheda attempted to resist him, slaughtered even Catholic women and children. In 1650 he conquered Scotland, and so succeeded where generations of royalty had failed—he forged a United Kingdom of England, Wales, Scotland, and Ireland. Two years later, proving himself as gifted at war on the seas as he was at cavalry charges on land, he defeated the Dutch, who'd continued to side with the old Royalists. In the later 1650s, the Lord Protector even won from Catholic Spain a number of the best islands of the former Spanish Main, among them Jamaica, a place John Beville had heard sailors describe as an earthly paradise.

The Lady Essex Beville had by that time managed a small, special protest against the draconian Lord Protector. The rich Sir Robert's widow had no shortage of suitors, and when she remarried she chose an earl of the Montague family—Cromwell's old nemesis. The new husband was, in fact, the very Montague who'd snatched up the property of Cromwell's bankrupt uncle.

The former King, still distinguished-looking despite years of war and imprisonment, was beheaded on January 30, 1649. The executioner's block was set up before the banqueting hall Charles's father had built at Whitehall: the very building whose ceilings Rubens had been hired to decorate, at the start of this unlucky monarch's reign.

The Lord Protector survived his lifelong antagonist less than a decade. And no sooner had Cromwell died, in 1658, than a new Parliament invited Charles's son to return to England as Charles II.

The same year, fittingly, saw the death of the last of the Chesterton Bevilles. In summer, the Lady Essex, the patient and sweet-tempered woman most responsible for John and Mary's happiness, succumbed to pleurisy. Her passing came as a signal to that younger couple, and to her namesake godchild and little John. The family had already begun thinking about emigrating to America.

John's tobacco business had provided him with extensive contacts not only in Virginia, but throughout the new English colonies. Sot-weed factors, or brokers, like himself were also busy in Maryland and Carolina. Many urged him to come to the New World, and rid himself of English taxes and regulation.

As for the settlements to the north, in Plymouth and Boston, those were Puritan like Cromwell's Protectorate; they'd try to control Beville's life and fortunes in England. No, if he were to go to America, it would be to Virginia. Who knows? John and his sons might even build a new way of life over there—something without the unfairness of the old system that had so betrayed him in his youth.

CHAPTER 6

Amy Butler Beville and Colonial Virginia

The seventeenth-century wars between Charles I and Oliver Cromwell concerned, at heart, the inadequacy of the ancient feudal way of life. Indeed, the system was breaking down all over Europe.

Even under less flexible governments than England's, emerging merchant and working classes no longer silently accepted the rule of aristocrats. Why, they demanded, should the mere accident of birth decide a person's destiny?

The New World loomed large in the search for better opportunity. The 1600s saw an explosion in emigration to the Americas, driven by a desire for a fairer apportionment of life's rewards.

John Beville was one of those immigrants. Along with Mary and Essex and John Junior, he sailed for Virginia in 1666—600 years after the Bevilles had arrived in England with William the Conqueror.

But if America were to offer a new beginning, it would have to be forged by the people who lived there. One such was the extraordinary pioneer woman who captured Essex Beville's heart. Our next chapter concerns her struggle for fairness, recognition and a better way.

A my Butler straightened up from her latest row, needing a breather. No sooner had she blinked the long morning's sweat from her eyes, however, than she saw her Indian help still hard at it. Even Contanchook, the Appamatuck Powhatan old enough to be her grandfather, jabbed and scraped with his hoe as diligently as he had when they'd begun. Amy, a lean-muscled twenty-six and no stranger to tobacco work, found herself impressed all over again at how soulfully these Virginia natives could commit to their lands.

Nonetheless, she took her breather. Stretching sideways and back, Amy fingered her fallen hair off her face. It was straw-colored, this hair, a fine straw that matched her farmer's hat. And when she tipped back this wide-brimmed headcover, she revealed pale sweat-trails along strong, sun-beaten cheekbones, white squinter's crow's-feet at the corners of forthright gray eyes. At first glance the young woman appeared dirty, at second lovely, at third unyieldingly determined.

When she'd finished her stretching, Amy needed to lean on her long-handled hoe. Dizzy from the heat, she surveyed her tobacco-field, a good fifteen acres of loamy Appomattox riverland. These acres were the only ones cleared for farming, only fifteen acres out of 400. And this summer was no less than Amy's sixth year of farming the sot-weed: the Year of Our Lord 1668.

"Sot-weed": like most Virginia colonials, Amy usually used this slang for her primary cash crop. But today "sweat-weed" would be more like it. May through July were the most trying months in the growing cycle, requiring hour after hour of pulling, hoeing, clearing. Some of the big downriver plantations had slaves. These were Africans mostly, plus a smattering of Indians or Irish. Besides that, indentured servants arrived in the colony almost daily. These hardscrabble former peasants came eager to sign up for five or seven or even ten years of servitude. To them, those years were the only chance they'd ever have at eventually owning land of their own.

But Amy Butler was a small farmer, her land at the edge of the upriver wilderness. Worse, she was a woman alone, orphaned and unmarried. She couldn't afford help, neither slaves nor indentures. The aging brown Powhatan Contanchook and his two teenage daughters received a kind of payment, room and board mostly.

No, Amy was no plantation lady. She hacked out her own living. The color of someone's skin or the number of their servants meant little to her.

And even on a steamy noontime like this, she was alive to her chosen home's beauty, the shock of the green Virginian sweep surrounding her. Her feelings for the place generally ran deepest at harvest time, after she and her three natives had collected and hung the tobacco leaves in the curing barn. Then she could lose long breathless minutes in the barn's doorway, drinking in the autumn-speckled woods around her, the flesh-pink wild roses, the beetle-bright grapes peeking beneath their rag-shaped leaves. After a while her gaze would drift northeast, downstream, downslope. Amy's 400 acres stretched for nearly a mile along the west bank of the Appomattox, a couple of hours' ride south of where it entered the wide, meandering James.

Yet Amy—especially in the middle of the year's most demanding season—didn't only notice the farmland's beauty. Also she scouted the landing-spots of the sot-weed smugglers. Yes, her riverside location was practical as well. After her very first harvest, six autumns ago now, the then sweet-faced young woman had learned quickly how to haggle with those smugglers, haggle hard.

Smugglers arranged for transport to foreign territories: to Dutch New Amsterdam, Spanish St. Augustine, the Danish toehold of Lord De La Ware. Such trade was illegal, under the harsh restrictions imposed by the Colony's home country, but if she didn't make it easy for the smugglers to land—and if she didn't make it difficult for them to cheat her, after they landed—she'd never turn a harvest profit.

Year after year, for a half-dozen years now, none of the grizzled men in the smugglers' boats or the powdered fops in the county assessor's office would've given tuppence for her chances. Yet Amy had held on. Today she stood in the middle of yet another crop, better than knee-high already.

"Miss Butler?" Contanchook called.

She faced him, this threadbare but durable Appamatuck to whom she owed so much. Methodical as ever, he'd weeded almost another whole row while she'd stood there dreaming.

"Miss Butler?" he repeated. "Not so bad. This year not so bad. Not this year, better stop."

Amy, reading the man's black eyes, couldn't suppress a smile. Contanchook had been raised in a village five miles upriver, a place where his ancestors had raised tobacco for millennia. Now, months before this year's harvest, his mind was already on next year's crisis.

"Next year," he repeated, "better stop. Dirt weak, no good soil, see? Weak. This year our last year."

With that, the morning's dust and heat overpowered her. Amy swayed heavily against her hoe, pulling her hat off. For a moment she couldn't see past the straw hair hanging before her eyes.

"In faith," she sighed, tossing her hair back. "I've had quite enough of this from you, Contanchook. 'Next year no good,' day after day."

She'd become a fine mimic, by now. Momentarily, Contanchook's small smile returned. "I'faith," she repeated, "I've had quiet enough. Let us leave off for lunch now, shall we?"

Contanchook signaled his two daughters, and Dorothy and Sarah hustled eagerly down the rows to the shade of a nearby oak. There they'd left the sun tea to steep. Just as they'd taken to the white man's Biblical names, so Contanchook's half-breed girls had come to love the English tradition of tea. Amy smiled again to see them rush for the kettle and cups, the day's bread, the honeycomb in its jar.

But then she noticed Contanchook stooping at the foot of one row. He'd taken up a handful of dirt, and as he rolled it between fingers and thumb, he kept frowning.

But then who was she, Amy Butler wondered as she ate, to think she could count on this land as hers forever? She was the interloper here. Sixteen hundred and sixty-eight was the tenth anniversary of her arrival in Virginia. Her family had begun its life in an England that was, looking back now, an almost unimaginably different place from this warm, wild, fertile world.

Her dear Pa had been one of the best-educated legal minds in their shire west of London. But "west of London" might as well have been "beyond the moon," when it came to using his learning to improve his family's place in the world. Her father's trunkfuls of books meant nothing to the cow-faced advocates whose positions in those towns had been carved in stone centuries ago. So parents and children—Amy once had two younger brothers—sailed for the Colony, with the onset of the favorable trade winds in the spring of 1658.

The Butlers' destination was a small town forty miles up the James, Varina. The name was a promotional device; Spanish-American Varina tobacco had briefly been regarded as the finest in the world—before the rise of the Virginia variety. Amy Butler's father had arranged through friends to purchase 200 acres of forested land along the Appomattox. Or mostly forested—so careful had been the father's preparations, the Butlers even knew beforehand that a small portion of the property had already been cleared by the Powhatans. Old brown Contanchook, Amy would later discover, had been one of those who'd originally pulled out the trees and brush on her essential fifteen acres. And when the Butlers had reached their contracted parcel of riverfront, ten years ago, they'd started planting.

Yes, Amy thought now, her father had planned wisely. They'd even enjoyed good weather their first two years, not so muggy as today, and had brought in profitable crops. But in 1660 her family had unexpectedly taken terrible blows—blows they'd done nothing to deserve.

The first had been economic. At the beginning of the decade, the Parliament back in England imposed the "Navigation Act." By this time, the Colony sot-weed had achieved a worldwide reputation as the best: the tastiest, the slowest burning, the most potent. The "green gold" had even become the local currency. So the mother country, greedy for every last tuppence it could extract from the Colony, required that all Virginians trade only with England. And on top of that, the Act levied a heavy import duty on the herb. That very summer, the smugglers' river rafts began to nose up the James and its tributaries, their bales of sot-weed disguised as boxes of Bibles, or as trunks of woolens.

The Navigation Act led inevitably to lower prices, but that was only the beginning of the Butlers' problems. That same summer of 1660, Virginia began to suffer a series of low-grade harvests. The problem was partly the weather, but also partly the sort of thing Contanchook was warning Amy about today. Like any other crop, sot-weed took a toll on the topsoil.

Native Americans were hardly alone in understanding the danger, of course. Back in Europe, untold generations of feudal agriculturalists had learned to rotate their farm-fields, renewing the soil's natural nutrients by letting certain acres lie fallow for a year. But too many English Virginians had believed that this former wilderness soil wouldn't need the kind of protection they would have given it back in the old country. And besides that, crop rotation wasn't an easy matter in a land still more than nine-tenths undeveloped. When Contanchook mentioned the soil's weakness, he was also reminding his mistress of her own weakness. Even so tough and determined a woman as Amy Butler couldn't cut trees and vines, pull stumps and creepers, all by herself.

For she was all by herself. The ruined profits, skimpy harvest, and insect-infested weather of 1660 had proven too much for the Butlers. In that single year, Amy had lost father, mother, and brothers.

How had she gotten through it? That time had battered Amy almost daily: her youngest brother collapsing into the deliriums of "summer-sickness"—the disease that visiting Spaniards called malaria—the afternoon after they'd buried her mother. How had she managed?

There'd been Contanchook and his daughters, taking up much of the slack, even arranging on his own for other native workers. Once or twice, Amy had come out from another night-long vigil by the sickbed, dazed and exhausted, and found five or six coppery Powhatans in her tobacco-rows where she'd expected only three. The first time it happened, she'd thought it was the onset of her own delirium. And then there'd been the farm itself—the green that helped her through the black. Sot-weed grows tall, and its broad leaves look almost clownish. After midsummer it needs little cultivation, but during those weeks a farmer must lop the better seed-pouches off the tops of the plants, in order to have plantings for the next season.

The next season! How wonderfully this understanding had struck Amy Butler, in that down-grinding year of four graves, four far-grimmer plantings. The next season meant another cycle of these shiny clown's-mitten tobacco-leaves, leaves that seemed to chuckle whenever the breeze stirred their stalks. Another woman might have found this vitality cruel in the face of her devastation. But Amy Butler could imagine no better place to face a loss: no better distraction, no more profound, soulful uplift. Yes, she was her father's daughter, set more on the future than on the past.

And finally there'd been her father's books. The man had made sure his daughter got an education—never mind the common, narrow-minded notions that women shouldn't read. And this learning too had helped see Amy through the season of graves; the books had gotten her through the nights, as the sot-weed had gotten her through the days. Many evenings she'd passed before the hearth-fire of her otherwise hushed and empty home, reading by the light of the flames. She devoured everything he had, more than fifty volumes, enjoying both the cool theorizing of Francis Bacon and the heated dramas of William Shakespeare.

Also the young woman turned to the Bible, taking comfort in the familiar King James translation. Certainly her tragedies recalled the suffering of Job, and she spent many a night sharing the troubles of that bereft, complaining man. But Amy Butler couldn't help feeling a closer connection to Old Testament women Ruth and Esther. Both Ruth's and Esther's were stories of eventual mercy. Both ancient heroines bravely made their way through crises to more just, more favorable destinies.

Over the years Amy had made her land work for her. She'd managed, without taking on the far greater labor of clearing the forest. Of course she'd done some of that, as time had allowed. She and Contanchook had cut down their share of trees. She'd broken enough farmland to allow for some crop rotation at least.

Still, sot-weed was a hungry herb, sucking up the soil's nutrients fast. Her steadfast Contanchook had been right, warning that she'd reached the end of what could be accomplished by half-measures. Even this coming harvest looked questionable. Amy would have to drive a hard bargain with the smugglers if she and her natives were going to have enough to eat this winter. And after that?

In her situation, the plantation factors downriver would have taken on more slaves or indentures: the old Lords of the Manor back in England would have rounded up a few more vassals. But what could she do—a woman alone in the New World, a small farmer with more books than hands?

She tried to relax, in the buzz of the insects, the gurgle of the Appomattox. Yet when a line of Scripture came into her head, a line from Esther, it was an unhappy meditation: How can I endure to see the evil that shall come until my people?

When a rider approached, a man, her first reaction was likewise cranky: Now what?

Amy's days didn't see much interruption. Varina, the closest community, was five miles away. Though hardly more than a crossroads, it was the center of county life, so that what little socializing the self-reliant young woman did was generally taken care of in town. Having a man come up to the farm on horseback, well . . . the young woman eyed him closely. Contanchook, with a native's unfathomable prescience, had already sent off his two daughters, one to the barn and the other to the house. There was a horse in the barn, a musket in the house. And her copper-colored handyman would have met that newcomer at the edge of the property, if Amy hadn't hustled to her feet and bid him stop.

She'd realized already that they had nothing to fear. Their visitor was clearly no larceny-minded highwayman. He bounced in the saddle too much for that, working against his steed rather than with it. Amy had seen horsemen like this before. Many who were new to Virginia looked equally ill at ease in the saddle. And seeing this, Amy had a pretty good idea why he'd come.

The man dismounted and came only so far as the nearest fence line. His walk was pained, his back stiff. Yet he was more than a little attractive, no older than twenty-seven or twenty-eight, lean and clear-faced with friendly, abashed eyes.

"Excuse me, ma'am," he said. "But might I enquire—would this be the Butler property?"

"It would," Amy replied, with half a smile. "Why d'ye care to know?"

Despite the stranger's obvious harmlessness, despite the magnetism of his clear and honest face, Amy kept her distance, several paces back on her side of the fence. She'd been through visits like this before. If a new colonial arrived with any sort of connections, he almost always could find work in the government. And the lowest government job was tobacco counter.

"Excuse me," the young man repeated. He looked, if anything, amused by her audacity. "I should have told you, my name is Essex Beville."

"Is it now?" she said.

"I've been riding all day," he said, "trying to find this farm. Would you be Miss Butler?"

"I would. And you would be here to count my sot-weed."

Essex Beville frowned for the first time since he'd come off his horse. "How did you know I had been sent to count your sot-weed?"

She allowed herself a laugh, and lightly made plain the things a seasoned colonial like herself could see in a glance. As the young woman talked, Essex fumbled through one of his saddlebags and withdrew paper, a quill, and an ink bottle. He even had trouble with the ink, leaking a bit between his fingers. Amy found herself charmed all over again. The immigrant counters who'd come her way before this had been full of themselves, striding around like they'd gotten their assignment from King Charles II himself; they'd sneer at her Indians—and leer at her.

It was all ludicrous, really. The reason these newcomers had been sent to a small farm like hers was that they weren't yet trusted with more important landholdings. The Burgesses were always careful to protect the feelings of the big plantation owners. Such owners didn't take kindly to time-wasting intrusions by inexperienced assessors.

In other words Amy was a test case for this young fresh-face. She'd been one before—but never so gaily. I'faith, her feelings were running high as the Appomattox current after the spring rains! She liked this man, this Essex Beville. He showed no traces of most new official's puffery; he asked openly for help.

"Do I count every one of yonder tall, raggy plants?" he asked, pointing past the gate.

"Oh la, esteemed sir," she teased him, "you would hardly be the first to add a few dozen weeds to my crop."

Essex proved a quick study, to boot. He learned the difference between tobacco and thistle and completed his count before sundown. Amy monitored his count, checking it against private calculations of her own. And by the time the two of them were through it was too late for the young man to find his way back to Varina before nightfall—or so Amy claimed.

More or less refusing to take no for an answer, she requested that he join the four of them on the farm for dinner. Contanchook's girls were sent off again to fix their guest a place to sleep, in the barn, and with their father they killed a chicken for the meal.

As they settled down to their food she asked, by way of beginning, how the man had decided to venture across the Atlantic. At first, Essex's coming to the New World sounded like a story she'd heard a dozen times before. His father's father had been the second son born to a nobleman, another of those younger offspring overlooked under feudal inheritance laws. But in Essex's family, for generation, there'd been more than enough of a fortune to provide a decent inheritance for even the later children. But all that—Amy's manly visitor shook his head, saddened but unembittered—all that had ended with Essex's grandfather. There'd been faulty investments, and there'd been a very strange last will and testament, left by a tragically unfulfilled uncle, which had once and for all deprived Essex's father John of the family's ancient lands.

"If we could have fought it in the courts somehow," Essex Beville said, before Amy's hearth-fire, "I'm sure my father could have prevailed."

"Y'don't blame the man, then?" Amy asked.

Again Essex showed no bitterness, shaking his head. "My Da's as hardworking and full of ideas as any man in the kingdom. But no one can fight a thousand years of bad law."

Now it was Amy's turn to shake her head. "My father too came to see the old ways held nothing for us. America, he used to say, must perforce be different."

The two shared a wordless gaze, mixing disappointment, loss, uncertainty—and hope.

In any case, the newcomer's story went on, John Beville eventually followed a few old friends to Virginia. The family had put up with one such friend in Varina: father John, mother Mary, himself, and his brother John, Jr.

"In Varina?" Amy asked. "I've heard naught of any new family in these parts."

"Good Miss Butler," Essex replied with a smile. "I sit before you only two weeks an American. I still had my sea legs when I had to climb up on yonder mule-headed stallion and began gallivanting all over the Virginia countryside!"

His father's friends, Essex went on as she was laughing, were the Farrars.

"The Farrars!" Amy exclaimed. "In truth, the Farrars?"

"Aye," Essex said, smiling. "William Farrar. He wasn't one of your counters who couldn't tell a thistle from the real thing, was he?"

"Not by a hundred-yard chalk, Master Essex. In Henrico County, the Farrars are the best friends a man might hope to have."

William Farrar, she went on to explain, was captain of the local militia and a member of the House of Burgesses. William's son, John, himself a militia lieutenant colonel, was a friend. Whenever she traveled to town, she paid the family a visit, and the Farrars never failed to include her in their parties and functions.

With a new stiffness in his voice, Essex asked about the Farrars' young man, John. "You say, Miss Butler, he's a friend?"

She didn't understand. "He's not an enemy, certainly. Virginia is a small place, yet, and one needs every last ally one can count on."

"I see. This John's been an aid in distress, then?"

Ah, now Amy saw what he was fishing for. This Essex was jealous, of all things; apparently he'd been feeling something like the same rush of affections as were careening through her. The idea set off yet more careening, round her heart. Hardly three hours after first laying eyes on her, Amy's visitor didn't like to imagine some other young man enjoying her company.

T he Farrars' party was only a week away, it turned out.

The road from Amy's farm to Varina was nothing more than a horse trail that became wide enough, here and there, to allow two buggies to squeeze past each other. The town itself was a collection of a half-dozen small streets with a few shops and homes. It had no mansions, no government buildings; those were down in the Middle Plantation, in the prosperous country where the James met the York. Likewise the social scene in Varina was subdued. Most activity took place at the Farrars'. Their plantation was among the biggest in Henrico County.

The family house was modest by the standards of downriver largesse, but it was exceptionally well-furnished. Captain Farrar had a large collection of swords, muskets, and pistols, all on display over the two fireplaces. High-backed leather chairs surrounded two large dining tables. Silver and pewter plates, platters, and goblets lined the wooden cupboards. And—another reason Amy liked him—the Captain took great pride in his library. William Farrar was as well-read as Amy's father, if not as open-minded. Many times she'd borrowed a tome of the Captain's, or shared one of her own with him.

This evening's gathering was the usual affair. A few other plantation owners and their wives had gathered to eat and talk. Tonight there were also several local Justices of the Peace. In outlying communities like Varina, Justices of the Peace got together every two months or so to address the problems of colonial administration. They resolve disputes, levied fines, hammered out policy, always striving to follow the rules set down by the House of Burgesses. Indeed, most Justices of the Peace eventually became members of the House of Burgesses.

William Farrar had two Indian servants who were excellent hunters, and dinner this evening consisted of a tasty mix of domestic stock and wild game. The native huntsmen had bagged two turkeys and one of the primeval brown bison that roamed the Piedmont hills; besides that, Amy and Essex were served smoked pork, corn bread, and squash with onions. The Farrars never skimped on the menu. All they expected in return was a lively conversation.

Having no newspaper, people throughout the Colony relied on gatherings like these to stay current on developments in England, English America, and Henrico County. Socializing like this was a form of education, in which the pioneers shared whatever they'd learned, often from bitter experience, in order to become better farmers, carpenters, doctors—whatever was required. At the table tonight, the conversation began with a discussion of new medicinal herbs from Europe, and whether those might be as helpful as the brews and roots these colonists had learned from the natives.

And then, speaking of the natives, tonight's group returned to a question they'd weighed before. Once again the Justices of the Peace were considering a measure to put up a college for the local Indians. The talk went round the table, slowly, gingerly. When it came to the natives, the feelings of these Virginia landowners remained profoundly mixed.

It fell to rangy John Beville, the newcomer, to address the matter head-on. "Captain Farrar," Essex's father said, "you've two of them working for you, in your fields every day. What do you think?"

"They are—clever," Farrar replied, carefully.

John Beville knitted his brows, waiting for more.

"Without the natives," his host went on, "this colony might not exist. A new arrival like yourself, you couldn't begin to know the things we've learned from the Powhatans and the others. This very corn bread—" Farrar indicated the sweet-smelling pan on the table before him—"it came to us from these Indians. But they've no idea what private property means."

"Precisely why a college might be a good idea," a white-haired old Justice of the Peace added. "With a college, they might come to learn how the world looks to us."

"May I point out something, Mr. Justice?" William Harris put in. "May I, please?" The burly Harris, though a farmer like everyone here, was more a military man than most. He ranked even higher in the militia than Farrar. "Let me remind you," he went on, over a raised fork, "why we have a militia. Its purpose is to defend our families and our land against those savages. Do we fear the French, down here in Virginia? Do we fear the Spanish, those wasted conquistadors, in faraway St. Augustine? No, I say. We fear these savages only."

A number of the guests were nodding their heads.

"True," Major Harris continued, "the Powhatans and their allies are clever. But they are clever savages. To educate them would only make them more clever, not less savage. To my way of thinking 'twould be best to move them all out farther west. Out beyond the Ken-tuck-ee ridges, out of our way altogether. A college, well. Quite the opposite, that would only encourage them to stay."

"Mr. Harris!" Amy objected. "Indians are human beings, they have the human soul and spirit. They deserve to be treated as we all do, as vessels of that spirit."

The woman's comment drew surprise from those new to the Farrar social gatherings. John Beville knit his brow again, and looked from Amy's face—undeniably fair, in this candlelight—to his oldest son's. Essex, too, was frowning, but intently, almost transfixed. As for the others, long since used to this articulate and strong-willed woman's opinions, they sat back prepared to hear her out.

"If we discovered ourselves in the position of the Powhatans," Amy went on, "i'faith, we'd do the same as they."

"The same as heathens?" Harris barked.

"Yes, Major Harris, I say yes. And as a military man you should understand this best." Amy faced her antagonist, raising her own fork to illustrate as if on a battle map. "Imagine a force of thousands, all coming into your own home territory. This force carries weapons with a power far beyond anything of your own. This force encamps on your lands, taking for itself your villages and farm fields alike, and there it builds stockades more durable than your largest lodge-tent. What might be your response, as a military man?"

Sourly the colonial soldier smiled. "Zounds, I'd do just as they did, young lady. I'd sue for peace."

"Ah, you speak of the payment these families received for these lands? Why, naught but the best baubles and trinkets and blankets we English could provide!"

"Oh la, gentle Miss Butler," Harris replied wearily. "Would y'have us all pack up and go, then? Give the lands back, lock, stock, and barrel?"

Amy Butler shook her head, a few strands flying loose impishly. "No such thing, Major. 'Tis history which carries we Europeans to these Americas, and history cannot be turned back."

A new murmur swept the tables, this one more approving.

"But I say," Amy went on, "we embrace the Indians too, in this history. Wouldn't it be easier by far to work with the natives as allies, rather than forever against 'em, as enemies? Major, even you must get tired of marching and killing. 'Tis to put an end to your unceasing labor that we should build a college. A college would allow the Powhatan and his brothers to understand us and to begin working with us e'en better than he has already.

"A college," Amy concluded, "would signify that the simple and generous native soul is to be included in the new-forged American soul."

After dinner, Essex and Amy escaped to the front porch. She took her ease before him, leaning on the railing over the James. The moonlight's willowy reflection in the current seemed to mimic her own unabashed languor, as did the purring throatiness of river wildlife. Essex found himself with nothing to day, nothing equal to the moment. What was happening to him? Could three weeks in a new country change a man so utterly?

"Wonderful," he said at last, "most, most wonderful. A Garden of Eden."

"'Tis a good country if you know how to work with her," Amy replied. "But many a settler's come with grand dreams, Essex, only to die ignobly. 'Tis beautiful, our Virginia, aye, But there's cruelty in her, cruelty and injustice."

Her companion, at these hard-bitten words, came out of his moon-smitten reverie. Matter-of-factly, Essex Beville questioned the woman on the economics of colonial farming. He was, he pointed out, a successful tradesman himself; for a good ten years now, he'd been his father's right-hand man.

Quizzing Amy, he even took the opportunity to demonstrate that she wasn't the only one brave enough to speak her mind.

"Contanchook has been your strong right arm," Essex said. "True enough. But he's old now, and you'll soon need better help than two girls in shirttails."

Amy Butler, her elbows still on the railing, looked back over one shoulder. Her gray eyes caught the candlelight coming through the mansion's porch windows; her face revealed a new respect.

"Oh la, Master Beville," she said quietly. "Where was this concern for me when Major Harris was on the march, over the dinner table?"

"You held your own nicely, I'd say."

Amy continued to take his measure, wordlessly.

"Miss Butler," Essex went on, "never think me one of those men who believe women must always remain docile and silent. My mother, you know, is no such creature. She's a reader like yourself, my mother. She's a preacher's daughter, and loves to dispute matters of theology, philosophy, and the nature of man."

"She'll have her chance here," the young woman said, after a moment. "In the Colony, we are generally desperate for conversation and company."

"Company, good Miss Butler?"

"Indeed. In particular we crave the company of those with some true refinement of character."

Essex Beville, mulling his reply, found himself wondering just what he and this provocative young woman were talking about—or rather, he wondered if they were talking about what he hoped they were talking about. But then, before he could frame an answer, the front doors opened. Their visitor was, of all people, the thickset William Harris. Even more surprising, his first words were kind ones for Miss Butler. The Major declared she'd argued her position admirably. He offered his apologies if anything he'd said had offended her.

"Not at all, Major," Amy replied, straightening up at the rail. "Y'know we Welsh women enjoy stirring up a good shindy now and then."

"'Deed I do," the big man said with a chuckle.

Amy chuckled too, keeping her lively eyes on her dinner antagonist.

"And let me add," Harris went on. "A little stirring, y'might say, is why I came out here. A little stirring up on your farm, I mean, Miss Butler."

Sounding very cut and dried, ever the military man, Major Harris pointed out that before dinner Amy had said she needed to clear some more land. And, Harris reminded her, he'd just finished the construction of a sawmill.

"Now, Miss Butler," the Major went on, "I'm sure you realize that a sawmill needs timber. And besides that, you live just upriver from the mill . . . ."

Major Harris would spare Amy the cost of hauling off the logs, if she'd let him have whatever she didn't use herself. At once Essex declared the idea a fine one, an excellent example of cooperation among colonials, the sort of thing he'd seen far too rarely back in—

"And who will help me fell the trees?" Amy asked coolly.

Essex was once more silenced by those gray eyes, that easy posture.

"Master Beville," she said, "Didn't you yourself say, not ten minutes ago, that my Contanchook was growing old and his two girls wouldn't be much help?"

"I did, good milady."

"Oh, good milady, tsh. I don't require soft words, Master Beville. I require a man who can take an axe and hack his way in our Virginia wilderness. Do you take my meaning?"

"I believe I do, Miss Butler. I quite believe I do. Shall I be there at sunrise?"

"I wouldn't smile so broadly about it, if I were you. 'Tis backbreaking work, mark my words."

She wasn't exaggerating. By the same time the next day, Essex Beville was more sore and tired than he'd ever been in his life. He'd handled an axe before, to be sure, but he'd never done it so much that he'd needed the protection of gloves. Eventually Contanchook showed the young Englishman how to wrap his hands in rags, but by that time Essex had already raised blisters from fingertip to wristline. And his legs had taken a beating too. The ancient Beville knack for climbing had helped him clear a few treetops, so the trunks would fall true, but in the process he'd suffered more than a few bad scrapes and pokes.

Yet all his pain seemed worthwhile when Amy took his hands in hers, at day's end. The woman was hardly gentle, doing so; she was lancing his blisters. Yet there'd been a new respect, a new intimacy, between them then. And when this colonial farm girl had soothed his broken skin with icy spring water, his heart raced at the sudden cold—and then kept on racing at the closeness of her exposed, well-shaped neck, bent before him as she examined his palms.

Essex became part of the routine on the Butler farm. He came by if he had to do tobacco counting anywhere within a day's ride of her place. The heat of August couldn't slow him down; the sudden rains after the trade winds changed only taught him to ride better. Essex even risked his lowest-rung government appointment for the woman, taking as much as a week off at a time in order to pull stumps and clear away brush. And the easy-bodied Amy labored beside him. She could knot a rope or yank on a rake as well as any man. As she worked, better still, she kept up her flashing-eyed banter, her educated judgments.

The entire time, Essex never lost the feeling he'd had out on the Farrars' porch—the feeling that he and Amy were talking about more than whatever subject they happened to be discussing. And that additional, unspoken element in their conversation (though it was some weeks before Essex dared give it a name) was in fact the most important part of every word between them.

The engagement and marriage of Amy Butler and Essex Beville took place in a rush that neither of their families would have allowed back in England. Yet, while the groom's father, John, grumbled—and mother, Mary, fretted—they managed nonetheless to put on a wedding that was the social event of the year in Henrico County. The Farrars hosted the reception, filling their broad farm-style home from porch to kitchen. The guest list included more than a few of the most influential people in Virginia, including powerful new families like the Washingtons and the Lees. Despite the suddenness of Essex's and Amy's coming together, their future looked bright.

With Amy's help, Essex easily made the transition from merchant to farmer. Thanks to all his work before the marriage, he had ten new acres to cultivate, and the first sot-weed Essex Beville could call his own grew fragrant and tall. They planted half the worn-out older field with corn. The other half lay fallow, with no more demands on it than a few grazing cattle—their manure helping restore the depleted soil. And before the second winter set in, man, wife, and Indians together built a smokehouse. No more would the lean months threaten death by starvation, as they had for Amy's lost family.

And as engagement and marriage had gone fast, so too the other rhythms of family. In the summer of 1670, new children began to populate the once near-empty farmhouse. The first was a son; by longstanding Beville tradition, he took the name of his grandfather, John. After him there were four more, and another son, Essex Junior, and then three daughters, Mary, Elizabeth and (at Essex's insistence) another Amy.

As the family grew, so did its status in Henrico county. Essex, though never neglecting his field work, had an office in Varina. From here he managed several fledgling tobacco counters. The man remembered how he'd started; he remembered that, out of ignorance, he'd almost lost the opportunity to meet the woman who became his wife. Essex Beville made sure his newly arrived underlings knew their sot-weed—and how to ride in open country.

By this time, his farm employed two indentured servants, in addition to Contanchook and his two daughters. Amy had overseen the indentures' contracts, and had gotten them as fair a deal as she and Essex could afford, with so many acres still undeveloped. Indeed, the property was half again as large as when Essex had first seen it. In 1671, after the new husband and father had put in his three years of hard work in the Colony, Essex too had been granted the customary 200 acres. Altogether the Beville farm came to nearly a square mile of forested river front.

Even the indentures had their own quarters, a cabin at woods' edge. Amy believed any servant of hers should be allowed some degree of freedom and privacy. Without that, she felt, they'd never develop any notion of what it took to maintain a decent home.

This hard-working mother never lost her sense of the "cruelty and injustice" in her beloved Virginia. Indeed, by the middle of the decade, there were new threats to the Colony—especially to more outlying settlers. In the early 1670s, a plague killed half the cattle in Virginia. Exacerbating the ravages of the disease was another cycle of bad harvests. And the whole while, the number of new arrivals kept shooting up. Close to 2500 came during 1675 alone. Food grew scarce once more; once more, the natives paid the price for the settlers' disappointment.

Coexistence between Indians and immigrants had remained grudging at best. For every relationship like Amy's and Contanchook's, there were a dozen others marred by broken promises and spilt blood. In the desperate autumn of 1675, a group of upriver settlers bartering with the locals for food and animal skins finally found the prices too high to bear. The frustration of the whites boiled over; several Appomatucks were left murdered, their food and skins stolen.

News of the violence spread quickly, and the young braves of Virginia went looking for revenge. Over the fall and winter, native war parties left more than 300 settlers dead. The response from the House of Burgesses was to set up small armed outposts in the wilderness, each with a few stay-at-home armed guards. Not surprisingly, these had little effect; the vast New World forests left plenty of room for slipping round an occasional log fortress.

Soon enough, disgruntled settlers took the law into their own hands. One Nathanial Bacon, a minor nobleman, organized a series of vicious attacks that bordered on wholesale slaughter. By the time news of his carrying-on reached Jamestown, it was being called "Bacon's Rebellion": a challenge to Governor William Berkeley and the Burgesses.

Amy Butler Beville shook her head. This rebellion, she could see, was at bottom neither more nor less than another effort to wrest additional land from the original owners. Nonetheless Bacon's star rose, astonishingly.

There were many deaths, white and native, and a considerable portion of Jamestown was once more put to the torch. Governor Berkeley endured a sudden series of humiliations at the hands of this upstart. Then Bacon died unexpectedly in 1676, succumbing to one of the unknown diseases of the time. Yet for a few brief months he'd very nearly taken over Virginia, and this sent a shock not only through the House of Burgesses, but into the Parliament of England. Together these two bodies hammered out a more representative government for the Colony.

Those changes meant in turn that the Colony's Justices of the Peace had to start doing their job. The incompetent layabouts that Amy had so often condemned, the ones appointed simply because they were someone's cousin or friend—these all needed replacements. In Henrico County, no man seemed a more natural choice for Justice of the Peace than Essex Beville. The bewildering swiftness of his life in Virginia held true; early in 1677, he was sworn in as an officer of the New World.

As Justice of the Peace, Essex held court in Varina with two other appointees. Assiduously, they worked through every case, trying to bring neighbors together or sorting out the best punishment for some small crime.

Once the children were old enough to let her go, Amy enjoyed observing her husband's court sessions. Listening to the proceedings offered an unmatched practical education in the legal system. As she sat in her husband's hearing chambers, much of English law came to seem to her sensible and well-balanced, particularly the more recent changes, the revisions spurred by the struggle between Oliver Cromwell and Charles I. To think that her husband's father had once been a hunting companion of the extraordinary Cromwell!

But the more Amy learned, the more one aspect of the system troubled her. The legal status of married women seemed terribly unprotected. As a single woman, Amy had been allowed to own property, but as a married woman, she had no such rights. As she audited the court proceedings, Amy discovered that if Essex should die, she could lose even her right to live on the farm.

Regarding orphans, too, English law wasn't always fair. Yes, there existed provisions to ensure the care and well-being of orphaned children. But unless special stipulations had been made before the parents' deaths, orphans lost the family property.

Yet the most disheartening hearings weren't, by and large, the fault of the law. Rather, they were struggles of friend against friend, brother against brother. Often Amy could only take such tragic cases as object lessons in what disputes over money and property could do. And she saw, too, how manfully and even-handedly her husband could adjudicate. A Justice of the Peace in such a small county nearly always knew the individuals involved in his cases; her husband's position was repeatedly strained by acquaintance and even blood relation. Yet again and again Essex would find a middle ground. If neither side was overjoyed about the verdict, neither side was devastated either. Justice Beville, slowly but surely, earned a reputation as Henrico County's best jurist.

Meantime, John Farrar had visited Jamestown and the Middle Plantation, calling on his father's old friends. Some of these were still Burgesses, while others worked as powers behind the scenes. While most had never heard of Essex Beville—still a new arrival, compared to the men downriver—they agreed with Farrar that the Colony needed Burgesses who could provide greater protection from the dictates of Parliament. This Essex Beville sounded like a man with ideas: a man who could make England's tight control of trade look unprofitable even in London.

In the first days of fall, 1682, hearty John Farrar approached Essex and Amy about making the trip to Jamestown. Farrar even offered to put up the children; his own kids, he said, would love the company. The couple jumped at the opportunity. Amy hadn't been there in twenty-four years. Happily they packed the children off to John's house, then took the ferry forty miles downstream to Virginia's capital.

Jamestown did appear prosperous, but after two days in the original settlement, Amy and Essex came away with mixed feelings. The seat of government had some decent buildings, but it remained grimy and bug-infested, the inevitable result of being built in a swamp. Nevertheless their meetings with John Farrar's friends went well, and Essex returned upriver confident that he would have support from some of the Colony's most influential representatives in the next election.

Yet two short weeks later, late in October, the forward-looking Essex Beville found even an ordinary farm task too much for him.

This was harvest time. The tobacco's floppy, manure-rich leaves had been cut and hung up to cure. In the Colony's moist climate, a farmer's next job was to smoke the curing house—roofed with sod, but open to the air—by means of small, carefully tended fires of hickory wood. This not only helped dry the leaves, but also gave them a pungent, distinctive flavor. Naturally the fires' effect didn't stop there; the work left everyone involved hot and stinking. But this October, Amy noticed that her ever-energetic husband, no matter how close he stood to the hickory fire, couldn't seem to lose a bad case of shivers. When she laid the back of her hand to his cheek, he seemed as cold as the Old Town Creek.

"Into the house," she snapped. Her hard year of nursing her dying family came back to her on the spot. "Into the house and into bed, husband. At once."

She got him to bed, under several comforters. Yet he remained a pasty winter-white, his teeth chattering and his body racked head to toe by bad shivers. It was "summer sickness," the swamp disease the Spanish called malaria. "Ah, God," Amy couldn't help but cry, "'twas Jamestown!" The mosquito-afflicted wetlands had claimed another victim.

Then Essex began to mumble. The words were nonsense: "buboes . . . Granma Lora . . . the Plague. . . ." This was the next symptom, to be sure—the delirium. Amy felt half-delirious herself, there on the edge of her marriage bed, holding the hand of an icy, quaking blatherer who only moments before had been her loving husband.

John, their oldest, came to the bedroom door.

"Tea," Amy said sharply. "Sassafras tea, at once. Contanchook's Sara knows how to make it."

With the tea, and with her constant light-handed care, the chills and their delirium passed before nightfall. But Essex himself, once he was back in his right mind, knew that what was to come next would be worse.

By morning he was deep in the sickness's fever. His wife removed all the covers; she cooled his forehead and chest with towels moistened at the creek. The fair-minded Justice of the Peace strove to hang onto his reason, but by nightfall he'd slipped into madness once more.

The next morning, Amy awoke on the floor beside the bed. She found she'd changed her robe but she didn't recall when; she discovered her husband's fever had broken but she'd no idea where the sickness' cycles might be taking him next. She knew only that they had to get help. In the murky dawn she tottered through the house, calling for her John.

Then the boy was before her, a raw-boned and bright-eyed twelve-year-old.

"Take the best horse," she told him. "Take Fibb."

"Fibb?" the boy asked, his eyes widening. Ah God, children! The things that matter to them!

"Yes, Fibb." And she smiled, suddenly grateful for the boy. "I don't care if you've never ridden him before. Take Fibb and run him like the wind. I need you to fetch Mr. Kent."

Henry Kent, the solitary neighbor upriver, arrived just as Essex began to descend into chills once more. The soaked sheets of the night before made him colder still, and in an exhausted trance Amy worked around him with her two oldest daughters, struggling to get fresh dry bedcovers in place. Then Henry was in the room—a bear of a man, built on the model of William Harris. It seemed to Amy that she no more than shared a look with this visitor, a tortured blear-eyed look, when her briefly sane husband croaked a request to have John Farrar brought out from town. Then Henry Kent was gone.

For two more days the cycle continued: chills, then fever, with madness at either extreme.

John Farrar, when he at last made it up the river, needed two tries before he could come fully into Essex's bedroom. The smell alone would have been enough to drive out most men: the fecund stench of a week-long dying. But for a friend like Farrar, his first time through the door, the worst was what he saw: the skullish face, sunken eyes, swollen joints, peeling skin. Farrar had seen this disease many times now; he knew that very few survived.

"Essex," he called softly, when at last he was in the room for good. "Essex, d'you know me?"

"John Farrar," Essex whispered, with a trace of his former smile. "Justice of the Peace."

At that Amy straightened up sharply. The lissome farm-woman had been slumped beside her husband's pillow, one arm loosely crooked round his blotchy head. But at the mention of their friend's legal role her chin came up, and she looked from face to face with the feral sadness of a trapped animal.

Farrar too understood Essex's meaning. A last will and testament—when time came for such a document—would be more efficiently read and served if some officer of the Colony took it on as a special duty.

"Certainly," John Farrar assured his bedridden friend. "Your justice, your peace, that I'll be."

Again that ghost of a smile played on Essex Beville's face. "Need make my will."

Farrar steeled himself, then arranged paper and writing materials. Essex began to dictate:

> *In the name of God, Amen, I Essex Beville, being very sick and weak of body but in perfect memory, make this my last will and testament. I bequeath my soul to God almighty. I give to my son John the land I now live upon called Old Town. I give to my son Essex, 200 acres of land on the north side of Old Town Creek. All the rest of my estate I give to my well beloved wife, Amy.*

Justice of the Peace Farrar added some legal language to ensure the property would be held in trust until the two sons came of age. He made certain, too, of the witnesses' signatures and the deposition of the remains. But there was nothing he could do for a woman's grief. Amy Butler Beville's first feeling, mother of five though she was, upstanding and popular citizen though she was—her first feeling was that she'd ended up alone again.

Her land remained more than half wild, at the edge of unknown woods. And so what if Contanchook was still with her? He and his Sarah and Dorothy added to her bereavement, if anything, the way they'd outlasted a love she'd believed deeper than the spring that fed Old Town Creek. And her indentures, and her children, all going on with their chores—they seemed like so much clockwork.

Amy retreated for a while to her library. She tried the Book of Esther again (Ruth was too happy, too much of a love story), and took solace once more in the courtesan's cry for mercy on her people. Small wonder that, in Scripture, Esther's was the book just before Job's.

But then came a day when she saw the good-hearted Henry Kent, over to help out again. She saw him teaching her young Essex Junior how to ride.

It was a day when the sun had broken through the February glooms. The breeze carried a hint of spring, flavored as always by the hickory of curing sot-weed. And the husky and bearded Kent wasn't merely teaching the boy how to ride in the little corral beside the barns. He was letting Junior try his luck on the most spirited mount in her stable—Fibb. Yes, Fibb: the feisty black stallion that her twelve-year-old John had been so impressed at taking, the night she'd made this same broad-beamed neighbor a part of their tragedy. Indeed, John was watching now, at the corral gate. Both boys took part in the fun, whooping in the sunshine, and Henry Kent growled between them good-naturedly.

Meanwhile, out in the nearest field, Amy saw the undying Contanchook and the two indentures. They were taking advantage of the day's warmth, turning the unexpectedly softened soil, preparing for the next season.

"Mama!" Junior cried, heading Fibb in her direction. "Mama, look at me!"

"Aye," she said, smiling. "Look, i'faith. Look at the whole whooping wild lot of you."

The woman's biggest problem—once all this New-World growth had hauled her again out of grief—was not the farm. No, Amy's problem was raising five children without a father. It was no coincidence, she realized soon, that the day she came out of her mourning, Henry Kent was visiting. The childless Kent was remarkably good with her kids, especially with the two boys. Teaching them to ride was just the beginning. He took them fishing in Old Town Creek; like Essex and Essex's father before him, the boys proved expert huntsmen, bagging fresh game every time out. Yes, Kent was a man's man, square-jawed and bear-pawed. He didn't do badly with the girls, either. Many times Amy had seen him bouncing little Amy on his knee, or playing the draft horse, carrying all three daughters on his broad back.

As season followed season, Amy began to have more serious thoughts about her neighbor. Granted, with Essex's death, some corner of her heart had closed down forever. The rush of love she'd felt when she'd first met the young tobacco-counter was out of the question now; Amy was past forty, after all. But given that sober new practicality in her, she understood that her five young ones would grow up best—and best-protected—if they had a real father around.

And yet Amy held back from open courting. She hadn't been the wife of a Justice of the Peace for nothing. Amy had visited the county court-house too often to forget the lessons she'd learned there—the widows she'd seen losing every penny. No matter what their husbands had decreed in their wills, once those widows remarried, every last stitch became the property of the new spouse.

"Not I," the pensive Amy muttered firmly, "i'faith, not I! Not in this new world."

And with that, she took out ink and foolscap and drafted a "deed of gift." She divided the property among the five children. She made sure each received his or her favorite horse, plus two cows, two sows, furniture, bedclothes, utensils—even a gold ring. Finally the document was finished. All that remained was getting it into the Colony records, into the law.

Amy brought her deed into Varina towards the end of summer 1683. For counsel she'd chosen perhaps the sharpest lawyer in the country, one Thomas Bott. Amy had seen the swaggering, wide-bellied Bott at work before Essex, many a time. She didn't much care for him personally, but she knew superb knowledge of the law when she saw it.

"Hm-nm," Thomas Bott kept repeating, that morning in early September. "Very keen, Mrs. Butler, very keen." He looked over her deed with a jeweler's eye.

"Spare me your blandishments," she snapped. "Can you make it binding?"

Gesturing at the paper, the man indulged in some legal jargon, the sort of folderol Amy had learned not to let confuse the issue. But the office round him, she noticed meantime, was undeniably lavish. Bott had built-in shelves and books enough to make her envious; he had, as well, considerable culture in every phrase he spoke. His suggestions boiled down to small matters of wording, but when he was through, Amy had to keep her face set, in order to hide how he'd impressed her. She gave the go-ahead with a lift of her chin. Then carefully Bott quilled the new sentences into place himself. In another moment both had signed, and the document had, as he said, "the force of law."

The lawyer called in his clerk, and asked for a copy. While he and the widow waited, the man sat back, showing her his wide belly. And at some moment during that time Thomas Bott began to smile.

"Woulds't be so kind, Mrs. Beville," he asked, "as to tell me something of life on thy farm? Haply a city man like myself may visit sometime."

"We do have visitors," Amy said warily. "Mr. Henry Kent comes by quite often, in fact."

Slowly he nodded, his wide neck folding and unfolding. His smile remained in place, thick and oleaginous.

"Hm-nm, visitors," the man went on. "Then 'twould be no imposition, Mrs. Beville, if I myself were to sometime acquaint myself with, as Scripture has it, thy habitation and dwelling place?"

Amy set her mouth, fighting to rise above the way this man's books and clerks had impressed her. "Would this be a business or a social call, Mr. Bott?"

"Hm-nm, a very keen question. Very keen indeed."

She kept her gaze level, her chin raised.

"My coming, Mrs. Beville, would be social."

I'faith, she thought, he does work swiftly. When she'd come in, Bott hadn't even recalled her from her visits to Essex's hearings. And more to the point—Amy reminded herself, as the clerk hurried back in with a copy of her deed—she already had plans for a new man in her life.

A my Butler Beville took another few months to make sure the deed was properly filed and recorded in Jamestown. She even paid one more call on Bott, checking the document's status. She had what she desired, the silver-tongued counsellor assured her, with narrowed, admiring eyes. No matter what happened, that land belonged to the Bevilles.

As spring came round again, her days and weeks seemed to rush by. The speed of her adult life was heightened, in fact, by its contrast with the slow business of drawing up her deed. And Henry Kent wouldn't keep coming by forever—not with her sons growing more self-reliant, and her daughters getting too heavy even for his muscular back. Amy knew he wasn't coming solely for the children, of course. There was no mistaking the yearning in the looks he'd given her.

But then, her neighbor was no Thomas Bott, his desires plainly stated despite the curlicues of his phrasing. No, Henry was just the opposite: terrific with his hands, clumsy with his heart. If Amy wanted the man for a husband, she'd have to take action herself.

Each year in late summer, there came a resting place in the growing cycle. The weeding season was past, and there was nothing to do except watch the sot-weed get bigger. But this didn't stop Henry from coming, of course. He hiked over from his lands with the same ready hands and good ideas as ever. One day in August, 1685, Amy made certain that Contanchook and John had the other children busy in the barn. She made big Henry Kent sit with her on the porch.

After a few minutes of small talk, Amy came round to the Book of Esther. Did Henry know the story?

The bearded man frowned, uncertain.

So Amy summarized for him: the orphan Esther, the favorite maiden of the great King Ahasuerus, must come to the aid of her threatened people the Jews. "But King Ahasuerus wouldn't meet with his fair Esther, just then," she went on, "on account of some protocol of his court."

"Huh," Henry said.

"She wasn't allowed to come see him, and he was beholden against going to her either, e'en though she was his queen. I'faith, is it not a silly protocol, Henry?"

"Ah," Henry said. "Uh-huh."

"So Esther went to a spot in the courtyard where she knew Ahasuerus could see her, all perfumed and lovely and bewitching. She stood out where he would see her and declare, Protocol be damn'd!"

Henry snapped his broad face towards her, startled at her language. And while he watched, Amy hitched her porch rocker closer.

"Now, can you see her there," she murmured. "Can you see your lovely, willing Esther, waiting for her man to act?"

"Ahhh," Henry said, or breathed, his yearning brown stare glued to her.

"Can you see her, Henry?" Her own gaze was gray and intent. "Can you call to her?"

"Yeh," the big man said finally. "Yeah, I can." He hulked closer still, till his face was hardly inches away. "Yeh, yeh, and I—"

He gnawed his beard; he swallowed hugely. "I want you for mine, Amy. I want you for a wife. Please."

"Kiss me, Henry Kent!"

A good husband and father Henry proved, and adept at running twin farms—hers had the work-crew, and his needed only weekly visits most of the season. Yet perhaps Amy's life had geared up to some improbable new speed after all. To begin with, she wasn't merely Amy any more, but Amy Butler Beville Kent. And Henry Kent wasn't just a neighbor any more, but father, lover, huntsman, farm overseer, chore-teacher, reluctant disciplinarian, and—tragically, as it happened—a soldier.

Nearly every male landowner in Virginia had an obligation to serve in the militia. Henry was no exception, making the bi-monthly treks to Varina for "training exercises." These awkward affairs were not much more than brief drills on loading and cleaning the new flintlock muskets, followed generally by a lengthy visit to the local pub. As long as Virginia's Indians remained peaceable, the militia remained easy duty. But in 1686, small groups from several native tribes had joined in a unified war party. These young braves were tired of the concessions their leaders continued to make to the insatiable whites.

As always, the settlers on the fringes were the most vulnerable. They'd had the least to begin with; they'd moved to the frontier because they had as little opportunity downriver as back in England. Yes, out at the woods' edge, there remained the outposts put up at the beginning of Bacon's Rebellion, but they still offered little protection from surprise Indian attacks.

News of the first raid that year reached Varina quickly. The redoubtable Major William Harris, along with the middle-aged John Farrar, called out their ragged militia crew—among them Amy's new husband, Henry.

"Henry Kent, do y'have to go?" Amy complained. "I'faith, we've hardly gotten started, here."

"Huh," the big man said. "Would y'have John and Junior learn they can ignore their neighbors?"

Yet some few days' ride to the west, that very obligation to one another broke down, among those in Henry's untrained unit. At an outlying post, the man on midnight watch fell asleep. And with that the young braves swooped in. The skirmish was brief; the three victims were killed instantly. Among them was big Henry Kent.

At the loss of her second husband—though undeniably she'd prized the man, her gentle bear—Amy felt more bewilderment than grief. She had little use for the condolences of the Farrars and the Varina parson. Yes, changing the sheets on her once-more-empty bed, she suffered the occasional bad pinch. Yes, there were tears one day, when she saw Essex Junior spring up on the spirited Fibb as easily as onto a rocking horse. But her ruling need in those days seemed more a farm manager's than a melancholy widow's. She needed to decide what next.

And so, after another year of making sure that harvest and sales went off without a hitch, Amy came back to Thomas Bott. By then, her sons John and Essex had begun working with the sharp-minded lawyer as they took on some of the farm's business responsibilities. Despite his reputation, Bott treated Amy's boys responsibly, even kindly. He always made a point, also, of inquiring after their mother. Was "the widow Mrs. Kent" in good health, up there on the farm? Was she not (if he might be so bold) a trifle lonely?

Swiftly, swiftly ran the machinery of an older woman's life. Amy was weary, yet her youngest, her namesake, was still only ten; her boys had grown up on a farm and the illiterate Contanchook was their only remaining father figure. And what did the warnings of Amy's heart matter, as once again Thomas Bott drew close, oily and poetic? What did it matter that she was only angling for a piece of his power, that she cared not a whit for his character? Her heart had shut down anyway, the widow told herself, so she might as well try to achieve a nice balance. And Thomas Bott—well, you could hardly imagine a man more the opposite of Henry Kent.

So the whirling clockworks of her life spit out yet another name. Late in 1688, she became Amy Butler Beville Kent Bott. And almost as soon as she'd given these latest vows, the new wife realized her mistake.

Immediately upon becoming her husband, the gluttonous lawyer began laying claim to all Amy's property, plus everything that she'd deeded to the children. Indeed, they had never set up household together before the problems began. By the beginning of 1689, he spent most of his days in the county court, summoning up every ounce of legal trickery in him. Yes, Counsellor Bott admitted, he'd officially witnessed Mrs. Beville's original deed of gift. But wasn't a husband entitled to protect his own interests, when dealing with such a changeable, unreliable thing as a woman landowner?

In one sense, this last suit for her land was the battle of Amy's life. Her hearings against Bott dragged on for two full years and left the twice-widowed Amy exhausted as never before. Several of her neighbors helped, showing support by bringing actions of their own against the fat and devious lawyer. Yet in another sense, Amy's trials during those two years were the culmination of all good work in the New World, and so more or less a moot point to begin with. Bott's suit was hopeless, at bottom. The crucial work had been done a half-dozen years before, when Amy had filed her deed. It was the power of New World versus Old. It was the strength of a system that made room for women, as opposed to the ancient dictates of rule of the lord.

The final decisions in *Bott vs. Bott* were handed down in August of 1690, and though she'd won everything she'd asked for—the land would remain the Bevilles' as long as they wanted to keep it—the victory left her suddenly frail, suddenly very old. Yet the woman still had a few good days to sit on her porch, look over her high, bright sot-weed, and think. She remembered those muggy long-ago days when she used to work the farm all but single-handedly, and would straighten up from weeding to look over the miracle of her clowny crop. So many times, those plants had restored her. So many times, the fullness of living growth had been proven to her. And yet, bewildered by the ever-quickening pace of human years, she'd denied that same renewal and vitality in herself.

Amy could put the problem simply, there on her porch. She could confess, simply, that she'd loved her kind and humble Henry Kent after all. She'd had room in her heart for him after all—not only, naturally, the same room she'd had for the young Essex Beville. But Henry Kent had meant something real to her, something genuine, and her mistake had been failing to recognize that: failing to allow herself to heal after the man was gone.

I'faith, she told herself, too much can be taken for granted, in the onward rush of years! Too much can be neglected, denied, ignored!

So Amy Beville went on thinking, exhausted and yet open again at last to whatever might come. On her favorite chair she rocked, in the late-summer breezes—the same breezes as stirred the flop-eared greenery of the New World.

CHAPTER 7

Thomas Flournoy and the War of 1812

Amy Butler Beville passed on in 1690. In that same year, Virginia's Middle Plantation, where her hard-fought legal victories had been recorded, was renamed Williamsburg, after England's new king, William III.

Actually Amy's accomplishment proved longer lasting than the big city downriver. In another hundred years or so, Williamsburg was a ghost town. The state capital moved inland to Richmond. The Bevilles' Appomattox acreage, however, remained in family hands well into the present century.

But the next two chapters—the closing historical episodes of Part One—take us away from the Bevilles. The Pamplin family tree has several branches (charted at the front of the book), and we move now to another two.

In the forthcoming episode we consider the Georgian, Thomas Flournoy, born in 1775. An esteemed legal mind and a commander during the War of 1812, Flournoy briefly rivaled the stature of Andrew Jackson. His tale is one of holding firm to principles despite frustration and broken promises. In the process, he came closer to God.

I t was the wedding of the summer. In the Augusta mansion known as Overton, the grand home of the Georgia Congressman John Milledge, extra drapes and flowers everywhere marked the occasion, from back parlor to front hall. Men wore their highest collars, their most sharply-cut coats. Women had plumped up their bodices boldly, then veiled their cleavage with delicate lace, or with handheld Chinese-style fans. Slaves moved among the crowd in thick velvet livery. This was the cream of society; the crowd included an aging signer of the Declaration of Independence. Nothing but the best would do for the rising young attorney Thomas Flournoy.

The wedding couple stood out even in this crowd. Vibrant, finely featured, the bride had a delicate manner and shimmering blonde hair. She was Sophia Davies, Milledge's cousin, one of the loveliest blooms this rural aristocracy had ever cultivated. And the groom was likewise striking, likewise bright-eyed and blonde—and a strapping six-foot-four. His excitement, if anything, called attention to his good looks, his exceptional height. Still only twenty-six, Thomas Flournoy couldn't seem to keep still. Yet whenever some well-wisher lifted another toast to the lucky Augusta lawyer, he was ready with a smile and a happy declaration of his own.

"The future!" the handsome young man would call out. "The future!"

"The future," his new wife would demurely concur. Beaming beside him, the former Miss Davies appeared unruffled by the hours of sweltering ceremony.

And tonight's high-powered crowd could well imagine that Sophia and Thomas would remain the toast of their prosperous Savannah River country for years to come. Today's celebrants included a few who could launch a career. There was Overton's master, Congressman Milledge, who'd served as the Georgia attorney general and had just helped establish the state university in Athens. There was the square-jawed William Crawford, another highly regarded attorney. Though only three years older than the guest of honor, Crawford already glad-handed his way through the wedding throng like a master politician. And there was Georgia's most famous statesman, Judge George Walton. Judge Walton was the one who'd signed the Declaration, almost precisely a quarter of a century ago.

Yes, the very date of the wedding was auspicious: July 14, 1801, just ten days past the twenty-fifth anniversary of the country's birth. And Thomas Flournoy's very youth seemed similarly propitious: he'd been born with the country, born the year after the Revolution had begun. All in all, a man so imposing and easy on the eyes appeared promising just standing there, even if he tugged at his collar or his vest a time or two more than necessary.

Now William Crawford asserted himself at the front of the line of greeters. He made a great show of kissing the lissome Sophia's hand, joshing loudly that he foresaw "Many, many healthy children out of such a partnership—a round *dozen* at least!" Thomas and Sophia roared with laughter, giddy, dazzled, but then the thickset political up-and-comer took the lanky groom's arm, and spoke more quietly. "It's a rare Georgia wedding that has Judge George Walton presiding."

The famous justice had been the one to pronounce Sophia and Thomas man and wife. More than that, Walton had done so even though the younger man had recently bested him in court.

"I heard of your suit against the old man," Crawford went on. "Well fought, I heard. Well fought and fairly won."

"My suit?" Thomas got back his smile. "It wasn't my suit, William. I represented a client."

"Oh really? An attorney representing a client? What an extraordinary thing!"

The two lawyers chuckled together, and Flournoy took time for two or three more guests. But William Crawford stood by, watching the groom's face. The bride, understanding, drew their well-wishers off a few paces.

Once more Crawford closed in on the happy Flournoy. "It may prove a mixed blessing, besting a former Governor and Congressman."

Thomas gave a shrug.

"No one admires the judge more than I," Crawford went on. "But no one will deny, either, that George Walton was born one of the stubbornest men who ever lived. On top of that, lately he's gotten more crotchety than ever."

"Crotchety. Well, William. I doubt any man's so crotchety he'll quarrel over the sort of money at stake in our lawsuit. A small amount, I assure you."

"I understand the old man still hasn't paid his settlement. Isn't that so, Thomas?"

"It's irrelevant. The plaintiff's out of the country." Another local success story, Thomas' client had accepted a presidential appointment overseas.

"I've heard that, yes," Crawford acknowledged. "But what about when your client returns? Suppose the judge won't pay then? You know our old Governor's a strict Republican."

"Republican?" Thomas frowned. "What has that got to do with it?"

"Walton holds the Constitution sacrosanct, does he not? He fought tyranny when he was younger, and upon my soul I believe he'd fight again, if he saw tyranny up north in our new national capital."

"Tyranny? When Thomas Jefferson is President?"

"Some don't trust Jefferson," Crawford said quietly. "Some say that his interpretation of executive power yokes us too tightly to a central government."

"Yes." Thomas, still confused over where the conversation was going, scanned the crowd beyond them. "Yes. I'm a Republican myself, William. Indeed. But I'm a Jefferson Republican."

"As am I, my friend. As am I." The shorter man laid a land on Overton's guest of honor. "From Virginia on down the seaboard, there's hardly a man who didn't cast his vote against John Adams and his New England Federalists."

Thomas nodded, still wondering. Were they discussing the previous November's election? Jefferson's party, agriculturally based, had enjoyed well-nigh unanimous support throughout these farm-rich southern states. Up at Monticello, after all, the Virginian author of the Declaration had proved himself the epitome of high-minded plantation gentility.

"You support the Virginian, then?" Crawford went on, carefully. "If the national executive office were challenged, you would stand up on its behalf?"

Thomas' eyes went wide. He cocked his chin.

"You would stand up, manfully," the other lawyer continued, "even if the challenge to central authority came from such a man as Judge Walton?"

Ah, Thomas thought. So this, at last, was the thrust of his colleague's maneuvering. Crawford needed to know if they thought compatibly, if they could function together in the machinery of the region that was currently running the United States. Should Thomas answer yes, no doubt he'd soon find work coming from this quarter—a quarter that, given Crawford's obvious ambition, might in time include the highest offices of the country.

"The new District of Columbia," the big groom declared, "is our capital. The government is there, the President and the Congress."

Crawford kept his hand on Flournoy's arm, his eyes on the big man's face.

"And my loyalties," Thomas went on, "must be with that Government. With our Commander in Chief and—" his look met Crawford's—"whoever he saw fit to work with."

Apparently this was all the assurance the fledgling politician needed. Crawford began patting the groom's arm, grinning more widely, more sincerely. His tone warmed and his questions turned personal. Wasn't Thomas himself from Virginia? the older lawyer asked. Virginia originally, and then Kentucky? Thomas acknowledged so. He'd been brought to Augusta by his brother, who'd helped raise the family after their father passed on.

"Yes, you lost your father while you were still a boy, isn't that right?" Crawford's look turned commiserating. "I've heard that too."

"Lost my father William, well. A man like myself, I have fathers a-plenty, I'd say. Why, Judge Walton himself, he's a father."

"Ah yes, the judge now, as to the judge," Crawford said. "Walton isn't so mulish as all that. This lawsuit, how much did you say was at stake? Fifty dollars, did you say?"

Young Thomas smiled back, but made no answer. He respected a client's confidence, he'd never revealed the actual amount—and more than that, he found himself unexpectedly giddy at having passed this brief but disturbing test. Was it the whiff of high office dizzying him? Was it the circuitousness of Crawford's approach? He blinked and looked once more over the other man's head. The crowd appeared for a moment like some sort of mechanical contrivance: the ladies' fans going tick-tock, the men's hair dark with oil.

Thomas Flournoy

"Even the judge won't fight over fifty dollars," Crawford went on lightly. "You'll have no need of dueling pistols."

In a farther room, a wide room deepening into shadow as the Georgia sun dipped lower, Thomas saw slaves standing on stools, lighting candles posted high in the corners. There too, musicians were setting up. Soon the dance would begin. He couldn't see Sophia anywhere. Instead, at the entrance to the ballroom, stood Judge Walton. White-haired and craggy, the man looked obdurate, erect as a nail. Seeing him gave Thomas an inexplicable chill.

"But I've taken enough of your time," Crawford was saying, "on this happy occasion. I have the answers I wanted, and I'm sure we shall speak again. For now," the older lawyer went on, "let me offer a toast." He lifted his glass. "The future!"

Thomas Flournoy realized, when later he reflected on his uneasiness with the well-intentioned Crawford, that just at that moment any possible political career had been the last thing on his mind. Indeed, he'd hardly had anything on his mind at all, other than his bride. She was a

Sophia-willow, this woman now rooted in his heart: a willow the color of a sun-struck peach and scented like a hot morning's rose. That was enough for any young man.

Yet the Augusta attorney was educated, even worldly. For one of his generation, born with the Revolution, he had exceptional training and a rare grasp of the world beyond the farm. He couldn't help but understand that, as well as winning his heart's desire, in Sophia Davies he'd also captured a valuable prize, socially speaking. Sophia was the sort of cultivated Southern beauty now coming to be known as a "belle"; the sophisticated landowners in these cotton and tobacco communities liked to sprinkle their conversation with French. And once the wedding was past, the young man's understanding couldn't help but trigger, in turn, long thoughts about where he'd gotten and where he was going.

The Francophile touches of the blossoming Southern style—including everything from a sparkling new drink called "Champagne" to a heated, gauntlet-flinging sense of *l'honneur*—suited Thomas Flournoy well. His very name was French. The first Flournoys, Huguenot Protestants, arrived in America in 1700. Huguenots had made a home for themselves not far from the capital of the Virginia colony, the sumptuous Williamsburg (though in those days many still referred to the city by its former name, the Middle Plantation). Thomas' father, Matthew, had been an adventurer. He'd been a frontiersman, unable to resist exploring the inland wilds of infant America.

To this day, Thomas believed that his *père Matthieu* was the first white man to build a home in the present Kentucky. Matthew Flournoy's first trip west had come in 1762, when he'd been thirty and newly married. Over time he made some thirteen trips to the country's receding frontier.

In later years, Thomas sometimes wondered when old Matthew had found time to sire his nine Virginia-born children. Thomas wondered, too, about his mother Elizabeth, a patient and spiritual Englishwoman. How had she been able to stand her husband constantly traipsing off? Yes, *père Matthieu* had been a strange childhood presence. Robert, the firstborn, enjoyed more time with the man; he was born soon after Matthew's first journey over the Appalachian Mountains. But Thomas was the eighth child, and the seventh son, coming into the world on January 3, 1775. Matthew was forty-three by then.

On his thirteenth expedition through the Cumberland Gap, in 1784, a Cherokee arrow felled Thomas' venturesome *père*. Thomas was only nine when the news came—nine, and he never really knew the man. But Robert, the Kentucky settler's oldest, was twenty-one, and *Captain* Flournoy by then. A war veteran, Robert had climbed the ranks while still a teenager.

Thomas' mother responded to her loss by withdrawing further into spiritual explorations, the church and community work that occupied older widows of that era. The boy's other older brothers appeared set already on carving out their own piece of the frontier. Thus it was Robert who took young Thomas under his wing. And Robert didn't share his father's enthusiasm for the West. He'd marched over a good deal of the colonial seaboard during his days under General Washington, and he rather preferred the quiet country spreads of the new Southern settlements. He liked a place called Augusta, Georgia.

Augusta had begun as little more than a rocky ford in the Savannah River, a crossing first used by Cherokee and Creek tribesmen, but by the time Matthew's sons came there the place was home to perhaps 1100 souls, and some 10,000 more lived in the surrounding countryside. Many were slaves, nearly all of them African.

The principal product was tobacco. Three redolent warehouses dominated the downtown. The Flournoy brothers found as well a wide variety of pioneer manufacturing: a tannery, a quarry, a brick maker, a "strong beer" brewery. There was a dramatic society and an opera house, and each November the Jockey Club held races to rival any in Virginia. All in all, the Georgia crossroads seemed precisely the sort of boom town where an enterprising young man like Robert Flournoy could prosper. And whatever was good for him would be good for his brother.

T he older Flournoy enjoyed exceptional luck. About the time he'd staked his claim in Augusta, a New England inventor named Eli Whitney came up with an intriguing new device. Whitney called his gadget the cotton gin.

An adaptable mechanism of stiff wire teeth and narrow metal slots, the gin removed seeds from raw cotton. At first glance, it seemed a simple innovation. Yet Whitney's machine triggered a revolution. In the warmer half of the young country, where the puffy white fiber could grow almost anywhere, the staple crop switched from tobacco to cotton in less than half a decade. Indeed, the gentle landscape of the Savannah River country proved especially congenial. Cotton loved open country and bottomland.

Thomas Flournoy saw the impact of Whitney's breakthrough firsthand. In his early twenties, many times he visited the filled-to-the-brim warehouses of his older brother.

"King Cotton," Thomas would say, marveling at the grassy stacked bales around him.

"King Cotton," Robert would concur, grinning up at the brother who already stood a good head taller than Robert himself. "And from here our king goes out to rule the entire world. Or the entire world that wears clothes."

Thomas laughed quietly, restrained even then.

By the end of the century Robert Flournoy had accrued a fortune, and he'd seen Georgia farmers go from dog-trot cabins to white-columned mansions in no more than two or three growing seasons. Eli Whitney may have been a Massachusetts Yankee, but it was Southern boys who'd turned his gadget to gold.

Yet Robert knew better than to ignore the advantages New England had to offer. Once he understood that Thomas would be no businessman like himself, Robert knew enough to send him to Connecticut for an apprenticeship in law. In the fall of 1797, twenty-two-year-old Thomas Flournoy boarded a ship bound up the coast. A successful businessman like his brother needed a well-trained attorney. More than that, the younger Flournoy had already shown a bent for scholarship, for philosophy, for the knotty questions of morality and human value.

For nine months, Thomas apprenticed under a respected lawyer in Litchfield, Connecticut. To enter the profession, Georgia like most states required only "good character." As for education, any rudimentary understanding of the law would suffice. An attorney with actual courtroom experience and settlement expertise, as Robert Flournoy insisted on for his brother, had an immediate advantage over nearly everyone else hanging out a shingle.

On his return to August, Thomas Flournoy wasted no time establishing a successful private practice. Given his brother's influence, his cases involved some of the foremost players in Georgia business and politics.

Soon he was making regular visits to the prestigious hilltop neighborhood of Congressman Milledge and other local leaders. Often he stopped to pay his respects to the aging Judge George Walton.

At one of the Congressman's many social affairs, Thomas met his bride to be: his heart's willow, Sophia Davies. Sophia embodied for him some of the emotion-enriched thinking he perceived in himself, a questing mind yoked to a feeling-full heart, resulting in quiet reflectiveness and a powerful sense of family. The young woman loved to read and talk over her reading, as did he. She shared his fascination, especially, with the various Gospel versions of the Crucifixion. With her shapely neck bent over her books and roses, Sophia looked like the single most perfect companion to his own inward-gazing soul.

One day in her family garden the gangling young man went down on his knees before this slim Georgia belle. Thomas knew that a suitor was supposed to ask a young woman's *father* for her hand, not the young woman herself. But there among the flowers his heart pounded at his ribs like a soldier at the door. It demanded that Thomas reveal his feelings first to Sophia.

"Eternity," he murmured. "I want eternity."

"Why, Mr. Flournoy," she answered softly, blushing. "Eternity is hardly in my frail power."

"Eternity," he repeated. "For family is eternity. It is the Savior's mustard seed, my Sophia. Tiny at first . . ."

"I know the parable, Thomas," she said.

"I want the herb that grows grander than any other in the garden. I want you, my mustard seed, my eternity."

When Sophia said yes, this undemonstrative lawyer with the sober New England education yanked her up into a sudden humming waltz between her father's flower beds. Together they whirled between rose and honeysuckle, all unbelievably bright against the vast white fields of cotton away in the surrounding lowlands.

Yet even a bookish couple must live in the world. Even the peaceable Thomas and Sophia were threatened by the Southern sense of honor—the ancient and bloody practice of dueling. The seeds of trouble had been planted even before they took their vows. And bringing its sorrow home to both of them, the honor at stake was that of the man who'd married them: old Judge Walton.

The quarrel was, from first to last, a tragically minor affair. It was the suit Thomas won against Walton—the very case William Crawford used to plumb the younger lawyer's suitability for working with the Jefferson Republicans up in Washington. On that occasion Thomas had staunchly refused to tell Crawford the amount of the settlement, but the sum was hardly worth the bother. The young attorney had bested the old judge over a matter of some fifty-five dollars.

The plaintiff had been one Matthias Maher, an Augusta official. At the time of the wedding the debt hadn't been paid. Maher, a Jefferson appointee, was out of the country on a three-year diplomatic mission. But eventually Maher returned. Eventually, petitions for payment began. By the summer of 1803, just two years after Walton had married him, Thomas began to dread every new letter he had to send the man.

"After having politely called on you twice for the small amount recovered against you by Matthias Maher," he began one request—and even with those words the attorney felt a familiar yet enigmatic unease rising in him. As he composed his demand, and the many that followed it over the next months, Thomas often had to rise and stride round the room. He tugged at the buttons of his office outfit, nervous as at his wedding.

Of course, as he'd told Crawford, Thomas knew Walton's reputation. The former Governor and Senator was nothing less than a father of his country, yet even the man's greatest supporters reserved judgment when it came to his character. Many complained about Walton's chilly hauteur, and his bitterness in conflict. As summer turned into fall, the judge ignored appeal after appeal, and closed his door on the lawyer's representatives.

Late in the fall the judge paid the fifty-five dollars, plus a token fee to cover the dogged lawyer's efforts. Yet within weeks the curmudgeonly patriot couldn't resist getting in one more shot at the young man who'd bested him. He made public a letter of his own, a bald-faced lie, declaring that the blackguard attorney Thomas Flournoy had extorted two fee payments for his services on the Maher case.

It was yet another irascible flinging of the gauntlet, over yet another ludicrously small amount. Indeed, more than likely the accusation was nothing worse than a lapse of memory. Walton was seventy-five, by then. But Thomas lost all but his last vestiges of self-control. "Will you stop here," he wrote to the judge, "and reflect how serious such a charge is?" His feelings were "wounded," his reputation "slandered." He asked to have the case heard in court—in Walton's own court, no less.

Sophia had done her best to stay out of the affair till now. She had enough on her mind as it was, with the imminent birth of their second child. But when she heard this last idea, the notion that her husband would explain his case against Walton the man to Walton the judge, she couldn't hold her peace any longer.

"Do you honestly believe the judge would agree to such a proposal?" she had to ask. "This judge or any other?"

Thomas was on his feet again, pacing and pulling at his collar. He struggled to explain. "Nerves," he said.

Finally he brought himself under control, drawing erect with arms folded. In truth, the sight of her calmed him. She was still his Sophia-willow, even with her great new belly.

"The old man won't listen to me, he won't see me."

"Oh now, Thomas." Sophia smiled. "It seems to me that his last letter proves Judge Walton *sees* you all too well. Indeed he seems to see two Thomas Flournoys, both sending him bills for services rendered."

Thomas relaxed a bit, chuckling. He took his seat.

Yet his request to have his case heard by Walton remained unanswered. Thomas fired off still more appeals, and late in January 1804, three and a half years after this same distinguished old-timer had presided at Flournoy's wedding, the attorney felt he was left with no choice but to see the business through to its grim conclusion: "Your late conduct to me," he wrote the judge, "has canceled the respect that your years would otherwise entitle you to. I therefore demand that you meet me prepared to decide in a summary manner the already too long protracted dispute."

Again, at home, Sophia had to question him. "Would you really shoot that old man?" she said. "Would you really risk his shooting you?" She was whispering, over the crib that held their infant boy.

Her husband shook his head, unable to answer.

T he confrontation never came to pass. Judge Walton died within the week.

Was the matter at last closed? The Georgia statesman left a widow and a son, neither of whom bore any ill will toward the much put-upon attorney. Indeed, seeing their haggard faces at Walton's funeral, Thomas understood that these last months had been a time of pain and incomprehension for them too. The widow's brimming gaze made clear that, so far as she and her son were concerned, the sorry affair was over.

Thomas' future seemed wide-open again, vast as the new Louisiana Purchase, with which President Jefferson had just doubled the size of the young nation. And closer to Flournoy's heart was the success of his brothers in Kentucky, now beginning to move into positions of power in that state. A couple seemed well on their way to serving in the Kentucky government.

Then, in the midst of this burgeoning happiness, Thomas Flournoy received two letters from a John Carter Walton.

John Walton was George Walton's Virginia nephew, a man several years Flournoy's junior. He'd come south to take over the hilltop estate, and in looking over the judge's letters he'd noted the "ungentlemanly conduct" of the attorney towards his uncle. Like that, Thomas Flournoy once more had a shrunken future, a way of life that pointed nowhere but toward the barrel of a gun.

"You are now called on to atone for the insults you offered my venerable relation," John Walton wrote.

Bad enough that Flournoy had nearly fought a duel with the old man. But this last perverse twist left Thomas suffering as if he'd been shot already. What sort of Divine Plan was this, which proved revelation but not justice? He had no quarrel with this impetuous youngster.

"You know, sir," Thomas wrote back, "I never wronged you." He reminded the nephew that the dead judge's son had let bygones be bygones.

John Walton took less than a day to respond—and Flournoy, reading, less than a moment to understand. Apparently the judge's nephew had all of his forebear's willfulness, without having developed the old man's grudging respect for less lethal alternatives. And the attorney was afraid. Of course he'd often been afraid, these last months, but not like this, not with tears in his eyes, not with his legs and arms going quickly motionless. He came utterly still over the rash young man's letter, just the opposite of his earlier twitching and stalking.

Three in the afternoon, March 7, 1804. Six men at the appointed location. These were duelists, seconds, and surgeons, all relatives and rep-

resentatives of what may have been, at that moment, the two most prominent families in Augusta. Everyone had dressed in their best. The pistols
were showpieces, hand-crafted with ten-inch octagonal barrels. The balls
were larger than most, .50 caliber.

The seconds, in keeping with the formality of the ritual, begged both
parties to reconsider. And then—neither Walton nor Flournoy finding it in
them to back down—the remaining rules went into effect: the ten stately
paces apart, the long countdown while close enough to detect the tremble
of the other's eyelash.

Thomas waited without moving, as still as he'd been after the
nephew's last letter. Walton worked his lips, his fingers fluttering against
the gunstock.

The shots echoed across the water: overlapping shots, an idiotic noise.
Then Walton lost his footing.

In moments Flournoy was bending over the victim, the poor deluded
youngster already bleeding terribly from a shot through his midsection.
What was this madness that had brought them here? Turning to call for his
carriage, the lawyer was struck breathless by the world's beauty, the talkative green currents of the gentle Savannah, the dreamlike browns and
blacks of the scrub woods at water's edge. And what was that human
geometry beyond the woods, the houses and industry that defined his
hometown? What was the even-handedness of law, the restorative calm of
reading? How could the very men who made regulations and wrote books
be captives of a primitive need to proclaim themselves king of the herd and
drive themselves to this kind of senselessness?

Now the surgeons were beside Flournoy, elbowing him out of the way.
They hoisted Walton and started towards the attorney's carriage. But the
boy was gone. Flournoy had seen enough death to know there would be no
saving him. Back at the Walton mansion, Sophia tried to nurse the
wounded Virginian. Sweet Sophia, then in her ninth month of pregnancy
with their second child, applied cold compresses and red to the boy out of
the Bible. But even the Bible seemed irrelevant just then. Even Scripture
was no help, against the animal urge of men's ambition. And who was
Flournoy to feel himself above that urge, standing here stained with a
thoughtless young man's blood?

Honor had been preserved, yes. Around Augusta, word was that Thomas Flournoy had no choice in the matter, and he felt this support in many ways. His wife's cousin John Milledge was now Governor, and within a month he appointed Flournoy Lieutenant Colonel of the State Militia. Not long after that Augusta's Richmond Academy, the area's fledgling college, appointed Thomas a trustee. This last recognition was especially telling, because the position had been held previously by old Judge Walton himself. And some seven months after the duel, its survivor was elected to the Georgia Legislature.

These affirmations were hardly meaningless to Thomas, still stunned at the way blood had stained his life. But he took greater comfort in the more spiritual reassurances of an old friend, Joseph Bowen. "I sincerely condole with you," Bowen wrote, "on this unhappy termination of your quarrel. Let the misery that you now must and do suffer hereafter induce a moderate line of conduct that will exempt you from further effections on this score."

How deeply Thomas himself wished to be so "exempt"! Hardly a week went by when he didn't, after supper some night, mourn to his Sophia over what had happened.

"If only," he declared after reading her Bowen's letter, "my own father had just once told me to take 'a moderate line!' If only!"

"You are yourself now a father," she told him, quietly.

Indeed he was. Many evenings he'd brood over the cribs of his infants Robert and Sarah, and pray quietly that they'd never fall prey to such corrupted family pride, such damnable self-promotion.

Yet the shooting—oh, corrupted values—continued to boost Thomas Flournoy's standing. Over the next two years he was elected to the Augusta City Council, then selected mayor by his fellow councilors. In achieving these posts Thomas received no small help from the two local leaders who'd put their stamp on his wedding party, John Milledge and William Crawford. And though his new career seemed to him grounded in bloodshed, Thomas appreciated the distraction of doing something for the community, as well as doing something for his soul. Better still, this son of a frontiersman discovered that he was adept at the sort of careful compromises civic administration required.

With the cotton boom showing no signs of abating, Augusta needed to come to grips with its growth. The number of streets kept increasing, but the local livestock roamed as freely as when the city was a colonial river-ford. Indeed, informal horse races occasionally broke up the midtown traffic. When an animal died, it simply rotted where it had fallen. Haphazardly dug drainage ditches either eroded the Savannah banks, making bridges impassable, or broke down into fetid pools. And the worst development, so far as the newly sensitized Flournoy was concerned, were the all too frequent gunfights.

On some of these issues, it was easy enough for Thomas and the other councilors to hammer out solutions. Augusta levied fines for firing guns within city limits, and dug out better ditches. Also the group created the Office of the Scavenger, responsible for getting rid of animal carcasses and other garbage. But when in the summer of 1804 a fever plagued the city's riverside blocks, Augusta doctors prescribed the relatively cleaner air up above town—a recommendation not much use to the ordinary working people who couldn't afford to move there.

But among those who had the means, life in the hilltop neighborhood of the Milledges and the Waltons had already become a perpetual round of summery pleasures. Indeed, by now the area was known as Summerville. The Flournoys' own Summerville residence went up in 1806. By 1811 his Sophia-willow was proving to be made of durable fiber indeed; she and Thomas had six children already. Only one died, the poor infant twin Julia. The rest all appeared as sturdy as their father. They scampered willy-nilly up and down the deep staircases of the broad new home. They laughed delightedly when their Dad entertained them with some of the more light-hearted moments out of the Gospels, or with one of the funnier incidents from his law practice. The children seemed likely to last as long as Thomas' own eight brothers and sisters.

T he events of 1812—the war which came to be named for that year—by no means sprang up unexpectedly. Indeed, the roots of the conflict went back thirty years, to the time when the United States had won its independence. That freedom had remained tenuous at best. Britain, with a far superior navy, vied for the position of most powerful nation in the world. Its rival was France, whose revolutionary government became the

Empire of Napoleon Bonaparte, the "little Corsican" who seemed ambition personified.

Even Indian tribes out West were pawns in the larger struggle. Several native clans elected to fight under the Union Jack, hoping to stem the rising westward flow of American whites. Yet in the larger sense England's wilderness allies were part of an attempt to undo Jefferson's Louisiana Purchase. The British, in enlisting native aid, were gambling that these immense territories might go to them as part of a peace settlement.

Likewise the war's spark, a few American sailors kidnapped and impressed into British service, had its beginnings in similar illegal activity among the French. Both John Bull and *Madame la Liberté* needed as many soldiers as they could get, in order to prove themselves the biggest bully on the block.

The issue had been repeatedly debated in the U.S. Congress. Thomas' longtime confederate William Crawford, a Georgia Senator these days, was one of the most vocal "War Hawks" in Washington. Indeed Crawford was enjoying a prominence rivaling that of his old mentor John Milledge.

Letter by letter the square-jawed Crawford kept his Augusta associate up to speed on developments in Washington. It seemed a good arrangement for both sides. Thomas saw to it that Senator Crawford was in touch with his support at home, and the Senator, in turn, touted Thomas Flournoy around the capital as a talent to watch. Soon Crawford and Governor Milledge had Thomas appointed a militia leader, since men in uniform were always quickest up the political ladder.

"A military man?" Sophia asked her husband, when the letter from Crawford came. "You know, Mr. Flournoy—" she tried to smile—"I never imagined you in braid and epaulets."

"Obligations," the attorney replied. "Crawford's a good man, Milledge is a good man. I have obligations to them both."

The task these two had in mind, however, seemed a bit much even for a dutiful friend. They expected Thomas Flournoy to conquer Florida. The long peninsula below Georgia was still in Spanish hands. Granted, the empire of the *conquistadors* was no longer what it once had been. Nonetheless a man couldn't simply round up a few Georgia farm boys and stroll down to St. Augustine. The militia had to be called up, to begin with. Rag-tag soldiers at best, they'd had nothing to do since the last spate of Cherokee raids. New recruits were needed as well, and everyone had to be fed and equipped and trained. And the Augusta lawyer couldn't even begin to imagine how he'd get them all down to Florida. Yet Crawford had written him that a Florida conquest would "reap a great harvest of laurels in the north."

"I'm not entirely sure," Sophia put in, "that my husband has a taste for laurels."

"Sophia." Thomas, at his desk, put the Senator's letter in his top drawer. "No one knows my heart better than you."

He stood and hooked one hefty arm around her shoulders. Fondly he cupped the other hand under the chin of the child in her arms.

"But you'll do," she surmised, "as your friends request."

"I'll do as duty requires," he said. "And not only because I'm a friend to Crawford and Milledge."

"Still the 'nationalist'?" she persisted. "Still a man who believes that whatever they might desire up in the District of Columbia is best for us all?"

Thomas eyed her more soberly, impressed again by her understanding. "Still," he said finally.

His wife frowned and smiled, softly jiggling the cooing infant in her embrace. Beside her, however, her husband grew still. He dropped his hand from the baby's chin. Over the next few moments Thomas became so motionless his wife recalled what she'd heard of his duel with poor young Walton—how he'd never moved a muscle, waiting for the countdown to end.

"My brother fought the British last time," Thomas said finally, quietly. "Now I must take my turn."

By early June of 1812, before his country had officially declared war, Militia Leader Flournoy had cobbled together a passable troop of about 1200. On June 18, Congress at last declared war, and Thomas Flournoy found himself one of a number of instant Brigadier Generals, wartime appointees of the President. Nonetheless, while all Augusta erupted in flag-waving, cannon-firing celebrations of the coming battlefield glory, the new Brigadier couldn't help but view the whole business with a skeptical eye. Just what did the seizure of a minor Spanish territory, with no small risk to American lives, have to do with a war against Great Britain? Just why were decent, full-grown men traipsing off into the woods, gun in hand, perhaps never to return?

Ｂut perhaps the young nation's leaders suffered some of the same doubts as the Augusta attorney. Congress, overriding Crawford and other Hawks, held off on final authorization for a Florida attack. Brigadier General Flournoy mustered his troops. Smartly they marched into southeast Georgia, hard by the border of the Spanish territory. And there the militia sat it out. No word came from Washington. The Georgians sat, the defenders in St. Augustine sat, more bothered by swamp rats and snakebite than by each other.

After some months the Brigadier's instructions to his officers began to express no little frustration. "The subject of your situation is such a delicate one," he wrote to one lieutenant colonel, "that I know not what to say to you with respect to it." Soon morale had hit rock bottom. Napoleon himself, Thomas reflected, couldn't win with troops so ill-equipped, ill-fed, and uncertain. All that General Flournoy could do was try to maintain a decent fighting edge. He encouraged his officers to a personal commitment. And the commander took his own advice. Many a morning Thomas rode past his company, noting with satisfaction how quickly and respectfully the files of troops snapped to. Six-foot-four and a solid thirty-seven the Brigadier cut an imposing figure, very straight in the saddle, practically motionless.

Ｌate in March of 1813, Congress and President Madison at last agreed not to mount an invasion into Florida. Recent naval skirmishes on the Great Lakes had produced a hero in Oliver Hazard Perry, and a memorable line in "We have met the enemy and they are ours." But when all was said and done, on that front too the fighting had gotten nowhere. Nowhere: just like Georgia's dispirited men.

Even William Crawford seemed to have abandoned the war effort. The very day that the President announced his decision against a Florida campaign, he also nominated the Georgia Senator as Secretary of War. Yet Thomas' friend didn't accept and chose instead the less volatile job of Minister to France, letting the War position go to yet another of the Virginia aristocracy, James Monroe.

Yes, the Senator's maneuver was typically sharp: a side-step that would hurt neither him nor his pet issues. Yet to Thomas Flournoy the move smacked too much of the callous ambition he'd come to hate. Crawford went to France with hardly a word about the campaign that had kept his friend so long on tenterhooks.

And yet, in the sort of bizarre stroke that Thomas was coming to see as the hallmark of this war, it was precisely then that his efforts seemed to be rewarded. When the Brigadier General and his troop marched back north to home, they found themselves celebrated as conquerors. The *Augusta Chronicle* noted "it must be highly flattering to the returning hero, to behold the tears of joy bedewing the cheeks of his fair countrywomen." Thomas, sharing the newspaper story with his wife, laughed with uncharacteristic abandon. Yet up in Washington, Thomas Flournoy was once more getting a boost from the men in power.

U.S. spies and scouts had ascertained that the British were preparing a major invasion into the American South. England too had been frustrated in this war. Americans could hardly claim that they were winning, but the British had no new territories or advantages to point to either. They needed a bold stroke. According to all reports, John Bull's most likely target was America's southernmost city—the former French port of New Orleans.

Congress and the President needed someone to drum up a decent defense for the region. Granted, there was already a commander in New Orleans, General James Wilkinson. But Wilkinson might well have been the most corrupt and destructive general in the entire mismanaged officer corps. He'd only recently, and by the skin of his teeth, survived a court-martial. He'd made a fool of himself at the treason trial of Aaron Burr. As reports of a British build-up mounted, Wilkinson was swiftly reassigned to the stagnant Canadian front. And just as swiftly, word came from the Secretary of War that the new Southern Commander would be Thomas Flournoy of Augusta.

"The Southern Commander!" Sophia exclaimed. "Why, it's as if, oh I don't know. It's as if Thomas Flournoy were King of New Orleans!"

Though headquartered in New Orleans, the Southern "district" comprised the states of Louisiana and Tennessee, plus the territories of Mississippi and Alabama.

Thomas sat, studying the unfolded notice in his hands. "A national command," he said after a while. "National, high-level. And me a man with such misgivings about a military career. Yet you know, Sophia, sometimes I believe those very misgivings make me a better soldier."

She narrowed her eyes, watching him.

"Better," Thomas repeated. "Better, because I care more. I care about matters like provisions and logistics, Sophia. Matters that wouldn't concern a commander interested solely in winning glory for himself."

"And this caring," his wife put in, "makes you the better officer in the long run."

"If troops are well-fed," Thomas said, "if they're rested and equipped and encouraged and well-fed, well then. They can defeat Napoleon himself."

Sophia smiled. "And if they know a command, once given, will be carried out."

Now Thomas' eyes narrowed, uncertain.

"Like the centurion in Scripture," she went on. "Doesn't my husband remember?"

"The centurion. . ." Thomas began.

"Our Savior rose to go to the Roman's house," Sophia said. "The man had a servant who was ill."

"But the centurion," Thomas went on, "told Jesus that wasn't necessary." Then together husband and wife recalled, out loud, the story from St. Matthew. The Roman commander explained that he needed only to know that Christ had given the order. With that, the centurion knew his servant would be cured. The Savior, astonished, declared that he'd never seen such faith, not in all of Israel.

"Do you think you have such faith, still?" Sophia asked Thomas, once they'd finished the Gospel story.

"Faith." Thomas pursed his lips. "My willow, James Madison is no Messiah."

"Certainly not," she agreed with a smile. "But do you have faith that orders given will be carried out? That now, for once, Madison and Crawford and the rest will stand behind their stated intentions?"

The husband and wife shared a long look. So many times the "national interest" had let them down. But slowly the set of Thomas' mouth grew firm, and he began to nod.

The New Orleans that Thomas Flournoy came to in May of 1813 was a rowdy and dangerous city, only a little more tamed than the wilderness beyond it. Eighteen thousand souls lived here at the mouth of the Mississippi: of all races, from several cultures, speaking a good half-dozen languages. A distinct French flavor.

But others called the place home as well: Spanish, Creole, assimilated Cherokee and Shawnee and Creek, Germans, Arcadian French out of Canada (called "Cajuns"), and free Negroes both from this country and from the Caribbean. Only recently had the more homogeneous brand of American, like the departing General Wilkinson, started to appear. And locals generally didn't take kindly to interference. Indeed, many saw no need to defend the city at all. They didn't much care which government claimed control. Several governments had come and gone already, while folks in New Orleans had kept their own unchanging set of rules.

Among those rules was a winking acceptance of piracy. Dealers in contraband held, if anything, a respected place among the city's businessmen. And these days sales were brisk. The British blockade just outside the harbor was as handy a market as a "privateer" could ask for. The war had so boosted the fortunes of illegal traders that the most famous men in the city may have been the pirate brothers Jean and Pierre Lafitte.

But District Commander Flournoy waded into this unruly maelstrom confidently. He saw three major concerns. First, there were the problems created by General Wilkinson, both in local politics and in troop morale. Second, there was the sudden increase in Indian raids to the east, in the loamy bottomlands of Mississippi and Alabama. And that increase was no doubt related to his third major problem, the looming British attack.

Any one of these three problems, left unsolved, could leave the city easy pickings for John Bull. To fix all three at once would require help from within the boisterous community itself. Thomas needed a man on the inside, someone to salve local hurt feelings while at the same time considering the U.S. defense. The one he had in mind was Louisiana's newly elected governor, a man of roughly his own age and background: William Charles Cole Claiborne.

As soon as he arrived at his New Orleans headquarters, Thomas met with Claiborne. He made certain it was a private get-together—one without former commander Wilkinson. The lax and greedy old general remained on the scene, in no great hurry to assume his new post. Thomas and

Governor Claiborne set up, therefore, an apparently informal meeting, a carriage tour of the downtown.

Though of medium build, plump and unexceptional-looking, for some time now William Claiborne had ridden the political fast track. During today's ride through New Orleans he and Thomas began by discussing the more outstanding developments of the Governor's career. While Claiborne was still young his father had taken the family west, like *Matthieu père*, and so his first successes had come in Tennessee. He'd become a state Supreme Court justice at twenty-one. A year later he'd been selected an interim Congressman; the man whose term he'd completed was none other than Andrew Jackson.

"Jackson?" Thomas interjected. "The firebrand lawyer? The man who killed Charles Dickinson in a duel?"

"One and the same," Claiborne declared. "Old Hickory."

The New Orleans statesman had an impressive circle of acquaintance. Even his brother, Ferdinand Leigh Claiborne, was an up-and-comer, currently serving as Governor of the neighboring Mississippi Territory. After serving out Jackson's term in Congress, the still-young William Claiborne had been appointed governor first of the Mississippi Territory, then of Louisiana Territory. When the latter territory became a state, Claiborne had swept into the top office easily. His worst setbacks had come recently, when he'd had to contend with General Wilkinson.

"The old man thinks of no one but himself," William Claiborne declared. "I tell you quite frankly, Thomas. If Wilkinson is an example of acting in the country's best interest, then God preserve us from such interest. The General has undermined my authority at almost every turn."

While the carriage pulled them slowly past reeking fishermen's docks, Claiborne explained. His foremost concern as governor had been to pull Louisiana's colliding cultures into a single unit. No one had so impeded this arduous task as Wilkinson. No civil ordinance was free from the General's consideration of its effect on his military stature. No local levy went into effect without his angling to take some share of the revenue.

The hard feelings between the civilian and military leadership, it soon became clear to Thomas, were more than could be soothed in a single carriage ride. At the end of the trip it seemed that what Claiborne wanted most from any District Commander was simply to be left alone. The very mention of training a city militia caused Claiborne's eyes to glaze over.

Going after the Lafitte brothers and their black-market colleagues appeared likewise more than the Governor could manage. In short, the meeting hadn't cemented Thomas and his carriage companion as unswerving allies. No; rather, it had established a truce, in which the military commander could try to get his own house back in order, while the civic leader attended to his.

W ithin the army Wilkinson's worst legacy was his unpredictable discipline. One day the general would be lax to the point of encouraging insubordination, the next harsh enough to recall some cruel lord of the Middle Ages. No sooner did Thomas Flournoy arrive in town than he signed a stay of execution for a private who, so far as he could see, was entirely innocent of any crime. The day after Wilkinson left for the Canadian border at the end of May, the new Commander began reviewing the most recent courts-martial.

The crimes ran the gamut: there was drunkenness, abusive language, officers assaulting enlisted men, guards sleeping while on watch. The lack of discipline appalled Thomas. But too often the crimes didn't match the punishment. Re-trying every case was impossible, but letting the old ones stand would further eat away at morale—not to mention at Thomas' conscience. Eventually the new commander drew up a compassionate general order:

> *The General feels no difficulty in stating that the persons convicted and sentenced to punishments aforesaid deserve to receive even a Greater Punishment than was awarded them. But at the same time he cannot consent to have a soldier in his command punished under proceedings so irregular and uncertain as they appear before him.*

As he finished composing the order, Thomas thought again of St. Matthew's faithful centurion. It was God who provided the "Greater Punishment," yes. But by the same token, God had given Thomas Flournoy his intelligence, his sense of justice. These gifts were like an order from Him, the Highest Centurion. And Thomas had to exercise those gifts now.

But this general pardon had repercussions far beyond the Commander's own developing sense of right and wrong. At a single stroke, the order both sent troop morale skyrocketing and showed the people of New Orleans something as well. The American military, the pardon demonstrated, now had a leader with humanity. Then within the same week Thomas handed down a very different order, a dishonorable discharge for a deserter who'd tried to cover his tracks by shouting a false alarm. This "shameful and cowardly conduct," Thomas wrote, "merits the punishment and disgrace awarded him." The soldier was drummed out of the ranks. This act, too, sent a clear message. The new commander knew kindness, yes—but he nonetheless expected discipline. Soon Thomas issued a third general order, spelling the point out unmistakably: "Soldiers must and shall be punished for every offense of which they are convicted."

"I'm impressed, don't you know," the ever-cordial Governor Claiborne declared, at their next get-together. "The way you can spare lives on one hand and enforce discipline on the other, well. I must say, I'm impressed."

Thomas nodded thanks, behind his wine glass. Relations with Claiborne had progressed to the point of the two men dining together, at the Governor's mansion. "Why," Claiborne went on, "it's starting to look as if New Orleans has a bona-fide army."

"Not a very large army," Thomas said. "Not nearly enough to defend the city if the British mount a full-scale assault. Your city needs a civilian militia."

Claiborne sighed heavily. He took a mouthful of wine.

"Your *country* needs that militia," Thomas said. "The national interests of the United States of America. Ordinary citizens must do their part."

Across the empty dishes, the empty glasses, Claiborne eyed his guest a while. Thomas couldn't be sure what he saw in those eyes, or what to make of it when at last the Governor worked up a new smile.

The biggest obstacle to getting the people of New Orleans on Thomas' side was the British money flowing through the city. Over the years, the crescent-shaped port had been a layover for many a ship that flew the

Union Jack, and commerce still went back and forth freely between dockside merchants and the nearby English blockade.

Thomas saw no point in simply declaring martial law. Wilkinson had already tried that, and the result had been increased sympathy for pirates like Jean Lafitte. Rather, the innovative Commander made contraband unprofitable. He placed guards along the shipping lanes, and ruled that no vessel could leave port without a complete manifest of its cargo and a written order from Flournoy himself.

There remained the smugglers' hideouts in the trackless byways of the Mississippi Delta. These misty and unmappable bayou swamps and canals had no easy shut-off valve, unlike the forts on the city harbor. And the unofficial overseers of those liquid back alleys were Pierre Lafitte and his younger brother Jean. Jean was the more famous, his cunning respected, his ferocity feared. Nonetheless many in the Crescent City considered the brothers heroes; they were seen as entrepreneurs who'd lived, in the best New Orleans tradition, by their wits. No one more openly flaunted the control of civilian and military government alike.

Governor Claiborne had once tried putting a price on the more notorious brother's head. He proclaimed a reward of $500 for the person apprehending Jean Lafitte. The young pirate, true to his swashbuckling style, countered with an offer of $5000 to "any person delivering Claiborne" to him. The outlaw posted his offer in handbills, just as the Governor had—though he had enough restraint to attach a memorandum at the bottom, stating that he "was only in jest, and desired that no violence should be done to His Excellency."

Beyond that, the Governor had accomplished nothing. No one dared go after Jean Lafitte for a paltry few hundred.

Thomas Flournoy, after he'd learned the lay of the land, came up with a very different suggestion. He laid out his plan in a letter: "Secret inquiry has been made and we have learned that Lafitte has a mistress in the city and that he plans to join her some evenings from now. I will order Capt. Blue with his company, at a late hour of the night to surround the house and make search for him."

This was the brainstorm of a lover, not a fighter, and it took his adversary by surprise. Blue and his men caught the young pirate with his guard down—his guard, among other things. But Jean Lafitte was nothing if not a bold improviser; he jumped from his mistress's window and ducked into a nearby well.

"I understand," Claiborne said at his next dinner with the Commander, "you heard from *Monsieur* Lafitte about that."

Thomas nodded, a hint of roguery in his eye. "A letter," he said. "Utterly brazen. The man had the nerve to say that he knew me very well." Shaking his head, the Commander couldn't suppress a bewildered chuckle. "He said he passed within a few feet of me very night. When I come to your home, for instance."

"When you come to *my* home?" the Governor said, in mock fright. "Good Lord. The Villain might be looking in the window this very minute!"

"He had the audacity to add that I had more to fear from him than he from me."

"You don't say."

"I do, William. And I must add, I think he's right."

B ut the Lafitte brothers were by and large a diversion from more important tasks. Earthworks and fortifications still needed improving, as did troop discipline. And there remained the unpromising business of organizing a citizen militia.

The most obvious invasion route was straight up the Mississippi. The city doesn't lie at the river's actual tip, on the Gulf of Mexico, but on a bay some 120 miles upstream. Thomas ensured, early on, that any attack could never come that entire way unopposed. He ordered the strengthening of Fort St. Philip, some ninety miles downriver from the city. If St. Philip and its two companion forts were properly braced and supplied, they could hold off even the British navy for weeks. At the same time the Commander took pains to keep the arsenal fully stocked. Artillery was paramount in any defense.

Late in 1813, after he'd won some civilian respect with his other measures, the Commander issued a proclamation which put everyone on notice that an attack was likely. The same document made it plain that if the war came to New Orleans everyone would need to work together. His statement read, in part, "hearty cooperation is expected from all who wish the prosperity and safety of the city." Yet when Thomas read his new confidant Claiborne this proclamation, the Governor rolled his eyes, openly doubtful.

"William!" Thomas exclaimed, drawing himself to full height. "Are you with me or against me?"

"I'm with *you*, my friend," Claiborne said. "And if the British come, I'll fight by your side."

"Well. . . ." Thomas frowned, mollified but confused.

"But is the British fleet coming?" Claiborne's look remained skeptical. "The reports *I* hear all seem to indicate that our enemy's not the British at all. The reports out of Washington seem to be directing us to fight someone else."

The heat rose in Thomas' face. "You mean the war on the Creeks," he said quietly.

"The war on the Creeks, indeed. The reports I see all seem to insist that our Seventh District soldiers should be fighting Indians, over in my brother Ferdinand's jurisdiction. Over in the Mississippi Territory."

Thomas met his friend's eyes again, aggravated at feeling so at a loss.

"Well, Thomas? Isn't that what Washington wants?"

He was right, this inscrutable Southerner. Earlier that year tribal war parties had gone into action again, in the undeveloped wilds to the east, as they did every year when the braves came out of their winter camps. By the late summer of 1813, however, the natives had drawn down on them the full firepower of western white America. And District Commander Flournoy, whether talking with the Governor or alone with his Bible, suffered wave upon wave of doubts about this bloody turn of events.

Not that the British had been entirely blameless. John Bull's encouragement was behind the Mississippi and Alabama raiding parties, no doubt, every time the tribes began burning down cabins and taking scalps. After all, war against the Creeks spread American defenses that much thinner. But the British command would never have been able to win Indian allegiance if it hadn't been for the oppressiveness and acquisitiveness of the westward-striving Americans. And this was especially true, Thomas realized, when the natives held something valuable: something, for instance, like rich, flat Delta soil perfect for plantation cotton.

At the beginning of the decade the great Shawnee Tecumseh (the name seemed to mean both Crouching Panther and Shooting Star) had

worked ada an alliance between the Creek tribe and his own. By the time
Commander Flournoy reached New Orleans, some 4000 Creeks in nearby
Mississippi and Alabama had pledged themselves to Tecumseh's cause.

Yet an up-to-date military man like Thomas realized that, in the
larger sense, even 4000 didn't present much of a threat. Only about one in
four of the Creek marauders carried firearms, typically out-of-date, and a
troop of braves rarely had enough powder or ammunition to fire off more
than a shot or two each. As redoubtable as the natives could be in hand-to-
hand combat, they were no match for a fully equipped army.

No, Thomas saw no need to waste much of his command in beating
through the woods after Tecumseh's latest converts. Instead he delegated
the Mississippi defense to the Mississippi militia, led by his friend's brother
Ferdinand. The militia was to protect local settlers, but not take any
offensive action.

Then in mid-summer 1813, the Creeks began to demand more of the
Commander's attention. A war party of 300 was reported massed in the
settlement of Pensacola.

"Pensacola!" a frustrated Thomas told William Claiborne. "Why,
that's in Spanish Florida." The two men were looking over a map in the
District headquarters. "Florida," he repeated. "You know I spent all last
winter camped outside Florida? Waiting to invade?"

"You don't say, Thomas." The Governor kept his eyes on the map.
"Why on earth would you do that?"

"Washington," Thomas said flatly. "Congress and the President kept
me dangling."

The last thing Thomas needed was to stretch his District's defenses
still thinner. He confined himself instead to what could be done by letter,
speedily posting warnings to both the Mississippi Claiborne and the Spanish governor. But the Creeks in Pensacola had already done serious damage
without so much as setting foot on American soil. They'd triggered a war
of nerves; they'd put fear in the hearts of local whites. Even as Thomas'
warnings went off to Florida and Mississippi, settlers around Fort Stoddard,
the closest settlement to Pensacola wrote pleadingly to New Orleans. "The
clouds thicken around us," their letter read. "Almost all the families within
fifteen miles of us have abandoned their homes." Another worried outcry
came from St. Stephens, some miles north: "Most of the citizens have gone

out under Colonel Caller and have taken with them all the arms which could be raised. We are nearly destitute, too, of ammunition."

Colonel Caller was a Mississippi militia officer. It was he who found the Creek war party out of Spanish Florida. Caller and 180 cavalry stumbled upon the natives east of St. Stephens, and in no time they drove off the unprepared braves. But the Colonel's undisciplined militiamen then fell greedily to dividing up the captured supplies. Soon they were the ones caught unprepared, as the clever Creeks came whooping back. The Indians had won the first battle of the Creek Indian War.

Nonetheless Commander Flournoy wasn't about to go off half-cocked. Tecumseh might have mythic status among his people, but his weaponry was as weak as any other native's. More than that, Tecumseh's well-known belief that every warrior under his command was a brother to him, unique and precious, prevented him from massing his forces in the way a white commander might. They were *brothers*, not *troops*. Likewise Tecumseh's allies might set fire to a settler's cabin, or a field of corn, but they'd never practice a true scorched-earth policy, as the Russians had against Napoleon. They'd never indiscriminately burn down sacred Mother Wilderness.

In other words, followers of the Shooting Star and Crouching Panther found the white way of war as distasteful as Thomas himself found the Southern system of duels. This the Commander knew already, or learned in conference with his scouts. He resisted mounting an attack into the Indian country east of New Orleans. "You must act on the defensive," he wrote to Ferdinand Claiborne, urging him instead to forge stronger alliances with the Choctaws, Mississippi Indians friendly to the United States. Yet it was this same Territorial Governor who, later that summer, sent a disastrously inept militia officer to a small eastern outpost called Fort Mimms.

Mimms wasn't much of a fort. A low stockade built around a single settler's home, the hamlet's population nearly doubled with the addition of these 120 militiamen. Like so many citizen soldiers, the men at Mimms had little idea of what the job required. Ferdinand Claiborne had ordered them to do a number of essential repairs, in particular to fix the stockade gate. But the men instead spent the hot August days playing cards and bagging the local rabbit and quail. They sent out no scouts, and when two Negro slaves reported sighting Indians in full war paint nearby, the militiamen refused to believe it.

The next morning a thousand Creeks, led by the mixed-blood William Weatherford, poured through the unrepaired stockade entrance. They slaughtered virtually everyone in Fort Mimms: soldiers and settlers, women and children.

The Mimms massacre got the white man's attention, galvanizing a full-scale federal response. The commander of the military district bordering Commander Flournoy's, Thomas Pinckney, called out the Georgia militia, plus more troops from the Carolinas. Some of Thomas' skimpy Louisiana force, over his heated protests, was ordered into the fight as well. And from up north came the Tennessee militia, led by the rough and ready Andrew Jackson.

Thomas tried to stick with what a dozen previous disappointments had taught him. A better soldier precisely because he didn't want to be a soldier, he concentrated on the basics of equipment and preparation. No one under Commander Flournoy would go hungry at winter camp in wilderness territory.

Yet his heart remained uncommitted. It wasn't just the way Washington's latest orders left New Orleans nearly defenseless. It wasn't just his distaste for mounting such a monumental assault on these natives. Yes, the massacre had been deplorable. But if the militiamen on the scene had shown the wit Heaven gave a flea, it never would have happened. But Thomas' misgivings went deeper.

"Like apes," he told his Governor friend over dinner. "The campaign has three Commanders, and already they're shoving and bellowing like apes. Fighting for head of the herd."

"Well, surely Washington knows what it's doing," Claiborne replied with another enigmatic smile.

Thomas shook his big head. "Washington doesn't seem to realize what we have to contend with, here in the South. Doesn't seem to care."

Claiborne allowed a long moment of silence, while the candles burnt lower between them. When he spoke, it was with that intimate, brimming quiet all his own.

"President Madison can read a map, don't you know," he reminded Thomas. "And he realizes, too, that defeating these half-naked savages is a simple business."

"I know," Thomas groaned. "William, I know. Then why does he allow this rampant waste to go on? Why, when we're in the middle of another war already?"

"He can read a map," the Governor repeated. "And he can see what doing favors for a man like Andrew Jackson might mean for him later."

"Politics," Thomas said glumly. "In the government they play the politics of the apes, all bellowing for leadership of the pack."

"Indeed they do, Thomas. The President doesn't want Jackson too powerful either, don't you know. He's taking care, you may be sure, to extend a hand to Thomas Pinckney as well." Claiborne took a swallow of brandy, then swirled the snifter a moment, studying the ripples of the brown liquor. "I understand," he said finally, "that now Madison's authorized Pinckney to take yet another of our New Orleans regiments."

Indeed he had. Never mind that Pinckney's headquarters was hundreds of miles to the east. The animal at the head of the pack wanted them, and the animal at the head would have them.

Then came the letter from Andrew Jackson.

As Tennessee militia leader, Jackson headed an army of some 5000— far more than the Southern District had ever seen. By the time Jackson's militia entered northern Mississippi, the Tennessee force was forced to forage for its supper. Jackson wrote that he faced "an enemy whom I dread much more than I do the hostile Creeks. You know I mean that meager-monster 'Famine.' Willingly would I endure the worst of all Earthly evils, rather than see my army starving in the enemy's country."

But Jackson concluded by asking his southern colleague for more than food. The man also wanted troops. For all its wit, his letter was another gorilla-like demand: *Me! Me! Me!*

Thomas took to his Bible again that night, though he'd pretty nearly committed the story of the dutiful centurion to memory. The next day, summoning up the last tatters of his commitment to "national interest," he arranged what he could for his fellow general. At the same time, he ordered Ferdinand Claiborne's Mississippi militia northward toward a hill village on the Alabama River, a Creek sacred place. Americans called the village "Holy Ground"; it was the home of the renegade William Weatherford.

"This is the highest place," Thomas wrote Jackson, "I think Ferdinand Claiborne dare penetrate to, with safety. This force will enable you to put an end to the Creek War in a short time." And then, sick of this chimerical war and the greedy men who strove to take advantage of it, Thomas found himself suddenly wishing Jackson the "fame, and reputation, which your conquest is calculated to inspire."

I n his orders to Ferdinand Claiborne, Thomas instructed his militia leader how to force the Creeks out of the Mississippi Territory. "Destroy all their property that can not be conveniently brought to the depots," the Commander stipulated. Not many braves were so bloodthirsty as to carry on a fight if their families had to go elsewhere for food. Andrew Jackson, however, hadn't brought 5000 Tennesseans south simply to shoo the Indians aside.

Even before Thomas dispatched Ferdinand Claiborne's militia to Holy Ground, the Tennessee commander had begun making his bloody purpose clear. In Tallusahatchee, he oversaw the slaughter of some 200 Creeks, virtually the entire village. Non-combatants weren't spared the frontiersman's rampage; the aged and the tiny died alongside the few battle-worthy braves. Five days later, at Talledega, Jackson's troop saw fit to kill more than 500. In the two encounters combined, the Tennesseans lost no more than a handful of their own. The natives' ancient muskets, bows and arrows, and tomahawks couldn't stand up to the white man's rifles.

Even Jackson's men recognized, afterwards, that their campaign was in fact nothing more than a series of massacres. By the time Claiborne reached them, the Tennesseans were calling the two battles "Big Bloody."

At least the dispatches from Holy Ground made it clear that the Mississippi militia, in contrast to Jackson's troops, had pulled off a largely bloodless action. Since the hilltop village was sacred to Creeks, most of its inhabitants believed the Great Spirit protected the place. Only the mixed-blood William Weatherford, raised in white society like Tecumseh, harbored no such notions. He and his band of warriors had been armed and ready when, two days before Christmas, the white men hiked up into the village.

The odds remained overwhelming, however, and swiftly thirty-three of Weatherford's braves lay dead. If a divine hand ever revealed itself during the battle, it did so via the miracle of Weatherford's escape. The *mestizo* chieftain rode at full gallop off one of the Holy Ground cliffs, fell headlong into the Alabama River below, and survived to rejoin his tribesmen later.

As for Claiborne's troop, it suffered precisely one casualty. More significantly, the battle had spared all the village's women and children and yet at the same time had made it plain that no Creek spirit, no consecrated plot of land, would keep The People safe.

To the natives the loss was demoralizing. To Thomas Flournoy, it was another proof that the entire "Indian War" was nothing more than a lot of career-minded strutting around. The fighting in Mississippi was plainly irrelevant, in the larger scheme of things. It would be laughable if it hadn't cost so many innocent lives and undercut, so badly, the defense of his country's most important southern port.

Then in March of 1814, Andrew Jackson concluded his sweep through northern Mississippi, with a slaughter rarely matched even in the dark annals of the Indian wars. On a stretch of the Tallapoosa River known as Horseshoe Bend, where the Creeks were outnumbered three to one, Jackson's militia roared in and killed virtually everyone. The final death count ran to more than 800: men, women, and children.

It was the final battle, if such ape-like smashing could be called a battle, of the Creek War—if such out-and-out genocide could be called a war. When news of what had happened reached Thomas Flournoy, he resigned.

I t was only after the Augusta attorney returned to Sophia and the children, weary but glad to be done with the insanity of this "second Revolution," that the struggle's last tragic irony worked itself out. If the War of 1812 saw one decisive victory, it was Andrew Jackson's Battle of New Orleans, early in 1815. The former frontier lawman—aided to no small extent by Thomas Flournoy's long-ignored planning and hard work—showed as little mercy for a British invasion force as he had for the natives in Mississippi. He got Jean Lafitte to help him as well, by the characteristically brutal tactic of holding his older brother hostage. The Louisiana battle ended the muddled conflict on a note of triumph for America. It more than made up for the British burning of Washington the year before.

Yet the fight outside New Orleans was unnecessary, the lost lives wasted. Great Britain and the United States had signed a truce on Christmas Eve, 1814. Only the slowness of communications provided Andrew Jackson the opportunity for the victory that made him a national hero.

Yet Thomas Flournoy found himself largely unbothered by this turn of events. Yes, he thought, let the violent Jackson go strutting and preening around the nation. Let him bash his way to the head of the herd, to the White House itself, for all Thomas cared. The Augusta attorney knew a deeper happiness, and a deeper certainty, freed from the clawings of ambition. He knew where his best self was, and to get at that best self, he didn't have to go charging off into the wilderness. He knew he was a Southerner, a Southerner first. Happily he'd committed to the nature and history of this particular place. Never again would he try to manipulate that place for some dubious larger national purpose.

Some years later Thomas stopped his carriage to let a group of Creek refugees stagger past on their way west. They were on a flat Georgia road bordered by vast plantation fields. Around the few dusky natives slogging down the road, there rose the plaintive rhythmic cries of the darker men and women working the cotton rows to either side. The song cut as deeply into Thomas as any music he'd ever heard, a night-colored melody as simple as weeping. What would become of a land, the song seemed to ask, which had done so much damage in the name of profit and expansion?

By then Thomas had begun to lose the companions that had so helped in his shaping. His older brother Robert died toward the beginning of the 1820s, his darling Sophie at the end of that decade. His old friend Crawford's presidential campaign, in 1824, got Thomas out on the hustings a bit, but the Augusta lawyer repeatedly made clear he had no designs on public office himself. And then the loyal Crawford too fell into ill health—his absence from the fray helped give the election, eventually, to John Quincy Adams. When the fiery Andrew Jackson at last was elected to the White House, in 1828, the news drew little more than a shrug from his Georgia contemporary.

Thomas kept to his Augusta homestead, enjoying an active social life and increasing involvement in the state's higher education. His long-ago trusteeship at Richmond Academy was followed now with other such posts. He kept up his letter-writing too, of course. Bent over in his leather and mahogany arm chair, before his mahogany rolltop desk, he kept probing and framing his beliefs for posterity. Religion, in particular, was much on his mind. In correspondence to a minister friend, he tried to bring together his own commitment to doing what was right with the unknowable purposes of the Divine Mind. One sentence seemed to recall the centurion of St. Matthew, the good soldier who needed only to know that the order had been given: "It is enough for us to know (according to my weak and humble faith) that Jesus Christ was the great Prophet and *sent* of God to bring light and wisdom to a benighted world, that he faithfully performed the duty required of *his God* and *our God.*"

All in all the aging Thomas retained, unalloyed, the sturdy self-awareness and intimately Southern frame of mind that he'd achieved during the private purgatory of the War. In the mid-1830s the still-handsome man was married again, to a Philadelphia woman some twenty years his junior.

Even after so much time out of the public limelight, his wedding was still news. One Philadelphia newspaper gushed the "petite Catherine Howell met the dashing General Flournoy and subdued that warrior with a glance of her eye." The ceremony, like the young Thomas' happy grafting to his Sophia-willow many years before, was attended by more than a few political and military celebrities. Once again the big man was the center of a grand public occasion, in a home among the finest in town. And as at most such galas since the last War, the band struck up a popular patriotic number written during the British raid on Baltimore and Washington. An adaptation of an old drinking song, martial and rousing, the tune was called "The Star-Spangled Banner." As the song was sung, the old groom stood with the rest, attentively honoring his country. But across his broad face there played an enigmatic smile.

CHAPTER 8

Athaliah and Ella Boisseau
and the War Between the States

T homas Flournoy, as explained at the beginning of the last chapter, was not a direct Pamplin forebear. Rather, this philosophic lawyer and soldier was an ancestor of Katherine Reese—the wife of the present Robert Pamplin Senior (born in 1911).

Our next episode considers yet another war, the American Civil War, and yet another thread in the Pamplin fabric, namely, the Boisseaus.

Ella Boisseau appears as a teenager in this chapter, but after the War she married into the Bevilles—the primary Pamplin forebears. Indeed, in the mid-nineteenth century the two families shared a number of similarities. Both ran successful Virginia plantations near the Appomattox River.

In the chapter before last, Amy Butler Beville courageously defended her property during the colonial era. Now, two centuries later, Ella Boisseau and her grandmother Athaliah poignantly must come to terms with losing their land—and their way of life.

A final note: this chapter is the last in Part I, which has dramatized the family history. The succeeding sections concern the contemporary Pamplins, Robert Senior and Junior.

A thaliah put down her sewing and, with a sigh, leaned back in her well-worn arm chair. Her long-time Mammy and maid, Emily, had just brought her some hearty, redolent tea, and before Athaliah tasted the stuff, she let the fragrance carry her back. Back, the soaking, steaming herbs took her: back to when sewing was a social affair and not a financial necessity, to when needles were made of metal and not hawthorn bush barbs. During that long fragrant moment she drifted all the way to the porch of Tudor Hall, her family home in Dinwiddie County. She sat out front of the heavy-linteled doorways of Tudor Hall, at the head of the steep porch steps, sipping afternoon tea. She smiled over far-rippling fields of Virginia cotton and tobacco.

But then Athaliah took her first taste of today's tea.

"Amazing grace!" she exclaimed. "This tastes just awful. Emily, come back here. Come back on *in* here."

Athaliah's kitchen-slave returned to the sewing room. A square-built daughter of Alabama Negroes, Emily had grown more gray than brown.

"Yes'm?" she asked.

"Emily, tell me. Just what have you put in this miserable excuse for tea?"

"Sorry ma'am," Emily said. "We all outa sugar. All's left for tea is raspberry leaves."

Emily's honesty was, to be sure, one of the things that had always endeared her to Athaliah. The grandmother and the slave shared a commiserating look—a moment's grim mutual recognition of the times they were in.

"All right Emily," Athaliah sighed, "all right now. Sorry for scolding you, dear. I suppose I just forgot where I was for a moment."

"Yes'm," Emily said. "Hard times, these days."

"Hard, indeed." Athaliah forced down another swallow, then forced up a smile. "Tell me, Emily. Has Lewis come back yet?"

"No ma'am."

"Well, do let me know when he does. We'll need the new provisions for supper tonight."

"Yes ma'am."

Emily turned her back before leaving the sewing parlor, something only the best-loved retainers could do. But Athaliah Goodwyn Boisseau never had been much for master-slave protocol anyway. And now she was old besides, seventy-one, and what had previously been an attractive leanness had turned to miserly skin and bone. Even simple work like sewing took up all the energy she had. Nonetheless, she wanted to sew; she wanted to help out somehow. Sewing brought in cash and barter, essentials in dealing with the terrible hardships brought on by the War Between the States.

Athaliah knew there were still a few pampered aristocrats up in Richmond, a little more than twenty miles north of here. And the wives of those aristocrats would pay dearly for Athaliah's hand-sewn "vanities." Just the year before, hundreds of well-to-do Richmond women, infuriated by rising prices and the scarcity of goods, had gone on a rampage. They'd smashed store windows and looted food and clothing. President Jefferson Davis had needed to call in Confederate troops to quell the near riot.

"Think of it!" Athaliah had declared at the time. "He has to call in troops, and all those thousands of poor Southern boys just cut down at Gettysburg!"

"Mama," her son Albert had replied, "times are hard in the cities of our South. I read in the paper—you remember when Vicksburg fell? Vicksburg, in Mississippi? It fell to siege, same time as the Gettysburg battle."

"I remember," Athaliah had snapped. "I read the same reports you did, *Doctor* Boisseau."

Yes, her Albert had been a godsend; yes, he and her other son Andrew had been very generous, putting her up here in this sparsely settled part of Petersburg on Adams Street since she'd moved out of Tudor Hall. And yes, Albert was a learned man, the town surgeon. But she did get tired of him—and Andrew too!—treating her with *quite* so much fawning restraint.

"All right, Mama, all right. But before Vicksburg fell? The people there were eating rats."

Athaliah had kept her narrow face set, refusing to squirm. "Eating rats out of hunger is one thing. But stealing a dress just because you're tired of your old one, that's entirely another."

"It's a scene we'll probably see in more cities," Albert had gone on. "Before this monstrousness ends, we'll see worse than a few windows smashed."

He'd been right, her Dr. Boisseau. In the nine months or so since then more towns had fallen, and now even lovely Atlanta was threatened. Every conquered city seemed to have tales more horrifying than the last. At least the twin railheads of Richmond and Petersburg had been spared till now. And there remained, between the two Piedmont cities, some opportunity for an old woman to help her ever-more-underfed family.

Clever Athaliah had plenty of raw material. She used her own old formal wear: the elegant gowns she'd worn only once to the many balls and social affairs that used to fill up her seasons in and around Petersburg. Silk, velvet, Belgian lace, these and other pretty, frivolous materials—these had been the embroidery of Athaliah's youth. Now she cut them up smaller and smaller, reworking them into fashionable bonnets, scarves, collars, or sleeves. By the spring of 1864, her items were in such demand that all she had to do was send a familiar slave, Lewis, to a few mansions in Richmond. The ladies there knew him, and always had cash and barter on hand.

The barter included such staples as corn and flour, ham and sugar, more valuable than the brown Confederate currency. The price of everything had skyrocketed. Inflation was running at ten percent a month. Flour cost $400 a barrel. So Athaliah persevered with her sewing, even as her own cheeks sank and her own stomach growled. When her old iron and whalebone needles broke from overuse, she made do with the barbs stripped from wild hawthorn. More than once the work drew blood from her dry and bony fingers.

Athaliah would have preferred teaching one of the slaves to do this. But what few slaves the Boisseaus had were either needed back on her Tudor Hall plantation, or had to go foraging around these nearby Petersburg homes of Andrew and Albert. Besides, between the two locations, the family had only nineteen slaves left altogether. Nineteen, out of the hundreds Athaliah had known in her time! Just three days ago, two more had run off.

Athaliah didn't honestly know how she felt about it. The war had forced many a Southern belle to search her soul, regarding how she'd treated the darker peoples of the earth. And Athaliah knew herself well, by this time. She knew that her soul wasn't yet at peace on the subject; she knew she was still searching.

The plantation she'd been born on, the gracious Tudor Hall she'd helped design, even these rooms of Andrew's in Petersburg—all of it, every corner of her life, had been attended by slaves. And like most women of her time and upbringing, Athaliah hadn't herself seen the worst of her serving-people's lives. Oh, she'd read her Exodus and her history books; she knew what slaves had suffered in the past. Part of the tragedy of her beloved South, indeed, was that the cotton- and tobacco-farmers in these states hadn't *invented* slavery, God knows.

The very natives who'd first peopled this land, the Appamatucks and other members of the Powhatan Confederacy, had made slaves of other tribesmen. Likewise, Athaliah's long-ago forebears had owned what were then called "vassals," back in England. Many an old Virginia family had done the same. For instance there were the Bevilles—why, the Bevilles went back to William the Conqueror. William the Conqueror! He'd made slaves of half of England! No question about it, American Southerners hadn't invented the problem. But once slavery had settled into place, there'd been no easy way to get rid of it.

No, Athaliah was no innocent belle. She'd heard of terrible things done in the name of "ownership." She heard of whippings, of parents separated from their children, of feet lopped off to prevent a persistent runaway from trying again. Nonetheless, in all her seventy-one years Athaliah had never been brought face to face with the harsher extremes of what slavery had meant. A plantation mistress didn't go after runaways or attend to their punishment. All Athaliah could say for certain, whenever she found herself agonizing again over this central issue of the war, was that the hardworking men and women who served her were wholly human spirits like herself. Her Emily had a soul, a mind, a place of dreams and frights, just as Athaliah did. When she and Emily shared a look, as they had a minute ago, they shared a common being. And Athaliah's Lewis, too, was made every bit as much in the image of God as herself.

Athaliah knew that much, positively. Her slaves' humanity lay stone-solid at the bottom of her agonizing. And by the same token, she didn't blame them for running off either, in this hard late spring of 1864.

With food in short supply, the slaves got still less than usual. With medicine needed at the front, the slaves received none at all. The Union army was nearby, and now the Bluejackets had started building Negro regiments, training slaves to be soldiers, giving them guns, uniforms, regular meals and ten dollars a month. That was more than enough to lure dozens more slaves off their plantations with every passing week—never mind that capture by the Confederates met certain death.

"Why, there are days," Athaliah murmured over her sewing, "when I'd leave home *myself* for regular meals and ten dollars a month."

She chuckled, but then grew sober enough to lower her latest piece to her lap. The very thought, she realized, had just brought home to her again the Negroes' humanity. She'd spoken the idea aloud: she'd do what they do.

"Amazing grace," the old woman murmured, even more softly. These were words from a favorite hymn, a song she'd heard once from a West Indian visitor to Tudor Hall.

Amazing Grace: the title rang, the melody sailed, and the lyrics went right to the heart. *How sweet the sound*, the words went, *that saved a wretch like me!* A wretch, yes—that's what the writer declared he'd been, openly and for all to hear. Apparently he'd worked as a ship's captain, this song-writer. Most often he'd been hired for the so-called "Middle Passage," the South Atlantic route that carried the slave ships to and from Africa. He'd run a slave ship, before he'd come to grace.

Athaliah's home plantation was itself something of a wretch, these days. With so few slaves left to work it, Tudor Hall was but a skeleton of its former glory. She and her husband, William Boisseau, had begun building "the Hall" way back in 1812—during an earlier, simpler war. William, a well-regarded Virginia tobacco inspector, combined land he'd purchased with property Athaliah inherited. The Goodwyns, her parents, had made sure to leave a fair settlement for their girl children as well as the boys; this wasn't feudal England, after all. Thus was created an estate of 1800 acres, five miles west of Petersburg. The centerpiece was a stunning mansion.

Two and a half stories tall, Tudor Hall had the peaked roofs and heavy-browed gables its name implied. Inside, the main features were the two immense fireplaces, one at each end. The stairways went up steep but wide, with swooping mahogany banisters. Around the place Athaliah and William had planted shade trees: cedar, maple, poplar, magnolia, and dogwood. Also Athaliah's favorite flowers had been put in: azalea, forsythia, and fragrant lilac.

She and her attentive husband had raised seven children in Tudor Hall, five boys and two girls. They'd had a life of enchantment, it seemed to Athaliah now, a life in the sort of Southern high style which was already being called *antebellum*. As a wealthy plantation mother of seven, her weeks had been filled to the bursting with parties, social visits, and sporting events. If she or her William hadn't scheduled some engagement, then young Andrew or Albert or Joseph or William Junior or. . . . Lord, just listing them exhausted her! In any case, someone always seemed to have arranged some to-do or other.

Of course, much of that came to an end log before the war. The social whirl Athaliah Boisseau had grown up with was gone forever after 1838— the year her good husband had died. William's death had meant, too, that more of the operation of Tudor Hall fell on the shoulders of Athaliah's sons. They too had needed to quit the Dixie roundelay.

Thus the 1840s had passed without Tudor Hall seeming like too much of a load for Athaliah to bear. Rather it was the next decade, which saw the deaths of two of her sons, that sapped the woman's vitality. In her sixties, she'd sat deathbed vigil for those boys, and arranged every detail of their funerals, too. And there'd been tears, oh Lord yes. Athaliah's tears had seemed dredged up from the bottom of her lungs, after her poor dear boys had passed on.

After that, the woman hadn't the strength for a plantation's demands. She'd moved into Petersburg, into the house of her youngest son, Andrew, anticipating a gentle easing into her own end. Even Andrew's wife Susan was family, after all; in the kind of liaison that was common among the constantly socializing Virginian clans, Andrew had married a cousin, one of Athaliah's nieces.

Another son, Joseph, had stayed on at Tudor Hall to run the plantation. Joseph was married, but he had no children and received some help from another Petersburg brother, Albert. But Albert was the family's most prominent member, and had little time for farming. Not only did he have a thriving medical practice, but also he'd served in the state legislature—until the war.

Now, even in this gloomy spring of 1864, Joseph strove to put down seeds around Tudor Hall as always. But with so few slaves, he could hardly cultivate the entire sprawling three square miles of cropland. In the past, cotton and tobacco had been just about all the Boisseaus had needed to turn a profit, but now running these raw materials out to foreign markets like England or France was next to impossible. The Union blockade deadened even grand old trade centers like Williamsburg—the former "Middle Plantation," for 200 years the center of Virginia's agricultural wealth. And finally, the Confederacy had ordered farmers to plant more food crops. "King Cotton" had been replaced by "King Corn." Or rather, King Cotton was being replaced, slowly, slowly. Too many plantation owners were reluctant to change, even to feed the starving boys in gray.

A ll in all, Lewis' return today was a terrific relief. First, it did Athaliah good just to see her man make it back safe and sound, stout and smiling, in his hand-sewn, homespun vest jacket. Better still, Lewis told the old woman that her sewing had assured them all of better eating.

"Ma'am, they sho'ly likes your handiwork up there in Richmond," he reported. "I gots even more than 'spected for some of them hats. Coupla sisters kept on raisin' the price, raisin' the price. Thought I was at an auction."

"Amazing grace," Athaliah said. "Lewis, that's just wonderful. Now what were you able to buy?"

"Well, we did all right, did all right. . . . 'Fraid the price for some things done gone up again."

"Oh Lord. Naturally."

"Nacherly, yes'm. Nacherly. Yeah but uh, we got us *some*, though. Got us ham peas, some sorghum molasses."

"Sorghum molasses! Oh Lewis, really?"

"Really, ma'am." She and her man shared a smile for a moment, just as earlier she and Emily had shared their sorrow. "I wouldn't mislead ya, ma'am. And we got us a barrel of flour—" the smile grew broader—"a whole *barrel*, too!"

"Amazing grace," Athaliah said. "Molasses and flour. Lewis, I think this calls for Christmas in June. You tell Emily to whip up one of her pecan pies."

"Oh, yes ma'am!" The man grinned still more and gave a body-length nod, practically bowing. But he didn't leave. "Uh ma'am, uh." Lewis' battered fingers played at the lining of his denim vest-jacket. "Uh ma'am, there's one more thing. Yes'm there is." One thick brown hand went under the denim. "Mrs. Armistead, she asked me to give you this."

From under his armpit Lewis fished out a square of paper. This he handed diffidently to squinting Athaliah.

"Lewis, honestly." She kept her look narrow. "Lewis, something like this—why, you took an *awful* risk, bringing me something like this. Some overeager sheriff could've had you arrested for carrying this around."

But Athaliah's gaze softened as she began skimming the news headlines. She realized the twisted irony that made it so dangerous for Lewis to bring her this day-old story. There were laws forbidding slaves to carry paper, even simple blank sheets. The logic behind the law was, slaves might use paper to help them learn to read and write.

After Lewis left, Athaliah read avidly. It was the latest Richmond newspaper. It was two days old: June 6, 1864. The headline shouted *Grant is a Butcher*; the lead story concerned a Union attack on Cold Harbor. Cold Harbor was actually an inland crossroads, not even near a major river, some miles northeast of Richmond. The place was flat, sandy farmland not far from the swampy Chickahominy River. Here the harassed Confederates had dug in, outnumbered three or four to one by the Army of the Potomac. For a month now Johnny Reb had undergone a painful, stubborn retreat towards the capital, despite having inflicted terrible casualties. Up in Spotsylvania Court House, and on a battleground called simply The Wilderness, the game troops under Marse Robert had mown down thousands of the Bluecoats, thousands. Still the dogged Ulysses S. Grant, plainly a tougher breed than earlier Federal commanders like McClellan, had kept slogging south. Just a few days ago, according to Athaliah's newspaper, the Yankee general had lost still thousands more of his boys in one fruitless charge after another at Cold Harbor.

With that, Athaliah read, at last the Northern advance seemed to be stopped. In just one month, Robert E. Lee's brave Army of Northern Virginia had cut down close to 50,000 Union troops—more than "the butcher" Grant had lost over the previous three years.

The paper, of course, played up Grant's bloodthirsty desperation, and the courage of the Confederate boys defending their capital. It even claimed that many young Yankees, their enlistment up, actually crawled off the battlefield in the middle of the fight. Yet Athaliah took such reports with a grain of salt by now. No innocent, she recognized the whiff of wartime propaganda. But she could see that both sides were plainly spent, after so much breakneck marching and hell-sent bloodletting. The armies were settling in for what looked like a long-term siege of Richmond. The war wasn't coming any farther south—any closer to home—this year.

A thaliah's reading was interrupted by one of her favorite sounds, namely, the cheery young voice of her granddaughter, Ella. Ella had been born a long way from the Boisseau estates, off in Alabama, where Athaliah's son William had set up a medical practice of his own. William hadn't wanted to compete with his brother Albert, which seemed a sensible decision at the time, and so his six children, including Ella, had started their lives in another part of the South.

But then ten years ago (when this vivacious Ella had been only six) William's wife had taken ill and swiftly died. Another man might have weathered the tragedy, but not William. The doctor couldn't heal his own beset beloved—nor could he save himself, it turned out. Within months the heartbroken William had also died. His children had come to live with Athaliah and the other family in and around Petersburg. Athaliah's deepest joy, in all the hard decade since, had been that Ella had chosen to live with her. Now the easy-bodied teenager burst into the sewing parlor, clutching a large bundle of tatterdemalion plants.

"Grandma, Grandma, look!" Ella exclaimed. "Aren't they just *wild* and delightful?"

"Amazing grace." Athaliah set down her paper, furrowed her brow. "If that isn't the strangest collection of weeds I've ever laid eyes on."

"Oh, Grandma." Ella drooped as she sighed: easy-bodied indeed. "They're not weeds. Honestly! They're medicine."

Behind the girl then came the husky Albert, deliberate and slow as usual. Naturally enough, it was Athaliah's living doctor son who most often took time with her lost doctor's daughter.

"I'm going to help Uncle Albert," Ella went on brightly. "We're going to make medicine and save lives."

"Is that so?" Athaliah looked up skeptically at her sober-sided Albert.

"It's so, Mother," Albert said. "Ella, tell Grandma what we found."

"Oh, yes!" the girl said. Eagerly she sifted through her treasure. "See, these are dandelions, Grandma, you probably already knew that. . ."

"*Probably?*" Athaliah snapped.

"Oh, yes Grandma, of course you knew." Ella did another endearing body-long droop. "But they're all just so wild and delightful, I quite forget myself! See, this one is pokeweed, this one is, ah, snakeroot. And this. . ."

The girl paused, studying her latest plant. Then she caught a whiff; she curled up her nose. "*This* is skunk cabbage. It does smell revolting, certainly. But Uncle Albert says it can make medicine, like all the others."

"Lord, Lord," Athaliah said. Her old eyes were fixed again on Albert, skeptically as before.

"Now Mother," he said. He'd had no trouble divining what was in her mind. "These plants can be helpful. You know medicine is in short supply. You know many more of our soldiers die in the hospital than go down on the battlefield. We need to use what we can, Mother. Why, our field hands have been saving each other's lives with this kind of woods medicine for generations now."

"Our field hands?" Athaliah asked.

"Yes. Hands like Lewis and Emily. You know."

The grandmother dropped her head, returning to her long thoughts on slavery.

"The field hands learned it from Indians," Albert went on, more uncertainly. When the old woman didn't respond, he asked: "Mother? Is something wrong?"

"Oh Lord." Bravely she smiled back up at them both. "Is there anything that *isn't* wrong, Albert? That's the question. Take a look at what

Lewis brought me," she said, lifting the newspaper from her lap. "Seems General Ulysses S. Grant simply doesn't know when to give up."

Albert read the thing standing up, or tried to. Beside him Ella freed a hand from her flowers and began pulling the paper down from before his face. "Let me see," she said. "Let me see."

Albert struggled to hold the thing close. He was past fifty now, his eyes weak, his hair pepper-and-salt.

"Easy there, young lady," Athaliah put in. "Easy there. It's about time you looked to your studies, I'd say. You pack up this 'medicine' of yours now and go sit down to your own reading."

"Oh Grandma."

"In your room, if you please, young lady."

"But I've already done my reading for this week," Ella protested. "Besides, Mr. Davis says I'm one of his best students."

For all her bobbing and swaying and trying so hard, the youngster wasn't exaggerating. She attended Southern Female College, an élite girls' finishing school, where compliments weren't handed out simply for looking pretty.

The College had been founded on the highest principles in the grim year of 1863. By the beginning of school that September Vicksburg had fallen and Pickett's Charge at Gettysburg had staked its place in the annals of military disaster.

Yet in a year when these horrors and more were erupting, a man named William Davis had decided to start a school for young women. The man declared his venture a "defiant assertion of civilization in the midst of barbaric carnage." Now Athaliah, mastering her joy at the teenager bouncing before her, tried to follow Davis' gentle example. No reason for Ella to hear today's hard news.

"Young lady," the grandmother said sternly, "this war will end someday. Things *will* return to normal, someday. And when that happens, your education will come in handy, very handy indeed, believe me. Now you get some work done. You go read until supper."

"Oh, Grandma." Yet Ella's last droop, and the way she dragged out of the room—that was an act. Athaliah knew how much the girl enjoyed reading. Ella's special favorites were stories about the far West, about Oregon Trail pioneers and all the adventure beyond the Mississippi. Today's jaunt in the woods, too, had been an expression of the same girlish enthusiasm for the wild. When she left the sewing parlor, she took with her the raw odor of her bunched herbs.

"I see," Albert said, able to finish the paper at last, "I see." He looked up from the report, the deep-set wrinkles round his eyes revealing again how much the last few years had taken out of him.

"Mother, I trust you see through the Richmond bias here." He gestured at the headline. "Grant may be a butcher. But that doesn't mean the Confederacy's going to win the war. What does it matter if Grant loses a thousand of his troops a day? The next day, two thousand more march down and replace them."

"Albert. Is this a doctor's diagnosis?"

"Mother, yes. This is a doctor refusing to deny what he can see as plainly as these headlines"—he flipped over the newspaper clipping in his hand—"before his face. The question is no longer whether we will lose. The question is whether it will happen without coming into our home."

Athaliah narrowed her eyes. Albert was frightened, of course. And Andrew too, and Joseph: they were all past fifty and ineligible to fight, but they were frightened nonetheless. Indeed, the same fear now gripped any Southern man who, for whatever reason, had been excused from military service. As the fighting appeared to be coming home—as the Yankee general Sherman, outside Atlanta, spoke of something called "total war"— these homebound men had to face the same horrifying possibilities as the soldiers in the ranks had been living with since the first Bull Run.

"Mother," Albert went on, "we must be realistic. Do you realize the hostilities could come to our very *doorstep*?"

"We all do, Albert. We all do. Amazing grace, we'll see it through somehow."

Her stocky, full-grown son met her eyes again. Heavily he sighed, a rueful smile stretching between his salted muttonchops. His posture relaxed; he laid a hand on her worn-down shoulder. "The question," he repeated more gently, "is whether it will reach us down here."

"Lord, yes," Athaliah agreed. "But that's not the most important question."

Her son frowned, tugging at a muttonchop.

"The most important question," the grandmother said, "is how did it come to this? What have we done wrong?"

T he next morning Albert rose early. He crossed the yard to his brother's kitchen, as usual these days, since the only house help either son had left were Athaliah's two. Still enjoying the fullness of last night's pecan pie, Albert did his best to drink down what now passed for coffee in the South.

"Emily, really," Albert said. "What is this concoction?"

"Rosie over at Miz Taylor's give me the recipe, Dr. Boisseau." The woman always sounded more deferential with her mistress' son than with Athaliah herself. "It's got chicory, dried peas, and beets. Don't you think it's better than that okra and corn?"

"It's strange brew indeed, Emily."

The gray woman remained quiet, waiting.

"But then, we're all sipping strange brews across the South, aren't we? These days we'd better get used to brews of an entirely different kind."

Emily didn't respond. The doctor took one last sip, grimaced, then gave his instructions: "No need to set a place for me tonight, Emily. I'll dine at Tudor Hall this evening." He went out, headed for the back door.

The doctor had been gone for no more than an hour, and the rest of the household hardly had time to judge Emily's latest "coffee," when he came bursting back in. Albert came through the front door this time, breathless after the sprint from his carriage.

"The Yankees," he gasped. "They're coming!"

Athaliah and the rest rushed out of the dining room, gathering around him and—trailing the doctor in the door—Lewis, that day's coachman. Though the news was hardly good, young Ella couldn't keep from bobbing round the edge of the crowd, like a girl at a carnival.

"The Yankees!" Albert kept repeating. "They're here already, by God. They're just outside the city."

"Are you sure?" Athaliah asked. "They're supposed to be up by Cold Harbor."

Then the clanging of the courthouse bell broke into their hubbub. Several church bells took up the warning next, tolling away as if men were dying already.

"*Now* do you believe me?" Albert asked, showing again the fearful anger of the night before. "The Yankees are everywhere, I tell you. They're up in Cold Harbor and they're down here as well."

Athaliah's thin lips drew narrower still. "We've got to get ready to leave. We may not have much time."

Ella shoved up beside her, bobbing. "Why would we have to leave?"

"Ella, Lord, Lord!" the grandmother said, exasperated. "Go gather up a case of clothing. One case, only! Albert, you—"

But her son was already making the arrangements, conferring with Emily and Lewis as the three of them hurried together towards the kitchen.

Outside, at first distant but then closing in, gunfire crackled as the fourth day of June, 1864, wore on. By late afternoon several Union regiments stood at the edge of town. The Bluejackets appeared wary of the Petersburg fortifications but nonetheless ready to fight, even after their hard twenty-mile march south. The town's only defenders, meantime, were 125 boys as young as sixteen and men as old as forty-five. Though Albert was far too old for this sort of thing, his heart still felt a tug when he thought of the men defending the city.

The man responsible for this motley band was himself something of an outcast: the former Governor of Virginia, Henry Wise. As Governor, five years before the war, he'd called for Virginia to secede from the Union. He had no military training and so had been sent to Petersburg mostly to keep him out of harm's way. Yet it was Wise's clever strategy that would hold off a much larger and better equipped Union cavalry for several hours.

He had long since directed slaves to dig out some ten miles of earthworks, trenches, gun emplacements, and other fortifications for the city. Now, though Wise's defenses lacked the troops to fill them—he was outnumbered a good four to one—he spread his ill-equipped soldiers under the command of Colonel Fletcher T. Archer along the entire range of defensive battlements, ordering that there be ten feet between each man. After that, he kept shifting them from location to location, creating the illusion of a much larger army.

The trick was a politician's, rather than a military man's. Nonetheless, Grant's shock troops came within 150 yards of the city streets. Their last barrier was a deep ravine, and there Colonel Archer bunched his ragtag men for a true defensive stand.

Meantime, Athaliah and the rest of her family loaded their buggy with provisions and prepared to ride west to Tudor Hall, away from the invasion. But as Wise's ruse continued to hold up the Northerners' advance, they chose to wait. Albert took up a position two blocks away, on a hill, where he could watch the battle. Towards sundown, with the Bluejacket swarms seemingly unstoppable, Albert ran down the hill once more and declared it was time to go. "Time," he shouted, "*time*!" But no sooner had Athaliah and the others piled up into the buggy than Confederate reinforcements began at last to reach the town.

The boys in gray came streaming down the Petersburg byways, moving at a trot after who knows how many hours of forced marching. As they came they shrieked, raising their massed voices in the infamous Rebel Yell, and even the discouraged Albert couldn't help but roar back, heartened by so many brave boys arriving in the very nick of time.

But these Confederate saviors were, on closer inspection, a sorry sight. Gaunt, bloody, ragged, exhausted, and often carrying only an improvised excuse for a weapon, these infantrymen bore the devastation of month after month of unrelenting warfare. Indeed, for some of them it had been year after year of this inferno—yet most were young enough to be Athaliah's grandchildren. Every now and then there passed a boy she knew from around Petersburg, but as he hustled by, the old woman would barely recognize him. Where did these battle-weary scarecrows find the energy for that infamous Yell? Drawn-out and yet sharply punctuated, hideous and yet courageous, Johnny Reb's holler never failed to inspire terror in the Bluejackets across the way.

The old woman herself wasn't up to anything like that, but she did what she could. "God bless you all!" Athaliah cried. "Amazing grace!"

Her shout elicited a few more yells from the passing hundreds. They kept bravely trotting by, making for the earthworks and the massing invaders.

Near the Boisseau house at Poplar Lawn, the park where the defenders mustered their troops, two smaller groups split off from the ranks. These were artillery, with horse-drawn caissons. These squads maneuvered cannons to the tops of two close-by hillsides. By then the Union cavalry had begun to work their way up the side of the city's last defensive ravine. Henry Wise's threadbare defense had only been able to do so much. But now the reinforcements got into it, their hilltop batteries unleashing a horrific volley. Deafening, skull-thumping, every blast seemed to suck all the air out of the surrounding city. From her buggy Athaliah could see Andrew's windows bulge and rattle, and all round her flocks of birds startled up hysterically.

Above the din, the old woman heard someone shouting. "Head for the cellar!" Then as she clambered from the carriage, Athaliah realized it was she who'd been shouting. Seventy-one years old, frail and breathless, she'd fallen back on some naked urge for survival. She'd ordered everyone to shelter.

The Boisseaus and their two slaves scrambled into the big home's English basement, half above ground and half below, and huddled there for the rest of the afternoon. Down there, in the dark and the banging and the smell of sulfur, it was unlike anything Athaliah had ever known. She'd had no real idea of what war was like—no notion of the shape, the feel, the impact of the end of the world. The obscure monsters of Revelation hadn't prepared the old woman.

After a while Athaliah noticed that Emily and Lewis appeared to be the quietest, the least shaken. Even the irrepressible Ella cringed, quivering in Albert's embrace, her hands clamped to the sides of her young face. But the two slaves sat reserved, hands on knees, their old mouths firm. Could they have seen something like this before? Or—Athaliah found herself wondering—had poor black Emily and Lewis seen worse?

Then Athaliah had to get out. She couldn't stand the hard thoughts that crowded in on her, down in that battle-shaken cellar: the guilt, the shame. She couldn't stand to be so enclosed, held back, enslaved—she didn't deserve it! And Albert didn't have hands enough to stop her.

The old woman was up and out of there in a moment. She emerged into sunlight streaming through cannon smoke, the triumphal cries of Southerners echoing through their city. The Confederate cannons had done their work—the Union cavalry had fled. Athaliah saw the blue-uniformed horsemen galloping away out of range of the big guns. Could she call them *enemies?* She knew those were boys over there too, boys and families. And most of those Union families had at one point or another in the past shared some loving kinship, some cousin or girlfriend or partner in trade, with the families she knew on this Confederate side. The grandmother was watching war between her own children, and her heart filled with sorrow to think that too often the most intense and longest lasting hatred is stirred between brothers.

And here she was, upright in her front yard—Athaliah Goodwyn Boisseau, lifelong slaveholder, staring clear-eyed at the last of the horror her own way of life had created. She hadn't invented slavery, neither she nor the demure minions like her, the respectable and liquid-voiced ladies with their blood and background and ingrained gentility of heart. Yet the horror Athaliah saw now had been lurking all the while behind that gentility; the chained-down human spirits on which her world had been built had broken free at last, vengeful and bloodthirsty. Indeed, those chained spirits had been waiting since long before Athaliah's world had been built—the South hadn't invented slavery, she told herself yet again. Rather the long-confined wretched of the earth had been climbing this way for millennia now: misery had been climbing the centuries. Was there no end to it? Athaliah wondered. Was there *nothing* but misery, climbing the centuries?

"Amazing grace," she whispered, through seeping tears. "Amazing grace."

T he Petersburg reinforcements threw back the Union assault, forcing them south. After that General P.T. Beauregard took command over the Rebel troops defending Petersburg, which now numbered more than 57,000. But then the Union's Grant defied logic, or so it seemed to the Confederacy's Lee. The bulldog Northerner ordered a march south from Richmond; with 112,000 Union troops, he prepared a full-scale attack on the well-entrenched Petersburg.

Grant reasoned that most food and essentials coming into Richmond had to go through the southern railhead, and to choke off supplies there would be easier than taking the Confederate capital by force. Army of the Potomac engineers threw a 2,100-foot pontoon bridge over the James River in only eight hours. Then the hundred-thousand-strong juggernaut lurched southward again, toward Petersburg. By June 9, the first assault group began keeping the city's defenders busy.

Petersburg had been, till then, a quiet place: bright Richmond's more restrained little sister. Streets here were orderly and tree-lined, houses tidy and unpretentious. The Boisseau homes had small front yards surrounded by low wrought iron. And if you could measure a town's religious character by the number of its church steeples, Petersburg must have been very close to God.

Like Athaliah Boisseau, most residents must have seen war's coming as some horrible act of God. If their city had been wicked, they'd never seen it; if they themselves had been sinning, they'd never known it. But now, just six days later, the Union advance troops mounted another, still larger attack. And again the Confederate defenses were reed thin, terribly outnumbered.

But the Yanks, as before, never pressed their advantage. One mile-long fortification east of the city fell to the Bluejacket infantry, spearheaded by a division of the U.S. Colored Troops, freed slaves led by white officers. And this was a key fortification, a linchpin. Once the Negro infantry stormed into it, nearly every remaining soldier in gray knew that Petersburg lay open—Petersburg and no doubt the capital of the Confederacy as well. Yet once again, the Union generals preferred to remain cautious. A secondary assault was ordered to wait until scouts could determine how strong the Confederate defenses were. Night fell on eerie quiet. And this respite—which stretched into several more days—gave General Beauregard time to call up more reinforcements and build additional trenches and earthworks.

What the Federal forces failed to take by action, they would try to gain by waiting. Both sides began to settle into siege warfare, a war of attrition, alternately boring and horrendous. And eventually even Grant—though at first furious at his generals' missed opportunity—realized that time was the Union's ally. His engineers set up a command center at City Point, at the junction of the James and the Appomattox, ten miles to the northeast.

Athaliah Boisseau, hearing of the new military headquarters, shook her head. Why, it was over near her old friends the Bevilles! That God-fearing, well-spoken family too was being shown the face of misery and sin. To what end? the old woman wondered. If these days were the Revelation for people like the Boisseaus and the Bevilles, then what Kingdom of God lay behind the moment's ruling shame?

Over at City Point the Army of the Potomac built a mile of wharves, an immense tent hospital, and row upon row of supply houses. Within a few short months "the Point" became one of the world's busiest seaports, handling 200 ships a day. The ships carried men, munitions, and food; the troops and material traveled to Petersburg via a brand new Army-built railroad line. The City Point bakeries pumped out 123,000 loaves of fresh bread daily; the delivery system brought it to the Bluejacket soldiers still warm from the ovens. The Army of the Potomac had every luxury warfare allows.

T he Boisseaus learned all this over the next several weeks. Indeed, Athaliah, struggling to find some good in her infernal vision of brother against brother, proved a quick study in problems of military supply and movement. The Union lines, she learned, remained about a mile off. Thus, during the third week of June, she and her family could still leave the city by going west to Tudor Hall or north to Richmond. But what Athaliah and her kin didn't know, during those first days of digging in, was that the Army of the Potomac had brought in three devastating new weapons.

These soon made their presence felt. One morning before month's end, Athaliah, Ella, Andrew, and his wife Susan had gathered as usual in the dining room, doing their best to manage a siege city's miserable excuse for breakfast.

"Uncle Albert is right," Ella said, over Emily's makeshift coffee. "This is indeed strange brew."

Wanly, Athaliah smiled. The girl remained a godsend, making jokes and hoping for the best. But Ella's teenage optimism had changed its focus; the granddaughter was struggling to become more practical.

"Well, Grandma," she went on, "I suppose this queer stuff will give me the energy to do more sewing. I mean, you and I must keep going with that."

"Indeed we must," Athaliah said. "We need to send Lewis back up to Richmond soon . . ."

An eerie whistling cut her off; a rumble rattled the windows. Albert looked towards the more densely settled part of the city and saw a cloud of smoke and dust rising. The family sat immobile at first, stunned, wordless.

"Wh-what?" Andrew began, reaching for his wife.

But once again the whistling came: a hunter's piercing signal to his bird dog, but metallic and inconceivably loud.

"The cellar! Everyone, quickly—the *cellar*!" At least this time Athaliah knew it was she who was yelling. Before they reached the cellar door, however, another muffled explosion came from city center; in the distance she glimpsed the wall of a house collapsing. Another family blasted to shreds. But Athaliah had enough of battlefield Revelation, for now. Though her family was out of range of Union artillery, nonetheless she forced herself to join the others in the root cellar. Once more they huddled in the herb-rich dark, arms linked, heads down. The banging they knew— but what was this diabolical new *whistling*?

"Strange brew," Ella repeated, during a lull. She was trying to smile, fixing crooked lips across a pale, frightened face.

Hollowly Andrew laughed. Athaliah, for her part, kept trying to blink away her vision of ancient injustices working towards redress.

"Every time there's an explosion," Ella went on, "I see the queerest things."

"That so, chile?" Emily said. She and Lewis had remained as calm as before, voiceless in the dark.

"Oh yes, Mammy Emily," the teenager went on. "The queerest things, honestly. They flash before my eyes bold as you please."

Athaliah, startled, stroked the girl's hair. "Amazing grace, my sweet Ella."

The pretty youngster turned her crooked smile the grandmother's way. "Amazing . . . grace?" she asked. "Do you mean you see such things, too?"

Andrew cut in, sounding sober as his big brother Albert. "Hellfire and damnation," he said. "That's what I see. Every time another of those bombs goes off, I see the Devil laughing in Hell."

"My son, my granddaughter," Athaliah said. "Please." Even she was surprised at the unexpected gravity in her voice. "Please," she repeated. "Whatever God gives us to see, he also gives us to comprehend."

Finally the shelling stopped and the family emerged once more into the sunlight. "Lord ha' mercy," Emily declared, then. "Is it still 'fore lunch time?" Athaliah laughed at that, heartened by what she saw. They'd all expected devastation, the utter ruin of their city, but in fact the damage appeared slight. The Dunlops had lost half their chimney wall, but all in all Petersburg seemed to have survived this first major artillery barrage of the siege.

"Lunch?" Lewis asked Emily, incredulous. "Big mama, you thinkin' bout *lunch*?"

Athaliah laughed again, more deeply, and this time her son and granddaughter joined in.

The barrage the Boisseaus and the rest of Petersburg had endured, they found out over the next few days, included some shelling from the "Dictator." This new "Dictator" had to travel mounted on a flat-bed rail car, it was such an ungainly weapon. Essentially a stubby mortar, it could hurl 200-pound exploding shells more than two miles.

General Grant's strategy had become to wear down Petersburg's citizens. It was a strategy he'd used effectively in the siege of Vicksburg the year before. So the Army of the Potomac lobbed artillery into Petersburg at unpredictable times, hitting all sorts of different targets, the shells whistling with varying intensities. But Petersburg's citizens—despite all their losses, their deprivations, their bad dreams—adjusted and went on with their lives. They learned to gauge the whistle of incoming artillery, to watch for the burning fuses of the cannonballs. In this way even the man on the street could predict where the shells would strike; they could know whether to take shelter or not. The Boisseaus soon appointed Ella to this watch duty, since the active youngster had the sharpest eyes.

For the troops at the front lines, however, it was a different story. Life in the trenches combined excruciating tedium and horrifying fear. In some places the opposing forces' trenches were no more than fifty yards apart, close enough to carry on conversations—or hurl insults and promises of a painful death. Meanwhile, rifles were so powerful and accurate that to lift one's head above the earthworks was to risk certain death. Soldiers built walls of sandbags with slits for their rifles, but even these could be unsafe. Snipers simply waited for an enemy head to block off the daylight behind the slit.

Next, Grant's well-stocked army introduced a second weapon that changed the face of war. It too had a sound like nothing else heard before in combat: a grating *rat-a-tat-tat-tat*, grinding on endlessly. It was, in effect, a rifle that didn't need to pause for loading, a whole rapid-firing rifle squad contained in a single emplacement. The new killing tool was called the Gatling gun, after its inventor, though those in the trenches called it by a simpler name: machine gun. A prototype had been tried at Gettysburg, and its use in Petersburg, though limited to a few emplacements, was still enough to spread fear.

Still, Beauregard's lines didn't budge. Trench warfare was proving static; even an undermanned, undergunned group could hold out indefinitely, so long as it maintained open supply lines. Life within the fortifications was by and large miserable, yes. Soldiers suffered from the Virginia heat, the persistent rats, the mindless tedium. But Petersburg remained in Confederate hands. So Grant's commanders came up with yet another new weapon, the third of this extraordinary campaign.

P etersburg had lived under siege for nearly two months, by the time this weapon was tried. By then—the end of July—Tudor Hall had brought in some crops at least, and the generous Boisseaus had tithed the Confederacy and their neighbors. In town, Athaliah and Andrew and Albert and the others had developed something resembling regularity, despite their unnaturally disrupted lives. Though the enemy artillery barrages continued day and night, Athaliah and her family had learned to sleep through most of them. But just before dawn, July 30, all of them were jerked from their beds by an explosion like nothing they'd ever heard before.

The blast went off at 4:40 A.M.; Athaliah, as was her habit, looked first at the clock. The thunder of detonation was so loud, even though it was toward the front, she wouldn't have been surprised if lightning had struck their backyard. Or was the lightning *underground?* The earth was shaking and it was raining dirt, gravel, scraps of wood and debris over the city. Lightning underground, earth overhead: it was the world turned upside down.

What had waked the old woman was a Union assault unlike any ever attempted. Miners from Pennsylvania had dug a 500-foot tunnel under Confederate lines. At the end of the tunnel they'd paced four tons of black powder; at 4:40 A.M., they'd lit the fuse.

The plan was to rupture the fortifications and, before the surrounding Rebels could refill the gap, send Federal shock troops through. The crater left by the explosion was immense, thirty feet deep and seventy feet across. An entire Confederate fort had collapsed into the hole, with nearly 300 men killed on the spot. For hundreds of yards on either side, Rebel soldiers scuttled back in amazement, in dread. Yet then, incredibly, it took nearly fifteen minutes for the Union troops to enter the crater. The division commanders assigned to the attack were back in their bombproof dirt shelters. One of the scrappy divisions of the U.S. Colored Troops, already seasoned and eager for more action, had been originally slated to make the first assault. But the North was afraid of what would happen to the former slaves if they were captured by their former masters. At the last moment the Colored Troops had been pulled back, replaced by far more exhausted whites.

When Union troops finally approached the pit, they arrived more curious than anything else. Unable to get around it, they clambered in— into what one survivor called "a cauldron of hell," trapped hopelessly under the guns of a furious Confederate rally. Belatedly, desperately, Federal commanders sent in the Colored Troops, and these fought with the bravery of men who have nothing to lose, often going hand to hand in the blown-apart muck. Here and there they even broke through the Confederate line, but they couldn't by themselves overcome several hours of inept management.

Union casualties were enormous. Though the battle had begun with the slaughter of 300 Secessionists, by its end the Army of the Potomac had lost three times that many, wounded, captured, or dead. On the Confederate side, fewer than a thousand died overall. General Grant called the episode "a stupendous failure." But again it was Grant who took the blame in the press, branded a butcher once more. Stung, exasperated, the Federal commander resorted again to siege. Risking no more lives, he slowly burrowed west around the city, extending his lines and forcing Lee to spread his threadbare troops even more thinly. By September those lines reached Tudor Hall.

Athaliah's son Joseph and his wife Ann had remained childless since inheriting Tudor Hall a few years before the War. They lavished their affections instead on the land, the livestock, the slaves and their families. They were old-style Virginians, in love with farming and the countryside.

By late summer, the Union's continual westward probing had seen some five forward fortifications put up within a mile and a half of Tudor

Hall. Not long after that Joseph Boisseau was interrupted at breakfast by a stern knock at his stately front doors. In years past, a slave would have answered. But no longer. Joseph Boisseau left his plate of fatback and went to the door himself.

His caller was no farmer. For today's visit this Confederate officer—for that's what the man at the door was, plainly—had pulled on his parade uniform, the elegant gray jacket with gold trim, gold buttons, a gold sash and a long gold-tipped saber. All this, Joseph understood after a moment, was out of respect to the grandeur of the house. Joseph himself stood a little more erect, tucking back his gray beard. But the visitor's regal garb didn't mask his fatigue. On second glance Joseph could tell that this was a man weary of battle, struggling to fulfill his obligations in the face of growing discouragement and dwindling supplies.

The officer introduced himself as a South Carolina General. "Samuel McGowan, sir," he said, "of the Sumter McGowans. Do you mind if I come in?"

"Please." Joseph tried to match the officer's formal *politesse*. "Would you care to join us for some, ah, some hot breakfast drink?"

McGowan seemed dumbfounded at the generosity. As the men moved toward the kitchen, Joseph could swear he heard his visitor's stomach growl. And once Joseph's wife had poured the Carolinian a cup of their own substitute for coffee, he drank it down without regard for what it was made of. Clearly, this was a man who'd grown used to strange brews.

The soldier took some fatback as well. Not till he'd taken three or four hurried, hungry bites did McGowan at last remember his business. He'd come, he said swallowing, to ask the two of them to make "a sacrifice."

"Many have made such sacrifices for the Confederacy," he said. "Many."

Ann and Joseph exchanged anxious glances. Both knew what was coming.

"You've heard the skirmishes going on near here, no doubt," the officer went on. "You've seen the Yankee forts nearby. That devil Grant wants to find some way to cut the railroads leading from Petersburg, since he can't break through our brave boys in front of the city."

"You want our farm," Joseph blurted.

"We cannot allow the Yanks into Petersburg. We simply cannot. Once he gets into Petersburg, our capital's but a train ride away. Your plantation," McGowan continued more gently, "well, its location is strategic, to say the least. Boydton Plank Road out there—" he gestured towards the parlor windows—"is the most important supply route into the city now that many rail lines have been cut, and it stands between Grant and the vital South Side Rail Road."

"General McGowan," Ann said, "we are no strategists."

"Ah, but you understand the need for food, don't you? You understand the need for regular supplies? The devil Grant tore up the South Side line two months ago, and we have only just repaired it. We desperately need the Rail Road, and we need the Boydton Plank Road, as well."

"How much do you want?" Joseph asked, his heart sinking. "You see we don't have much." With a shaky hand he indicated his wife and himself, sitting in the servants' side of the house, eating food they'd prepared themselves.

"We need your sacrifice for the Confederacy," the Carolinian said, more gently still. "We need your land, your house, everything." His voice seemed almost to age into greater kindness. "Mr. Boisseau, I'm very sorry. But the war has come to your plantation. It has come to so many, you know. It has come to mine."

"You need *everything*?" Joseph asked, angry.

The general turned businesslike. "We need to build defensive positions, and we plan to use your house for a hospital. We need not move into your home at once, but there will soon be hundreds of soldiers living on your property."

"Everything," Joseph repeated, angry still. But his rage, he realized, was directed mostly at himself, at his own childish yearning to burst into tears and beg for some reassurance. Lord, he thought, we are fragile.

"General," he went on, striving to master himself. "General, we do have one request."

The soldier met his eyes, levelly.

"This home means the world to us," Joseph said. "My parents built it more than fifty years ago, my sisters and brothers were born here, we all grew up here. My request is—" again he struggled for control—"please treat it with care."

McGowan said he'd do what he could, formal as ever, straightening his buttons and sash. But after he'd remounted his horse and left, Ann and Joseph needed several minutes arm in arm on the front porch, gazing out

over their beloved Tudor Hall. It was still harvest time and their slaves were
hard at work picking cotton, tobacco, and vegetables. The sunlight filtered
through a haze of dust kicked up by the workers. Joseph remembered how
his mother Athaliah used to love such scenes—how she'd sit in her rocker
of an afternoon, sipping the real tea they'd had before the war, smiling over
the tranquil fields. Yet now there was nothing tranquil; from where he
stood, Joseph could hear gunfire. Would this be the last time a Boisseau
stood on that porch, looking over land he was happy to call his own?

Before midday, Confederate soldiers began arriving. Engineers
walked along a steep ravine across the property, a natural defensive bul-
wark, and there staked out a lein for fortifications. Earthworks were built
fifteen feet across, wide enough to absorb Union artillery. Trenches went
deep enough for troops to stand with their heads out of harm's way, while
at the same time keeping a clear view of approaching forces. The Rebels cut
down trees and made sharpened stakes to plant pointed end up, a bristling
infantry obstacle called *abatis and fraise*. Cannons rolled into place. Tudor
Hall became an armed camp.

Yet even this late in the war, officers of the Confederacy did what they
could to maintain some semblance of Southern civility and grace. Through
the frightening nights that followed, General McGowan and his high
command proved surprisingly genial guests. The perceptive South Carolinian could see that the Boisseaus felt more and more like strangers in their
long-time family home, and he tried his best to rekindle the spirit of Tudor
Hall. McGowan and the other generals enjoyed many a long hour of whist,
joking and laughter around the dinner table. Some nights, before the
fireplace, the Boisseaus and their visitors listened rapt as McGowan recited
poems of Milton or whole passages from Shakespeare. There wasn't much
light to read by, and few books other than the Bible had survived the
family's need for items of barter.

Still, despite the comfort of these evenings, every day the Hall felt less
like a home. McGowan said that Grant's attack would come, paradoxically,
from the south, and so before long Joseph and Ann packed what they could
and moved the opposite way, north toward the still-tranquil Appomattox
River.

L ewis' trips to Richmond had become less and less productive, as winter settled in. Prices kept skyrocketing, and more than a few unscrupulous shop owners refused even to sell some products, waiting another day or so for prices to rise still more. Basic foods such as beans and rice were available, but many things now became luxuries out of most people's reach.

Life for the soldiers was worse. The winter of 1864-1865 proved one of the coldest in memory. Sleet and snow turned the trenches into quagmires. The mud, sometimes two feet deep, alternately froze and thawed, creating a sickening slop. And despite the miserable conditions, the work of war had to continue. Confederate soldiers tried tunneling out mines of their own, as the Federals had done last July, but they never got far enough to blow any of them up.

Rations, meantime, were cut to a pint of cornmeal a day. Soldiers sometimes went for a week or more without meat. Neither side had winter clothes—each wore the regulation wool uniforms they had been issued. Plus in winter as in summer, the stench that ruled their days was a combination of latrines impossible to clean and bodies impossible to bury.

Many deserted, many, as sober and clear-eyed about the Confederacy's doom as Albert Boisseau. Up to several hundred a day fled the Petersburg entrenchments. And this dispirited dwindling was, of course, just what Grant and his commanders had been counting on.

Those Confederates who remained tried to keep their spirits high. When they received their pay (typically, four months late), they spent with abandon. Petersburg dance halls and taverns did a booming trade. And when the Confederate dollars ran out, they bartered for goods. Indeed, in one of the most bizarre developments of a campaign like no other before it, Johnny Reb bartered with Yank, trading goods between the opposing lines. There was an unwritten agreement that soldiers from both sides could hold swap meets in a few designated places, and that at such times no shots would be fired. It was during those exchanges that the two sides' contrast in supply became abundantly clear. The Federal soldiers had everything they wanted, the Confederates much less—and still less reason to stay and fight.

That November, President Abraham Lincoln declared a national holiday of Thanksgiving to be held on the last Thursday of the month. Union soldiers celebrated with a feast of turnkey or chicken, pies and fruit. The Confederates, meantime, had their usual cornmeal. But both sides, in a poignant show of honor between mortal combatants, declared a single-day cease fire.

These stories of humanity in the midst of horror, of compassion in an inferno, touched Athaliah Boisseau most deeply in the last days of her life. Her household, after all, hardly had it easier than the troops at the front. Tudor Hall was gone, Tudor Hall and all it had offered.

"Amazing grace," Athaliah murmured, when the reserved Albert brought the news about the Hall. "It's bad as Petersburg over there."

The old woman was spending most of her days in bed by now. During her talk with Albert she sank back into the pillows, too sick to take the news sitting up. "The Lord does take everything," she told her son, "doesn't he?"

"Oh, Mother," Albert said, broken-voiced. "I wondered if I should tell you at all."

"No, I'm glad you told me," the old woman said. "I needed to know." Though too weak to raise her head again, she fixed him with a dead-serious look. "You think the soldiers in the trenches here have the truth hidden from them?"

Albert eyed her worriedly, a doctor once more.

"The soldiers know the truth," Athaliah said. "They've looked the worst in the face. And I must too."

Albert called for Ella, and told the girl to bring the best tea they had left, plus any kind of fruit. Ella by then had begun to work with Lewis on foraging after food, making a startling combination of spunky white youth and canny black age. They proved a remarkably successful twosome, but even Ella and Lewis had trouble finding meat during that hard winter. The Boisseaus, like many others, had to live with a diet of cornbread and black-eyed peas.

Now the girl came running up the steep stairs with an herb tea she'd learned about from Emily and an apple from the relatively unaffected orchards north of town.

"Ella, Lord," Athaliah said, after the youngster had given her a few sips of the tea. "You are a godsend."

Albert took out his pocketknife and cut up the apple. Together he and the teenager got some nourishment into the grandmother, and in a few minutes Athaliah was sitting up again. Albert tried to bring up one of the happier times he remembered from the old days at the Hall, a harvest dance when father William had insisted on scratching off the names of everyone else on Athaliah's card. But his mother didn't want to lose herself in the past. Instead she asked Ella to sit beside her on the bed and, taking the girl's hand, declared she wanted to know if Ella still "saw things" when the Union bombs landed nearby.

"Sometimes," Ella said, bobbing a bit as she nodded.

"And does your Uncle Andrew," the old woman asked, "still claim to see hellfire and damnation?"

Ella frowned, and shared a look with Albert. But Athaliah kept her fingers tightly meshed with the girl's, her look kind but free of jokes.

"We mustn't flee the hellfire we see," she told her granddaughter, there in her faded bedroom. "We mustn't, because it comes from within us. It is a part of us."

"Mother . . ." Albert began.

"Albert, *please*." For a moment she was the disciplinarian of Tudor Hall again, certain of the rules and brooking no impertinence. "I'm not some doddering, dying fool, Albert." Athaliah coughed and sank into her pillows once more. But she maintained her grip on Ella's hand, and she took them both in with an unshaken look.

"Dying?" Ella asked. "Grandma, you're not—"

"Of course I'm dying," Athaliah snapped. "I know that, of course. But because I know that, I also know something more." Her look remained tough, a soldier's, but her voice grew more gentle. "I know, too, that the hellfire is within us. And the grace to overcome it is within us as well. The grace to overcome *anything*, children."

"You mean," Albert tried, "just as our Southern system contained its own fatal flaw . . ."

Athaliah nodded. "Just as our beloved South contained the seeds of its own destruction, in the wounds and injustice we laid on poor souls like Emily and Lewis, so we each in us contain a horror, a wretchedness, a hellfire."

Ella squeezed the old woman's hand. "But I'm working with Lewis now, Grandma. He's no slave to me, that wonderful old man."

Albert stared at his bouncing niece, blinking. Yes, she was the new breed, and every generation must give way to the new breed. But it still took a man by surprise, when he saw it taking place right there before him.

"Why, without Lewis," Ella went on, "we'd starve."

"And knowing that," Athaliah said, "recognizing that, is the power of grace within us. Amazing grace, how sweet the sound. It is the power that keeps these soldiers in our trenches human and rich in soul, though every day they face a hellfire worse even than we do."

"Amen to that," Albert said quietly. "I see the poor wretches in surgery. Never seen such strength of souls. Tell them they're going to die in the next ten minutes, they never utter a word of complaint."

"Lord, no," Athaliah said. "And I'm not going to start complaining now, either. Not when out there—" she cocked her chin towards her window— "there are soldiers in gray and soldiers in blue . . ."

"Soldiers with black faces," Ella put in, "and soldiers with white faces."

"Lord, yes," Athaliah said. "And all of them, all of them keeping their spirits alive through inferno after inferno, by the power of God's amazing grace."

"Amazing grace," Albert echoed, a deep sadness coming into his look.

But Ella repeated the words with a laugh, and bent to hug her dying grandmother.

A thaliah died in early December, a bitterly cold time when the Boisseaus' fireplaces were barely enough even for young Ella. On the eighth of the month, during a Union barrage aimed at the Boisseaus' neighborhood, the old woman refused Andrew's offer to carry her down to the cellar.

"It's nothing but a lot of strange colors and smells and noises," she told her son. "Nothing but a strange brew. That's all these bombardments are."

"Mother . . ." Andrew began.

"Go," she said. "Save your worrying for Ella."

And young Ella was the first to discover her afterward. Athaliah was upright at her headboard, her sewing on her lap. The old woman had quit this task at some point; no point trying to do needlework with a hawthorn barb when there's a bombardment on. Instead, she'd folded her grandmotherly hands, as if in prayer. The funeral was simple, as were most during the Petersburg siege. Even during funerals, after all, the Army of the Potomac continued shelling. Even during the hymn afterwards: *Amazing grace, how sweet the sound* . . . .

But Ella Boisseau, sixteen years old and in fine voice, sang the song as if she never noticed the incoming artillery. She performed with the spry retainer Lewis over Athaliah's grave, and the harmony of her girl's soprano and his old man's bass sounded so liquid and gentle it was a if they had somehow managed to rise above the entire 250 years of Southern slavery.

But then, too, the girl was leaving. To the less magnanimous at the funeral, the ones too damaged by malnutrition and heartache to lose themselves in the beauty of Ella's singing, the only plausible explanation for how happily she sang had to be that she was getting out of Petersburg. While Grant's vast insatiable animal went on gnawing at the city's eastern defenses, Ella Boisseau—lucky girl!—was heading the other way. Albert and Andrew had arranged for her to stay with relatives in a road junction well to the west, far from the hostilities. She'd see out the duration in a crossroads called Five Forks.

It took hardly a day for Ella to get packed, hardly a half a day to have Lewis drive her out to the quiet crossroads. Yet it seemed to the teenager as if she'd gone to another world. The place was Burnt Quarter. A mansion before there even was a Union, it stood bright and welcoming, its tall chimneys towering over a roof that sprouted dormers, windows with green shutters, and a porch with white pillars. Its name was a mystery—perhaps named after a nearby creek—perhaps because the British had burned the slave quarters in an earlier war.

Greeting Ella on the portico were more of her family—the Gilliams—distant relatives, but people she could count on, nonetheless. "Come in, come in, Ella," beamed the warm-faced widow, Mary Gilliam. "I'm so sorry to hear about your grandmother. She was a fine lady."

Ella nodded, softly smiling, entering the house. Her eyes fell on her cousin, Albeena Gilliam, now twenty-three years old and in the full bloom of her womanhood. Ella herself was a pretty girl—people always told her so. But Albeena was more than pretty, she was a Southern beauty. Her wide brow was crowned with long curls that tumbled to her low-cut bodice. And her eyes. Ella loved to look into those blue eyes that were so beautiful, so kind.

The Widow Gilliam noticed Ella's admiring gaze. It was a look she had seen many times before. Her daughter had the reputation of being the most courted girl in the Confederacy. "If you observe a fair number of our Southern officers paying us a visit, well, you may understand why," the widow said proudly.

One of those visitors was a dashing young cavalry general, William Fitzhugh Lee, a son of General Robert E. Lee himself. "Everyone calls him Rooney," Albeena told Ella. "The poor man's wife died last year, and he has no one else to talk to. He misses her very much—he is a very lonely man."

The man had other reasons for coming. Mary's other child, sixteen-year-old Samuel Yates Gilliam, knew the back roads in that area better than just about anyone, and he personally escorted the troops along the hidden routes.

Sometimes Ella would watch as the handsome young widower strolled through the garden daffodils with her lovely cousin. He in his gray uniform with gold-braided sleeves, his sabre at his side, and she in her hoop skirts, her bodice cut low. They seemed perfect together—almost too perfect. The brave man faced death day after day, and found refreshment to carry on in the sweet companionship of Albeena. Ella wondered if there would ever be so dashing a figure as Rooney Lee in her life. She wondered if she would have the warmth and support to offer a man when she became a woman, the way her cousin Albeena had.

Samuel Yates Gilliam was the same age as Ella. Lanky and sometimes awkward, he made Ella laugh when he seemed to trip over his own feet. But Ella admired his courage. When fighting erupted near Dinwiddie Court House, it was Sam who led the Confederates to just the right place to surprise the Federals. He came home jubilant: "We whupped 'em!" he crowed. "Ol' Pickett chased Sheridan back to the Court House. We're goin' to run 'em all the way back North."

And in the glow of that moment, the family circle sharing in the Southern triumph and in Sam's part in it, Ella could almost believe that it might really happen. "Perhaps," she let herself dream in this small window of hope, "perhaps somehow it will all work out for the best."

The dream was shortlived, however. At the end of March, 1865, there came days of sheet-like rain through which beaten-down files of gray-clad infantrymen tramped like ghosts. Despite the victory at Dinwiddie Court House, Southern men were being pushed aside by the vast Northern juggernaut.

Ella clung to each spring day as if it might be the last. The peach trees behind the house were now in full bloom, their bright pink blossoms like clouds in a peaceful sunset. It was as perfect as the fine oil portraits that hung on the walls inside. The family was so kind, the house so lovely, the garden so peaceful. Ella's heart ached to hang on to this serenity, and to avoid forever the violence she had known back in Petersburg.

But for now, the peace she longed for existed only in her heart. The morning of April 1, Sam ran up the porch steps, flung open the door and dashed into the parlor. "It's happening," he said. "They're here."

The ladies rushed to the windows and saw gray-clad horsemen jumping the split-rail fence beyond the cornfield and thundering for the peach orchard behind the house. Moments later, the Bluecoats were right behind them, hordes of them, their horses knocking over the log rails as if they were nothing, the men shouting and charging into the cornfield.

In an instant, the shouts were drowned out by an ear-splitting fusillade of carbine shots from the Confederates in the peach orchard. The women held their ears and watched in horror as men and horses fell bleeding onto the grass. The shots rang back and forth between the two sides. One of the windows shattered—a bullet hole appearing on the wall behind.

One young Confederate sharpshooter was behind a big tree at the side of the mansion, picking off Yankees as they charged through the field. Albeena was watching from the parlor, and could see the boy was cut off from the rest of the troops. "He'll be killed if those Yankees ever get their hands on him," she said.

Albeena pushed wide the front door and yelled to him: "Come on! Run!" Through a hail of gunfire, the soldier—not much older than Sam— scampered across the grass, onto the porch, all the way through the house and out the back door to rejoin his unit. The Widow Gilliam was holding her heaving chest, while young Ella beamed at her courageous cousin.

By one o'clock the fighting had died own, each side withdrawing to regroup and get reinforcements. But the yard was littered with dead and dying soldiers and horses. The women and the slaves helped Union soldiers bring the wounded, blue and gray alike, into the dining room. They pushed the table and chair aside and laid a dozen bleeding men on the floor while a Union doctor tended them. Ella and Albeena washed wounds, brought tea and water, and spoke tenderly to the fallen.

The Widow Gilliam looked out the shattered window to see that the great clouds of black-powder smoke had wilted her peach blossoms as badly as a killer frost. "And look at this blood on the floor," she exclaimed. "It will take weeks to scrub it clean." She had had quite enough of this war, thank you. They could just take their foolish fighting somewhere else. Closing the doors to the dining room to keep out the groaning, she sat down and wrote a letter to Union commander Philip Sheridan. "You can move your battle," she wrote. "I cannot move my house." She put the letter in the hands of a trusted slave and sent him off.

She got her answer from her own side of the fight. Soon another slave arrived with a letter from the Confederates: a letter to Albeena from Rooney Lee. He thanked her for all the kindness she and her family had shown him, and apologized that he was unable to keep Sheridan's forces far from her farm. He felt she would be better off if she and the others left Burnt Quarter immediately, because the fighting she had seen that morning was a mere skirmish compared to the battle that was coming. He had taken the liberty to dispatch an ambulance to take her and her family to safety.

Albeena clutched the letter and allowed herself a quiet moment. She appreciated being cared about and protected by this Southern gentleman, but she hated to leave her home. When she told Ella they would have to flee, Ella smiled sadly. "I have been through this before and I know what you're feeling," she said. "Everything will work out fine—trust me."

The rout at Five Forks came on April 1—perhaps destiny's grim reminder that the joke was on the formerly comfortable South, given its foolish dependence on slavery. In the days that followed, while someone—vandals, soldiers, whoever—slashed the lovely portraits on the walls at Burnt Quarter, Ella learned that as soon as General Grant heard that his troops had overrun Five Forks, he marched straight into his tent and wrote out the orders for the final assault on Petersburg the next day. To her horror, she also learned that this last scene of pain and sorrow was played out where her family had spent so much happy time—at Tudor Hall.

The key assault had come before dawn on Sunday, April 2. In the darkness, the front-line shock troops had crept forward on their bellies.

Most of the 4000 last-ditch defenders at Tudor Hall were caught asleep. In the semi-darkness, the Yankees silently swept over the top of the earthworks, their banner floating against the gray sky. Then, their guns and their cheers erupted, destroying what remained of the night, and of the last defenses of the South. They captured Southern cannons, swung them around, and opened fire. In less than half an hour of chaos, they had torn their way to the last lifeline of the South, Boydton Plank Road.

In the groaning weeks that followed, Ella Boisseau helped blue and gray alike, anyone who could make it to the hospital tents where she helped. And she heard many a Yankee infantryman, flat-voiced but victorious, call their Tudor Hall attack "the wedge that opened the home of the Confederacy."

The home, yes. Petersburg had finally been laid open to the Federals. The breakthrough came on back-to-back days, Saturday the First and Sunday the Second, and by some sudden startling flash of history's torchlight, each time on Boisseau property. The first was at Burnt Quarter, the second a few miles away—at Tudor Hall. It was as if once the Union had conquered this family, they'd won over the entire Old South.

N ot that Ella understood all this on April Fool's Day. The best the courageous girl could do, that entire terrible weekend, was understand that she'd never suffered such close exposure, such a profound test of her new-forged compassion and goodwill. It was as if she'd inherited the eyes of her visionary grandmother Athaliah. She saw the kind of human devastation the old woman had told her about. And, as these last days of war wound down, she continued seeing to the wounded. Circulating tirelessly among the moaning, the dying, the teenager strove to recall every root and herb her Uncle Albert had taught her. She sent for old Lewis again, needing his memory, his advice. Together she and the old black man labored over the veterans of that final battle.

Together too, they heard of the war's end. The closing acts came, in another oddly fitting wrinkle of fate, during Christian Holy Week. The breakout at Tudor Hall was the first of a series of momentous events on succeeding Sundays. The next was April 9, Palm Sunday, when at Appomattox Court House Grant and Lee signed the documents ending hostili-

ties. And the final awesome stroke came on April 16, Easter Sunday. That
evening Ella was shocked to hear from a cavalry courier that Abraham
Lincoln had died the day before, shot while attending a play, by a deranged
actor. At a play, by an actor! It was like some cosmic reminder that this
intrinsically American conflagration, so different from earlier European-in-
fluenced wars, was itself a drama played out in the palm of God's hand: a
reminder that the Divine Mind had briefly but blisteringly focused on
these few mid-Atlantic farmlands and hillsides—and on this family.

Through all the news good, bad, and inspiring, Ella and Lewis labored on. They concocted poultices, sleeping potions and fever reducers. To
Ella there came to seem a special justice in their remedies. For how often
had sick slaves, deprived of the white man's doctors, required the sort of
woods medicine she and Lewis were brewing up these days? And now how
much strange brew would her tragic new South need to drink in order to
purge its system of its former disease?

Sometimes, as the pretty teenager and her seamy old friend circulated
among the cots of the wounded, in the front rooms of the old plantation,
the two of them would begin to sing again. Their twinned voices soothed
the men around them. *Amazing grace*, Ella and Lewis sang, *how sweet the
sound.* . . . And as their voices rose, it seemed sometimes to patients and care
givers alike as if they were all afloat in the air, some unimaginably peaceful
summer air. Sometime the soldiers couldn't help joining in with rough
harmony of their own: *that saved a wretch like me!* It was as if their linked
voices were timeless, as if the yearning towards the hymn's salvation had
been going on for centuries. The singing seemed to be climbing the air,
climbing out of those fetid sickrooms, out of the human inferno altogether,
as if its beauty were climbing the centuries.

PART 2
ROBERT B. PAMPLIN, SENIOR

CHAPTER 9

Robert Pamplin, Senior:
A Virginian's Beginnings

SUMMERTIME LINGERS in Virginia's Piedmont farm country. Afternoons remain muggy and breathless well into September. On one such afternoon in 1916—hot enough to turn the richest topsoil to dust—five-year-old Robert Boisseau Pamplin sat by the side of a road with his cousin Dee, tearing apart his schoolbooks.

"I guess we figured out what these are for," Dee kept saying, ripping out another page or two. "I guess we did!"

Little Robert giggled, crumpling a sheet and chucking it at the boy beside him.

Books and education were still brand-new to Robert, as he sat by that dirt roadway between Sutherland's two-room schoolhouse and his own farmhouse. This was Dinwiddie County, deeply rural though hardly a day's wagon ride from cities like Petersburg and Richmond. And though Robert had been raised to respect propriety and order, though he knew his name was "Robert" and not "Bob" or anything less formal—he was Robert Boisseau Pamplin, yes sir!—still in many respects he remained a country boy. What Robert knew and loved were the woods and the fields and the pleasures a five-year-old could have there—a five-year-old and his dog. What he liked to carry was a string of fresh-caught Appomattox river shad, not a bag of schoolbooks.

Freckled and full of grins, with home-cropped blond hair, Robert had certainly looked like a country boy when his father had brought him to the schoolhouse that morning. And now as he sat in the roadside weeds tearing his first day's homework to pieces, he was clearly a boy who'd forgotten what his father had told him.

"Boy," Robert said again, as he ripped out a map page. "I was sure tired of carryin' these."

"Uh-huh," Dee agreed. "Was way too hot for sure."

All this, when little Robert's Papa had promised to "switch" the boy if he didn't take his schooling seriously.

Papa was John Robert Pamplin, a presence that loomed over the boy's life like one of the granite war memorials that dotted the scarred Virginia countryside. The father was a farm-hardened fifty-five that September of 1916—yet with a switching arm to be feared. Fifty-five, yet energetic enough for a wife thirteen years his junior. And not only was John Pamplin's wife a good deal younger; she also had the more imposing family tree. Little Robert's Mama was the former Pauline Beville, from one of the oldest and best-known clans in the Appomattox River Valley. Even preschool Robert had been made aware of such things. His cousin Dee was a Beville too, after all, and he lived in a farmhouse just across the road from the Pamplins'. Likewise, Robert was aware in his own boy's way that his solidly built, independent-minded Papa had kept wife and family cared for and satisfied since the turn of the century.

Robert had, all in all, the child's essential comfort of knowing he was loved. On top of that, he enjoyed the self-reliance of knowing a man could prevail despite hardships. Again, the idea was hardly something a five-year-old could put into words. But Robert could repeat, for instance, what he'd heard uncles and grandfathers tell him: that times weren't like they used to be in the South, and that a farmer had to be something special to do as well as his Papa had. Even Robert's assault on his schoolbooks, this afternoon, came out of that same self-reliance.

"What d'we need these for?" he'd asked his cousin. With that the two of them had set to work, tearing into their readers and arithmetic books.

But this morning—if only Robert had understood!—his Papa's piercing blue eyes had been even more resolute than usual. This morning, on the steps of the Sutherland School, the old man had been determined that his boy would know a better way of life than his own.

"This is my son," old John Robert had told Miss Clark, the school teacher. "If he's bad, you whip him. Send him home and I'll whip him again."

Robert had looked up into his father's face. The boy could rarely be sure of what emotion he found up there—the old man's handlebar mustache hid his lips too well. Sometimes the wrinkles at the corners of the eyes

would grow, and then Robert would know there was a smile inside somewhere. But not this morning.

J ohn Robert Pamplin was born the first year of what was still called, in
most Virginia households, "the War." By the time he had learned to talk,
among his first words were "Reb" and "Yankee." As a toddler he saw the
wagons hauling men in gray from the front: dead men and dying, in the
gray clothes that signified they were somehow his kin, Southerners. As a
little boy (holding his own father's hand just as, this morning, the five-year-
old Robert had held his) he'd heard the rumble of the horses and wagons
on the road north—the road to Appomattox Courthouse, where the Surrender had been signed. John Robert had started school in a country under
occupation, when the Bluejackets and their guns seemed to be everywhere.
He'd been able to stomach only a few sessions of the Northern propaganda
taught in those days.

And yet though the pre-teen farm boy quit school after only three
days, even then he'd had an inarticulate sense that school would sooner or
later be necessary. Education might not have worked for John Robert just
then, but it would have to work for someone in his family, sometime, if the
Pamplins were ever to get back the comforts they'd once known.

Not that the Pamplins had been rich before the War. Nearly every
generation had owned its own farm, however, which meant that most
Virginia Pamplins had owned slaves. Slaveholding had been, when all was
said and done, the root of the Dixie Armageddon. For John Robert's family,
as for all others in the South, the system had been a tragic necessity. Local
tobacco growers had hardly been the first to use slaves. The practice was as
old as Moses—as old as humanity itself. But once the system had been
established in Virginia and other nearby states their economy had come to
depend, ruinously, on this labor.

John Robert Pamplin, canny and realistic farmer that he was, could
understand all this without the benefit of schooling. The facts were all
around him, after all: not just the iron-littered battlefields, but the de-
crepit, collapsing former mansions. More's the pity, the Secessionist states
had been full of good souls who'd despised slaveholding. John Robert, like

every man in Virginia, knew that General Lee himself had spoken out against the practice more than once.

Nonetheless the War had ruined all, all. The Pamplins had not only

John Robert and Pauline Beville Pamplin at home in Dinwiddie County, Virginia, 1904.

lost farmland and a few slaves. They'd been driven from the very town that carried their name.

A small community along the road to Appomattox, Pamplin had been, before the War, the home of the family's clay pipe factory. Pamplins had a skill at clayware that went back centuries. Their roots were in Essex County, England, in towns like Thaxted and Widdington, just inland from the ancient Roman port of Colchester. The locals in that part of the Old Country had long excelled in domestic wares of all kinds, from cutlery to porcelain. The beginnings of this craftsmanship went back to Spanish immigrants who'd once favored this corner of England, bringing with them the best iron goods and skills in Europe. The Virginia Pamplins knew that their own line went back to an immigrant from Pamplona. And John Robert had heard, as well, that this original forefather had himself been the victim of racial injustice: he'd been hanged as a traitor in part because his looks didn't quite suit the local Norman overseer.

More recent forefathers had emigrated to colonial America. John Robert's family had been in this country almost as long as his wife's. But now Pamplin, the town, had almost no one left from Pamplin, the family; they were gone with the pipe factory that had sustained them. Union forces had torn up the railroads, blown up the bridges, made Southern industry impossible. Worse, the Piedmont land itself was devastated, worn out from so many seasons in the grip of a single crop. Land value crashed to four dollars per acre at the end of the War; it was little more than ten dollars on young Robert's first day of school.

The sons of the South found themselves doing slave work. John Robert grew to manhood working for fifty cents a day.

All in all, John Robert's deepest recollections from childhood were of humiliation and loss. On his farmhouse mantle he set a jar full of Minie balls, old square nails, arrowheads and other mementos of times past. *Vanity*, the old items in the jar seemed to say, after Ecclesiastes; *all is vanity. What profit has a man for his labor under the sun?* Yet out of this same abasement, in men like John Robert at least, was born a bitter determination to do better.

Little Robert Boisseau Pamplin had come to school with some notion of his father's background and commitment, on that September day in 1916. Robert, too, had heard of Billy Yank and Johnny Reb, of the artisan Pamplins and the estate-holding Bevilles. He'd dug up buried Minie balls himself, and bent them round his fishing lines as weights. His was a sprawling but close-knit clan, like more than a few others of these depressed Virginia generations. The Boisseaus, Bevilles, and Pamplins had of necessity learned to rely on each other, and in the process they'd swapped many an old family tale.

Yes, Robert had heard his share of these stories, and had made his share of promises to Papa. But he was only five. He couldn't remember everything, through the heat of the day and the droning of Miss Clark.

Not that the teacher wasn't doing her job. Early on, seeing the quiet attentiveness of the dozen other kids in the room, Robert had come to understand that the silver-haired Mamie Clark wasn't to be fooled with any more than his Papa. She had insisted on the name Miss Clark, and she hadn't allowed Robert to whisper with his cousin, either. The two five-year-olds had wound up spending most of their time staring out the window, lost in daydreams.

When the first graders were at last let out, Robert and Dee walked through the choking dust at the roadside: dust stung to white by the hard September sun, wherever it poked through the oak and maple that canopied the fence row.

Then the boy asked Dee, "What are we supposed to do with these books?" In another moment the damage was done. The two hunkered by the road, ripping their unwanted weight to shreds.

His load lightened, Robert Pamplin made the rest of the way easily. He approached his family home on Cox Road, a nearly new house built half a century after the War. It stood as a personal triumph of hard work over humiliation. The place was a fresh, glaring white, with bright green shutters. Two steep stories high, it had no less than four bedrooms up top, and a sitting parlor below.

Robert skipped blithely across the wide front porch. His mother gave him no reason to worry either—at first. She offered him a glass of milk; she asked what his day had been like. The little boy found the house cool, the drink refreshing, and his Mama's steady gaze soothing.

A thin-waisted woman with a gentle smile, her wide, clear brow crowned by auburn curls, Pauline Beville Pamplin looked every inch the offspring of Virginia nobility. Indeed, her nobility had been earned; she'd prevailed despite the collapse of the old Piedmont plantations. Like the great Beville forebears she'd grown up hearing about—extraordinary men and women, going back to the Crusades—Pauline had been forged by hardship into sterner stuff. Indeed, this fine new house on Cox Road was her doing, too. She ruled the parlor and the kitchen as her husband ruled the farmwork and the trips to market.

And Pauline's mother, had likewise proved her mettle in a trial by fire. The little boy had often heard how his grandmother Ella had braved one of the last great battles of the War, the Battle of Five Forks. He'd seen the house called Burnt Quarter, where the teenaged Ella had nursed wounded and dying Confederates; the walls were peppered with bullet holes.

Robert's own house was quiet, his milk soothing. But when he'd finished his drink, his Mama asked about his books.

"Where are they, Robert?"

The boy swallowed down a last mouthful of milk, then swallowed again, dry-throated. After that, wordless, he dropped his head, staring at his dusty bare feet. Pauline Beville Pamplin said nothing more, taking her middle boy's measure, arms akimbo.

Her older son John William—Robert's brother Bill—had been in school for three years now, working with this same Miss Clark. Bill had always made a great display of the books he'd brought home to study. He was studying right this minute, still at school with the other older kids. And Pauline and her husband had made it plain that the youngest, Claude Allen, would be going in another two years. As soon as baby Claude turned five, he too was getting an education!

All this came back to little Robert as well, as he stared down guiltily at his dirt-smeared toes. He recalled as well the promises made to him and his teacher both: *You whip him, and I'll whip him again.* Then no sooner had what was coming begun to dawn on the boy than he heard a clatter from the nearby barn. His father had returned from the fields.

Robert found himself checking the apple tree just visible out the kitchen window. His father used the apple's branches for switching; they were pliant yet strong. Indeed, the little boy started to wince at his father's heavy footfalls up the path to the house, each thud of those work-weary boots like a switch of a fresh-cut branch. When the screen door squeaked open, the boy began to tremble.

The aroma of a man's hard day in the fields overpowered even the brunswick stew simmering on the stove. Thick-chested, wide-faced, broad-handed, John Robert Pamplin filled the kitchen. Little Robert, hoping against hope, watched his parents make eye contact, and he caught the least hint of a shared smile, giving him a moment's relief. But then his father's stare hardened, and focused on him.

"Where are your schoolbooks, son?"

In a moment, Robert had torn up the books. Now, in another moment, he was out under the apple tree taking his punishment with as little crying and carrying-on as he could manage. Once the boy had realized what he'd gotten into, he'd understood that there was nothing to do but look his Papa in the eye and confess. Then once again Papa's look had shown him that hint of something better, sympathy or respect, but the man had hauled him out of the kitchen and torn off the branch with bare hands, hands not yet washed for dinner. After the usual ten strokes Robert's father tossed aside the switch, allowing his son a few moments to collect himself. Then the man walked the boy back into their home.

Old John Robert Pamplin never let a broken rule go unpunished. Over the years, that family apple tree lost nearly all its lower branches, as Papa took his boys out for switching time and again. Little Robert endured his share. However, it was younger brother Claude who received more than Bill and Robert combined, since he was the roughhouse and the risk taker among the three.

But over the years Robert, Bill, and Claude also saw, more than once, that their taskmaster father had good reason to make sure they grew up tough. One unforgettable example—one proof that a Virginia boy needed to be strong—came when the middle brother was eleven.

It came on a late-summer day, after the boy's morning chores were through. Robert had crossed the rutted dirt of Cox Road and fallen into some game or other at his cousin Dee's. The two rarely missed a chance for fun, one of the greatest advantages of growing up in the large extended families of the Piedmont. Dee's father was Frank Beville, brother to Robert's Mama, and Robert's playmate was the fourth of ten children. Between the two houses, they could field a baseball team.

But on this day in summertime, there was no chance for ball. Robert had hardly reached his cousin's yard when the wide farm skies were suddenly obscured by clouds—and not just any clouds. These were heaping, clustering clouds, as dangerous as fists, clouds with knuckles in them. Sunlight first turned to ribbony streaks, then to an ominous, discomforting amber.

Robert had seen storms before; his Appomattox homeland was only a hundred miles from the Atlantic, after all. But he'd never seen one like this. Winds started the poplar leaves rattling, then, all at once, started to rock the trees themselves. The boy had barely made sense of the first heavy splots of rain in the dust (manure-dark, silver-dollar-sized), when the downpour turned to solid sheets, made more solid still by pockets of hail.

Across the road, barely visible through the explosion of weather, Robert's mother pulled the green storm shutters over the windows. Farther off, his father was trying to handle their mule, Daisy. The man had hold of the animal's bridle, and struggled to haul it into the barn.

The noise kept getting worse, a train bearing ever closer. Robert's father was caught out in front of that train, like some horrible scene in a nickelodeon, and now the rain and hail were a curtain closing on the screen. Lightning flashed, turning the Pamplin's rooftop rods briefly golden, splitting one of the trees in the yard. Once again Robert caught a glimpse of his Papa. The mule had been abandoned; the big man lay in the furrowed muck, clinging to his heavy plow.

The boy, spying his Papa bent against the rain, couldn't help thinking of himself, bent to take his switches. This storm, this entire unpredictable world gave worse punishment, far worse, than anything his father meted out.

And hardly had Robert put together this thought when, as quickly as the storm had hit, it now began to ease off. Virginia storms were like that, a tail or finger of weather, rather than an entire two- or three-day blow like they got down in Florida. The hail lifted; the sheets of rain grew more and more diaphanous. Robert took off from his cousin's porch. He tore across the muddy road towards his father. The way had never felt so long, a good 150 yards from the edge of one plowed field to the edge of the other.

The big plowman was hauling himself to his feet: drenched, mucky, shaking.

"Papa?" Robert ventured. "Papa, you all right?"

His mother joined them, her apron flapping in the wind, breathless from her run.

"Bob," Pauline gasped, "Bob!"

Then the man wetly embraced wife and son. His touch felt new to the boy, at once cold and warm, shivering and powerful. The three stood like that for a long moment. The rain continued to ease off, becoming little more than a drizzle, and off in the east emerged the beginnings of a rainbow. Then Robert's father returned to himself, breaking off the embrace. He saw his home still standing, and the path of devastation through the apple orchard, where every tree for fifty yards was flattened.

"That," the man said, "must have been a tornado."

These were times when a man had to keep hold of whatever was solid, reliable, and firmly in place. Little Robert and his brothers knew few frills growing up. In summer they went barefoot every day, and when they stubbed their toes or cut their soles, their mother merely washed and wrapped the wounds. If a boy's shoes should wear through, as happened from time to time, the father would take a piece of leather, soak it, cut a half sole, and nail it in place.

Such a repair job was good enough for church and school, the only occasions when shoes were needed. Everyone of course dressed up for Sunday, each boy in the one suit he owned. Robert's mother insisted on that, and kept up the suits as needed. For school the three brothers had corduroys and white shirts. Otherwise, it was overalls every day.

Yet young Robert had never known better, after all. Most of the time his day felt like no great hardship. The chores varied with the seasons, sometimes dirty and full of aches, other times sunstruck and stinking of perspiration. But even farmwork nearly always allowed him a few hours for ball with his relatives, or for hunting with his dogs.

Despite his love of whacking a baseball or playing Johnny Reb, Robert had always been in other ways a very sensitive boy. After dinner, whenever his mother told tales out of the family's history, her stories often left him disturbed, his full stomach churning. For instance when Pauline told him proudly of the ancient grandmother who'd endured the Black Plague, back in England, the thought of so much ugly death gave Robert nightmares.

But the most upsetting time—the most profound learning experience—came on a day when Robert's father took him into nearby Petersburg to deliver a calf to the slaughterhouse. They generally sold livestock to the Jackson brothers, who butchered the animals in the mornings and by afternoon could offer the meat as veal. The Pamplins took home some of this veal as part of the transaction. It was an important moment in a farmer's year, one of the days when he worked out what his family would have to eat. To young Robert, his coming was always a thrill and a challenge; Papa was always seeing just how grown-up his boy could be. And part of what made the trip interesting was that, though most of the Jackson brothers' customers were white, these butchers were Negro. Indeed, in the Jacksons' neighborhood of Petersburg, there were a number of such successful Negro business people.

John Robert took his middle son to the Dinwiddie County Court-house. On the ride over he explained why. The father wanted Robert to see the way things were done, he explained, or at least to see where they were done: the imposing courthouse with its Greek-style pre-war portico.

When he was a boy, old John Robert explained after a moment, this same venerable, white-pillared edifice had been the site of a battle. In the early spring of 1865, the courthouse grounds had been filled with dead and wounded, the air thick with smoke. Here the brave Confederate Pickett, who had led the last doomed charge at Gettysburg, had driven off a regiment of Bluejackets under the war-loving George Armstrong Custer, who later fell victim to his own arrogance while fighting the Sioux out West.

"You mean we won this one, Papa?" Robert asked.

Slowly the old man nodded. "We whupped 'em good," he said. "Custer and that devil Sheridan—whupped 'em both."

Next the boy saw a memorial to the struggle, a twenty-four-foot granite monument topped by the figure of a Confederate at parade rest. And then, a minute or two later, came another reminder of what the War had been about—a more terrible reminder by far, and one Robert would never forget.

A Ford pickup stood parked next to the Courthouse, surrounded by a crowd of gawkers. Robert, curious, left his father to work his way through the bystanders. It didn't take him long; the people seemed almost eager to give way. On the truck bed, inside a rough wooden box, lay the corpse of a big Negro man. His eyes remained open, lifelessly studying the sky, and a swollen purple-black tongue hung out of his mouth. His face was a color the boy had never seen. But his neck was scraped raw in a way Robert recognized. He knew rope bums when he saw them.

"This here's a piece of the rope we lynched him with," boasted a man by the truck.

One boot on the truck's running board, the man must have been a leader of the lynch mob. He kept waving the frayed length. "See it, son?" he asked Robert. "See what we used on him?"

Robert noticed then that others in the crowd also had pieces of the rope.

"This nigger," the man went on, "he went to the store down the road and robbed and killed the owner, which was a *white* man. This one wasn't one of our own. Came from out of town. None of us ever saw him before."

Robert's hands had closed over his stomach. His mouth had turned to flannel, and he couldn't swallow.

"We stretched his black neck good for him," the man with the rope crowed. "We didn't need any trial."

A s for the officials in Dinwiddie's proud county courthouse, they seemed to think justice had been served. Robert got the story as he rode back home beside John Robert; in the old man's tone, the boy could hear how his father cared for him. Once more, he was making sure his son got the facts, the way the world worked.

But as Robert listened, on the road back from the courthouse, his stomach kept roiling, viciously. His head felt saturated still with the vision of the recently dead. Just seeing a dead man was unusual enough, upsetting enough, for a sensitive boy like him. But a *murdered* man, hanged without fair trial, hanged maybe for his color alone—that left Robert devastated as never before. Over the coming nights he was assaulted by his worst dreams yet, and over the coming days and weeks he couldn't stop thinking about what he'd seen.

To young Robert Pamplin, Negroes were friends, teammates, neighbors. His farm was bordered on two sides by Negro landholders. Indeed, about half the local countryside belonged to former slaves and their children. One of them, Johnny Harris, had bought thirty-five acres from Robert's Papa, and Papa had trusted the man enough to take his note for the property. Robert and his brothers had played with Harris' sons many times, swimming in the same swimming hole, fishing the same creeks.

On the other side of the Pamplins lived the Parhams, another colored family. John, the oldest Parham son, worked beside Robert, Bill, and Claude in the Pamplin fields. Robert's Papa had an arrangement with John's—the boy would work the Pamplin farm, and Papa would pay his wages directly to Mr. Parham. Some years older than the Pamplin boys, John Parham was a deep, handsome brown, easy-bodied and quick to laugh, forever bringing a smile to the faces of the hard-driving Pamplin boys. He'd been living in the old Pamplin house, the one they'd moved out of before Robert had started school, and he generally ate his meals in the new Pamplin house. Like the Harris boys, John too played with Bill, Claude, and Robert, enjoying the same swimming hole.

Swimming, in fact, was the only activity that little Robert had ever been told *not* to share with his Negro "big brother" John. This happened after Papa had driven young Parham into Petersburg for a day. Young Robert didn't entirely understand what had happened there, yet; all his father would say was that the teenaged John had gone to "the wrong sort of house," in town. At this "house," somehow, he'd caught a disease. And though Robert still didn't know just what kind of a disease this was, he knew better than to argue when his father ordered him and his brothers not to swim too close to their easy-laughing co-worker.

"You swim upstream from him," Papa had insisted.

But other than that, young Robert couldn't remember any segregation in his upbringing. Aunt Cora Parham, the mother of the family, had been Robert's "black mother." When Robert had been born, she'd come to the Pamplin home for about a week to care for him while Pauline regained her strength. In the years since then, Robert's parents had pointed out many times that Aunt Cora was his "black mother," and she had to be treated with the same respect as Pauline Beville Pamplin herself. Likewise the Pamplin boys were raised to call older Negro women "Aunt," older men "Uncle"; if their parents ever heard them do otherwise, the switching tree was the next stop.

One of Robert's favorite "uncles" was Uncle Moses, the freed slave who had built their house. Uncle Moses was the best carpenter the boy knew; he planed rough wood he got cheaply or for free, making it suitable for even the finest homes in the county. Locals had been so impressed with the job Uncle Moses had done for the Pamplins that a nearby family, the Leonards, had him put up one for them exactly like it. And Uncle Moses later built Olger's Store, about a half-mile up Cox Road, a favorite place for country people to gather and talk.

All in all, what Robert had seen by the Dinwiddie Courthouse simply did not fit. For a long time—the rest of his life, really—he would wrestle with the image of that murdered black man.

B ut there's other trouble besides troubled sleep. Not long after his shock at Dinwiddie Courthouse, on an afternoon that began with a baseball game beside his little schoolhouse, young Robert found himself crushed against the ground and unable to walk.

He was backing up home plate, trying to catch a long throw from the outfield. At the same moment the school's two teachers, Miss Suitor and Miss Webb, were nosing their Model T into the yard. They didn't see Robert racing into position, bracing himself against his outstretched left leg. The Model T went over him, over the leg, shattering the bone. Robert collapsed, yelping, and twitching; the two teachers tumbled out of the car and screamed for help.

"Here comes a drummer!" cried Miss Webb. " Stop him!" The traveling salesman pulled over by the schoolyard. A few minutes later he had the injured boy on his lap, while Miss Webb drove the Model T to the Pamplins'.

"Oh, dear God!" Miss Webb cried, as she and the salesman carried Robert toward the front porch. The boy's broken leg hung at an impossible angle. The femur—the ragged bone end of a compound fracture—had ripped through the muscle, and Robert's skin and pants bulged unnaturally.

Pauline and John Robert came running, then drew up in shock. Their boy lay on the porch with his leg at the angle of a broken doll's.

Robert was rushed to Petersburg hospital. His leg was forced into a splint, and then for an agonizing two weeks Robert lay helpless in a hospital bed, waiting to see if the device would do the job. No: when the doctor unwrapped the bandages, blood spurted from the broken leg anew. The wound erupted with such blindingly painful force that the blood hit the ceiling. Robert ended up spending another six weeks in a cast—and it was only after the cast came off that the family and their doctor discovered that the boy's knee had also been injured. Walking had become a stiff, bitter, halting process, and only very slowly did the muscles of Robert's leg adapt and grow strong again. By the time the boy was through with hospitals, casts, and learning once more how to walk, he had missed an entire year of school.

The father did what he could to make the trying process easier. Most of all, he got the larger family involved. Aunts, uncles, and cousins took part in the boy's slow recovery. The county-wide support of family and friends came in handy, too, when the father asked Miss Webb to pay half Robert's $100 medical expenses. Miss Webb had been the driver at the time of the accident, and paying half the cost was the least she could have expected. Papa Pamplin told the woman that if she refused, he would have to take it up with the school board. Fifty dollars was a lot of money in the 1920's, but Miss Webb wasn't going to anger the whole family.

Young Robert, meanwhile, would settle wincing into a chair at the family get-togethers. Listening, piecing together the stories, he began to get a sense of the world beyond his home county. Over in Europe a war against the Kaiser and his Austrian allies had recently ended. "The war to end all wars," the struggle had been called, but most of Robert's older relations rolled their eyes at this idea. They spoke of earlier conflicts in which the family had taken part, not just the Civil War but a number that had taken place much longer ago as well. All those wars too had promised a new and better world. The boy heard also about his Crusader ancestor, Sir Robert Lawrence. Another athletic youngster with a leg injury, Sir Robert Lawrence hadn't let his bad luck keep him from becoming a hero.

The young Virginian's clan was skeptical, as well, of the many new inventions of the dawning "Jazz Age." The gramophone brought music from far away, nickelodeons were luring people to the cities, and some people were actually going up in airplanes. There were so many good things to be had that many people gave up saving and took up spending. All round the South—all round the country, Robert heard—people were saving less and less of what they earned. But John Robert Pamplin and most of his relatives weren't so eager to invest their hard-won income on these city-folk diversions.

"I don't need electricity," John Robert announced to the gathered kin around the dinner table. "These kerosene lamps have always been good enough, and this old ice box keeps food just as well as an electric refrigerator."

Another time, Robert's Papa let him know that, broken leg or no, he wasn't going to pamper his boys with any newfangled heat or plumbing. "If it gets too cold," he said, "we can just throw another piece of wood in the stove like we've always done. And y'all can use the outhouse same as me and my old Papa before me."

Robert's father kept the Pamplin farm going with a single horse and a single mule; all his equipment together wasn't worth more than $2000.

Of course he and his sons knew, as the twenties went on, that most farmers were modernizing. Tractors, especially, had begun to make their smoking, gear-grinding mark on the nation's agriculture. By the end of the decade, successful farms tended to be much more productive. There were fewer and fewer of them, but they were feeding more and more of the population at large. Meanwhile, a lot of the sons and daughters of long-time tobacco- or corn-growing families were moving to town. All in all, by his late teens Robert had come to see that, in this day and age, a successful farmer had to be a sound businessman.

B ut while Robert's Papa didn't have the new equipment of the modern farmer, he didn't have the debt, either. In that sense—that crucial sense—the man proved himself a better businessman than many of the more high-rolling types around him. For when the national economy crashed at the end of the twenties, more than a few rural Virginia properties were lost, their mortgages foreclosed. These farmers couldn't pay for their new tractors. But those without debt worked their way through the crash, and through the Depression that followed.

Indeed, there was only one new device John Robert Pamplin was willing to pay for. A reliable automobile was essential transportation, a tool to make him more competitive. More than that, Papa had been fascinated with moving machines since he was a boy. Often he regaled his family with the story of his first experience with trains. The young John Robert had never seen a train before he and his brother Ethan had hauled some wheat to a mill in Lunenburg County. There John Robert had taken a dare and climbed a steep hill near the tracks to wait for a train. His teenage eyes had grown big when he'd seen the belching black smoke coming through the forest. He hadn't been able to believe his ears when he heard the chugging locomotive. Finally, when the train had been directly beneath him, so close that he could smell the coal smoke, the whistle blasted.

"I ran down that hill so fast," Papa Pamplin finished the story, "you could have played marbles on my shirt tail."

Yes, electricity, indoor plumbing and central heating were luxuries John Robert could live without, but a car was a necessary investment and (though the old man would never admit it to his sons) a point of fascination for him. Early in the twenties the Pamplins bought a new Model T. It was of course the family vehicle, ferrying everyone to Ocran Methodist Church up what used to be Cox Road but now appears on the maps as U.S. Highway 460. More than that, the Model T became their farm carryall, hauling produce to market every Wednesday and Saturday during the school year, and every day but Sunday during summer.

The car also gave the old man an extra zest, bringing out his playful streak. Once, when a policeman in Petersburg told John Robert he couldn't park at a fireplug, Papa simply smiled and said: "I've already done it!"

And naturally, John Robert made sure that his three sons knew how to use the "tin lizzy." Young Robert got his first turn to drive one Sunday when he was ten. Like his older brother before him, Robert was to take the family to Ocran Methodist. Robert exchanged a grin with his younger brother Claude as he took the driver's seat. He slid up in his seat so his feet could reach the pedals, then pushed the forward one and pulled down on the spark advance as he'd been taught, and sure enough the Model T began loudly but steadily to chug away from the farmhouse, grinding along at the majestic pace of fifteen miles an hour. His brothers jiggled and hooted in the back seat; John Parham rushed from the old house and leapt onto the running board for a quick grinning ride.

Robert was so short he had to peer under the top of the steering wheel to see the way ahead. But he had no trouble seeing his father at his side, no trouble seeing those widening wrinkles at the corner of the old man's eyes, the unmistakable evidence of a proud smile.

The road wandered through fields of green cornstalks stretching sun-ward, past tobacco plants that spread their clown-like leaves wide. Like nearly every other road in Dinwiddie County, this one was nothing but dirt and gravel. As always, ridges caught the tires of the Model T. But Robert's grip on the steering wheel wasn't as good as his father's, of course, and the car twisted out of control.

"Watch out!" his Papa shouted. The old man grabbed the wheel, but too late to stop the car from lurching over the road's embankment and into a cornfield. There Robert was at last able to brake the rattling, black, shoebox-shaped vehicle, amid a few broken green stalks.

Humiliated, doing his best to ignore his brothers' smothered giggling in the back, the ten-year-old forced himself to meet his father's glare. "Are you gonna whip me?"

The old man heaved a heavy sigh, plainly disappointed. But his glare softened.

"You did your best," Robert's Papa answered at last. "You learned something from this experience, I expect, and no one's hurt. But get on out, now, and help me and your brothers push this thing back into the road."

By the time Robert was twelve, he was counted on as a contributing family member. To the Pamplins, this meant doing chores. Some of his friends got new clothing in the fall, for going to school. But for Robert the time for new clothes was when school was over, at the beginning of summer. Then he always got new bib overalls and a new straw hat, the clothes a boy would need working in the fields.

The muggy, still days were the ones Robert hated most. Out of 200 acres of property, the family farmed thirty, and on those oppressive days their entire rippling cropland steamed, its underground nutrients sending up pungent vapors. The sweat dripped off Robert's nose onto the rows of cantaloupes, watermelons, corn, butter beans, tomatoes, and other family produce. Everyone had freckles from the sun—freckles, just for starters. Sooner or later he usually ended up sunburned, blistering and peeling.

In the growing season the Pamplins rose before the sun, had a big, sustaining breakfast of biscuits and strawberry jam, eggs, and pork, and then headed out to the fields for the next several hours. Day after day from the time he was eight, Robert worked the land until sundown, alongside his brothers and father and the strapping young Negro John Parham. Like most Virginians, old John Robert recognized that sometimes it was just too hot to pull weeds or pick tobacco suckers, and on those days the five of them would nap from noon until two in the afternoon. But during most of the season, everyone put in a ten-hour work day. And during the school year, young Robert worked an hour before class and two hours afterward. At harvest season, he sometimes went longer. "Work till the job is done"— that was his parents' guiding rule. "A thing that should be done now," Pauline and John Robert would say, "is done now."

Never once did his father or anyone else suggest that this kind of struggling in the dirt was beneath them. Just the opposite, the Pamplins believed that the work was honest, honorable, and forged their character as a family.

Robert worked the rich brown Virginia soil with a plow, a hoe, and his own hands. There were no pesticides; insects were plucked by hand and squashed between fingers. There were no permanent cattle ranges; Robert drove the cows out to pasture in the morning and brought them back to the barn after school. He fed the pigs morning and evening. He brought in wood for the stove and helped churn the milk to make buttermilk and butter.

The boy's favorite crop was butter beans. He loved to stake them in place, and then to watch the vines wind their way up those stakes, eventually so thick they were like a hedge. He used only the best seeds, the most richly prolific. At harvest, twice a week and sometimes till late at night, the whole family gathered by kerosene lamplight to shell those beans for market.

Vegetables were, all in all, the outstanding example of "work that should be done now." The farmer who brought the freshest beans to market had the most customers; the farmer who tried to pass off old produce could hardly make a sale. So the Pamplins picked cantaloupes and watermelons the day they went to market. They didn't keep eggs beyond two or three days.

Robert likewise learned to plow corn rows with a craftsman's precision. He held the plow very near the plants, pushing the weeds away while at the same time not damaging the corn. In time the boy realized his skill at this must be something special, because he heard his father boast about it. "My Robert," Papa would say, "plows corn better than anyone I've seen." Compliments like that were rare from the old man; nothing so filled his son with pride.

Robert came to know his land's cycles with an intimacy and sureness that few youngsters ever enjoy. He prepared the soil, planted, weeded, nursed the crop to maturity. Then he took part in the harvest, and in the subsequent hearty dinners or the trips to market. And the boy was just as involved with animals. He watched pigs have their piglets. He fed them, saw them grow from the size of his palm to 300 pounds and more. He helped slaughter them, too, and of course took pleasure in the pork chops and the profits that followed. With chickens and cows it was the same, except these included the additional bonuses of eggs and milk.

He shucked corn and shelled butter beans by hand. He fed cornstalks to the cows and shoveled their manure into a wagon and hauled it to the fields. He fed the hogs that were kept in pens, and he got to clean up after them, too. Chickens wandered at will around the yard. It was a style of living that could have existed a hundred years earlier—or a thousand.

After season upon season of this sharing in the cycle of nurturing and harvest, Robert developed a special sense of what it meant to be maturing physically himself. He came to see himself as in that cycle: in the community of those whose life is meant to be of use. At the same time, he had rare dual roles in that community, as both a witness and an enabler. Certainly he watched the things under his care come to fruition, but more than that, he had a calling to shape, to make, to create. He saw his parents grow older, and inwardly acknowledged that their time in the world was limited, but more than that, knowing what it meant to help something grow, he understood how much his parents had been helping him find his own place and direction. One day they would be gone, and then the care they'd given him would exist only within himself At that point, it would be his turn to provide that same guidance and support for others.

Yes, hot as the work sometimes was, sweat-soaked and grubby as it sometimes left him, the farm labor nonetheless inspired young Robert. Even after he'd begun to pick up some of the stories of his forebears, after he'd heard that his people had once owned vassals who did this very sort of work for them, he himself never expected that his day-to-day experience would be anything other than demanding and dirty. And—whenever the Piedmont heat wasn't too much for him, at least—that life was the one he found most fulfilling. Indeed, there were times when he couldn't imagine a better life. There were times, as he hoed or picked or plowed, when the songs they sang in church would come to him:

> *Oh Lord my God, when I in awesome wonder*
> *Consider all the worlds thy hands have made,*
> *I see the stars, I hear the rolling thunder,*
> *Thy power throughout the universe displayed.*
> *Then sings my soul, my savior God to thee,*
> *How great thou art, how great thou art.*

N onetheless there was one part of the farming that Robert didn't much appreciate. This was tobacco, Virginia's original money plant, the "sot-weed" which had provided the area's essential economic base since colonial times. Tobacco could bring in as much as half a small farm's cash, and Papa himself liked his daily Apple brand. But the crop required such special attention, such mind-numbing work.

The family raised Bright tobacco, which was processed into cigarettes in Petersburg. These plants had to be started as early as possible in the spring, and yet they needed to be protected from the cold. They couldn't survive in open fields, so every year Pamplins had to clear some woods in order for the plants to have the protection of surrounding trees, and so that logs could be set around the seedbeds. They even put canvas over the enclosure.

Then as soon as the tobacco had grown large enough, Robert and his brothers and father carefully pulled them up and replanted them in the field. The boys had this replanting down to a routine, in which they formed a line and each had an assignment: make the hill, drop the tobacco slip, plant the slip. It was an agricultural assembly line, a sharing of the load based in plain common sense, and the system made an unforgettable impression on the middle boy.

But the tobacco cycle remained nothing short of backbreaking, nonetheless. The brother at the end had it worst, constantly stooping to plant. The rows were set four feet apart, the plants themselves spaced two and a half feet or so from each other—and then began the real work. The Pamplins had to hoe out around the plants regularly, and when the plants had reached the proper height, they had to break the tops off to keep them from going to seed. Besides that, two "suckers" grew from every point where a new leaf emerged from the stalk, as they do on tomato vines. These suckers sapped the vitality of the leaves themselves, and so Robert and his brothers had to pluck them almost every week. At the same time they had to go after the green tobacco worms, picking these pests off the leaves and snapping off their heads. In short the boys had to be out there week after week, every time gumming their hands and clothes with tobacco stains. Afterwards they had to wash their hands with gasoline.

Harvest time came when the leaves started turning yellow from the bottom. Then the father or someone else would lead a mule dragging a sleigh down the rows, while the boys, right behind, broke off the leaves that were ready to harvest. When the sleigh was full, they went into the tobacco barn, where three leaves at a time were tied to four-foot-long sticks (no more, no less) and hung to dry and cure. The curing took about three days and three nights, during which Robert and his brothers had to keep supplying wood for the barn's flue fires. Then the barn doors were left open and the now-golden leaves (they were pretty, at least, glowing in the shadows) were softened for carrying by a day or so of exposure to the air. And getting ready for market was a dirty, exhausting task as well. The leaves, still on their sticks, were steamed again to make them even more pliable, then separated by hand into grades, a measure of their quality, and then finally bundled by grade.

And on top of all that, the hard work of planting, caring, harvest, and preparation, the family faced a problem when it came time to sell. Robert often rode to Petersburg with his father and heard the auctioneer call on one buyer and then another, trying to drive up the price. But John Robert Pamplin's situation was hampered by more than market forces, because he had a contract with a co-op. This co-op alone handled his tobacco. And since the crop needed to age two to three years before it could be made into cigarettes, Robert's father got his sales price doled out to him in thirds, a portion every year for three years. The son couldn't recall a time when there hadn't been a delay collecting their money.

Finally there came a certain late-winter family dinner—a dinner at about the time the boys needed to start thinking of clearing forest land for this year's tobacco. After the meal was done old John Robert laid down his fork and made an announcement.

"I've signed a contract with that co-op to let them sell my tobacco for me," he declared, "but I didn't sign anything saying I had to grow it."

His three sons eyed the big man at the head of the table, hardly believing what they were hearing.

"I'm through with tobacco," John Robert announced. "Through!"

Not wanting to do anything to change their father's mind, the three boys held their tongues. But after the meal was over, once they were well out of earshot, the three brothers celebrated, whooping and clasping each other round the shoulders. That night Robert and his brothers promised each other that when they grew up, there would be no tobacco in their lives.

Still they'd never forgotten their hard labor: the demands of even a so-called "cash cow" like Virginia tobacco. Their father underscored the point again and again, for instance by his lack of sympathy for anyone who didn't seem willing to pull themselves up by their own bootstraps. Whenever a panhandler approached John Robert Pamplin for a handout, the old man would reply, "I'm working this side of the street, you work the other."

He told his boys, "If you give someone something for nothing they don't appreciate it a bit. They just want more."

Marcus Aurelius once wrote: Give a man a fish and he'll eat for a day, but teach a man to fish and he'll eat for a lifetime. The aphorism was the sort of thing you'd see stitched into framed samplers, on the parlor walls of old Virginia homes. Classic, stern, and yet humane, the statement seemed to express the view of Robert's father as well. For this same unsmiling farmer could also be enormously generous. By their teens, all three boys knew that he'd pay for their college expenses. And from time to time, there were setbacks for friends or neighbors who put in an honest day's work: suffering that came as an act of God, no fault of their own. At such times John Robert Pamplin was always swift to lend a hand.

At one sweaty summer dinner, as if to get everyone's mind off the heat, Pauline Beville Pamplin had fixed one of the family's favorite side dishes: tomatoes with mayonnaise, sugar, and vinegar. And as they ate, still trying to take them all away from there, the mother began to reminisce about the past. The boys found themselves leaning forward over neglected dinners, hearing how their grandmother Ella Boisseau, then hardly older than they, had aided the Rebels during the siege of Petersburg.

All in all Pauline Pamplin's gambit was working. She was distracting her menfolk from the heat, keeping them happy. But then, abruptly, the evening's spell was snapped. The mother broke off her story with a gasp, pointing out the dining room window. The others turned and at once saw what had frightened her, an orange smear on that hot night's blackness. There was a fire out there somewhere, and few things could ruin a farmer's livelihood more quickly or more permanently. No sooner had the father made it over to the window than he realized what had happened: it was the tobacco barn of the Wells, about a quarter mile up the road. Yet though

John Robert and the boys quickly joined more than fifty other neighbors in the glow of that barn, in the stench of uncured tobacco, there was nothing any of them could do to save the place.

So Robert's father had shown his workingman's generosity—the other side of his refusal to help a beggar. "You know I don't have much money," John Robert told his neighbor after the building was gone and the fire had been contained. "But if you want to rebuild, I'll help you in every way I can."

In a matter of hours, neighbors black and white converged on the Wells farm, and together they built the family a new barn.

Nor was raising a barn the only cooperative venture in young Robert's community. Slaughtering hogs also brought the neighborhood together. When the Pamplins or a neighbor wanted to kill hogs in the winter, the neighbors helped each other. One or two would quickly kill the animals by cutting their throats, while others propped at an angle a big barrel half full of water. This water was then heated with fire-warmed rocks and scraps of iron, dropped in sizzling and hissing. Then the men heaved the huge hog carcasses into the barrel, where the water softened the skin and bristles, enough for the farmers to scrub off the hair with ordinary stones. Then the hog could be hung up and later taken apart.

The group's effort provided Robert and his neighbors with chops, of course, and with ribs, bacon, and sausage. But they got a lot more from their shared slaughter besides. Yes, Virginia ham was one of the crowning glories of their farm system, cured in smokehouses like the ones in Surry County and then shipped throughout the world. But Virginia ham was only the beginning. Nothing was wasted. The pigs' fat became lard for cooking, the roasted rind cracklings for crackling bread, the large intestines chitterlings. Brains were eaten with eggs. Even the ears, snout and feet were put to use, often in recipes learned from the former slaves of the area. Generally these leavings were cooked thoroughly and then left to congeal. Sliced for frying, the result was almost as tasty as the ham.

Small wonder the Pamplins loved their pork. When a doctor advised the aging John Robert not to eat such rich meats, the father declared, "I'll eat what I want."

A s the years went by, Robert grew to appreciate the difference between the way his family lived and the way some others did. The Pamplins were by no means rich. They weren't the Candlers of Atlanta, who'd invented Coca Cola, or Buke Duke and R.J. Reynolds, both of whom had made a fortune in North Carolina tobacco. But their farm was well-kept, their house comfortable and, by local standards, still new. Their crops nearly always turned a profit.

The secret of his father's success, Robert began to see, was that he had a philosophy: modest yet strong, specific to his background yet pervading everything he did.

John Robert, for instance, preferred to grow only as much as he knew he could cultivate well. "Some farmers plant twice what they can look after," he said, "and then they don't look after anything." Corn, a usually reliable cash crop, was particularly tempting to a farmer without John Robert's restraint. Most planted their corn too thick, too close, and in a dry year such a crop would produce nothing. The price of corn would be double, those years, and the Pamplins would be very nearly the only ones with corn to sell. In a wet year, while they wouldn't enjoy such a monopoly on the market, they'd still make a profit.

Robert's father even had a favorite proverb to describe his philosophy. *The desire of the slothful kills him*, he would remind his boys, *for his hands refuse to labor.* Yes, if the family's working the land supported them physically, their Bible study supported them spiritually. The little country Methodist Church up Cox Road may have been so poor it couldn't afford a full-time pastor, but come the end of the work week there was always some recognition of the day consecrated to God, even if it was only a children's Sunday School. When the preacher was at work Robert knew enough to sit quietly through the sermon, and occasionally a line or two sank in. A lot of the time he spent daydreaming about the cannonball hole in the wall, another souvenir of the Five Forks battle. The Federals had used the church as a hospital.

Whenever he could, Robert slipped away to hunt for squirrel or rabbit among the loblolly pines and hardwoods that covered two-thirds of his home county. In that wilderness he often saw the transportable, steam-powered sawmills that turned trees into big slabs of lumber. Also he fished at a river branch near his home. It was for these trips that Robert scooped old lead Minie balls out of the fields around his home and pinched them round his fishing line for sinkers.

The family swimming hole was also nearby, shared with young friends. One blistering-hot July afternoon, Robert took a dip with his brother William. They swam and played for what felt, to judge from the ache in their arms and backs, like an entire summer's vacation in that single afternoon. Afterwards William said he'd start driving the cows back towards the barn. But Robert was exhausted. He went straight home and came in through the back door, unseen There he lay on his bed to rest—only for a moment, he thought. In no time however the wear and tear of the day and the early-evening breezes had put him to sleep.

When he awoke it was dark. Despite his foggy wondering at what time it was, he couldn't mistake the commotion in the yard. Something was wrong, some crowd had gathered. Rising, blinking, Robert looked out the window and saw a dozen or more of his relatives out on the lawn, most of them carrying lanterns. He scrambled downstairs to find out what was the matter.

"Look!" someone shouted as he struggled, bleary, into the yard. "There he is!"

"What. . . ?" But Robert barely got the question started before his father had him by the arm. Right there in front of friends and kinfolk, the old man hauled him away under the familiar apple tree. Robert was still wiping sleep-sand from his eyes, and his father was breaking off a fresh switch.

"No one knew where you were!" the big man said. "We thought you were lost! Robert, Robert. You've got to learn to think about other people, and I am going to teach you."

Yes, the youngster got his share of switchings; some summers the tree's lower branches looked naked. But that couldn't stop him from going out into the woods, preferably with his gun. Virginia had too many rabbits and squirrels for that. Every morning and every evening, when Robert took the cows out to pasture and when he drove them home, he had the perfect opportunity to get in a little hunting. Of course, there were times when hunting, too, caused him trouble. Once, when Robert was working the mule team, sitting on a mowing machine (his father's continuing profits had by then been reinvested in extra farm animals and machinery), a young rabbit ran out of the hay. Robert first tried to rein in the mules, but then took off after the rabbit. His running frightened the mules and caught old John Robert's attention—and then it was back to the apple tree.

Nor did the father approve of the time Robert came running home from school and, taking only a moment to drop off his books and pick up his shotgun, lit out after his dogs, which were pursuing a rabbit. The boy caught up with the rabbit. He took his kill to his Uncle Frank's country store across the road, a place that seemed to always have a few country people gathered round the rocking chairs on the porch. Inside, the walls had posters for chewing tobacco and beer, and there was an ice box from which a man could take what he wanted to drink and pay for it later. Neighbor dogs wagged their way up the steps, only to have the men on the porch shoo them back home: "Hey Jimmy, you get, now! Your master's a-lookin' for you."

On this afternoon Robert strode up to the store, in his straw hat and bib overalls, his rabbit hanging from his belt and his dogs romping behind him. His cousin Dee was among those sitting on the porch.

"What you grinnin' about?" Dee asked.

"I just shot this rabbit," Robert declared.

Dee was dutifully impressed. "Well," he said, "let's celebrate." He ducked into the store and brought out a can of sardines and some crackers. Then the two youngsters sat eating together, laughing and swapping stories with the men around them.

But when Robert got back to the house, his father wasn't laughing. "When I heard the gun go off and you didn't come home," John Robert said, "I figured you might have shot yourself." The boy was switched once more.

Then there was Robert's accident driving the school bus, which happened when the boy was fifteen. This "bus" was little more than an expanded Model T, and Robert took over the driving when he was entering the seventh grade (after a year as the only sixth grader back at his original school), considered high school at that time. On this afternoon, after taking other students home, the fifteen-year-old began showing off for his cousin Calvin. He started weaving back and forth across the road, he and his cousin laughing like crazy. Before long, creaking and jangling, the unwieldy old vehicle went out of control and fell over onto its side.

Robert and Calvin scrambled out and ran to the front to check the engine. Then suddenly Calvin was bellowing and hopping away, holding his bare foot. The radiator had leaked scalding water. But Calvin's injured foot was just the beginning of Robert's problems. The whole episode had been witnessed. A group quickly gathered and hoisted the Model T back up onto its wheels, but these same neighbors saw to it that word reached old John Robert even before his middle boy got home.

In those days, "whupping" was the norm when it came to disciplining an unruly child. But there was a significant additional element in the Southern boy's upbringing, namely, that a good father supports his son with the same fairmindedness as he uses when it's time take a switch to "the young'un." In Robert's teen years there was an instance, for example, when the father had to stand up to his neighbors on behalf of the boy.

In driving the children to school, Robert followed a regular route. He had to rove the countryside, stopping at a few homes that were off the beaten track, and his riders were always supposed to be waiting in front of their house. If the children weren't there, Robert would honk, and then the children would come running. But one morning he came to a house where the two kids he was picking up lollygagged on their way to the bus, dawdling over various roadside distractions.

Robert quickly reached the end of his patience. If getting to school wasn't important enough to these kids for them to hurry into the bus, it wasn't important enough for him to wait. He advanced the throttle and chugged away. Over his shoulder he glimpsed the children starting to run after him, taking him seriously at last, but he kept on anyway. From that house to the school was four miles, he knew, but it was time those kids were taught a lesson.

That night the children's parents showed up at the Pamplins, asking to talk with John Robert. Briefly, angrily, the children's father summarized what had happened that morning. Robert, listening in the other room, once again heard the unhappy word "whuppin'." This time, however, it was the other father saying it.

Robert's Papa, however, saw the incident the same way his son had.

"He did just what he should've done," John Robert declared. "If he waits for your children he'll have to wait for everyone. Then he won't get anyone to school on time."

The other father grumbled again, though more quietly.

"My boy can't give in to things like that," Robert's Papa insisted. "Why, then there'd be no discipline at all."

Though Robert was coming to understand the need for discipline at home and in his chores, when it came to school, he continued to feel far more lackadaisical. Not that he was a difficult case in the classroom. Indeed, from the first young Robert had been one of most reliable and easy-to-manage boys in the thirty-five-student Midway High School. Nonetheless, he frustrated his teachers.

"Your son could do so much better if he would try," his instructors would tell his parents, year after year.

But Robert remained a farm boy at heart. He didn't see much use for most of what was being taught in school—for English, especially, with all its love sonnets and long sentences and such. In that course and in too many others, Robert did just enough to get by. As soon as he could be sure of making seventy-five out of a hundred, he would quit working.

"If you pass, you pass," he'd say. "What's the sense in a higher score?"

He never finished a book or an assigned paper. Playing sports was more his style, and since Midway High was too small to afford a coach, the responsibility for setting up teams quickly fell to him. Robert was the one who put the teams together and, not surprisingly, was the one who served as captain of baseball and basketball. In baseball he usually pitched. Of course, as with his school work there were some things about sports that bored him. He didn't practice at all. But because he did so well at keeping athletics up and running, his classmates soon chose him as Student Body President as well.

So most of high school went by, with Robert giving time to what he liked and avoiding what he didn't. But as his senior year approached, the young man began to think long thoughts about college. His father, after all, had long since made it clear that he'd pay the cost, and now Robert realized that he in fact had a desire to go. Some part of him had always known that farming wasn't his entire existence. Good as his countrified childhood had been for him, strong and loving as it had made him, none-theless it wasn't in him to give everything he had to that way of life alone. And if Robert expected his demanding old Papa to take him seriously as a college boy, he had to improve his grades.

He did bring them up enough to make the honor roll. He managed this even though he still took no homework to the house. He had too many chores at home for that, and there were still no electric lights to read by. But he still didn't have the discipline to study things he considered "foolishness." Shakespeare's *Hamlet* gave Robert his worst experience in that regard—the experience that finally taught him.

His English teacher, Miss Evelyn Abrahams, wanted the class to memorize the "To be or not to be" soliloquy. To Robert, this seemed like the biggest waste of time in the world. "What good can that ol' speech do for me?" he asked his cousin, Carrie DeShazo. Scornful, bullheaded as always, he didn't even try.

But the teacher gave him an F for the month. And even before that failure, Robert had only been number six of twelve students in his class.

"I told you you'd get in trouble," cousin Carrie scolded him. "What's your Mama going to say?"

But—in one of those odd lucky breaks that can define a life—Miss Abrahams overheard this exchange. After class, she took Robert aside.

Miss Abrahams had always dedicated herself to her students extraordinarily, ever since she'd come to Midway in 1926. She taught not only English, but also French and Latin, public speaking and debate, and dramatics. She never married, in part because a married woman would have been asked immediately to resign. Southern school boards tended to believe that a woman with a husband belonged at home. Indeed, Miss Abrahams' own father had been a Baptist minister, the sort of man who ordinarily would have thought that girls shouldn't be educated beyond high school. But this woman had made up her mind that no matter what the other girls were doing, she was going to the Women's College at the University of Richmond. And now, in 1928, she saw a potential in the teenaged Robert Boisseau Pamplin that she refused to see go to waste.

After class, when Miss Abrahams took him aside, Robert waited with hanging head. He expected his teacher to scold him. Instead, her tone was gentle, encouraging.

"Robert," the woman said, "I believe in you. You may be as hardheaded as they come, but anyone who's seen you organize these kids and get them working for you has to admit that you're a young man who can get things done."

Robert raised his head, not sure what to think.

"You're a born leader," Miss Abrahams went on, "and people listen to you. That means that if you put your mind to it, young man, you can accomplish something with your life. That's if you put your mind to it. Now listen to me, Robert."

"Yes ma'am," said the boy.

"There's a forensics competition coming up. That's a debate, Robert; forensics means debating. The topic is whether judges and auditors should be elected or appointed." The woman paused soberly, then smiled. "I want you to take part in it," she said.

"Oh, Miss Abrahams," Robert protested. "I'm no good at just standing up and talkin'."

But the teacher insisted. "I will be with you to coach you and teach you everything you need to know. If you can compete and win in sports, Robert, you can do it in forensics. Or in anything else for that matter."

The boy's cousin Carrie, who till now had been standing off at arm's length, closed in eagerly.

"C'mon," she said, "do it! You don't want that F to be the only thing you bring home today!"

Robert eyed her, thinking.

"We'll be a team," Carrie went on. "We'll debate together. Come on, Robert."

The big teenager didn't have much choice in the matter, finally. He took the two women up on the offer. Over the next several days, practicing with them during study periods, he built up his confidence and his speaking skill, and shortly thereafter entered an entirely new field of competition. Before an audience of other students and parents, before a panel of judges, he applied himself to his arguments as he had never applied himself before to any activity that didn't include a ball. And just as Miss Abrahams had thought they would, he and his cousin Carrie won debate after debate. There are a hundred counties in Virginia, each with four or five high schools, and in that year's forensics tournament Robert Pamplin and his cousin came in second in the state. Miss Abrahams said later he was the best debater she had ever had.

As for the F on *Hamlet*, that never showed up on his report for the year. In 1929, Robert graduated from Midway High with honors.

Old John Robert and Pauline were proud of their son, and happy that he'd accomplished what they'd wanted for him all along. But their happiness had, as well, a taste of regret. Their boisterous but good-hearted

Robert was slipping away, with every passing milestone, and his graduation was only the latest. Already, the boy had begun dating. He and his brother Claude had taken girls into Petersburg. Often the boys went to movies; they liked cowboy movies.

O f course John Robert had set rules regarding those dates, just as he'd set rules for everything else. His boys were to be home by ten o'clock. There were nights, however, when ten came too early. Claude and Robert learned to speed up just before they reached the house, then cut the lights and motor and let the car coast past the house and into the garage.

Once they coasted in this way on a gorgeous August night, when the Milky Way streaked the sky like an up-flung spatter of whitewash. When the car was in the garage, the crickets and cicadas filled the night, punctuated only by the boys' own anxious breathing. They slipped off their shoes and crossed the creaking porch planks. Gently they closed the screen door behind them. Then they were at the top of the stairs, they were past Papa's bedroom, they were almost into their rooms . . . .

"Didn't I tell you ten o'clock!" boomed the voice from the half-open door of their parents' bedroom. John Robert was now sixty-seven years old, but the boys knew he could still switch them good in the morning. Indeed, though their father often went to bed by eight, and didn't always wake up when they came in, he still knew if they had been out too late. "I saw your tire tracks," he'd tell them. "You came in after the dew fell."

But despite this close watch he kept on his children, John Robert remained convinced that they had to go to college. College was the way off the farm, the way out of the hardscrabble life he'd striven all his life to rise above. Robert was encouraged to go to Virginia Polytechnic Institute and State University, over in Blacksburg. His mother and father reminded him again that they'd pay his way—his and all their sons'. In doing so, the Pamplins were reaping the benefit of all those years they'd lived frugally, saving money on heating and plumbing and the other newfangled developments that had seduced so many neighbors. They'd never lived lavishly, and never borrowed a dime. Playing the stock market may have been all right for some people, but John Robert didn't believe in anything he hadn't earned by the sweat of his brow. So, just about the time the market crashed in October, 1929, the father nonetheless had enough money to send his middle boy to college.

John Robert's oldest, William, had already graduated Virginia Tech by now, with a degree in engineering. William was still the most studious of the boys, five years ahead of Robert in schooling though only three years older. He'd finished high school at fifteen, college at nineteen. Robert, on the other hand, had been held back a year because of his broken leg. Now as Robert prepared to start college himself, it was William's encouragement that meant the most to him.

"Robert," William told him, "I know you can succeed at Virginia Tech. Believe me, I know."

The younger brother smiled, pausing over his half-packed bags. He needed these reassurances.

"But," William went on, "you'll never be the kind to study things that don't have a practical application. I'm that kind. I like scholarship for its own sake. But not you, Robert. You'd do best in something down to earth. Something like business."

Robert was well aware of his shortcomings. The entrance exams he'd taken placed him at the top in math, but at the bottom in English. Students from city high schools were clearly far ahead of him in academic skills. On top of that, Virginia Tech was perhaps the most demanding college in the state. A military school, it had a strict code of honor and a tough system of demerits. Anyone caught lying, stealing, or cheating would be quickly expelled. The same punishment awaited anyone caught failing to report another cadet for one of these offenses. Not surprisingly, then, Tech had a high rate of attrition. During one freshman assembly, the speaker said, "Look to your right and to your left. Those people won't be here for graduation."

Yet right away Robert liked being part of such an old and honorable establishment, such a big, committed team. He began going to activities at the YMCA, the Christian arm of the school, and began taking part in sports.

Life at Tech had rigors he'd never dreamed of back on the farm. As a freshman, Robert was a "Rat." Lowest in the pecking order, Rats were the errand boys of the school, quickly scurrying off to fulfill just about any whim that might cross an older cadet's mind. Not only did they have to maintain their own rooms impeccably, but they also had to take care of upperclassmen's.

One crisp autumn night, Robert heard the cry every freshman dreaded: "Rats down here!" It was from a big red-headed bully of a boy on the upper floor, and all freshmen in earshot had to drop whatever they were up to, run to his room, and do his bidding. This time he wanted a sandwich, and Robert had the honor of going to fetch him one.

Other times the freshmen had to play "Railroad": shoving a match stick across the floor with their noses. Every time the freshman crossed a crack, he was required to holler for "wood," the signal for an upperclassman to whack him on the backside with a broom. Then the hapless freshman would have to yell for "water," to be rewarded by an upperclassman dumping a bucketful over him.

Still, there were days when the hazing felt like a welcome break in the routine. The regular schedule at Tech was no small trial in itself. The drum corps blew reveille at 6:00 A.M., and cadets had to be dressed and in formation by 6:20. They stood at attention in neat rows, eyes focused forward, chins in, their shoes and hat bills buffed bright enough to reflect an officer's face, their company banners fluttering in crisp morning light.

"Owens?"

"Here, sir!"

"Palmer?"

"Here, sir!"

"Pamplin?"

"Here, sir!"

After formation, they were dismissed for breakfast. But cadets couldn't relax then either, the freshmen in particular. Young Robert had to march to breakfast, lunch, and dinner, and whenever he walked on the quadrangle, he had to walk "braced up," chin in and shoulders back. From eight in the morning until four in the afternoon, he had to be in his room or at classes. If he wanted to go to the library, or somewhere else on campus, he had to sign out as to where he was going on a card, mounted on the back of the door. When he returned he had to erase this off the card, and if he failed to do so after he returned to his room, he would receive two demerits. From 8 P.M. to 10 P.M. he had to be in his room. From 10 P.M. to 11 P.M. he turned his bed down; as a freshman, he had to do the same for the upperclassmen. All lights were out at 11 P.M.

Given the strictness of this system, then, a little hazing could seem like a relief. One day when Robert was a freshman, marching "braced" towards his room, a sophomore told him, "It looks like it's going to rain tonight."

Robert knew that comment had to do with more than the weather. The soph was doing him a favor, tipping him off that the upperclassmen were going to raid the Rats. Not much later, the door to Robert's room silently opened and four shadowy figures appeared. The "rain" came from buckets of water they dumped on him and his roommate. Robert immediately jumped out of bed and flipped his mattress over to keep it from soaking all the way through. He didn't want to sleep on bedsprings. Then he brought out his real blankets—the ones he had hidden out of harm's way.

Mattresses were a Rat's most vulnerable spot. When freshmen had class meetings, they sometimes came back to find their mattresses had been thrown out their windows. Upperclassmen also confiscated freshman mattresses a month before school ended—and burned them. Robert tried to soften his springs with layers of newspaper.

All in all, the young man found Virginia Tech the most arduous four years he ever spent. He came away with respect for anyone who made it through even the first couple of semesters. And, adapting to the schedule as well as to the distractions, he rose at last to the same level of intensity he'd enjoyed during the debating tournament under good old Miss Abrahams. By the time he was a sophomore he'd caught up with most of the rest of his class, and at the end of four years he graduated with honors.

And as he became more comfortable with academics, Robert also made room for sports, his first love. In fact, since the young man was still growing, he proved an even better competitor than before. In the Tech intramurals, thanks to a newly perfected curve ball, he pitched the Companies A & B baseball team to the championship. In one game he struck out the first nine men, in another he pitched a no-hitter. He also played on their championship volleyball team, and was named co-winner of the award for best all-around intramural athlete. Around the fieldhouses and playing fields of the college he was known as "Bull" Pamplin—a title enjoyed first by his older brother.

He also came away from the school with a new friend, one of the closest friends he'd ever have outside of his family. This was his long-time roommate, Julian Cheatham. The friendship proved in time to be another of those odd strokes of fate which can affect an entire life. For during the years at Tech, Julian's brother Owen often came to visit. Owen Cheatham was outgoing, witty, always an enjoyable visitor. Robert learned soon that he had started a small lumber company in Augusta, Georgia.

R obert graduated as a First Lieutenant in 1933, among the one-third of Tech's entrants to make it through all four years. He was assigned to a tank corps, but after attending Reserve Officers Training Camp two weeks one summer, he decided to resign his commission rather than be placed on inactive status. Bull Pamplin didn't want to be at the military's beck and call. These were the depths of the Great Depression, and he had to get on with making a living as quickly as possible.

Instead, on $650 borrowed from his still-generous father, Robert spent a year in business school at Northwestern University in Evanston, Illinois. He ignored several of the courses required for a Masters degree, but took those he felt would have the most practical application. In particular, he learned accounting. Immediately after putting in his time at Northwestern, he tested for a certificate as a Certified Public Accountant, and passed handily.

Evanston, however, was a cold place for a Piedmont boy, and Robert went back to Virginia. And it was there, interviewing for a position in Richmond, that he received a wire from Owen Cheatham—the good-natured brother of his Tech classmate Julian.

It was an offer for a job with Owen's company, Georgia Hardwood Lumber of Augusta. The city was 400 miles away, but as soon as the wire came Robert remembered what his father had told him: "A thing that should be done now is done now."

"I will be in your Augusta, Georgia office tomorrow morning at 9:00 A.M.," Robert telegraphed back.

He persuaded his younger brother Claude to drive him. All night the two young men pushed south, over roads paved and unpaved, and digging up change for the occasional toll bridge. Robert made Augusta in plenty of time, and even had time to freshen up a bit for his meeting.

He found his old friend's brother as charming as ever. Right away Owen and Robert re-established the camaraderie of Owen's visits to Virginia Tech. More than that, the company owner quickly understood that this young CPA's attention to detail and analytical ability would provide a very useful balance to his own talents in sales. Similarly, Robert could see that behind Owen Cheatham's informal, good-ol' boy manner there lurked a savvy and dedicated businessman.

The two men had similar backgrounds. The Cheathams too were rural Virginians, with many of the same values. Both believed there were more important things than success in business, but both also knew that success in business made such things possible. So Robert was hired, the fifth employee of a firm that then had a net worth of about $50,000. He wore the many hats typical of a new man at a small company: office manager, accountant, traffic cop, and postal clerk. Indeed, of all those tasks, opening and reading the mail turned out to be the most useful. In this way he got to know everything that was going on in the company.

Twenty-two years old, he began at a hundred dollars a month. This was hardly wealth, but it was enough for a healthy single man in the depressed America of 1934. His room in an Augusta boarding house cost only sixty dollars for the entire year. He found he could live on sixty-five a month, and right away set up monthly payments to old John Robert, reimbursing his father for the Northwestern expenses.

Nor was everything dollars and cents for young Robert. He was in a new city, beginning a new life. He even took on a new name—"Robert" became "Bob," a moniker more in keeping with his employer's easygoing ways. Of course, Bob continued reading the Bible. He kept up his prayers, and his respectful letters back to Dinwiddie County. Nonetheless, he was always aware of new horizons—on which there often stood a lovely Georgia woman or two.

Bob had a roommate, another economizing measure. This was E.A. Scott, Scottie to his friends. He worked in a bank, and though his take-home pay was less than Bob's, he'd bought a Plymouth. Bob preferred to invest his money in Georgia Hardwood stock rather than a car. Thus, gas for dates was his responsibility. And Scottie helped in another way, too; he paid attention to pretty girls who made deposits in the bank. Often he passed their names and addresses on to Bob, and soon the two were double-dating nearly every night.

Dating in the Depression consisted of going to a dance or a movie, then out for a Coke and a hot dog. The whole affair could cost as little as fifteen cents. And there were plenty of girls available, especially for a young man with a job that appeared secure. But some of the girls smoked or had unfamiliar, un-Virginian notions. Though dating was to a large extent a harmless diversion, the young man's practical nature nonetheless soon had him evaluating each woman as a potential marriage partner. That's why he was so pleased to meet Katherine Reese at a dance one night in 1936. He and Scottie had come without dates, to try their luck under the mirrored ball. And as that ball dappled the waltzing crowd with unexpected reflections, it made this young woman's smiling eyes sparkle. She was surrounded by young men who seemed to dote on her every laugh, her every word. But as she stood enjoying the attention, her right eyebrow often flicked upward—a sign that she didn't take these suitors and their flattery too much to heart. Even from across the hall, catching Robert's look, she seemed to pick up on his relative seriousness and restraint. And Robert understood it was time to shed the last vestiges of his country-boy shyness. If he were to stand a chance with this belle of the ball, he would have to act now. Boldly he crossed the floor.

"May I have this dance?" he asked.

That was the beginning. Katherine, for her part, enjoyed Bob's athletic coordination, as useful on the dance floor as on a ball field. She admired, too, his special gravity, the mature tone with which he spoke of job and family and home. And Bob, over the nights that followed, soon became convinced that she was head and shoulders better than any of the other girls he had dated. Katherine Reese didn't drink or smoke. A country girl from a Christian home, she shared his values.

Her family, Bob learned, worked a cotton and dairy farm of more than 200 acres, eight miles outside Augusta. His new sweetheart—for that's what she was, he soon realized—had grown up in a clapboard house not unlike his own, and now she shared a small Augusta home with her grandmother, Carrie Robinson. This grandmother had told her tales of her much-honored Kentucky forebear Thomas Flournoy, just as Bob's grandparents had passed on stories out of his own ancestry. Katherine respected a man with an education; she herself was attending a local junior college.

Bob felt comfortable around her. Katherine Reese, he came to believe, would understand why he had to work as hard as he did, and why his

Virginia people would always mean so much to him. And despite this deepening of his feelings, every night that he went out with her Bob also seemed to have the time of his life.

After graduating from Augusta College, Katherine wanted to go to Winthrop College in Rockhill, South Carolina, and get her degree in home economics.

But once Katherine got to Winthrop, the witty and sharp-eyed young woman found herself forced to wear a blue-and-white uniform. The place required written permission just to get off campus. "Bob, this is like prison," she once confided. "I hate this!" She was so unhappy, her health faded. Half the time she seemed to be sick, and it was almost as hard for her to graduate on schedule as it had been for Bob at Virginia Tech. Afterward she took a job teaching school in a small Southern town, a place at least a little closer to Bob in Augusta. She even established the school's home economics department.

Yet this remained a hard time for Bob. Katherine wasn't the only one Bob cared about whose health seemed to be collapsing. As the years passed, the young man grew more and more concerned about his father. Old John Robert, who'd never been sick a day in his life, contracted Bright's Disease, a kidney ailment, in 1936. He refused to follow the doctor's instructions and as a result his health deteriorated rapidly. When the phone rang on March 16, 1937, it was Bob's brother Bill who gave him the news.

Bob had known it would have to come one day—that even the mighty oak at the center of his life would one day have to fall.

He swallowed hard. "I . . . I'll be there," he said.

At home, Scottie said, "Take the Plymouth, Bob. I'm sorry, very sorry. Take the Plymouth." Once more Bob drove through the night, heading homeward.

Later the next day, without having had a moment's sleep, he went with the family to Morrison's Mortuary in Petersburg. He said his good-byes to the big figure in the coffin, a corpse still farm-hardened, strong enough to suggest that grief was only one of life's many cycles, and that a job well done included sorrow as well as reward. Indeed, the old man in the coffin silently prompted Bob to think about the family that remained. The place was of course full of mourners, most in black. Bob exchanged nods with his uncle Mervin DeShazo and his daughter Lelia. Uncle Mervin had married Pauline Pamplin's sister, who had passed away some years before, and now he was staying with Lelia. Uncle Mervin at least had his daughter to keep him company. Bob's mother would now live alone in the family's home, a place suddenly much too big for her.

A
s Bob made the sorrowful drive back to Augusta, he realized he would need to get back to Petersburg more often. His business experience had gotten him named executor of his father's estate; the older brother Bill's engineering skills weren't right for the job. So Bob was the one responsible, should his mother or brothers have any problems. Besides, now that he was dating Katherine steadily, he needed good transportation and he didn't feel right about continually borrowing Scottie's car. He needed one of his own.

A new car, yes: a yardstick to measure his new independence, to demonstrate that he understood how life's turning continues past grief.

He knew exactly the one he wanted. Bob walked by the Augusta Packard showroom on his way to work, and often had paused to gaze inside. He admired the rakish Phaetons and the big limousines with their spare tires mounted up front. The Packard had an upright grill topped by a gleaming chrome swan, and red hexagons on the hubcaps. In the mid-thirties these were the hallmarks of an up-and-coming executive. And in the showroom there was one exactly right for him, a gleaming blue 120 model. At $960, it was the lowest priced four-door available. But it was still a Packard, and Packard was the car to beat.

Bob bought his 120, and found pleasure in taking it around Georgia and the rest of the South. But he was never one to love a mere car. For him as for his father, quality was a matter of getting the most use for the money. Bob never became particularly attached to the things he owned, neither clothing nor tools nor even property. If a piece of land had some history attached, yes, that mattered to him. History mattered, because history meant people—people who were special to him. And most special to him now was Katherine Reese.

The courtship deepened after old John Robert's death. The greater independence brought on by Bob's new Packard was no small help, either. On June 15, 1940, in First Presbyterian Church in Augusta, the couple took their marriage vows. The Reeses had gone to First Presbyterian for many years now, and Bob made it a point to transfer his membership to the First Presbyterian Church. It was time, he had come to understand, for him to be thinking about his place in the world. His bride was twenty-two, he himself twenty-eight. His salary with Georgia Hardwood had increased to $300 a month. And an ocean away, in a matter of days, Nazi armies had overrun France. The "war to end all wars," it seemed, was about to be fought again. Bob's own small part in these vast dramas, he realized, was to be a conservative one; he was to confine himself to a single small practical step at a time. To begin with, he and Katherine would live with her family before they got their own apartment a few months later.

The wisdom of this approach was borne out only three months after the wedding, when Katherine called him unexpectedly at the office. Weeping, she told him her father had had a heart attack. He was dead before the day was out. In a few short years, both Bob and his wife had lost their fathers. With them, the young couple lost a way of life. Farming had been in Katherine's family for generations, as it had been in the Pamplins'. Her

Robert Pamplin, Sr. and Katherine Reese on their wedding day June 15, 1940.

father had actually come back to agriculture after a dual career in dentistry and pharmacy. But now the man was no longer there to care for the land. Robert, now the man of two houses, declared that the place had to be sold. Good as farming had been for him, for Katherine and him both, their fathers hadn't put them through college to see them picking cotton and milking cows. The whole point of young Bob's upbringing, like that of many a rural Southerner of his generation, had been to build the character of a farmer without suffering a farmer's harsh limits.

Katherine understood; her parents too had both honored the family farm and, at the same time, pointed out its shortcomings. The young Pamplins got in the cotton crop as best they could themselves, using the help still living on the Reese place. Then Bob leased the land to another farmer and auctioned off the livestock and equipment.

Eventually they traded the acreage for something closer to Augusta. Later still, as the Second World War swept up the U. S. as well, Katherine's mother bought a house in town. The daughter and son-in-law rented an apartment in town as well. Farms had passed away but family had remained, closer now than ever. And Bob Pamplin—offspring of a man so durable he might be called Virginia hardwood—was free to concentrate on Georgia Hardwood.

CHAPTER 10

Robert Pamplin, Senior
Family Life

B OB PASSED THE BOOK to Katherine. "It's your turn to read, dear," he said.

From the earliest days of their marriage, this was how they'd gone to sleep—lying in bed and reading passages from Scripture to one another. Bob and his wife might choose from anywhere in the book, but Bob usually preferred Proverbs. Proverbs was the good stuff, the practical stuff. The very brevity of the verses, like pithy utterances from the wise, appealed to Bob. Pith and practicality came in especially handy over at Georgia Hardwood, where his responsibilities were growing.

Katherine already knew some of Bob's favorites. Tonight she opened to a familiar page: "Humility and the fear of the Lord bring wealth and honor and life," she read. And the young wife met his gaze, smiling. Katherine was learning already the truth in that Proverb. Her husband was a man who took his spiritual life seriously, and it seemed the more he did so, the more the family prospered.

Bob had decided to accept the Biblical responsibility to tithe, that is, to give ten percent of what he made to church and charity. He didn't give to get anything in return, but he kept getting back anyway, in income and in other gifts.

"The king's heart is in the hand of the Lord; he directs it like a watercourse wherever he pleases," she read on tonight. "Now you, Bob," she added after a pause, "you're not a king." Once more she smiled. "But it does seem the Lord is directing your heart sometimes."

Bob nodded, chuckling. "Yes," he said. "Like when he directed my heart to you."

She joined him in laughter, putting away the book as he turned out the light. For most Americans the close of 1941 was a sober, even tragic time. The country's involvement in the current World War loomed ever closer, with increasing anti-U.S. belligerence from both the Nazis in

Europe and the Japanese across the Pacific. But for Bob and Katherine Pamplin these months were full of gladness. A year and a half after they'd married, they became parents. Family members on both sides shared in the excitement, Bob's two Virginia brothers in particular, for the child was another boy, and another Bob.

Mrs. Reese, the former Kate Coffin Robinson, loved the idea of being a grandmother, undeniably. She'd had two children, two daughters, but one had died as an infant. Bob's wife had grown up an only child. But the mother, on the other hand, had shared a house with a sister and four brothers. Mrs. Reese enjoyed the notion of her bloodline continuing, and of having children around.

So on September 3, when the twenty-three-year-old Katherine Pamplin felt the first contractions, Mrs. Reese suggested they make a phone call to "Grannie Robinson." This Grannie was of course her own mother, the new baby's great-grandmother. The old Augusta matron had given birth to twice as many healthy youngsters as her daughter Kate Coffin; she seemed like the most sensible person to call. Soon Bob got a call at work. On his way to the hospital, he picked up Grannie. Even as he pulled up in his dark Packard, the petite widow was emerging from her home. She wore her gray hair topped with a pillbox hat, standard headgear for a Southern matron. And in her case that hat was black, as was her dress; she'd worn nothing but black since her husband had died in 1934. Her manner, however, was considerably brighter, talkative and reassuring.

"Don't you worry about a thing," Grannie Robinson told Bob. "Everything's under control."

"I'm not worried," he said.

The woman smiled, letting that one pass.

But then, Bob Pamplin was one waiting-room Dad who hardly had time to be worried. Katherine's labor lasted just two and a half hours. Finally, the white-smocked doctor emerged from the delivery room. It was a boy, he announced, and mother and child were both doing fine—and after that things went on behind a fog for several long moments, as Bob and his womenfolk were ushered through to the nursery. The new father couldn't be sure what he was hearing, what he was seeing. He was amazed at that tiny life on the other side of the nursery windows, at once innocent and wizened. Like all newborns this one had blue eyes, very blue, so blue that Bob couldn't quite take them in.

Only slowly did he return to himself, a common-sensical man, a man who liked information. "Don't worry about those red marks on his face," the doctor was saying. "We had some problems in delivery, and we needed to use forceps. Those marks will disappear in no time."

Then there was the question of the baby's weight, under six and a half pounds. The doctor reassured Bob and the two women with him about that, too. Likewise the mother was still a bit weak, given the suddenness of the delivery.

"She'll bounce back in a hurry, though," the doctor went on. "Don't you worry."

Since the baby was a boy, there could be no question about the name. Robert had been prominent in the family tree as long as anyone could recollect—indeed, one had even been a hero in the Crusades.

But now, nearly a thousand years further on, this latest Robert came home to no vast Crusader castle. Indeed, the little Pamplin apartment groaned for space, for the rest of September The new parents had one bedroom, the mother-in-law the other, and in the living room slept young Bobby and the licensed practical nurse the family had taken on when it became clear young Katherine wasn't recovering as quickly as the doctor had predicted. On top of that, most days Grannie Robinson came over to pitch in. With so much company, well-intentioned though it was, no wonder Katherine felt exhausted. It took weeks for the mother's strength to fully return. She had so little milk that the baby had to be given a supplement.

Finally Katherine recovered, and the nurse could leave. After another two months, during the first week of December, little Bobby and his mother both seemed healthy enough for a Sunday visit with the Pamplin grandmother up in Dinwiddie County, Virginia. The threesome left early, since the weather that December 7 was bad enough to add some time to the trip. For long stretches of the way north, the windshield wipers were the only noise in the car; mother and child were tired, and Bob had never much liked the distraction of the radio.

The reunion was happy, the conversation concentrating as always on family affairs. The still-vigorous Mrs. Pamplin seemed to be spending a fair amount of time with Uncle Mervin DeShazo, the father of Bob's high school forensics partner, Carrie. The two old people were alone now, he a widower and she a widow. They had a lot in common, including a considerable circle of family and friends. That Sunday evening, the new grand-mother and great-uncle went with their Augusta visitors to a late service at a Methodist church in Petersburg. Joining them there was Bob's older brother Willie, happy as the others to find so many of the scattered Pamplins together again. Willie had just finished a year of military service with the Corps of Engineers, and he was heading home to Bartow, Florida.

The jovial group found a pew. They noted the first hymn numbers on the church walls. But the pastor strode to his pulpit before any music started; something was up.

"My friends," the pastor began, "my friends and neighbors, I must begin with bad news. It brings me great sadness to do so, but as your pastor, your shepherd, the responsibility is mine. I know, for instance, that many of you do not have radios and so have no way of knowing."

The pastor paused. Bob and Katherine shared a wondering look.

"Here in Virginia," the minister went on, "it is evening now. You see the Lord's tranquil darkness descending outside, after a day's hard rain. But in a faraway place called Hawaii, it is Sunday morning. Some of you may remember hearing of our naval base there, in a place called Pearl Harbor. My brothers, my sisters, the news from Pearl Harbor is terrible this evening. Even as we sit here, the evil forces of the Empire of Japan are striking at our fleet there."

Katherine gasped, instinctively clutching the baby tighter. Bob caught her eye again, uncertain, then turned to catch his brother's. Willie—the thought flew faster than understanding—was still officially in the service, an army engineer. Before them, meanwhile, the preacher had raised his hands, stilling the sudden horrified murmur.

"It's true," he went on, "all too true, my brothers and sisters. The Japanese struck in surprise, with no warning at all. Our ships are destroyed, our sailors murdered before they were out of bed. Our President Roosevelt has gone on the radio by now, denouncing the attack. He calls December 7 'a date that will live in infamy,' brilliant words for a dark moment. He's asking that Congress declare war on Japan and its allies."

By now the entire Pamplin group had begun exchanging worried glances, needy touches, guess-filled whispers. War! The country was at war! And just when they had new life in their midst, new life and health.

William Pamplin's discharge was held up, as he and Bob had guessed in that first shocked moment. Back in uniform, he stayed with the Army Corps of Engineers for the duration of the war, teaching classes in engineering near Washington, D. C. Bob himself had already served his country for some four years, as a First Lieutenant in the Reserve Officer's Training Corps; he'd officially resigned the commission in 1937. Immediately following Congress' Declaration of War, while he was still thirty, he drew a high draft number; when he was called later, the military no longer wanted anyone over twenty-eight. Later still, the rules changed again and men up to thirty-six were accepted for the draft. Bob's number was called, but being in an essential industry, he was given a deferment until the war's end.

During the war, like every other American, the new father made many sacrifices at home. Gas, for instance, was rationed, limited to three gallons per car per week. Tires were not to be replaced. In Bob's case, the shortages felt like no great hardship, since he'd spent so much of his life living on so little. He got himself a used Model A Ford, a car with better mileage than the Packard.

Indeed, in one regard things even eased up a bit, as the war went on. After little Bobby turned two, late in 1943, the mother-in-law Mrs. Reese decided it was time for her to get a place of her own and bought a large, old home. Soldiers and their wives stationed at Fort Gordon, Augusta, were desperately in need of housing. By renting rooms to them, Mrs. Reese realized needed income.

These early years of marriage were difficult for Katherine. Her frail nature and many pregnancies forced her to spend hour upon hour in bed. Fortunately, Bob was able to see that Katherine had full-time help.

During these same early war years, Bob and Katherine began trying to have another child. Bob wanted at least one more, preferably a girl. He'd come from a family of five, and grown up surrounded by hosts of aunts, uncles, and cousins, with the natural result that family mattered to him enormously. And Katherine, the only child who'd trained to work with roomfuls of schoolchildren, felt the same. Yet though the young woman got pregnant twice, each time resulted in a miscarriage. It soon became obvious that these miscarriages had to be the result of something more serious. The worst—the most heartbreaking—came five months into the second pregnancy.

Her obstetrician was William Thurmond, a successful professional, brother of the rising young politician Strom Thurmond. On Christmas Day, after Katherine had been ordered to bed for several weeks, Dr. Thurmond examined her. He operated on her that very day. Though the fetus was removed, it had developed into a freak of nature, a hydatidiform mole. It would take the doctors six months before they knew whether Katherine would develop cancer, and Katherine herself was unaware of the possibility. Fortunately, her test results remained negative.

"The problem is something called the Rh factor," the doctor told them. "We didn't even know there was such a thing until 1940. It's called 'Rh' because Rhesus monkeys were used in the tests that discovered it. You, Mrs. Pamplin, are Rh-negative. Your husband is Rh-positive. Now, your first child, Bobby, inherited your husband's Rh-positive traits, and before he was born, Mrs. Pamplin, some of your Bobby's blood cells entered your body. And your body, being negative, had to build up antibodies to fight off the foreign blood type your boy had introduced."

With every pregnancy since, the doctor went on, Katherine had probably been exposed to more Rh-positive blood. In this she'd faced worse danger than more miscarriages. "Your blood could clot," Dr. Thurmond went on, "and you could become seriously ill. You could die. But if you do succeed in bringing a second child to term, the antibodies in your blood may build up enough to harm the fetus."

The man concluded by reminding them that, as yet, the profession didn't know much about the Rh factor. "But it does seem to be responsible for your miscarriages," Thurmond had to repeat, "and does give any child you might have a high probability of turning out deformed."

Numbly, Bob and Katherine returned to their apartment. Only when they were back in the privacy of their own home did the still-young wife allow herself tears, the long nightmare of miscarriage and sickness having depleted her emotional reserve. Bob, dizzy with disappointment himself, staggered briefly around the little apartment. Then he came back to his weeping wife, back to his senses.

They consulted the Mayo Clinic, and the doctors there said the couple had only a 50-50 chance of a normal baby. "We can't risk it," Bob declared. "We can't even consider another baby. It's just common sense. Anything else is too dangerous."

Katherine blinked, fighting for control. The only child was seeing the same for her own boy. But after some moments she mastered herself. She nodded.

"We can adopt," she said, striving for good cheer. "We can always adopt."

With that possibility as a hope, they pulled themselves together. Bobby was waiting for them, they knew, over at his Upma's (Bobby's special name for his Grandmother). He remained very much the apple of the old woman's eye, despite her need to set up a place of her own.

L ittle Bobby Pamplin's grin came easily. He was happy, bright, active. The boy's smile came from his mother's side, his pale blue eyes—unlike most newborns, he'd retained that color—from his father's. And the startlingly open look in his eye seemed from somewhere else entirely, some place neither parent could identify. Bobby had already revealed greater reservoirs of love in Katherine and Bob than they'd ever known were there, and now, with the news from Dr. Thurmond, those same reservoirs seemed to grow still deeper.

That same day, picking him up at Mrs. Reese's, Katherine had crushed the boy in a hug and said repeatedly how "thankful to God" she was for him. Afterwards, Bob had explained the situation to the boy as best he could, and over the next few years father and son did whatever they could to cheer up the disappointed mother. Little Bobby tried not to say anything to do with having any brothers or sisters of his own. When the war ended, in 1945, the family took comfort in the victory. And at night, when Bob and Katherine read the Bible to each other, he selected only those passages he thought would help.

Then came a day in '47 when the man could give his wife some truly good news. "Katherine," Bob announced one morning, "The war's over, the economy's booming and Georgia Hardwood's doing well." The company had just gone public, the still-young executive explained, and he owned more than six percent of the shares. "Those shares are worth quite a bit right now, honey," Bob pointed out. "Don't get me wrong, we're not rich like Rockerfeller, you and I and Bobby. But we sure don't have to live in an apartment any longer."

Katherine, sitting across from him at the small table where they'd shared so many meals, didn't know what to say. She smiled open-mouthed, dazzled.

"We can have our own house," Bob declared. "Now, why don't you go out and pick yourself the loveliest place you can find?"

The house Katherine found was at 3002 Lake Forest Drive, a white-painted brick Georgian with green shutters and a pillared alcove entryway. Stately pine, maple, and magnolia graced the yard. Not only did she get to pick out the house, but over the next months she arranged all the furnishings. The paneled living room was decorated in charming Victorian style, with a fireplace and floral curtains. The tufted Victorian couches and wing chairs had tapestry footstools. Oil portraits of Bob and Katherine in gilt frames hung on either side of a window. In no time the exceptionally appointed home became part of the Augusta Council of Garden Clubs tour. Guests passed through smiling and nodding; pictures appeared in the Augusta *Chronicle.*

And yet there was always a quality of the down-to-earth about the house. It had the sense of a place lived in, played in, worked in, rather than of an ornate bauble no one should ever disturb. The place was intended to help make Katherine happy again, and to establish the threesome's pride of family for all to see. This was what the guests felt, coming through on the homes tour, and this was what, finally, had those strangers nodding.

Bob himself, in fact, would more than likely have been equally content to stay in the apartment. Still, he knew this was the right move, and like any working man he took pleasure in being able to buy things for his loved ones. But at bottom, Bob Pamplin, Senior, remained the sort of man who wasn't defined by what he'd been able to buy. Those were what Scripture called "earthly treasures"; they didn't impress an old farm boy. In his middle years Bob remained impervious to the attractions of a more free-spending way of life.

He made his cars work for him longer than just about anyone he knew, going six or even eight years before a trade-in. He wouldn't break down and buy a new suit or a new pair of shoes until Katherine had reminded him it was time. And the yard of the new house, though it was meticulously maintained, had a piece of the old Dinwiddie County farm in it. Bob had his own personal vegetable garden, where he grew the butter beans and other food he'd loved as a boy. He was never much interested in flowers—they couldn't be eaten. When it came to hunting and fishing, too, he was out for meat rather than for sport. If he was going to go to the bother of catching a fish or bagging a deer, then he was going to eat it. Collecting, too, held no appeal for him, though like most successful Southerners he'd picked up one or two Civil War mementos. Over time he added a few older items as well, museum-quality pieces from across the Atlantic: artifacts that had some connection to the ancient family of which he now realized he was a part.

But those items had the value of bloodlines. They deepened spiritual connections to the world and to others. They were the opposite of the Bible's "earthly treasures." And within the man, too, though by the beginning of Bob's forties he had more money than he'd ever dreamed of as a boy, his deepest excitements had little to do with costs and sums and payoffs.

A s for money, that gave him two principal pleasures: it was fun to make and fun to give.

At heart, the former "Bull" Pamplin remained an athlete. For him the point of business was to play by the rules—and win nonetheless. Money was the way a man kept score. The more money, the greater the victory. Yet by the time Bob and Katherine were ready to buy their new home, the former Tech Rat's old competitive fires were no longer entirely satisfied by what he could do at Georgia Hardwood. At Georgia Hardwood, he'd come to realize, most of his best plays and sweetest victories had wound up benefiting the people who employed him.

Granted, his old friend Owen Cheatham gave Bob a good salary and stock options. For those he was grateful. But as primary finance officer Bob had built up the company tremendously by the end of the war. His decisions revealed the special practicality that comes of seeing the big picture, a perspective inspired in part by his and his wife's reading in Proverbs night after night. His explanations had the same irrefutable simplicity as what he'd said during his greatest crisis at home, the discovery that he and Katherine couldn't have more children.

"It's just common sense," he'd say around the office, as he'd said at home then. "It's just common sense."

So, given all he'd brought to the company, Bob began to have thoughts of getting more in return. His own share of dividends and appreciation from the stock no longer seemed an entirely fair share of the profits.

Early in 1946, Georgia Hardwood owned some five lumber mills in Alabama, Arkansas, Mississippi, and South Carolina. A company with a net worth of about $50,000 when Bob had signed on had grown to a net worth of about $1.2 million—a twenty-four-fold increase in slightly more than a decade. The corporation's first public offering of stock increased that worth by half again, some $700,000. These additional funds were invested in Georgia Hardwood's first property in the opposite corner of the country, the Pacific Northwest. The company picked up Bellingham Plywood, out of Bellingham, Washington. And of course Bob and Katherine, at the same time, used their own profits from the stock offering to buy their home on Lake Forest Avenue.

In the late 1940s, too, Georgia Hardwood laminated its first sheets of veneer into plywood. Within five years, given no small boost by the postwar boom in new families and new housing, the firm had captured ten percent of the U.S. plywood business. Bob and his colleagues had built a place that was second in total sales and first in firwood plywood manufacture. The former star intramural pitcher got a terrific kick out of these figures: precisely the sort of victory margin he liked to see. Over these same years, the company began the transition from merely manufacturing and selling lumber in the South to making plywood in the Northwest and selling it all over the country.

In 1940, lumber had been the whole company, and half of that had been exported. But by 1950, lumber accounted for only fifteen percent of its business. Timber processed into plywood, as Bob had understood early on, has two or three times the value of simple lumber.

The second step in the company's westward migration came in 1948, when it acquired the Washington Veneer Company. Owen Cheatham's strategy, one approved by Bob, was to acquire going concerns; in this way Georgia Hardwood avoided the delays and costs of building new mills. By 1951, the company had likewise acquired the C. D. Johnson Lumber Co. in the tiny coastal community of Toledo, Oregon. Though no more than a dot on the map in Bob's road atlas, Toledo had one of the largest sawmills in the Northwest and, nearby, some 66,000 acres of prime Douglas fir timber. With that single purchase, Georgia Hardwood became the nation's largest producer of Douglas fir plywood.

The company's holdings in the Pacific Northwest were now so significant, the name was changed to Georgia-Pacific Plywood and Lumber Company. To Bob Pamplin the change was, naturally, "just common sense."

But the husband who'd done so much to help his unhappy wife after her miscarriages wasn't concerned only with the game-playing side of moneymaking. Running up the score against other lumber companies gave Bull Pamplin great pleasure, to be sure. But those same profits could help deserving friends and family, and such giving provided him a happiness far more profound.

After the late 1940s, Bob found his Georgia-Pacific stock piling up, and this allowed him to send regular assistance to other Pamplins elsewhere. For one thing, he could share the stock itself, especially with the families of his brothers Willie (now known by the more adult name of Bill) and Claude. Bill was back in Bartow, Florida, solidly employed as a mining engineer with Southern Phosphate. Claude worked in chemical engineering with DuPont. But despite these jobs, since both brothers had only recently finished their service in the war, neither had great assets. And both Bill and Claude had an extra responsibility that Bob still dearly wished he could share—they both had more than one child.

One night, as Bob and Katherine studied the Bible before sleep, Bob read a passage from Ecclesiastes:

> *Two are better than one, because they have a good return for their work: If one falls down, his friend can help him up. But pity the poor man who has no one to help him up.*

Then turning to another part of the Bible, Bob read the famous passage from the Gospel: *It is more blessed to give than to receive.*

Bob slept on these thoughts, and awoke knowing what he must do. He had received much, a wife and a son, and wealth, position, and respect. And Bob's own father had made those gifts possible, by means of a gift of his own. His father John Robert had paid for all three brothers to get an education; the sweat of his field work had created a better future for the entire succeeding generation. But now, without resources to match their father's, two of John Robert's boys might not be able to provide the same essential hand up for their own children.

Pity the poor man who has no one to help him up. And Bob Pamplin, Chief Financial Officer with a booming firm, would have only Bobby Junior to help up. So that morning Bob called each of his brothers. He announced he'd give each of his nieces and nephews 200 shares of Georgia-Pacific stock, which could be used, if needed, for their college education. By that time, late in 1948, the stock was worth $9 per share. And the gift embraced some five youngsters altogether: Claude's Allen, Jeanne, and Carol, and Bill's Janice and Jack. Given the way the company was growing, who could say how much it would be worth by the time those children were out of high school?

Then there was Bob's commitment to the First Presbyterian Church, where he was on the Board of Deacons. The church was the center of their spiritual and social life, much like Ocran Methodist had been for Bob back in Dinwiddie County. But First Presbyterian of Augusta was considerably more impressive than his old country church. The sanctuary was the oldest original house of worship in the old Savannah River city. The congregation went back to some twenty-five years before the Revolution, and the church, begun during the town's cotton and tobacco boom in the first years of the nineteenth century, had taken fully a decade to complete. At the beginning of the War Between the States, Presbyterians of the South had renamed themselves the Presbytery of the Confederacy in this very church. The pastor then had been one Joseph R. Wilson, a distinguished theologian whose son was none other than Woodrow Wilson, the twenty-eighth President of the United States.

On lovely summer days, palmettos in the First Presbyterian's church-yard would sway in the breezes, while the sun-gold weathervane high atop the steeple would pirouette. Graceful magnolia caressed the tall gray walls with their shadows, and created rippling patches of sunlight through the Gothic-arched windows. It was where Katherine's family had worshipped, where she and Bob were married, where Bob became a more integral part of the Augusta community.

One such Sunday in the late 1940s, the Pastor introduced a special guest speaker: the Reverend Billy Graham. This talked-about young evangelist was staying in the minister's home while he was in Augusta. There were many new faces in church this Sunday to hear him, and the sanctuary softly buzzed with anticipation. When Billy Graham rose to speak, his soft and comforting North Carolina accent at first had people wondering what all the fuss was about. But the words Graham spoke soon began to sink into the hearts, the natures of those listening, at once familiar and disquieting. Bob, Katherine, and Bobby (now eight), learned that just living a good life wasn't enough. "To be saved," Graham proclaimed, growing louder, "you must accept Jesus Christ into your life, must invite the Holy Spirit of God to live inside you."

Young Bobby, his father could see, was struck as never before by the man's quiet yet insistent zeal for Jesus. The boy's pale blue eyes seemed almost otherworldly.

"Those of you who have made a decision to commit your lives to Christ," Graham called, "stand up, leave your seats, and walk down the aisle to join me in prayer. You come!"

And Bobby did. Of course the boy caught his father's eye as soon as he stood up in the pew, checking for approval, and Bob Senior somehow found the presence of mind to nod. Then the child went to the front of the church and prayed with Billy Graham.

Nor was the family's spiritual life limited to church. Every morning they gathered at the breakfast table for a devotional; there they'd get occasional previews of Katherine's Sunday School message. Little Bobby so enjoyed these get-togethers—his mother's own private service, really—that he occasionally brought by playmates from the apartment building. The little knot of boys together got the benefit of his mother's college-trained teaching. Bobby would sit in front of a small home stage, and Katherine would bring out the fruits of long labor.

Often she made illustrations of Scripture and its characters: Joseph and Potiphar with the pyramids of Egypt; Moses with the burning bush; Jesus healing the lame and sick. And she cast these Biblical characters in the developing drama of their culture, defining them by details of their place and moment. His mother's work made the story as real for Bobby as if these sages and prophets were striding the room before his eyes.

As a Sunday School teacher, by the late 1940s Katherine knew all too well that the education facilities of First Presbyterian badly needed renovation. Bob, more and more moved by the spirit of giving, became the prime mover in getting the work done. In 1951, Bob's income was $73,298, including salary and stock—a very healthy piece of change for the times.

But according to estimates it would cost some $150,000 to redo the Sunday School. So Bob issued a challenge to the rest of the church. The Pamplins would match the congregation dollar for dollar, he and Katherine announced, for up to half the cost of the renovation. His fellow churchgoers hadn't been so fortunate as Bob Pamplin, though, and so over time the man ended up giving at the high end of his challenge pledge: a year's income. Yet the church he loved wiped out its debt and began to renovate its Sunday School rooms and facilities, thanks to his gifts, and to Bob's way of thinking that was reimbursement enough.

The old Virginian also found ways to help his mother. By then the former Mrs. Pauline Beville Pamplin had married his uncle, Mervin DeShazo, who'd been keeping her company since John Robert died. That made Bob's old debate partner Carrie also his step-sister. Mrs. Pamplin DeShazo and her husband now lived together at the Pamplin family farm.

The whole family was happy for them both, of course. But the forty-year-old farmhouse seemed to Bob less than his mother deserved, these days. The place had been modernized, with the electricity and plumbing that Bob's conservative father had so long opposed. And old Uncle Moses, the Negro carpenter, had done a fine job, originally. But now Bob wanted better.

"God's been good to me, Mother," he said when the old woman tried to protest. "And you were good to me. I can afford to do this and I want to." He built them a fine new brick house between the old one and Ocran Methodist Church. It was a single-story home, in order to spare the aging couple the trouble of climbing stairs. And, since Ocran Methodist was so close by, Bob decided that after his mother passed on he would donate the place to the church, as a manse for the pastor. His giving would go on and on, from those closest to him out to the rest of the world.

W hen it came to his boy, Bob Pamplin tried to provide the same combination of hard-headed practicality and genuine caring as his father had given him.

A singular test of his child-rearing skills came when Bobby was in the sixth grade. The rambunctious eleven-year-old found himself unexpectedly bedridden, a victim of hepatitis. His father, remembering the broken leg that had kept him out of school for a year, realized that, all things considered, the time off had done him a world of good. He and Katherine decided that the best response to an illness this serious would be to keep the child out of school for an entire year.

Throughout that year, every night Bob would come into little Bobby's room and pull up a chair beside his son's bed.

"Are you feelin' any better today, Bobby?" he'd ask.

His child would nod, weakly in the first days and more heartily later on. Then after they'd covered a few of the day's events or made some other small talk, Bob would add his own remarkable personal touch to the bedside visit:

"American Telephone and Telegraph Corporation," he'd begin reading, "annual report. First, the report to shareholders, then a review of the balance sheet." And when he had finished reading through the AT&T annual report—or some other company's, depending on what might have come his way in the office—he then read the boy, say, the U. S. Steel pamphlet.

"Now," he'd go on, on the weekdays, "let's look at *The Wall Street Journal*. Center column, there's the major business news."

This was bedtime reading at the Pamplin home. The father who'd almost flunked English as a teenager never had much use for fairy tales, and Katherine handled much of Scripture reading, especially in her home services. But business understanding was a unique gift, something nobody could give Bob Pamplin's son so well as Bob Pamplin himself.

Yet the father also had skills of a very different sort to pass on. The former country boy knew how to hunt and fish like few Augusta men, and he made sure to share that knowledge with his son. The ancient crafts of gathering food, of survival in the wilderness, were part of the way even a generation born in the shadow of the atomic bomb could join the unending chain of all those before it.

Similarly, Bob saw recreation and business as links in an integrated whole. As a "meat hunter" and "meat fisherman," the man made these pastimes businesslike. He expected something to eat for his efforts. He couldn't understand the appeal of fly fishing, for instance, that is almost purely recreational. Thus, the business of sport balanced for him the sport of making money, in which expenditures and returns were the box score.

Little Bobby, too, was made to see these balances, this interactive whole, on his many hunting trips with his father. For Southerners of the father's generation, taking a gun and a game bag into the woods remained a way of life. Bobby was five when his father gave him his first BB gun. Not long after that Bob took him on longer hunting trips in the swamps, along with men friends from Georgia-Pacific, the church, and elsewhere. The boy bagged some game himself, and helped with the cleaning. Bob found himself proud of the job his son did.

But for the better part of a year now, Bobby could do little more than lie in bed, weak and jaundiced. For all Bob knew, the boy's very illness might be exacerbated by the same complications of the blood that had meant he could never have a brother or sister. And as this deeply spiritual man passed evening after evening by his son's bedside, his emotion developed new muscles, and carried him to windy new summits. On one hand Bob reached a greater gratitude to God than ever: gratitude for a wife and a son, and for that son's slow but steady recovery. Yet the powerful executive also felt vulnerable. The same God Who'd given him success and a fine family could take it from him at any moment. Bob had no permanent claim to any of what he'd been given, he realized. Once again he understood he couldn't invest all his love in one place; once again his circle of caring began to grow beyond his immediate family.

He returned, naturally enough, to thoughts of what he himself had been doing at about his Bobby's age. He certainly had never taken schoolwork as seriously as his boy appeared to. If it hadn't been for the dedication of Miss Evelyn Abrahams, back at Dinwiddie's Midway High, Bob Senior would never have gone on to his many present accomplishments. Indeed, what Miss Abrahams had given him was more valuable than money. Miss Abrahams had improved his personality, not merely his pocketbook. Thanks to her insistence that he go out for forensics, Bob was now able to argue his points persuasively. He could make people see things his way, whether he was proposing a stock exchange for a merger or convincing a foreman of a better system for producing plywood. Persuasion was nothing less than essential, if those under him were to work together effectively.

And Miss Abrahams had given up so much for the students at Midway. She'd never married; she'd had no family. Besides that, she'd been at the high school longer than any other teacher, and still enjoyed an overwhelmingly favorable reputation. Whether the teenagers were shy or outgoing, athletic or bookish, she found ways to give each of them the skills to present themselves effectively to the world at large. Now a man who owed her more than most, spurred by his reawakened awareness of childhood's fragility, felt compelled to demonstrate his appreciation. Midway High had by then been replaced by Dinwiddie High, but Bob Pamplin knew where his money should go. In 1953, with a thousand-dollar check, he established a trust fund in the name of Miss Evelyn Abrahams. The income was "to purchase medals to be given to outstanding boy and girl forensics students."

Yet it was with this latest gift that Bob discovered his Proverb-quoting Katherine had her misgivings about their generosity. He didn't tell his wife what he'd done until the check had been sent, and when he made the announcement before dinner that night, he expected her to be as proud and happy as he was. But instead, there over her kitchen preparations, he saw a cloud pass across her face.

Quickly his loyal Katherine recovered, and put on a smile. "Well," she said, "isn't that nice."

Bob knew her better, though. He studied her a while, then: "Honey," he asked, "what are you really thinking?"

"Well, dear," she began, "I just don't know how you can give money away like that." She frowned briefly, then went on in stronger voice. "I realize Miss Abrahams was good to you, Bob. I realize she deserves the honor. But what if we need that money later? I mean Bobby and I—your family? What if something happens to Grannie, or to one of your relatives? Heaven knows. . . ."

She faltered again, biting her lip. "We give away so much, Bob," she finished quietly. "So much."

The husband took this in without comment. He remembered the stories Katherine had told him about her childhood. The daughter of a man who'd tried to be both a dentist and pharmacist, Katherine had been hit harder by the Great Depression than Bob. The Reeses had staggered back and forth between the comforts enjoyed by a family of professionals and a near desperate scraping by. Bob, on the other hand, had known only the demanding but sustaining life of the farm. To Katherine, the possibility of losing their present affluence remained more real, more frightening than her husband had realized.

And then after dinner, the man went back upstairs to his afflicted son. The boy could barely smile at first.

Dear God, Bob thought, how threadbare You've spun these webs of family and character! How vigilant, how strong a man has to be to keep them in place!

Bobby's illness left Bob that much more determined to prosper, to provide. Before long even his beloved Packard, after eight years of meritorious service, gave way to a more luxurious Lincoln. Yet his increasing wealth felt more than ever like God's rather than his. His success in the business world stemmed as much from reading the Bible, he firmly believed, as from studying accounting. Thus simply holding on to his money—much as the most important woman in his life might want him to—seemed to Bob Pamplin tantamount to sacrilege. What the Creator had put in his hands should be given gratefully back, in part at least. To share his money was to remove its power over him, and restore the preeminence of the One from Whom All Blessings Flow.

On another night when he and Katherine were alone, he tried to explain his thinking to her.

"I know that giving away money disturbs you," he said. "But remember what it said in Proverbs? The Lord directs the king's heart. Remember?"

Katherine sighed and nodded, her eyes narrowing in thought. Plainly she'd been pondering these same issues.

"And have you noticed," the husband went on, "that the more we give the more we seem to have?"

Katherine was so in accord with her Bob that he needed to say no more. After that, she never forgot that showing restraint and generosity when it came to money was as much a gift from God as the money itself. And she understood better than ever her wealthy husband's remarkably austere ways. He wanted so little for himself. For all his love of hunting and fishing, he never cared for collecting guns or fishing gear. In the garden he used only hand tools. His dress at the office was unpretentious, even severe.

"That first steak tastes good," Bob Pamplin liked to say, "but the second one you have trouble eating and the third one makes you sick. It takes a lot to make some people happy. It just doesn't take much to make me happy."

With her, however, Bob grew ever more generous. Katherine understood this, too—understood that there was more to it than his love for her. Gifts for the wife were part of the role of the Southern gentleman. That role extended as well to the wife's relatives. During these same years of increasing comfort and security, Bob suggested that Katherine give thousands of dollars of Georgia-Pacific stock to her mother. Over the years the two Pamplins gave so much to a trust for Mrs. Reese that in time the total mounted into the millions.

And they gave her more than cash. When they made a substantial gift to Augusta College for a new library building, they did it in the name of Kate Coffin Robinson Reese and her husband, John Thomas Reese: The Reese Library, as the students knew it. Likewise the new Sunday School facility for the First Presbyterian Church was named after Katherine's mother and father.

By the couple's middle age, the Pamplin tithe had grown to some three times the original amount. They'd adopted a policy of giving some thirty percent of their annual net income before taxes, rather than the tithe's ten percent. All Augusta—indeed, the entire South—honored the husband and wife for their generosity. And throughout Bob's business community, too, his power and influence grew.

The executive found himself traveling frequently to the Pacific Northwest, the best new source for his company's necessary raw materials. By now, well more than half of Georgia-Pacific's holdings were in those distant green states. Bob's knack for smart acquisitions allowed vast stands of timber to be harvested.

Also, he understood that the industry was badly fragmented in places like Oregon and Washington, and that with better management and organization it could be far more profitable. On top of that, better management would mean better conservation of the natural resources. The industry should apply a farmer's conservative approach to their cropland, this former farm boy thought, cycling their harvests carefully and being sure to allow forests to renew themselves. All in all, Bob's most promising future seemed to be here in the Northwest. His old friend Owen Cheatham agreed, and in 1953 the two men decided to relocate the corporate headquarters to Olympia, Washington.

"Bob," Cheatham said before the move. "I want you to go to Olympia and take charge of things. You're the only person who can do what needs to be done. You get along with everyone—you get on their level. You're tough, you're honest, and you work harder than anyone else I know. You look out for the stockholders and I know you'll make the employees and their communities happy in the Northwest as well. It's something that needs doing, and needs doing now.

"And Bob," Owen concluded briskly, "I want you to be Chief Operating Officer."

Chief Operating Officer! The man who made nearly all the decisions, who handled the entire day-to-day operation! It meant a raise, of course, but more than that it meant an opportunity to show what he could do. Bob told Owen he'd try the new position for two years, providing he could hand-pick his staff, some ten or twelve good people. With those people, he'd have the best chance of succeeding out West—the best chance of perhaps one day running the company himself. For Bob still had that ambition. And the desire to run the show, in a man like Bob Pamplin, never goes away either.

Bob told Owen that if the company in the Northwest accepted and supported him he would remain and run the company. If after two years he was not accepted, he would return to Augusta. For that reason he did not sell his home or move any furniture to the West Coast. The family home was still there, a refuge they could return to whenever they needed it.

Yet it was the COO's wife, more than the man himself, who needed the reassurance that they still had a home in Augusta. Katherine was losing more than he, in this momentous move. To her, the home and the circle of friends and family that went with it were like her career; they were what occupied her days and provided her definition. Could she still perform her private devotionals out West? Could she reign over a house that was featured in the paper and was part of a city's pride?

Katherine had no idea, but she understood that, just as she'd always taken the good that had come with Bob's success, so she should also take the bad—or what appeared to her to be the bad. Besides, she told herself, it was only for two years.

So, on a warm spring day in 1953, Bob and Katherine and Bobby boarded the train for the West. The ride was exciting at first. Bobby got up on his knees in his seat, watching the farmland and forest of the South roll by. Katherine tried to keep up an enthusiastic front, though she'd gotten homesick almost as soon as they'd pulled out of Augusta. Nonetheless, as the landscape became more and more unfamiliar, it became harder and harder for the woman to remain upbeat.

After a few days the train carried them into the worst territory yet, the Badlands of the Dakotas. This barren, eroded scrub land extended bleakly to the horizon. It seemed to get worse, if "worse" were possible, the farther west they went.

Finally, Katherine's fear and unhappiness boiled over.

"I can't believe you took me away from my home and life in Augusta for this!" she exploded, gesturing out the window. "This is horrible. I want to go home!"

"Excuse me!" came a woman's voice from the seat behind her. "Excuse me, I don't mean to be nosy." The family turned to see a middle-aged woman whose lined and tanned face revealed a life spent mostly outdoors.

"I couldn't help overhearing you," she said. "And I don't blame you for not liking this area. The Badlands are awful." The outdoorsy woman waved a dismissive hand at the window herself. "But believe me," she went on, "it changes when you get farther west. Just wait'll you get to Butte, Montana. Now that's some beautiful country."

Katherine wasn't entirely sure how to take this. The outspoken stranger seemed nothing special—just another woman carrying around a copy of a 1953 bestseller, *The Power of Positive Thinking*. But Bob's homesick wife recalled the patience recommended by Proverbs and Ecclesiastes, and managed to keep a lid on her uneasiness. Over time the dirt and gravel outside the train's windows took on a cover of grass, and then the grasslands sprouted occasional groves of trees. At Butte, Katherine and her menfolk went up to the observation dome, trying to find whatever it might be that the Montana woman believed was so beautiful.

The most prominent thing Katherine could see, however, was a vast hole in the ground. An open-pit copper mine—the work of Anaconda Copper Mining Company, Bob told her—wound down and down out of sight, seeming to burrow halfway to Hell. Beyond that stood filthy smokestacks, belching fumes into the air. The countryside was nothing but rocks and stunted scrub pine.

"Bob," Katherine told her husband, "that woman must have been teasing me. Butte is just as ugly as the Dakotas."

But then, from their perch in the glass dome, the small family saw the rangy, weathered woman emerge from the train. No sooner was she down the steps, than she dropped her bags and ran straight into the arms of a man across the platform: a man in blue jeans and a cowboy hat. Then behind emerged an older lady, likewise suntanned. Beside her, there stood three boys. One by one, the woman who'd tried to cheer Katherine up, hugged each of these people, oldest to youngest, largest to smallest. All the while her seamy face glowed with happiness.

As the train pulled out of Butte again, rising into impressive gray-green mountains, Katherine Pamplin thought about what she'd seen. She thought about how joyful the woman had looked, simply at finding herself in Butte, Montana. Even the title of the book the woman had been carrying seemed to speak to Katherine: *Positive Thinking.* . . .

Then somewhere in the splendid northern Rockies, Katherine found that, there facing her husband and son, Augusta seemed suddenly like another lifetime.

"Bob," she announced without warning, "I can see why that woman thought Butte was beautiful. Anywhere you call home is beautiful."

Bob's eyes grew bright, full of hope that his wife had taken to the move at last. "Dear," he said, "I wouldn't take you from Augusta to a desert. Never. I care about you and Bobby too much for that."

The boy was asleep, his head on Bob's shoulder. Carefully husband and wife reached out from their facing seats, linking fingers in midair.

"You've seen the worst," Bob went on. "Soon, dear, you'll see the best."

After another night, she knew what he meant. The three of them climbed up to the observation dome again as the train snaked its way along the mile-wide Columbia River. It was blue-green, not brown like the rivers she was used to. Forest-feathered mountains rose right out of the river, their tops cloaked in mist. Waterfalls cascaded threadlike yet potent, white and gleaming down rock faces hundreds of feet high. And the Cascade Mountains brooded around them, dark blue-green with Douglas fir; among these loomed the airy whitecapped skyline of Mount St. Helens, Mount Adams,

Mount Hood. Around the newcomers also unfolded villages and farmlands not unlike some quainter, more temperate version of Georgia.

Little Bobby was particularly excited by the towns. He kept pointing out the sturdy white homes.

"But," Katherine laughed, "I don't see any teepees!"

Bob Pamplin Senior, smiling, extended his arms round his wife and his son. In a three-way embrace, the family began the last miles toward their new home.

CHAPTER 11

Robert Pamplin, Senior
Making It Work Out West

B OB AND BOBBY PAMPLIN swung their guns and bags onto the check-in counter with a satisfying thud. The hunting trip of a lifetime—several days in the great north country of Canada in August, 1955—began for them when they boarded the graceful four-propeller airliner and its greyhound frame droned briskly out of Portland's airport.

Yet for the forty-four-year-old father, much as he enjoyed going after rare game with his son, the journey was tinged with regret. Even airborne, he couldn't stop thinking that when he returned to Oregon, he'd be facing the end of his career with Georgia-Pacific.

To the right of the father-and-son team passed the perfect white-capped cone of Mount St. Helens. Then came the more canine Mount Rainier, followed by the rugged, snow-slashed heights and ravines of the North Cascades. To their left was the mile-wide Columbia River, then Puget Sound, then the Olympic Mountains. The sea-swept air of August made for an utterly faultless panorama of the sumptuous territory that Bob had hoped to call home.

But as Bob gazed out his window, he kept wondering how his twenty years with this company could end so abruptly, so unsatisfactorily. By that summer of 1955, he was Administrative Vice President of Georgia-Pacific. The corporation, according to the business press at least, was the nation's largest producer of plywood. Yet, incredibly, only two years after G-P had moved its headquarters to the Northwest, profits had deteriorated and morale was low.

Indeed, Bob's own move from Georgia—his appointment as Chief Operating Officer out in this part of the country—now appeared to have been, in part, an effort to forestall these very difficulties. Of course at the time the new COO hadn't worried much about possible problems. His new autonomy and authority had been too exciting for that.

Yes, in 1953 Bob had been happy to have the job. The appointment
had meant that one day he might take over the company from its founder,
his old friend Owen Cheatham. Bob had promised to give the new location
at least two years. He'd picked the people to accompany him out to Olympia, Washington. With the right staff, Bob believed, he'd set everything
swiftly to rights. And yet today as his plane passed over Olympia, Bob
couldn't help thinking that he and his people had never really gotten the
chance.

After all, though Bob was by now halfway into his fifth decade, he
still hadn't lost his dream of running his own business: of reaping the
benefits of his creative management himself. His farmer father hadn't
raised his boy to be a sharecropper.

Even over the last little while, when so much of Bob's energy had been
going into staving off a G-P collapse, he'd approached a few of his best
people about setting up a new lumber business back in Augusta. For as
soon as this hunting trip was over, it seemed, Bob and Katherine and their
son were headed back to Augusta—back to their house on Lake Forest
Drive. Thank God, Bob thought as he gazed out over the black-freckled
stands of Northwest fir, he'd never sold his old home.

Not that he had expected such an ignominious return. He'd expected,
for starters, that the business would remain in one place. But after only ten
months in Olympia, the headquarters had been relocated again, southward
to Portland, Oregon. Bob didn't disapprove of the move, since it brought
the management closer to its principal landholdings. But the transition
had been handled poorly, creating the sort of confusion and missed connections that a well-run organization wanted to avoid. The real trouble had
begun even before that. Bob had been in Olympia only a few weeks when
Owen Cheatham called about a retired brigadier general named Lewis Pick.
Pick was interested in joining the operation, and Owen thought the former
officer would make a useful associate in the new headquarters. In fact, he
wanted Bob and Pick to work on an equal basis.

The conversation was one of the most difficult Bob ever had with his
old friend. "I don't think that will work," he told Cheatham frankly. The
deal with Pick smacked of broken promises, since Bob had moved all the
way from one corner of the country to its opposite on the assumption that
he alone would be in charge of the western operation. But loyalty runs deep
in old Virginia boys. "If you want to do it, Owen," he told his long-time

employer finally, "I guess it's okay with me and I will stay on in keeping with my agreement, but I will leave the company at the end of the two years."

And his initial impressions of the new man weren't bad. At first meeting, the former General seemed pleasant enough, a tall and presentable man in his late fifties, full of military-style organizational strategies. Bob turned everything over to him except the financial end of affairs. Pick then hired a few people of his own, in effect supplanting Bob's hand-picked staff—and the company's effectiveness and worth began immediately to deteriorate. Month after month showed little or no profit, both before and after the disorienting move to Portland. By mid-1954, Georgia-Pacific lost more than six dollars a share off its initial 1947 offering price of $8.20. Overall profit dropped to less than $2 million, a miserable return on investment for a business of its size.

Three weeks before the two-year period was up, Bob took a three-week vacation go big game hunting with his son in Canada.

F ather and son spent their first night at Prince George, on the Fraser River in central British Columbia. Over the airport tarmac loomed the solemn, deep-hued Caribou Mountains, brown and green with startling touches of blue. Young Bobby took in the scenery with mouth agape—a look he'd been wearing practically the whole flight. The flat and swampy South was nothing like this.

The executive had made arrangements with a bush pilot to fly them from Prince George, taking them into the wilderness where their guides waited. But he'd never expected transportation quite so rustic, so frail. The Prince George pilot had a single-engine pontoon plane that bobbed like a cork in the Fraser River currents. Going up was against Bob's better judgment, but he figured that if he could survive the last two years, he could survive anything. He and Bobby crammed their gear into the cargo bays, strapped themselves into their seats, and waited while the engine spat, choked, sputtered, wheezed, and then fell finally into a steady blue-smoked coughing.

Apparently this satisfied the pilot. He checked a gauge or two, then grinned at his passengers. "This the first time you folks been up in a bush plane?"

Bob confined his reply to a nod and a wave of his hand: Okay, okay; let's go.

Loudly, slowly, the plane pulled away from the pier. Facing into the wind, the pilot brought the machine to full speed. But the suction of the water was too strong. The thing couldn't get airborne.

"You guys," the pilot shouted over the engine. "I want you to rock back and forth together a few times."

The man rocked in his own seat momentarily, left-right, giving them the idea. "You start her rocking, see, we can pop her out of the water."

Bob and Bobby, together not much more than 250 pounds of swag, did as they were told. After three long minutes of rocking, they felt the airplane lurch free from the water and at once pick up speed. It lifted into the sky with remarkable grace. Soon the two hunters had a smaller version of the previous day's panorama. Spruce-clad mountains walled in the Fraser River steeply, and the upper granite reaches were marked by occasional blinding palm-prints or finger-streaks of snow.

The DeHavilland Beaver had horsepower enough for this kind of work, the pilot cheerfully explained, but was at just about its weight limit. Bob and Bobby tried to relax; it was more than 400 miles to their base camp. And the last quarter of the trip turned out to be the toughest. They found themselves facing a bank of clouds within which, somewhere, lurked a mountain range.

The pilot remained as full of grins as ever. "Not a problem," he declared, spiraling downward toward a shimmering lake at the mountain's foot. He pulled the pontoon DeHavilland up at a lake-side storefront with an attached house, buildings so tiny that Bob and his son would never have seen them from overhead. This, they learned, was an outlet for the Hudson's Bay Company. Everything else for hundreds of miles around belonged to the native Athabascans, much of it unchanged since the Stone Age. Relieved, even charmed, the Pamplins remained nonetheless impatient to get on with their hunt. They had to wait two days at the store before the clouds cleared. They found themselves actually glad to be back in the airplane. From there it was only an hour to Cold Fish Lake.

Athabascans were hired as their guides and camp crew. There were four, and the leader seemed to be Don White Eagle. White Eagle had lost his teeth, though he claimed he wasn't too much older than Bob himself, while another of the group appeared to be in his twenties. The foursome gathered the Pamplins' gear and strapped it onto their pack animals. The party still had two more days of travel, on horseback this time, before they at last reached the actual base camp.

The Pamplins had ventured so far towards the Arctic Circle that, even now in the height of summer, the temperature dropped below freezing every night. When they washed their faces in the morning, they first had to break ice in the wash basin. The leaves on the aspen were turning gold already, and occasional snow-heavy cloud banks skirted the horizon. But the legendary north-country mosquitoes, unfortunately, had long since grown used to the cold. Bob and his son had to sleep under a net.

Their camp, so Bob had been told, would put them close to some of the most exotic game in North America: moose, grizzly bear, bighorn sheep, mountain goat, caribou. And the site, when they finally rode into it, was spectacular. There was a creek with delicious water (delicious, but cold enough to pop a taster's eyeballs), and plenty of close woods cover. The timberline, where game was sure to forage at some time or another, was only a short ride away.

The first day after arriving, Bob and Bobby and the two guides took the horses high enough to make the animals skittish. There the guides scouted for game with binoculars. It wasn't long before one of the Athabascans spotted a hefty moose, just at the timberline.

"You can get close enough to him to get a good shot," toothless White Eagle said. "But you have to get downwind. If the moose smells you, he'll run off."

The hunters and the natives had to take their mounts still higher, as far up as the animals would go. The last bit of slope—gravelly, slippery talus—they climbed on all fours. As quietly as they could, the foursome made their way to a point about fifty yards above the moose, and about 250 yards off to one side.

"Get ready," the old Indian whispered.

Bobby had the better eye at this range. He leveled his .30-.06 at the hulking animal, getting the broad neck in his crosshairs. The shot's ear-splitting crack kicked Bobby a good foot or two back along the slope. At first the moose was probably as much frightened by the echo as stung by the bullet. The creature bolted for the safety of the woods, clattering downhill faster and more gracefully than seemed possible for such a big, ungainly beast. Only its webby antlers betrayed its lack of control, break-ing off tree limbs as it tore along. Father and son then both fired, hitting the moose again and again. The ton of animal turned a cartwheel, collaps-ing.

Bob couldn't keep from grinning. This was just the sort of excite-ment he'd needed to get his mind off the trouble at Georgia-Pacific. Even after the kill, they had to race the clock. The guides set to field-dressing at once, even partially skinning it.

"It's getting dark," explained Don White Eagle. "We have to get back to camp."

They didn't haul out any of the moose till the next morning, when they could bring up the pack horses. And in the bright sunshine after breakfast, as they neared their kill, White Eagle warned them of worse dangers.

"If a bear's found that moose," he said, "he'll fight us for it."

But the guide found no sign of bear, and smoked moose became their mainstay meal throughout the rest of their stay in camp. The meat was cut in strips and hung on wire lengths over a slow fire. The trophy head was wrapped and kept separate, out of harm's way. And within another day Bob and Bobby had bagged a caribou.

Hunting every day except Sunday, it wasn't long before father and son had bagged the government limit on everything except moose—hunters were allowed two—and the dangerous, elusive grizzly bear. Moose held no more appeal for them, since they'd been eating it for two weeks now. But Bob and Bobby still wanted a bear. And their return appointment with the bush pilot, back at Cold Fish Lake was coming up quickly. When the group celebrated Bobby's thirteenth birthday, by firelight on the night of Septem-ber 3rd, the boy announced, smiling, that the only present he really wanted was one of these huge and shaggy northwoods predators.

The guides tried taking the two Southerners to a place where berries grew, a place grizzlies often visited. The foursome spent the entire day there, scouting all the likely feeding grounds, but nothing turned up. It looked as if the Pamplins' getaway would end unfulfilled. Granted, the bond between father and son had grown more powerful, more mutually respectful, over the course of their adventure. But he and his boy couldn't help feeling a little let down.

But that night Bob and Bobby were wakened in their tents by an unmistakable noise. They heard a padded but heavy footfall and raw, snort-full breathing just outside their canvas walls. Sharing an excited look, the father and son said nothing. They knew better than to jump out and confront the hungry carnivore at close range, in the dark. While the beast moved through camp, each kept a hand on his rifle.

In the morning, Bob's first concern was for the horses. But both pack animals and riding animals remained where they'd been tied. Instead, the grizzly tracks led through the camp, down the hill toward where the foursome had thrown last night's dinner scraps. Swiftly the guides set about clearing a target area around their dump. They left one narrow tree standing, and from it they hung a rope holding fresh meat.

"He'll be back tonight for dinner," White Eagle said, grinning close-mouthed. "You'll get your bear."

Then the guides left to keep watch above the camp. All day the father and son waited by their rifles, under cover most of the time, and at dusk the stealthy return of the guides signaled that they'd finally seen what they'd been waiting for. "The bear," the Athabascans whispered. Yet even after that, Bob and his son couldn't get a clear shot. Now and then they spotted the grizzly in the bushes, in the dark, but not well enough to draw a decent aim.

"Better wait," White Eagle said. "If you can't kill him quick, better leave him alone till daylight."

Daylight meant their last day at camp. Snow had already come to the higher elevations, and was threatening down at their level. The two hunters slept spottily, anxiously. But at dawn it was the old Athabascan who woke them.

"The bear," he whispered again, in the gray clarity of an autumn sunrise.

Instantly alert, once more Bob and Bobby took their rifles out into the cold and slithered downhill. They could see the trail where the grizzly had dragged the meat into the bushes. They could see his brown bulk in among the leaves. But its vitals, the places where the animal might be quickly stopped—these they couldn't be sure of.

"*Shoot*," the guides hissed, "*shoot*! You're not going to get a better chance."

Bob could see white on a tree next to the bear. He used that mark to line up his shot, and then he and his son began. They each fired three times, and the 500-pound predator reared up, roaring, lurching round the bushes trying to find the source of his pain. For one terrifying moment it faced the hunters, claws up, jaws open. But already the damage had been done. In another moment the grizzly collapsed in the brush, groaning and thrashing and at last growing still.

This was the last trophy for the vacationing father and his birthday boy. The next day the party loaded the horses and headed back to the lake. But they had stayed too long; the snows descended the mountains with them. Above the timberline it was hard to make out the trail, and in places the horses' hooves poked through several inches of snow. The first night of the trip back, they had to set up winter camp. They had trouble finding enough dry firewood.

The next day, pushing hard to keep the blood circulating, they reached Cold Fish Lake by mid-afternoon. And how appropriate that name seemed now! The snow kept following them, as if some vast and assiduous cleaning-woman were nosing a blue-white broom down the forested slopes. Bob had hoped that their devil-may-care pilot would be waiting at water's edge, that he'd somehow gotten in under the weather. No such luck. The snow-bordered lake was empty.

That night, after another scavenging trip to bring in dry wood, Bob did his best to hide his mounting fears from his son. As night came on, the sky remained ashen. Serious cold could set in any time, cold that would freeze the lake and make landing impossible. Even with the Athabascans along, the father and son felt terribly isolated, their only evening company the eerie cry of the loon. Bob remembered the pilot's hell-for-leather style. A man like that could get into a lot of trouble. What if something had happened to him?

And even after the pontoon DeHavilland at last emerged over the mountain crest the next day, Bob's relief was short-lived. Yes, he and his son were happy to get their trophies aboard, to bid a respectful good-bye to Don White Eagle and the others. Indeed, the Athabascans looked relieved as well. What were they going to do, after all, with a white man and his teenage boy stranded in the north country for an entire winter? Nonetheless, getting back into the plane wasn't the end of their troubles. After a while aloft, as they were passing over Big Bear Lake, the engine suddenly quit.

Bob swallowed hard and began praying as the plane slowly lost altitude. His son Bobby, beside him, dropped his head and followed suit. Meanwhile, the pilot frantically fiddled with the controls, and after a few dizzying prayerful moments, the engine coughed once more to life, belching a fresh cloud of smoke.

B ob and Bobby pulled back into their Portland driveway tired, mosquito-bitten—and full of fresh energy. The son couldn't stop talking about the things they'd done. The father knew he'd once more forged confidence needed to face the coming challenges.

Before the hunting trip, he and Katherine had begun the preparations to move back to Georgia and begin a new chapter in their lives, probably with a new start-up company. Katherine, for her part, was delighted with the prospect. And Bob Floweree, one of his closest associates, was also making plans to leave the company. And yet within a few short weeks of his Canadian hunting trip, as the fall rains settled over Portland, Bob's larger trial in the wilderness unexpectedly came to a close. It was now the last quarter of 1955, and Owen Cheatham hadn't gotten where he was without learning how to read a financial statement. He could no longer ignore what he saw there; he could no longer deny that he'd made a mistake with General Pick. Reading the Georgia-Pacific financial statement, in this case, was like reading the proverbial writing on the wall.

And at the same time, Owen Cheatham was forced to see that the one person who could turn things around was Bob Pamplin. Bob had the expertise within the firm, the connections outside of the firm, and that same unbeatable "common sense" which had served Georgia-Pacific so well in the past. Judging from his record, Bob might even be able to get the company headed in the right direction again fast—by tax time in 1956, hopefully. So, no sooner had the hunter returned than he heard that "Mr. Cheatham" needed to talk with him.

Polite and deferential as ever, Bob went to his long-time superior. The witty Cheatham was so concerned he even skipped his usual opening joke.

"The company is in pretty bad shape, Bob," he conceded at once. And he confessed what he'd realized during the three weeks his Vice President had been gone. Bob Pamplin alone, he said, was the man who could save Georgia-Pacific.

"You tell me what it will take to make you stay," Cheatham concluded. "You can be the President, if you want. You can write your own ticket."

Bob couldn't answer right away. He had already made his plans, already begun to picture himself running his own company. He'd imagined many times how it might work, building up equity for himself and his descendants. Of course, a start-up was always a risk. But the same know-how that had brought him Cheatham's new offer made him believe that he could make a go of any new venture. And there was his family to consider, Katherine in particular. She'd be disappointed—not to say heartbroken—if they didn't return to Augusta.

But he'd been in management long enough to know that a man in charge of a company like this had responsibilities that extended beyond his wife and children. There were some 8000 employees who looked to a well-run Georgia-Pacific for their security. Besides those, there were the thousands of shareholders, including himself and many of his extended family, who depended on dividends and stock appreciation for part of their incomes. Throughout the region, in fact, whole communities relied on the payrolls from Georgia-Pacific mills. If the company were allowed to continue its slide, employees, shareholders, and communities would all suffer.

All in all, it was no easy choice.

Finally, however, the man's only moral option was clear. There in the office that morning, Bob and his old friend began to hammer out a plan that would do right by the employees and shareholders, and by the communities that depended on the company. What else could he do, in the end? What else offered the same combination of loyalty, practicality, and ethics? As for Bob's dream of running his own company, that would have to be set aside, for the time being at least.

"I don't want to be President," Bob told Owen. "Not when there's so much turmoil already. Maybe a couple of years down the road," Bob said. "But right now it doesn't make sense."

But Bob would have to be Executive Vice President and Chief Operating Officer, he explained, with everyone reporting to him. At the end of two years, if G-P had settled down the way he'd expected, then he'd take the presidency.

Also Bob had a few practical concerns. The company had to buy him a house in Portland, a house he'd have the option to pick up himself later. And he had certain figures in mind, of course, for pay and stock options.

Afterwards, the meeting left Bob with the sort of mixed feelings he'd never felt before. He felt he'd won and lost at the same time; he'd triumphed and been defeated. And what, *what* was he going to tell his wife? Everything was ready for the move back South; Bobby was even enrolled in an Augusta school. By the time Owen and Bob had hammered out their new deal, it was the day before Katherine's and the boy's departure. They were expecting Bob to follow them in another few weeks. How could he explain it?

Though full of these worries, he allowed Katherine an unbothered evening, and a restful night's sleep. The next morning, as planned, the new Executive VP drove Katherine and Bobby to Union Station, a brick tower looming over the Portland rail yard. The porter wheeled their bags through the marble lobby to the waiting trains. There on the platform, Bob asked his son for a moment alone with his mother. Bobby, seeming to understand, hugged his Dad and climbed aboard.

"Katherine," the husband began awkwardly. "Katherine, dear."

She'd been expecting a few kind words, a good-bye kiss. Now her pretty eyes narrowed, concerned.

"How would you like it," Bob asked slowly, "if we made Portland our permanent home?"

The woman frowned. "I don't understand, Bob. What do you mean?"

He explained what had happened, briefly, without emotion. He emphasized what was good about the plan. "I just don't feel right about leaving the company now," he concluded. "Georgia-Pacific needs me too much."

As Bob's words sank in, Katherine felt like the world had just given way beneath her feet. Disappointed, hurt, she was tempted to make the obvious retorts: *Your family needs you. You said you would. You promised.* But she'd seen this man do what was best for her so many times before. She held her peace. Tears welled in her eyes, but she made no scene. "Really?" was all she said, or murmured. "Really?"

Deeply Southern and deeply spiritual, like Bob, Katherine understood by now that there were moments in a marriage when one partner had to yield temporarily to the other. She remembered too the woman who'd loved Butte, Montana—a town with a hole that went halfway to Hell. If that woman had found the place beautiful simply because her family was there, why, surely Katherine Reese Pamplin was capable of the same. And finally, she knew that if this was a decision Bob thought was morally correct, neither she nor anyone else could sway him.

"When will we see you?" she asked, her eyes downcast.

Bob said he would make it a point to come to Augusta every month. He suggested, too, that the aging Mrs. Reese come and stay with her and Bobby.

"It'll work out for the best," he said.

"I'm sure," she said. "I trust you."

Then with the conductor shouting, "All aboard! All aboard!" Bob tried to thank her, to tell her again how he loved her, to let her know that he realized she was making a tremendous sacrifice. . . .After that he was left watching his wife and son wave to him from the window as the departing train pulled out of the depot.

As it turned out, having no family responsibilities for a while was one of the smartest moves he could have made. He shared an apartment with his friend Bob Floweree, who was likewise without a family for a while and, more importantly, likewise understanding after Bob explained the change in plans. Their apartment was in the city's West Hills, one of Portland's most elegant neighborhoods. But the two men had little time to socialize. Often, after a stop at home for dinner and a head-clearing walk back downtown, they went once more up to the office to work late into the night.

The two of them were a good match, with a healthy regard for each other. Pamplin watched the numbers and Floweree made the operations work. There was so much to do that they had little time to feel lonely. And with both of them going so ferociously, the company quickly began to come around, just as Cheatham had hoped.

There's no arguing with the numbers for what Bob Pamplin accomplished over the next twenty years. Georgia-Pacific became one of the biggest forest products companies in the world. Its stock was listed on the New York Stock Exchange as the best gainer in the country, beating out hot competition like IBM and Texas Instruments. To a man for whom business was a sport, it was great to see such a winning score posted day after day in *The Wall Street Journal.*

Yet fiercely as he competed, to Bob it was just as important to be fair. Any money he earned had to be honestly won. "Money you get dishonestly is worth nothing," Bob said. "I would much rather have a good reputation than all the money in the world."

Bob knew that everyone in the company was taking their cues from him. They knew that he would not tolerate dishonesty. Bob recognized that whatever he thought was fair dealing, right or wrong, they would feel entitled to do as well. And if he took a big salary, they would want a big salary. If he had a chauffeur-driven limousine, a company airplane or yacht, if he took company time for golf or for thinly-veiled vacations, then order and discipline would suffer all the way down the ranks. Thus, any advantage Bob took for himself he made available, at some level, to other employees. He set an example, working harder for less pay for his contribution than anyone else in the company.

Most of this operating philosophy was based, by and large, on his old fundamental trust in "common sense." In this, of course, he owed much of his gift to his father and the farm life he'd grown up loving. To his way of thinking at least, he ran a giant company the way his Papa had run the old Dinwiddie County truck farm. Papa set the example of working hard and doing things when they needed to be done. If Bob's leadership set a good example now, it was because John Robert had set a good one before him.

Bob's first rule in building an organization likewise adopted his father's farm principles. He strove to be the kind of person good people will work for. "A good man will work for a good man and no one else," he often said. "A sorry man cannot keep good people—a good man is not going to work for a sorry man." Pamplin put a premium on setting strict but reasonable policies and guidelines: the kind any worthwhile employee could see the value of. Everyone had to know what was expected of him, and everyone had to see the fairness in the company discipline. At the same time, Bob needed to inspire a team: as leader, he had to push for bigger scores in production and profits, all while never losing the corporation's moral grounding.

Then there was Bob's work ethic, likewise inspirational. The Vice President figured that most people worked at about fifty percent capacity, and so he doubled many employees' work loads. He felt they would be happier performing at their peak. Also, in another echo of the farm ethic, he required that anything that needed to be done today be done today. Key managers might work until midnight, if there were deadlines looming.

In addition, Bob's management showed the benefits of a strong religious faith. It was easier to trust his judgment, his sense of rightness, given his long study of the Bible. He didn't need to take destructive paths in order to see that they led nowhere. In Scripture he'd read example after example of bad decisions. This too helped him think innovatively, creatively, trusting that after reading so much of God's Word, some of it had rubbed off on him. An idea didn't come entirely "out of the blue," to Bob. The thought was always moved by a divine Hand.

To Bob, a bad decision was better than no decision at all. With a bad decision, at least something was happening. Failure to make a decision, on the other hand, meant paralysis—always deadly for an organization. Besides, the kind of good people he valued learned from their mistakes, and such learning was always better than dodging a hard choice. He would help make the choices when necessary, and there were clear guidelines within which they were to be made. But it was always up to the individual manager to act.

In that way, too, Bob's people couldn't hide behind committees. If something went wrong, there was always a clear track of decision making to follow. Committees, on the other hand, made organizations slow, top-heavy and afraid. The new Chief Operating Officer made it a rule that there were to be no committees in Georgia-Pacific. All decisions were made by individuals, and all of those individuals were responsible to him. Granted, Bob himself chaired a committee, the Operating Policy Committee, composed of key executives. But this met only once per quarter, to review the latest developments and discuss future possibilities, and it didn't make decisions. It transmitted information, nothing more. In the same way, managers at the headquarters office and at each of the four division offices would meet for breakfast or lunch every Monday.

Just as committees seemed to Bob like a way of avoiding responsibility, so were consultants. To him, a company that used consultants was admitting it didn't know how to run its business. It also risked having what it was doing passed along to the competition. That's one of the reasons the Chief Operating Officer wrote all the company's pension plans himself, with the help of the legal department. Nor did Bob call in outsiders to invest the pension funds; he did that himself

Even Bob's experience fishing and hunting were part of his formula for Georgia-Pacific. The outdoorsman in him understood that if you had the right gear, came to the right place, and worked at the right time, you had a good chance to bag a trophy and have meat for dinner. And there was a touch of the old ballplayer's thrill in that, again: the excitement of making the big score.

Then there was the military-style discipline Bob had picked up at Virginia Tech. After 1955, for instance, alcohol was no longer served at any Georgia-Pacific event. Managers who had a martini or two at lunch likewise knew better than to return to the office. Such laxity interfered with the important business of setting a good example. For the same reason, Bob always came to company parties wearing his dark suit. Even picnics required, for him at least, a coat and tie. To Bob, success was serious.

That Tech-like discipline showed, too, in his handling of annual and long-term goals. He made sure the goals were precise and easy to understand, preparing new standards before the beginning of each operating year. Included in the standards was a projected profit and loss statement for the coming year, showing all cost items broken down by units. Bob reviewed the standards with each operating manager. He set the policies from headquarters, then delegated to managers elsewhere. And every year, trying to inspire the corporate team, Bob reserved his highest standards for himself He aimed for Georgia-Pacific to double sales and profits per share every five years. This was accomplished from 1955 to the day of his retirement in 1976.

Shortly after Bob took over as Chief Operating Officer, he established a policy that no one from the family of an officer could be hired unless he approved. His reason for this was that he felt an officer's relatives would have to work harder than anyone else to prevent criticism. He did not feel that this was fair to the individual. On the other hand, if they did not work as hard, it was not fair to the company.

Also, he felt that if a person wasn't doing a job, that person should be replaced immediately. He believed that as a general rule those not performing would want to leave to strike out in another direction. He often said, "Nine times out of ten that person would find something more suitable for his ability." He didn't enjoy letting people go, but he didn't hesitate to take action when he felt it was necessary. Among Georgia-Pacific's staff, it became a matter of pride to survive under Pamplin.

B ob saw the success of the company, in its simplest form, as a three-legged stool. It was a balance of the stockholders, the employees, and the communities in which they lived and worked. To Bob, the interests of these three elements were equal.

Stockholders, as owners of the company and the ones whose money is at risk, are entitled to a fair return on their investment. So Bob insisted, and thus he pushed to double earnings and assets every five years. To protect the stockholders' earnings, he chose to finance expansions through debt rather than by issuing new equity, and he paid off the debt as fast as he could because, naturally, the old farm boy didn't believe in debt unless it resulted quickly and directly in company growth. To build the assets of the company for stockholders, Bob drove for investment in new and modernized plants.

"Our philosophy," he'd say, "has been that if we don't have the cheapest costs we're going to get them. And I'll spend any amount of dollars to get them."

As for the employees, Bob's great contribution to management was to regard them as essential. This simple fact would seem self-evident—that companies need their employees—but so many American executives appeared not to notice. Bob Pamplin, however, always made sure his people received competitive wages and benefits. And he understood that one of the points of company growth was passing along the profits and opportunities to the employees. He set up incentives for employees to perform at their peak. If they did well, they shared in the profits of the company through the Georgia-Pacific Stock Bonus Plan. As the corporation grew, so did the employees' equity. And employees were allowed to buy stock on their own, equal to another ten percent of salary.

Thirdly, Bob took an active interest in the communities where Georgia-Pacific operated. These were the homes of the company employees, after all, and everyone in those communities made it possible for the company to succeed. Therefore Bob encouraged employees to be active in the towns and cities where they did business, and made sure the company was always a good corporate citizen. Georgia-Pacific donations sustained many a local scholarship or high school function. More than that, Bob involved himself in political affairs that affected the company, even speaking out when he felt he had to. In this, speaking at Rotary Clubs, Chambers of Commerce, church and industry gatherings, his experience as a debater came in handy as ever.

Yet while he was establishing the company's success, putting his philosophy in place, Bob somehow found time to return to Augusta almost every month during 1955 and early 1956. He'd visit his family, of course, and he'd put in a few hours at the old headquarters as well. Then Katherine and Bobby came back out West in the fall of 1956, back to Portland's Dunthorpe neighborhood, where a year before they'd lived as renters. In G-P's resurgent success Katherine and her son had seen once more, unforgettably, what this man could do when he put his mind to it.

Bob's position as head of the company, now one of Oregon's fastest growing corporations, actually made the family's transition to the new community somewhat tricky. The firm's quick rise branded it an upstart in Oregon's conservative business climate. Many local leaders predicted it would be a flash in the pan: that it would cut the timber and run. Bob sensed that this far outpost at the western edge of the country was different from New York or California, where neophytes could more quickly make a place for themselves.

Portland had a different ambiance. Family reputations and social circles built more slowly. Nonetheless, thanks in large part to his many good works within the community, the Pamplins were soon accepted socially. Besides that, Bob's and Katherine's Southern accents didn't stop them from being excellent bridge players, and they were soon playing round the card tables of many fine Dunthorpe homes. Bob earned a reputation, not surprisingly, as an extremely aggressive bidder no matter what the hand.

Also the Pamplins joined organizations with which they were sympathetic. Bob particularly enjoyed the Arlington Club, an ivy-covered men's club in downtown, with stuffed leather chairs and private dining salons. There the city's elite power brokers gathered to deal. And he and Katherine were welcomed into other exclusive organizations, such as the Town Club, the Waverly Country Club, and the Multnomah Athletic Club.

In the same way, in 1956 Bob became a trustee of Lewis & Clark College, a private liberal arts school near their home. His lifelong commitment to education made the position a natural fit for him. He also served as trustee of Portland's First Presbyterian Church and became involved on the Board of Directors of the Greater Portland Council of Churches.

By 1958 Katherine had found a house that was just about right, at 404 S.W. Edgecliff Road. This gracious, white Georgian-style house was built on three and a half acres overlooking the Willamette River. After a bit of remodeling, the home looked as if Katherine had brought a little piece of Augusta, Georgia, to the Northwest. Robert even had the entryway rebuilt just like their house in Augusta. Also he added a wood-paneled den with fine oil portraits of the family members.

The formal gardens had rock terraces and restful glades where Bob, Katherine, and Bobby sometimes studied Scriptures together. Indeed, those gardens were another link to the family's past, since the English love such places, whether they live in England, America's South, or the Pacific Northwest. Bob and Katherine often walked out of the east wing onto the slate patio, and strolled along the stone walkways, under the purple flowering wisteria or flowering cherry trees. From there the gardens sloped eastward, toward the Willamette and Mt. Hood, through flower-filled terraces. One might have roses, another geraniums and dusty miller (artemisia). In summer these beds were transformed into something completely different with bedding plants. Bob's favorite spot, however, was behind the garage. There he spent his quiet time spading and hoeing the soil with hand tools, growing butter beans and the other vegetables that had meant so much to him back on his father's Dinwiddie County farm.

On August 1, 1957, after having been with the company for twenty-three years, the forty-five-year-old Bob Pamplin became de facto President of Georgia-Pacific. After two years at the helm, he had increased profits from $1.7 million to $7.4 million; he had met his five-year goal of doubling profits per share in less than one-half of the allotted time. The man just plain had the knack for making money.

By December of 1960, inside the upper reaches of the company, age and illness had begun to take a toll. More than once, while Bob and Cheatham were discussing some problem or detail, Cheatham would become suddenly distant, unfocused.

"Owen? Owen?" Bob would ask. "Are you all right? Have you heard anything I've said?"

Cheatham, coming back to himself, shook his head. "I have to sit down . . . I'll have to talk to you about this later." Then Owen, a former bon-vivant now in his sixties, would go home and rest. The next day he would be all right again.

This went on for six months. Owen kept losing concentration, needing unexpected breaks. And Bob wasn't the only one to observe the change in Owen; other top managers would discreetly bring up the problem as well. But in the end everyone had to shrug the matter off

Without prior warning, Owen's neck began to swell while he was on a plane trip to Washington, D.C. He was rushed to a hospital there and was operated on immediately. Bob learned the news while visiting his brother Bill in Florida. By the time Bob arrived in Washington, Owen was in critical condition and for a long time afterward he couldn't talk, couldn't think, couldn't communicate. The problem, the doctors told Bob, was the equivalent of a stroke. Owen had a blocked artery in his neck.

Bob turned for advice to Dick West, a long-trusted Georgia-Pacific attorney. The only workable solution, both men agreed, was that Bob become Acting Chief Executive Officer as well as Chief Operating Officer. And, sensitive to the fears of stockholders and employees, the men at the top saw to it that the transition took place quietly. The Board of Directors met swiftly and voted for the changeover, and thereafter kept the matter under wraps. Indeed, for the rest of Owen's life, out of respect for his feelings, no one ever told him. The stockholders didn't know either.

About a year after his first operation Owen Cheatham returned to work. He continued to come to board meetings, and he looked like much the same fun-loving person as ever. But Bob and those close to Owen knew the man had changed irrevocably. And they made it a point to cover for their old founder when he couldn't remember the name of a close associate he was talking to, or meant to say one thing but would say something else. Every effort was taken to keep things looking respectful and under control.

Georgia-Pacific had a mandatory retirement age of sixty-five, and by the end of 1957 Bob was already planning for the day. The same year he became Acting President, he organized the R. B. Pamplin Corporation. He placed some 20,000 shares of Georgia-Pacific common stock in the company as its capital, then balanced those dividends with income from newly purchased real estate. This kept the R.B. Pamplin Corporation from being a personal holding company, and provided tax protection for the dividends from the G-P stock as well. And as he kept giving Georgia-Pacific his best effort—the same effort as had saved the firm in these last two tumultuous years—his eyes would drift from the papers on his desk toward the aloof and solitary mountains on the horizon. One of these days, he'd think. One of these days. . . .

CHAPTER 12

Robert Pamplin, Senior
Running Georgia-Pacific

I T'S EASY for a style of management to work well for a while, just as it's common for a style of clothes to look appealing briefly. After that style's season, however, many fashions look ludicrous—and many out-of-date managers, likewise, quickly find themselves out on the golf course. Then how did Bob Pamplin's management wear on Georgia-Pacific? Did he grow as the company grew, change as the industry changed? Certainly, in the early years with Owen Cheatham, Bob had never imagined that the corporation would become so big.

But he hadn't come so far from his father's Dinwiddie farm merely in order to stop moving now. He hadn't learned to set such clear and mutually agreeable goals in order to now lose sight of further opportunities ahead. By the end of the 1950s Bob was finding he could spot what others missed. He could see how materials others wasted could be put to use, or how costs that limited other operations did not have to keep Georgia-Pacific down.

It was the old thrill of sport for Bob, the kick he got from outsmarting the competition. Bob's men kept close tabs on virtually every sizable piece of timberland in the areas they operated. They knew who owned them, how much timber they had, and how close the owners were to selling. When it was time to purchase, more than once the G-P representatives came up with a dollar figure for the lands that was higher than that of the owners themselves. Bob took pleasure in figuring out how to give a smaller company as much or more than it wanted, and still be sure of making money on the deal.

Bob particularly preferred old, established companies, with boards of directors who were ready to retire. These companies usually had valuable assets on the books at relatively low cost. In such cases, rather than buying the assets of a company, such as its timber, he bought its stock. Then he could sell off those assets he didn't need, such as lumber yards or real estate or even some of the timber. The sale of assets alone almost paid for the

stock. In effect, Bob's Georgia-Pacific bought woodland wholesale and sold
it retail. Unlike later "corporate raiders" (the 1980s wheelers and dealers
who Bob himself came to despise), he paid for his maneuvers by selling
actual assets, rather than "junk bonds," and he never dismantled companies
outright, but integrated them into a larger whole. And he made as much
money as most corporate raiders anyway. His acquisitions left him with big
holdings of timber at very low cost.

Not surprisingly then, by the late 1950s the company was building
five or six mills a year. Still riding the housing boom incurred by America's
larger postwar families, G-P had assets of some $200 million. It had
twenty-one plants across the country and more than twice as many wholesale warehouses and worldwide sales offices. Through insurance companies
such as Prudential and Metropolitan, Bob had lined up long-term operating funds. And through banks such as Bank of America and Chase Manhat-
tan he'd arranged short-term loans of five years or less. Approval for such
loans always came smoothly. Bob never closed a deal for a company until
he'd secured enough contracts for its assets—timber, machinery, whatever—that he could be certain to pay off any debt incurred within five
years.

Even Bob's smaller deals, the kind he started with in 1957 and 1958,
did better than anyone expected. When Georgia-Pacific bought the Booth
Kelly Lumber Company in Springfield, Oregon, with its 120,000 acres of
timberlands, it was done by buying the entire stock, 100 percent. They
arranged the same with Coos Bay Lumber Company's 180,000 acres and
with other companies. Once a purchase price was agreed upon, Bob then
took the sort of innovative step that set his management apart from the
crowd. He asked for a ninety-day period before closing, and during that
period he sold five-year harvest contracts for approximately half the timber
reserve. These deposits and contracts went to the bank at the same time as
G-P's new purchases were closed.

The closing on Coos Bay Lumber Company was typical. It took place
on one of those mild, half-sunny San Francisco days, a day that could come
at any time of year in that lovely city. A troop of men in suits descended on
the Bank of America building, some forty or more, all unusually efferves-
cent and light of step for men coming to a purchase closing. They'd been
instructed to show up at nine and to have their checks with them.

Inside the board room, the suits surrounded an immense oval table. On this table today's serving was a feast: a deal with something for everyone. Pamplin and his group stood at one end, alongside representatives of the Bank of America.

"Gentlemen," Bob began, "I don't have to tell you why we're here. And I guess I don't have to tell you what to do next, either."

The businessmen chuckled and drew out their certified checks. Bob then worked his way around the group, gathering the crisp rectangular slips and, at the same time, signing documents that gave the businessmen rights to harvest timber on the Coos Bay properties. When Bob had gathered all their checks, amounting to some $10 million dollars, he presented them to the bank officers along with his own check from Georgia-Pacific. So closed his purchase of the company.

And what had Bob himself gained, as the head of that morning's feast? While picking up the Coos Bay stock, Bob had bought standing timber for about thirteen dollars per thousand board feet, and simultaneously sold half of it for twenty-eight per thousand—more than twice his unit cost. After the harvesters got their timber, and the owners got their fair price, Georgia-Pacific wound up with vast holdings.

The company President and/or Acting Chief Executive, in keeping with the Directors' deference to the disabled Cheatham, grew more generous as he grew wealthier. By 1960 he was making $150,000 per year and owned more than 200,000 shares of Georgia-Pacific common stock. Meantime, however, he hadn't forgotten his old forensics inspiration, Miss Abrahams. The woman remained at Midway High. She had been there more than thirty years now, and had touched the lives of hundreds of Dinwiddie County youths. None of them, it would seem, so appreciated the help she'd given as her former debate student, Bob Pamplin.

One day the aging teacher got a phone call. "Miss Abrahams," said the voice on the other line, "this is Robert Pamplin."

He had been in touch with her over the years, of course, especially when he'd sponsored that forensics award in her name some years before. She had never married nor had children, but the student who himself had wound up with fewer children than he'd wanted had tried hard, over the years, to show her a child's love. Now he offered a special honor. He said he'd endow two scholarships every year, one for a boy and one for a girl. Each scholarship would be worth $2000 towards a four-year college education for a Midway graduate. The money would go to someone who had the capacity to make good use of a college education.

"And Miss Abrahams," Bob went on, "I want you to head up the committee to select the winner. The scholarships will be given in your name, of course."

Overwhelmed, enormously grateful, the woman nonetheless retained enough of her old classroom self-control to ask if Bob wasn't already doing enough. After all, he'd been setting aside G-P stock for her for some time now.

"I want to do this, Miss Abrahams," the man repeated. "I want to do all I can."

For while Bob was happy to honor this fine old woman, he also had other reasons for setting up the scholarship program. With this gift he was remembering the lynched black man lying in the back of the pickup truck by Dinwiddie County Courthouse. He was remembering Uncle Moses, who had built his family home, and his "black mother" Aunt Cora, and all the African-descended friends and neighbors he'd swum and played with. He hoped to help restore friendship and trust between the races, in his own small way, in order to avoid the kind of thing he had seen beside the Courthouse.

Before the U.S. Supreme Court had begun to enforce integration, back in 1954, Bob had given scholarships both to Dinwiddie's "colored" high school and to its "white" counterpart. Now, with integration, Bob was seeing too many white families in Virginia and elsewhere around the old Confederacy abandon their neighborhood schools. Instead, these parents sent their children to private schools. Bob could see big problems ahead if integration failed. He could see that only affluent whites could afford to put their children in private school, while the poorest whites were getting left behind.

The purpose of integration was not to create a new minority of whites, Bob realized, with typical forward thinking. The purpose was to teach children to accept and respect differences while they are young. So Georgia-Pacific's new President reasoned that if he offered scholarships only at the public Midway High, never at the private schools, whites would be more motivated to keep their children in public schools. Bob Pamplin couldn't single-handedly reverse centuries of discrimination, of course. But his wealth, used wisely, could make a difference.

The Midway scholarships, solidly in place by the beginning of the 1960s, had no small local impact. Over the next couple of decades Bob built up a trust fund of over a million dollars, providing scholarships to as many as thirty graduates a year.

His special care for high-schoolers moving on to college was perfectly understandable, for those who knew Bob's family. Back in the late 1940s, after Georgia-Pacific's first public stock offering, Bob had given some 200 shares to each of his brothers' five children. It had then been worth nine dollars per share, enough to ensure that Bill's and Claude's kids could go to college, just as old John Robert's boys had done. Bobby knew all about the gift to his cousins, of course. But that earlier gesture of his father's would prove to be minor, compared to what was about to happen.

In the summer of 1961, on successive nights, Bob rented a hall at the Holiday Inn in Petersburg. He invited each of his thirty-four first cousins on his mother's side to a dinner on Friday night, and each of his twenty-four first cousins on his father's side Saturday night. If the cousin had passed away, Bob's letter stipulated, the living spouse or children were to come. These kinfolk thought it was a nice idea that Cousin Robert wanted to treat them to dinner; they thought buying a good meal for more than sixty people was generous enough.

The hall was laid out so everyone had a clear view of the head table. Bob greeted each person as they came in with a handshake and a smile.

"Why is Bob *smiling* like that?" Inez Beville asked her husband Dee— the cousin with whom Bob had once, so many years before, torn up his schoolbooks.

"Smiling like what?" Dee replied, finding a seat.

"Oh, you know," she said. "Like he's the cat who swallowed the canary or something."

Dee shrugged, having learned long since not to try and guess what his cousin had on his mind.

Anyway, it wasn't long before they found out. Both nights, once Bob's cousins took their seats, he and Katherine and Bobby took their places at the head table. Beside them settled the sturdy grandmother Pauline Beville Pamplin DeShazo, plus *her* husband and brothers and sisters.

Bob gave an opening prayer. Then afterwards, as the plates were cleared, he invited each cousin who wanted to share something to speak up. Though a bit embarrassed, most relatives nonetheless had their say. "I want to thank you for the fine dinner," said one, and others murmured assent. A few discussed what their children were doing, or how their parents' health was progressing.

When everyone who wanted to speak had spoken, Bob himself got to his feet. "I'm glad you enjoyed the dinner," he began, "and each others' company." But, he went on, he had to let them know now that there was another reason he'd invited so many of them to Petersburg that weekend.

"God has been very good to me," he declared. "Not only do I have a fine family"—his gesture swept across the room—"but I've also had some success in business."

A few of the cousins laughed, perhaps guessing what the man was leading to.

"Today," Bob Pamplin said, "I want to share that success with you all."

He took up a stack of envelopes then and began handing them out. "Each of these envelopes has 100 shares of Georgia-Pacific stock," Bob declared as he came to the first table, "which is worth about $5,000. I want you to keep these shares as the start of your nest egg—your savings."

Cousins around the big room gasped. In another moment there was pandemonium, with dozens of kinfolk talking at once. "Dee," Inez Beville declared, when the envelope came to her, "I can't believe anyone could be that generous!"

Each night, after enjoying a moment or two of the delighted hubbub, Bob raised his hand for silence.

"I'm just glad," he said, when the crowd had quieted. "Glad that God has given to me to do this."

O ver the years each of Bob's many cousins used the shares as they saw fit. Some took cash as they needed it, others held on for future earnings. Certainly Bill's son Jack benefited from the second approach, leaving his old 1948 gift alone until Bob retired from Georgia-Pacific in late 1976. By then, thanks to Bob's repeated success with his clearly-stated five-year goals, Jack's original 200 shares had repeatedly "split"—that is, each share had become the equivalent of two, and then each of those two had become two more, and so on. Jack's holdings, at first worth some $1800, came to roughly 120 times that amount in the late 1970s—almost $220,000. And that was in addition to the annual dividends.

Few cousins did quite as well as Jack, naturally. But Bob Pamplin's deepening commitment to family, to the Bevilles and Pamplins and others who'd helped make him what he was, shaped and drove his company management. Family was, to him, an inspiration and a resource, a special advantage that very few other high-level executives could claim.

He never wanted anything for himself in return. Bob asked only that, as they could afford to, his family pass on as much of what he'd given to others who needed help. And when the G-P President had business back in Virginia, he often wrote to cousins, inviting a few to join him for breakfast or lunch, to share their lives with him. When any of them told him they had done something benevolent with the money he had sent them, he expressed his appreciation.

"The Lord expects us to share and to pass on what we receive," he explained to his relatives. "Money can buy you a bed, but it can't buy you sleep, and I want you to know I sleep well at night."

And in time, Bob tried to encourage his wife Katherine in the same way. "What about your ten cousins?" he asked her. "We don't have to wait till we're dead to start helping them, you know. It would be fine with me if you were to give them a monthly check."

Katherine, as she had years before when he'd endowed his first Abrahams Scholarship, expressed some reservations. "You just think differently than I do," she conceded. "I see things in dollars and you work with millions."

"Well," Bob chuckled, "if you wait too long, the people you want to help might start dying on you."

She came around to his way of seeing things, over the next few years. By the middle of the 1960s she was sending checks to her cousins. One of them wound up in a nursing home, eventually, and the $1000 per month Katherine sends helps enormously. Another has an invalid husband; Katherine sends her an extra thousand monthly as well.

These direct regular payments were, again, Bob's idea. As his cousins grew older, he began to supplement his earlier gifts with $500 per month for each of them. Some cousins received even more if they were in particular need, or were actively helping others. Calvin Beville, for instance, got extra supplements because he headed an organization to help the local poor. Inez Beville, Dee's wife, received an additional $250 per month for her expenses in visiting fifteen shut-ins.

And, never forgetting the woman who'd changed his life, Bob saw to

Pamplin Family gathering in 1969. From left: (seated) Kate Reese (Katherine's mother), Katherine, Margaret (Claude's wife); (standing) Robert, Claude, Marilyn and Robert Jr., Helen and William.

it that Miss Abrahams became a sort of "honorary cousin." She too began receiving $500 a month.

As Bob grew older, concerned that some of the people he cared about might outlive him, he set up a trust in each of their names. The old accountant carefully saw to it that the interest off the principal would continue the payments throughout his relatives' lifetimes. The man whose own family consisted of "a wife and a son," as he humbly put it, over the years extended himself to embrace a family twenty times that size and more.

And Katherine, getting more into the spirit of giving, came up with a project of her own. The idea occurred to her once when she was back in Augusta, on a humid evening in 1961. It was the kind of night when teenagers usually took whatever car they could find and went out cruising. But not tonight, however. Tonight the kids had come to Augusta Senior High, where they sat fanning themselves in the gymnasium. A platform had been set up under the basketball hoop, and it held a number of adults. There was Mrs. Elizabeth Bradley, for instance, principal of Belvedere Elementary School. And there was one person the students did not recognize, a trim and refined-looking woman with graying hair.

As the ceremony progressed, students learned that the stranger was Mrs. Katherine Reese Pamplin. Tonight, they found out, was the first presentation of an annual scholarship in the visitor's name. Finally Mrs. Bradley called on Marya Moseley to come to the platform as winner of the first Katherine Reese Pamplin Scholarship. At that, the students broke into thunderous applause. Marya was one of the best-respected girls in school; she also received the Outstanding Christian Character award that evening.

No one felt better about how the occasion went than Katherine herself. She talked about it all the way back to Oregon with Bob. Then she made plans for the Knox Scholarship, in the name of the principal of her high school. Smiling at her study desk, beginning to seriously enjoy this giving business, Katherine wrote out plans for funding the scholarship. Eventually, the amount came to $400, 000.

Best of all—as it had been since their first small tithing to the Presbyterian church back in Augusta—the more Bob and Katherine gave away, the more his efforts at Georgia-Pacific bore fruit. "It has been the hand of God on this company that has made it grow so fast," Bob told Chamber of Commerce and Rotary audiences. "He has seen to it that I've received benefits far in excess of what I've given. For me not to give still more in return would be like stealing from the Lord."

Indeed, in the fifteen years following its first purchases in the Northwest, Georgia-Pacific had grown to be the largest company in Oregon. By October 1961, it employed more than 6000 in that state alone. By that time, more than one business journal had pointed out that Bob's drive for additional profits was like a football quarterback driving for one more touchdown. The man's competitive fire wasn't satisfied with success in the Northwest or the country generally; he wanted Georgia-Pacific to become a player internationally. And within two years the company had a new plant in the Philippines, hundreds of thousands of acres of timberland in Canada, and some eighty distribution centers supplying retail dealers throughout the country. That year sales showed a 200 percent increase over what they'd been in 1955, the year Owen Cheatham had at last handed the company's reins over to Bob. More than once in those same eight years, the new President had already surpassed his goal of doubling profits per share—a goal he'd originally intended to meet every five years.

And in a bold move into a new product, Bob once again looked to the South. This was G-P's home territory, of course, and Bob's heartland as well. Yet his acquisitions in this region were motivated, typically, more by a canny sense of an industry opportunity than by anything less practical. The first Southern purchase came in 1962, when the company acquired 560,000 acres of pine and mixed hardwoods in Arkansas. By that time Bob's firm was in such a healthy financial position that it no longer needed to sell timber cutting contracts to finance the deal. Before the purchase was closed, this hands-on President as usual spent some time on the site. He looked over the stands of Southern pine, over the decks of raw logs waiting to be milled into lumber.

And he asked himself a question: What if, instead of lumber, that pine could be used for plywood?

He'd already been able to undercut the competition in the Northwest by using white-speck logs to make sheathing plywood. This innovation had kept Georgia-Pacific profitable in plywood when others had been losing their shirts. Now, if he could produce plywood in the East, where the great bulk of his customers were, he could save the cost of transportation.

Keeping his ideas entirely hush-hush, as always, he asked his Research & Development people to run some secret experiments. Other companies had tried to manufacture Southern pine plywood in the past, but the product had never gotten past the testing stages. No one had been able to glue the recalcitrant pine veneer into plywood. But in 1962, both the logs and the labor were in good supply in the South, and Georgia-Pacific was brewing new glues of its own for the process. Back in Oregon, working on sample Arkansas pine, Research & Development was able to come up with a satisfactory product. The key was G-P's new glues, better and stronger than anything tried before. With that, Bob wasted no time putting in an Arkansas plywood plant.

Southern pine plywood, a completely new branch of the industry, shipped its first commercial load early in 1964. Over the next ten years, Georgia-Pacific moved to put a plant within a fifty-mile radius of all the available timber supplies throughout the South—where most of its new acquisitions were.

In turn, the entire region soon joined Bob Pamplin's many cousins and in-laws in recognizing that they had a new hero and patron in this inventive executive. More and more Bob found himself invited to share his insights with younger people. Particularly meaningful to him was the commencement address at Augusta College in June, 1962. He urged students to get started soon and maintain good Christian habits thereafter.

"Do the best you can at the job you have at the moment," he advised the graduates. "Sooner or later, better opportunity will come along."

A few days later he also gave the commencement address at his old alma mater, Midway High School in Dinwiddie County. Word that Robert Pamplin was coming had gone through the county like a wind. Although there were only twenty-six students graduating, the auditorium was packed. Once more, the grateful graduate stressed humility and diligence: "Patience, hard work, genuine interest and a strong faith are the keys to success," he told them.

In the middle of that same decade Arkansas Governor Orval Faubus proclaimed Bob an "Arkansas Traveler," a high honor, making him an Ambassador of Goodwill for the state. That same year Arkansas Congressman Jack Edwards had one of Bob's speeches at a Rotary meeting included in the nation's Congressional Record.

Nor had all these Southern accolades made Bob forget his newer but nonetheless strong ties to the Northwest. As the decade went on, Bob found himself particularly impressed with the advanced education his son was receiving at Lewis & Clark College. Bob Junior went on to the Portland school after he'd transferred from Virginia Tech in 1962. At Lewis & Clark Bob Junior received degrees in business administration, accounting, and economics. On top of that, he served as president of Alpha Kappa Psi, a business fraternity. His career at the college was crowned, finally, by an Economics Student Achievement Award from *The Wall Street Journal*. In light of all this, Bob took a more active interest in the school. Already on the Board of Trustees, he became such an active participant in helping to frame the place's future direction that he was twice named Board Chairman. In 1963 the faculty presented Bob with a testimonial for his many contributions:

> *Robert Pamplin: Soft-spoken Southern gentleman, your zest and tireless effort have brought many to the support of our school. Diplomat par excellence, you have won the praise and gratitude of peers and students, and brought the admiration and generosity of many in the community. You have been a key man in our hopes of expansion, and for this service, I knight thee Sir Robert.*

So read the Lewis & Clark award. Its echo of the noble stature enjoyed by Bob's Beville and Lawrence ancestors—a stature unknown to the college faculty and still only vaguely understood by Bob himself—was precisely the sort of serendipitous coincidence that graces a life blessed by Unknowable Providence.

The 1960s, however, were a time of trial as well as triumph, for a natural-born Virginia conservative like Bob Pamplin, Senior. Early on in the decade one of the Georgia-Pacific board meetings had a rare visitor, a California acquaintance of Bob's—Richard Nixon. The former Vice President, just recently defeated in his run for the top job, came to make sure he could count on G-P's support in the future.

Bob was never interested in running for office himself, not with all he had to do at the company. But Nixon was far from the only powerful politician who came into Bob's widening circle of friends and connections. Inevitably, a businessman as broadly based as Bob took an interest in national affairs, especially as they affected the timber industry.

The executive became, in his own quiet way, a spokesman. In an early-1960s speech to business leaders, Bob proved himself something of a prophet by calling for a free market between the U. S., England, Australia, and Canada. This free-trade zone, he hoped, would lead to the eventual union between these English-speaking nations all around the globe. "With such a market," he claimed, "we would be leaders of the world for many, many years to come, particularly if we as countries and in turn our leaders of industry and labor work together taking advantage of our know-how, markets, and resources."

After the assassination of President Kennedy, the United States went through a notorious period of upheaval. Many long-held beliefs and values were questioned, or even rejected, as a dispiriting war dragged on in Vietnam and demonstrators swept through America's streets. At the same time, long-dormant minority resentments flashed at last to the surface. American inner-city blacks, in Detroit and Newark and elsewhere, wrecked their own neighborhoods in a desperate cry for help.

As for Bob Pamplin, Senior, he had a profound support for integration, and a natural disapproval of an unprovoked war in a distant nation. Nonetheless, the man embodied much that the country's dissenters were objecting against. He was white and, to those who didn't understand business, old-fashioned—a believer in the dominant spiritual and political wisdom of the century. And, of course, he was someone who'd grown very wealthy by cutting down trees. As the "movement" of the 1960s and 1970s moved from questioning the war and the white power structure to raising concern about the environment, Bob Pamplin found himself at odds with many new groups, in ways he'd never been before.

Not surprisingly, since as a boy he'd been so sensitive to other people's feelings, Bob felt offended and disturbed by the developing counterculture of these decades. He began questioning long-held allegiances.

Bob had been in charge of fundraising to build a new Interchurch Office Center in Portland, and had been honored at the ground breaking in June of 1963. The building eventually became home to the local affiliate of the National Council of Churches. But when the Watts riots erupted in Los Angeles in 1965, he found that he and the National Council were on opposite sides of the issue.

Statements from the Council claimed that the conditions the rioters opposed were so bad that the rioters were justified in their actions. Bob agreed conditions were bad and needed to be changed; he had worked most of his life to help change them. But to a son of John Robert Pamplin, nothing justified a breakdown of law and discipline.

"Look at this," he complained to Katherine, waving the Council's statement. "These people tore up half of Los Angeles and the National Council of Churches wants to take their part. They're trying to justify what they did, to excuse it. I can't go along with it."

And with typical single-mindedness, he launched a one-man campaign against the NCC. He let loose his first volley in Little Rock, Arkansas, at a Rotary meeting. The Rotarians were prominent Little Rock business and civic leaders who met weekly for a luncheon and some lighthearted fellowship, perhaps a few songs and jokes. But this week they received a heartfelt argument, buttressed by impressive debating skills, from a man whose faith had been shaken to the roots.

"I was taught and still believe that the Bible is the infallible Word of God," Bob proclaimed, "and that the chief functions of the church are to save souls for Christ, to administer to spiritual needs of its members. I was also taught and still believe that the Christian way of accomplishing things is through prayer and setting an example." With that he launched into a castigation of the Council's "liberal group." Rather than emphasizing "spiritual salvation and Christian living on a personal basis," Bob said, this group seemed to be more interested in "attempting to legislate every facet of man's environment."

He was, Bob went on, "calling for prayer and action that our church life not slide into religious socialism." And he urged the Rotarians to press their individual denominations to pull out of the NCC at once.

"I am in sympathy with giving minorities equal rights," he concluded, well aware of how his argument would be attacked, "and Georgia-Pacific has been among the leaders in fair employment practices, but I am not in sympathy with the program that this group has been following—advocation of breaking the law to carry out its ends; for if law and order break down for this purpose, then law and order will break down for other purposes as well."

Bob's remarks were widely reported in Arkansas, and shortly drew a noncommittal reply from the Council. More than that, he caused others who had paid little attention to the Council to reconsider its activities. An Arkansas Judge, Ed F. McFaddin, was prompted by Bob's speech to launch his own investigation into the NCC. He came to the conclusion that its social activism had "created an unbridgeable chasm between the various Christian denominations."

Bob pushed on, using his position with the Greater Portland Council of Churches to force a reassessment of social activism and its place in church life. And he knew, throughout the entire struggle, that his strong stand had caused hard feelings. But this was a matter of principle. "You can't be everything to everyone in a church," Bob explained to his son, who as a member of the younger generation had many friends among the more liberal thinkers. "You have to go by the Bible."

B ob butted heads as well with two ministers on the Board at Lewis & Clark. A number of athletes were found to have been drinking wine and the coach wanted to suspend them from the football team for the season. But the ministers thought the students should be forgiven, and they appealed to the board for leniency. Bob ruled that the Board had to follow the recommendations of the coach. "You will have no discipline unless you support the coach," he insisted, echoing almost word for word the lessons of his father.

And yet, as Chairman, Bob many times allowed alternative points of view at the college. In the early 1960s, Gus Hall, secretary of the U.S. Communist Party, was scheduled to speak on the campus. John Howard, the college President, felt that academic freedom required the school to allow him to speak, and Bob agreed. He didn't care for Hall's message, but Bob said: "A country that believes in itself is strong. Let him come. Communism will be self-defeating." Though he could have bullied the Lewis & Clark administrators, as one of the school's largest contributors, Bob took pains to respect a diversity of opinion and free expression.

At church, Bob continued to find himself on opposite sides of issues from several of his spiritual leaders. At one point, for instance, he learned that homosexual students at a Presbyterian seminary were seeking dates by posting notices on school bulletin boards. Bob couldn't have disapproved more. And yet this same staunch Portland conservative was also one of the leading industrial opponents of the fight in Southeast Asia.

"The Vietnam War is a terrible mistake," Pamplin declared at another speaking engagement. And, clearly understanding the war's connection to the contemporary turmoil, he added, "and we have compounded that mistake." He called the Vietnam War "the longest, most fruitless and illogical" in American history, and perceived it as the cause of unrest in the country, including the riots he hated. "It's not a question of what the war is costing us today but what it will cost us in the future, financially, in lives and in breakdown of the nation's morals."

Ultimately, the distraught philanthropist took the sort of positive action he knew best. To increase opportunities for young people, Bob gave more scholarships, heading a scholarship drive at Lewis & Clark and giving a $250,000 challenge grant that raised millions more for construction, including $2.2 million to replace the gym. The grateful school named the building Pamplin Sports Center.

Similarly, he began giving scholarships at his alma mater, Virginia Tech. Bob and Bob Junior also endowed a professorship at the University of Portland: the Pamplin Professor of Business Administration. A few years later, the college awarded him an honorary doctorate, and Northwestern University, where he had gone to graduate school, gave him the merit award as an outstanding alumnus.

I n the 1960s Bob also suffered a number of new personal demands, compounding the worries of the societal turmoil. His mother, Pauline Beville Pamplin DeShazo, died in 1964. For all his forensics expertise, Bob found it impossible to speak much of the loss; his mother had always seemed the young one, the playful one, compared to Bob's stern father. Her dying called to mind the Rebel young cut down on her grandmother's farm, a hundred years ago now, and those who knew Bob best heard some of his pain over the loss in his outcry the next year against a changing church.

Also her death left empty the house Bob had built for her after the Second World War. As planned, he passed on the property to the Ocran Methodist Church where he'd learned so much as a child, learned in spite of his dreamy nature. He asked that it be used as a home for the pastor.

And Bob's mother, who'd in general lived as frugally as her first husband, left securities to Bob Junior, then a senior at Lewis & Clark College. By now, including money he'd received when he'd turned twenty-one, Bob's son had some $265,000 of his own. One hundred and sixty-five thousand was in marketable securities and the rest stood as a beacon for the future—it was stock in the R. B. Pamplin Corporation, then still technically in utero.

Bob Junior, while at Lewis & Clark, took a course by correspondence from the New York Institute of Finance on the stock market and stock investing. After that, he quickly put his newly acquired knowledge and childhood tutelage from his father to work. He used his marketable securities as collateral, borrowing against it to buy stock. Playing the market, Bob Junior demonstrated he had the old man's gumption and brains for investing by earning his first million dollars by the end of 1964.

All in all, the dedication of Lewis & Clark's Pamplin Sports Center in 1969 was a watershed event for the Pamplin family, a celebration that suggested a new generation would carry on the family's successes, and that their new home would accept them for what they were. Bob Junior flew back to Augusta to accompany his grandmother, Mrs. Reese, to Portland for the ceremony. And some of Bob's cousins, also came to Portland from Petersburg to take part. By then the family's commitment to athletic activities, particularly outdoor activities, was well-known throughout the community.

At Georgia-Pacific, too, by then, there had been a changing of the guard. Though Bob Senior had been de facto President and CEO since Owen Cheatham's 1957 stroke, to outsiders the company's founder had remained its head man. Bob, as one of Owen's oldest friends and a man who understood public relations, had gone along with this charade uncomplainingly. Nonetheless, he was relieved when, in December 1967, at last Owen retired from the company. At fifty-six, Bob Pamplin was publicly declared the company Chairman and President and Chief Executive Officer.

By now Georgia-Pacific had assets in excess of $1 billion. This included some 5.5 million acres of timberland, the equivalent of Connecticut and Rhode Island combined. It was the nation's largest plywood producer, second largest in lumber production, and third largest producer of gypsum products such as wallboard, and a major producer of paper products and chemicals. There were over a hundred G-P building-materials centers across the country, selling products of all three types. The firm had 35,000 employees, and had made many, many stockholders rich—including more than a couple of Bob's relatives.

Bob's greatest satisfaction, indeed, was the strength of Georgia-Pacific stock. When G-P first started acquiring companies, most of them wanted cash because they did not have enough confidence in the young corporation to take its stock. But by 1964, the company had done so well that almost everyone wanted the company's common stock. Getting stock was better than getting cash, in fact, because stock came in a tax-free exchange. Similarly, Bob's philanthropic impulses, therefore, often took the form of gifts of stock.

And of course, success breeds success. Georgia-Pacific now had a trading advantage over other companies. In most cases, when Bob's people acquired another company they were able to work out an agreement paying about eighty percent of the purchase price in stock. Georgia-Pacific itself, meantime, put enough common stock in reserve to cover the remaining twenty percent of the cost.

Georgia-Pacific even gave these companies an economic safety net in such deals. At any time during a three-year period after the sale, Bob's people could evaluate the eighty percent of common stock given to the seller If the value of the stock was less than the purchase price, G-P would issue enough shares from the stock reserve to bring the value of the shares to the purchase price. Over the next ten years, Georgia-Pacific acquired perhaps twenty companies this way, and only once had to issue a small number of shares from the reserve to cover a deficiency.

Finally, Bob made sure the company would have a steady, renewing supply of raw materials. He used helicopters to re-seed cut-over areas, another innovation in the industry. He also sent out teams of people to replant by hand where necessary, thinned places where regeneration was too thick, and developed improved seedlings that would grow faster. To him, the forests were like Papa's truck farm, only with a longer harvest cycle.

And yet even at the top of Georgia-Pacific, the only company he had ever worked for, Bob's dream of independence never left him. The same year he became CEO of Georgia-Pacific, he became interested in textiles. It's not that this industry was any more fascinating than timber, but he could see that the stocks were undervalued. His nose for hidden assets quickly sniffed out that there was more in some of these old companies than the value of the stock indicated.

Now, making his first moves as the head of the R. B. Pamplin Corporation, he began buying common shares of Mount Vernon Mills. This solid and longstanding firm had the additional appeal of being headquartered near Bob's old stomping grounds, in Greenville, South Carolina. Before he retired from G-P, Bob managed to accumulate more than 10 percent of the Vernon Mills stock.

Bob also took a more active interest in those spiritual institutions that seemed to reflect his own beliefs. When Billy Graham's crusade came to Seattle, Washington, Bob remembered the time Reverend Graham had spoken at his church in Augusta, and how his then-young Bobby had responded to the Reverend's call. So Bob was pleased to serve on the crusade's finance committee, raising funds in the Northwest for a program at Wheaton College. He and Graham stayed on each other's Christmas card list from then on.

In addition, there were further honors for the new President and CEO. The Governor of Virginia appointed him to the Board of Visitors of Virginia Tech. Two years later Dr. Marshall T. Hahn, Jr., President of the school, gave him the Distinguished Alumni Award. The building housing the College of Business at Tech was named Pamplin Hall in 1969.

But Bob discovered there is such a thing as too much success. By 1970 Georgia-Pacific was headed for $2 billion in sales, matching gigantic Weyerhaeuser. Much of this good fortune was due to Bob's breakthrough innovation in Southern pine plywood. However, demand for G-P's plywood had grown so much that most of the small sawmills in the South banded together to complain to the Federal Trade Commission that they couldn't compete for raw materials. They claimed that Georgia-Pacific was able to outbid them because wood used for plywood produced yields two or three times the value of lumber. Of course, not everyone in the South was hurt. The Southern pine plywood had increased the value of many smaller timber holdings.

Nonetheless, Bob began hearing rumors that the Federal Trade Commission was coming after him. When the FTC took action against Georgia-Pacific, ruling that the company divest itself of about half its timber resources and plywood production in the South, he had a quick and determined response.

"There is no place for the Federal Trade Commission in America today," Bob stated at dedication ceremonies for a rebuilt plywood plant in Emporia, Virginia, early in 1972. "We have the antitrust law which looks after the same thing. That law is all we need." Bob said his company was being penalized for being too efficient, and that the FTC wanted to bring him down to the level of the inefficient.

The Commission, nevertheless, stuck to its guns, insisting that Georgia-Pacific divest itself of eight plants in the South, and the timber holdings that went with the plants. In response, some of Bob's friends in politics tried to take his side. The Governor of Virginia, Linwood Holton, questioned the FTC ruling. "It's incredible to me," Holton wrote, "that a giant supplier of jobs and materials has to stop and defend itself against such an order. I ask now that the FTC reconsider its order." The legislature in South Carolina and other Southern states passed resolutions condemning the Commission for its interference. To them, it seemed once again like the North meddling in affairs of the South.

These protests were of no use, finally. Bob's struggles with the Council of Churches and others hadn't caused him to lose his lifelong respect for discipline and playing by the rules. A good ballplayer, he knew, once in a while would lose on a technicality. And yet, now sixty-one and facing retirement, Bob came up with one more ingenious stroke in order to meet the FTC requirements while at the same time protecting his stockholders' interests.

This gambit also set a precedent; other companies did the same in coming years. Bob knew that the whole FTC action had been inspired by competitors who wanted to acquire efficient Georgia-Pacific plants at bargain prices in a buyers' market. But now, instead of just selling off the assets, Bob divested G-P of several key timber and production holdings by spinning them off into an entirely new company. The idea called for 92,500 of his stockholders to receive one share of stock in the new firm for every four shares of G-P they owned. It was the equivalent of a twenty-five percent stock split.

Thus was born Louisiana-Pacific, in 1972. Harry Merlo, a 47-year old Georgia-Pacific Executive Vice President, was the new President. Louisiana-Pacific, the first company spun off in response to an FTC action, started with twenty percent of Georgia-Pacific's assets. Thus, nationally, it was third in lumber and sixth in plywood production from its inception. This made Louisiana-Pacific a strong, viable company and the spin-off hurt neither employees nor stockholders. Employees got all the benefits at L-P that they'd had at G-P. And the value of the stock in both companies grew faster than Georgia-Pacific's would have alone.

The Federal Trade Commission also placed restrictions on Georgia-Pacific preventing the company from purchasing assets from any other company in the plywood business. But these restrictions did allow G-P to buy timber and timberlands, under certain conditions.

Over time, the consent decree worked more to Georgia-Pacific's benefit than to its harm. The company was able to acquire a lot of additional land, while the decree prevented the FTC from bringing action against them for it. And now, of course, there was Louisiana-Pacific as well. Said one of Bob's rivals: "It's bad enough having one G-P for competition, let alone having two."

N ot only were there now two Georgia-Pacifics, there were also two Bob Pamplins doing business. Bob Junior was thirty years old in early 1972. Like his father, he had a feel for sound investments, and he'd already been successful on his own, trading in stocks, timberlands, and farms.

Most of the money Bob Junior had inherited from his grandmother was in the form of securities, and that, of course, was one reason he'd developed an interest in the stock market. But the primary engines behind Bob Junior's aggressive investment program had started running years earlier, when he was sick with hepatitis and his father began reading stock quotations to him from *The Wall Street Journal.* As Bob Senior's father had inculcated him with the common sense of good farming, so Bob himself passed on the money sense of a winning market player.

In early 1972, then, this rising young investor wrote his parents a letter detailing his progress with his inheritance. He began by speaking of his early ambitions for the money. "I would dream of how great it would be," Bob Junior wrote, "if I could build this into a fortune, one like you read about in books on business tycoons. I am sure this was important to me because of the benefits money could bring, but probably more important was my continual, lifelong ambition to do things that would earn my parents' respect and admiration, and make them generally glad they put me on earth."

Then he made clear that, in fact, his dream had come true: "Being a son of such outstanding parents, it becomes imperative to me to be a man of achievement and improver of those things (money) which are given me. I think perhaps to some degree I have done this. To you, my parents, my deep-felt gratitude for allowing me the opportunity to experience what success I have. Without your assistance, little of this would have been possible."

A letter like that, of course, would mean a great deal to any parents, at any time. But to Bob Senior and Katherine these kind words came at a particularly good moment, when the company's problems with the Federal Trade Commission had been compounded by greater questions of integrity and basic values—questions that came into the Pamplin home.

Bob Senior gave $30,000 to Nixon's reelection campaign in 1972, and raised another $40,000 for him from others in the company. After that election, Bob and Bob Junior were invited to a dinner for business leaders at the White House, a proud moment for the old barefoot farm boy. At dinner Bob found himself at a table with H. R. Haldeman, a top aide to the President.

Within the next year, however, the so-called Watergate crisis unfolded, with revelations of all sorts of dubious tactics on Nixon's part. Throughout 1974 the President came under mounting, unprecedented pressure to resign. Bob, characteristically, remained loyal to his old friend and sent him a letter of support. Nixon wrote back: "Many times in the past I have had occasion to thank you, but I want to say once again how much it means to know I have been able to count on the loyalty and understanding of so many good, long-time friends. At this time in particular, I am deeply grateful for assurances of continued support."

In public, too, though defending Nixon was extremely unpopular, Bob stood up for him. "The press and Congress have been making it difficult for President Nixon to run the country properly," he declared.

Not long after he made that statement, the Portland CEO received an unusual visitor. Bob's office was in the top floor of a marble and glass highrise built in downtown Portland in 1970: a new city landmark aptly named the Georgia-Pacific Building. Gleaming white statuary rise from the center of a plaza fountain out front. Out his windows Bob had a sweeping view from the exclusive residential West Hills all the way to the older Northeast quadrant of the city. On clear days, snow-capped Mount Hood towered on the horizon. One morning in 1973, Bob was at his desk as usual when his secretary came on the intercom to say there was a gentleman to see him—a man who "says it's very important." Instead of her usual cheerfulness, the woman had a note of apprehension, of fear in her voice.

"Show him in," Bob said.

The man was in his mid-thirties, dressed in a gray suit and wearing a slight smile.

"Mr. Pamplin?"

"That's right."

"Mr. Pamplin, I am with the Federal Bureau of Investigation. You have the right to remain silent. If you choose not to be silent, anything you say can and will be used against you in a court of law. You have the right to have an attorney present. If you cannot afford one"—the man's smile widened slightly—"the court will appoint one for you. Do you understand?"

Did Bob *understand*? It took every ounce of his Virginia-Tech-trained self-control not to jump up and try to bite the man's head off Was he under arrest?

"I don't want a lawyer," Bob said, levelly. "Just tell me what you want."

The agent wanted company records, especially expense accounts. He explained that he was investigating illegal campaign contributions. "One of the things we look for are personal contributions to candidates that are really corporate contributions, made up for elsewhere by false entries on expense accounts."

"Well," said Bob, still flat voiced, "you won't find any of that here."

He was right, of course, but the agent spent days poring over Georgia-Pacific files before he was satisfied. Bob liked to help politicians he agreed with, and he wasn't afraid to speak out on behalf of an increasingly unpopular President. But to him an election was no different than the many small contests within his business. It had to be done within the rules.

This kind of integrity, so kindly spoken of by his son in that recent letter, brought the man more honors and awards toward the end of his career with Georgia-Pacific. He was picked by *Fortune* as one of the nation's leading industrialists, and as one of *Financial World's* top Chief Executive Officers. Sales and Marketing Executives International named him Marketing Man of the Year. He was even recognized by *Environment* magazine for G-P's successful process to remove mercury traces from industrial sludge.

And in 1976, the year he retired, *Financial World* named him Chief Executive Officer of the Year in his industry, while the Virginia Press Association chose him Virginian of the Year, given to a Virginian who has

moved from the state and brought distinction to himself and favorable
attention to Virginia.

T hen came retirement, on November 25, 1976—Thanksgiving Day,

*Robert B. Pamplin, Sr. and Katherine
Pamplin.*

or close enough. He had a lot to be thankful for. When he'd started with
the company in 1934, he was making $1,200 per year; when he retired in
1976, he was earning $250,000 per year—a cutback actually from the
$275,000 he'd been making two years earlier, before he'd, in his opinion,
"begun to slow down." And then there were, of course, the amazing things
he'd done for his company.

In 1957, the year Bob became President of Georgia-Pacific, the company had sales of $121 million and profits of $7.4 million. When he retired
in 1976, the year-end figures showed sales of $3 billion and profits of $215
million, well on the way to becoming the largest forest products company
in the world.

Equal to the corporation's amazing growth in sales and profits was the appreciation of market value of stock. If a person had purchased $10,000 of Georgia-Pacific stock when it came on the market in 1947, its value including stock splits and stock dividends, would have been $3.2 million on December 31, 1976. In addition, cash dividends of $482,000 would also have been received.

Growth of this magnitude is exceptional. Some factors can describe how such expansion happens, such as imagination, hard work, dedication, perseverance, luck, faith, and intelligence. But, behind such a success story, one usually finds the tight intertwining of a business philosophy and personal beliefs. This was so with Georgia-Pacific and Bob Pamplin.

To most other men, retirement from such success might have meant a time to head for the rocking chair, the motor home, or the golf course. But Bob Pamplin was never one to put up his feet and dwell on the past. It was the future, and the fulfillment of an old dream that energized him now. Gifted people tend to go on doing what they're good at, painting till they can no longer hold a brush, playing piano till their fingers will no longer work the keys. Bob's gift was making money, and he intended to go on exercising it.

CHAPTER 13

Robert Pamplin, Senior
Saving the Best For Last

N O SOONER had Bob Pamplin retired from Georgia-Pacific than he rented out space in his old building.

His R.B. Pamplin Corporation set up offices only a few stories down from the ones he'd occupied just a few months previously. He remodeled the new space so it looked just like what he'd enjoyed at G-P, with the same corner location and panoramic view, except that now he was on the eighteenth floor instead of the twenty-seventh. Along the walls ran the same type of wood paneling as before, and across the floor the same style of oriental rug. Yet there was one difference between this office and his previous one, a crucial one. Now his son Bob Junior was in the office next door. The sixty-five-year-old father was corporate Chairman, and the thirty-five-year-old son corporate President.

From the first, the two Pamplins put their heads together on all decisions. One of their earliest moves was another company acquisition, following the first-rate model the father had established at Georgia-Pacific. The company they picked up was Ross Island Sand and Gravel, one of those older, asset-rich firms Bob Senior liked so much. RIS&G mined gravel from the island for which it was named, a small place on the Willamette River, and sold that plus sand, concrete, pre-mixed sack products, and asphalt paving. The two Pamplins had been studying the company a while, so well laid were their plans for their own corporation. They knew it was worth more than the owners were willing to accept. Soon they signed papers to buy the firm's entire stock for nearly $7 million; father and son remained as fair about paying a good price as the father had been, earlier, at Georgia-Pacific.

Bob Senior and Junior made back this entire purchase cost in less than a year. They used Ross Island's own cash on hand, proceeds from the sale of some of its assets, and cash generated by its operations. In short, the deal was a classic pickup, as slick a piece of fielding as anything Bull Pamplin ever pulled off on the fields of Virginia Tech. More than that, it proved at once that the R.B. Pamplin Corporation was playing with the big boys, and playing for keeps. Almost fifteen years further along, Ross Island Sand and Gravel remained one of their subsidiaries, with some 250 employees and sales of $30 million.

T he R. B. Pamplin Corporation continued to buy up Mount Vernon Mills common stock, and by 1982 Bob Senior and Junior owned about a third of the company. "It's not that I'm particularly interested in textiles any more than I was in timber," Bob once said of this acquisition. "What I'm interested in is being successful in business, and textile stocks are currently undervalued."

It was time, they felt, to test their new power at a board meeting. Mount Vernon's chairman was Tom Bancroft, a sound businessman based, like his firm, in New York. It was Bancroft who'd invited the Pamplins to join the board. But now he was pushing to buy new looms for a mill at Tallassee, Alabama, and more than one of the other board members felt that this wouldn't be a good move. The new one-third owners agreed; the mills would take far too long generating the income to pay off the cost. Father and son came to New York, hoping the board would see it their way.

The Pamplins, as always, came not with a sword but an olive branch. Or at least, they came with something green. "We would rather buy the remaining stock of Mount Vernon Mills," Bob Senior said, "than see the company buy that equipment."

It didn't take the principal stockholders on the board long to see the advantages of the Pamplins' offer. The buy-out would mean money in their pockets, and given Bob's unparalleled skill in management, the company and the employees would be better off. After negotiation, the board stockholders agreed to take $53 per share, and the remaining shareholders speedily accepted the offer as well.

R.B. Pamplin Corporation needed to borrow $25 million for the deal, borrowing this from the First Interstate Bank. But once again they had the debt paid off in seven months, by cash flow from the company, and reducing staff and liquidating assets. Bob and Bob Junior went to Greenville, South Carolina, to look over a few of the seven textile mills they had bought. They met with everyone from top executives to mill workers, and sensed, predictably, uncertainty about what the future might hold under R. B. Pamplin

The two men set at once to assuage these worries. Bob told David Meek, a financial officer at the tender age of twenty-seven, "Pay attention to what we do and you'll get an education in business. At Georgia-Pacific we doubled sales and profits there every five years. I'll bet we can do better than that here."

The young officer realized that, seventy-one years old or not, his new superior still had a ballplayer's enthusiasm for the game of business. And such dedication and high spirits proved contagious, throughout the Pamplins' latest acquisition. Where there'd been drift and indecision, the father and son instilled focus and direction. As before, Bob made sure to set clearly defined goals, so that the employees knew exactly where the company was headed.

"And I'll tell you something else," Bob announced to the staff at Mount Vernon. "If you need a decision today from either Bob Junior or me you'll get it today." Actually, as the staff quickly learned, they most often had their decision from the Pamplins before they got off the phone. Information systems were kept simple, right down the line from Bob to the mill hands.

Also, as he had at Georgia-Pacific, Bob insisted on a hard-nosed commitment to company-wide sobriety. Signs were posted around the mills: "If you're on drugs, don't apply! " Even now, if anyone is caught coming to work on drugs, they are let go immediately. "It's not fair to the other employees," Bob maintains. "With all this equipment around, even the slightest incapacity is too dangerous to them and to the other employees."

And in a surprising development, this stripped-down approach to running a business proved to be, by the mid-1980s, a very contemporary style. Bob's direct involvement with his product's entire process had now become a buzzword, or buzz expression: "Total Quality Management," a notion that some would think had been introduced by the Japanese. Also, "Management By Objective," another idea supposedly on the cutting edge, was just another way of describing Bob Senior's long-standing system of explicit and mutually agreed-upon annual goals. The man had never intended to become a New Age management type, of course. Rather, it appeared the age had caught up with him.

Mount Vernon Mills quickly became an industry leader in new electronic data interchange programs such as "Quick Response" and "Just in Time Delivery." K-Mart, a major customer, can send a thousand store orders for Mount Vernon Mills infant clothing and bedding products on a Sunday night, and count on these products being put together, packaged, and shipped to all thousand stores by the following Thursday.

And once again, the only committee at Mount Vernon Mills is the Operating Policy Committee. This includes the top financial, marketing, and manufacturing people, who meet with the Pamplins for a single day after each quarter. The principal purpose of the meeting, as at Georgia-Pacific, is to review and inform.

N one of this, to be sure, took place without some cash outlay. In order to make Mount Vernon Mills a "low-cost producer," paradoxically, Bob Senior and Junior had to spend quite a bit up front. Indeed, their young financial officer, David Meek, was afraid the broad-based capital investments would strain the company's cash flow. From 1985 to 1992 the Pamplins invested more than $300 million in capital expenditures, principally in new equipment. But it wasn't long before Meek became a believer.

"Capital expenditures cleaned up the balance sheet faster than the conservative approach would have," Meek said in the early 1990s. The Pamplins' spending had proven again the power of positive thinking: good had followed good.

The investment in state-of-the-art textile equipment immediately resulted in higher productivity and a product nearly free of defects. This in turn has enabled the company to better serve its customers. The expenditures haven't proved all that different from old John Robert Pamplin's investment in a Model T, years ago, in order to get his butter beans to market while they were fresher than the other farmers'.

The Pamplins make it a goal to run all their textile-producing equipment twenty-four hours a day, seven days a week. If Mount Vernon isn't working at full capacity, it's frittering away the very benefits of its expensive new technology, since the more units you produce, the less the fixed cost per unit. But to have the plants operating at capacity requires close coordination between marketing and manufacturing. The company's marketing people must develop a keen sense of what the customer is going to want years in the future, so the manufacturing people can buy equipment accordingly.

The proof of this information advantage lies in Mount Vernon's ability to thrive despite an industry-wide slowdown. The textile industry has been ravaged by irresponsible leveraged buy-outs (very different from Bob Pamplin's style of acquisition, which traded in assets rather than junk bonds and never dismantled companies outright) and by the booming import trade. Yet the Pamplins' company has continued to grow. Mount Vernon has focused on supplying those key customers who want a swift-acting, world-class manufacturer. They've become a "preferred supplier," counted on for the highest quality at the most cost-effective prices.

Within the company, the motivation is likewise crystal clear. As always, the Pamplins aren't much for big salaries, but they provide employees an opportunity to earn a lot more based on return on investment. This incentive program tends to keep people working toward a greater goal, rather than simply putting in their hours toward a monthly check. Then too, many of Mount Vernon's employees are, naturally enough, committed Christians like the two men at the top. They appreciate working for a father and son who've set examples of being equally committed to success in business and to their good works as Christians.

T he R.B. Pamplin Corporation has made some other key acquisitions as well. And in 1991 the company acquired the Harmony Grove textile mills with two plants. This brought the total number of Pamplin-owned plants to seventeen, in a network spider-webbing the entire South. Bob Senior retired from G-P in November 1976. Since then he and Bob Junior have been devoting full time to R. B. Pamplin Corporation, and the performance of the company has been much better than what Bob Senior enjoyed at G-P. The results of R. B. Pamplin Corporation at four-year intervals were as follows:

For Fiscal Years Ending May 31 (thousands)

	1981	1985	1989	1993
Net Sales	$19,700	$116,100	$408,400	$685,000
Net Profits	$1,000	8,300	25,500	55,500
Cash Flow	1,100	14,300	43,300	100,000

R.B. Pamplin Corporation, too, has set a new standard for corporate responsibility and generosity. It has been giving about ten percent of pre-tax profits to over 100 tax-exempt organizations. Contributions for the fiscal year ending May 31, 1993, totaled over $10 million. Indeed, the Pamplins' generosity remains legendary in the South and Northwest. Their desire to help and ability to provide has made a major difference in building better communities. For example, in 1989 Mrs. M.A. King Talley, director of social services in Bob's native Dinwiddie County, wrote to him asking for help in funding companion services for the elderly and shut-ins. She would have been delighted with a contribution of, say, $10,000. Instead, Bob set up a trust fund with stock amounting to more than fifty times that amount, generating an annual income of approximately $50,000. The county social services have their own endowment, a situation well-nigh unique in the nation.

One Saturday morning in 1991, janitors in Dinwiddie County's administration building saw an elderly but solidly-built stranger walking alone through the corridors of the two-story brick structure. It was Bob Pamplin, Senior, on another business trip through the South. He wanted to see his portrait, hanging in the building his grateful home county had named after him in 1984—the Pamplin Administration Building. Another of Bob's old boyhood friends, Judge Gus Mayes, had arranged to have the portrait put up, in order to show the county's appreciation for all that Bob had given to so many local institutions and individuals.

But Bob Pamplin, Senior, isn't just a portrait yet. At eighty-one he remains intimately involved with the day-to-day running of a major corpo-

Robert B. Pamplin, Jr. and
Robert B. Pamplin, Sr.

ration. He remains as well a committed father, working side by side with his only son, and a loving husband with an active social life shaped to no small extent by his overwhelming generosity. Figures alone can't convey the enormity of his giving, but a few are called for nonetheless. Bob's donations to church and charity have held unyieldingly at about thirty percent of his annual income. In 1966, when he made $136,476 in wages and dividends, he contributed $50,061. By 1971—true to his G-P plan—those figures were roughly doubled. And twenty years further on, bringing in over $3 million thanks to his new venture, Bob Pamplin gave away over a million.

Bob always made sure to give back to people and institutions that gave to him. Remembering how the discipline of his days as a "Rat" at Virginia Tech had molded him, he and Bob Junior endowed the college of business which was named after them, the R.B. Pamplin College of Business. And in the mid 1980s, when the school called upon father and son to raise $50 million for its "Campaign of Excellence," the two put their hearts into the effort, and wound up generating $118 million instead. So exceptional was their dedication, they were awarded honorary degrees for this and other contributions. These degrees were a most special recognition. Since 1929 only three degrees have been given, with two of the three being awarded in 1987 to Bob Pamplin, Senior, and Bob Pamplin, Junior.

In short, Bob's life is the opposite of the millionaire stereotype, the Citizen Kane whose selfish ambition leaves him disconnected from the world, rich in material goods but destitute in spirit. No small amount of this triumph over the dangers of wealth is thanks to his humble beginnings—indeed, "humble" is an understatement—which instilled in him an unshakable sense of money's limits. His first considerations remained, ever afterwards, issues of principle, willingness to work, and faith in God.

His greatest success, in other words, isn't reflected in a balance sheet, but rather in the rare mutual regard he shares with his namesake son. Today Bob Junior owns or controls seventy-five percent of the stock in the family corporation. It's hard to imagine a greater testament to the trust of father in son, and the fidelity of son to father. Bob Junior has never wavered an iota from the honor he feels toward his father—feels, and demonstrates daily. To the Pamplins, which of them owns the stock is a mere legality, not the reality of moral authority. As Bob Junior puts it: "My father knows with clear assurity that after open discussion and compromise I will follow his direction."

PART 3
ROBERT B. PAMPLIN, JUNIOR

CHAPTER 14

Robert Pamplin, Junior
Early Years

I am Bob Pamplin, Junior. American-born, I was raised in the South; today I carry on my life's work in the country's Northwest. That work is as father and husband, preacher and businessman, outdoorsman and ducator, philanthropist and horse-breeder and writer. And it's my voice, my own first-person vision, that will now take Heritage through to its conclusion.

I realize this means a radical shift.

Throughout the two previous Parts, hundreds of pages by this time, my family has presented itself at the comfortable distance of the third person. But now, in Part 3, I remove that distance. I present instead myself: my flaws and fears and dreams, my challenges and struggles and triumphs.

My purpose is not to preen my feathers, not to indulge in chest-thumping braggadocio. Just the opposite. There's no more honest way to finish Heritage. There's no way that's less self-promoting, less a glossing-over of sore spots and hard choices.

My ancestors Robert Beville Armiger and his descendants appear in a lovely church carving, as we saw in previous chapters. But I am no church carving, no finished sculptor's beauty. As I write this I am still only Bob Pamplin, Junior, a transplanted Southerner trying to do his best in this world of compromise and limitations.

And that is how I must present myself to you, if my book's to have the utter sincerity I want for it.

For who isn't, like me, seeking to work out his or her own heritage in personal terms? Who, truly? We're all trying to keep our balance at the summit of a long climb through the centuries: trying neither to betray our past nor to hide from the clamorous demands of our present. Every one of us works ultimately in the first person, improvising as we go.

Consider the dilemma faced by my forebears Athaliah and Ella Boisseau. These two women had the Old South in their very bones. Yet with the end of the War Between the States, both recognized that their beloved Dixie *was passing—passing with good reason, to some extent. Both had to find a way to carry their guiding childhood precepts into a complex new world.*

Yes, like Athaliah and Ella, we're all improvising as we go. Therefore I want my Part 3 to provide more than simply a summary of my own experience. I'll do that, too, of course. I'll tell you about everything from an African safari to a bout with cancer. But, more than that, I need to conclude with philosophy: with my own guiding precepts for constructing a future in harmony with our past. Out of that ageless harmony, I firmly believe, will arise personal success in any world.

Thus my Part 3 will itself be in two sections. The first will present my own experience; the second will summarize the lessons I've derived from that experience, lessons shaped throughout by my ever-growing knowledge of my greater family story.

My own life, after all, has been marked by the same elements as my entire family's struggle through the last millennium. I was born in 1941, a time when war was once more ravaging the civilized world. I've had to contend against tragedies that compare with Southern slaveholding, and against scourges as terrible as the Black Plague.

In other words, I've had to create, under pressure, a code of living that synthesizes present and past: that brings together today's harsh reality with tonight's dream of better.

Hence my desire, my driving desire, to record that hard-won code here. It's not braggadocio, no. It's the urge to bring the same benefit to anyone who takes the time to read and understand. It's the attempt to carry forward the good work Norman Vincent Peale did in his Power of Positive Thinking, *to provide everyone with a few precepts for achieving both success and peace, worldly reward and spiritual sustenance.*

I finished my last corrections of these proofs in April 1993. You read them at a time unknown to me, in places that I can hardly imagine.

Yet by the miracle of this book, in my own humble way I am with you, wherever you are. I am providing what guidance I can, what company I can. And in this I try to follow—in my own humble way—the teachings of the greatest guide and companion, Christ our Savior, Who reminds us that He is with us always, till the end of the age.

E.C. WAS THE GREATEST FISHERMAN on earth. That, at least, was my firm conviction when my Dad first took me fishing in the swamps of the Savannah River, in eastern Georgia.

E.C. didn't have to use a lot of the tricks other fishermen did to catch jack, his specialty. He didn't have to spit on the bait, or hold his mouth right, or even wear a special fishing hat—although "all that might help," as he used to tell me with a wink.

E.C. just used a bent old cane pole, with a simple cork bob. He baited his hook with worms. But he could catch more jack than all the other fishermen in Georgia put together. That's what he claimed, at least, and it never so much as crossed my mind to doubt him.

I was six years old when Dad introduced me to the swamp. We went on weekends, nine times out of ten, sharing a one-room shack with E.C. and whoever else might have had a taste for fish that Saturday. And it wasn't just us men, in that shack. River rats holed up in the pot-bellied stove. These had to be chased out, their claws making a sudden racket on the stove's cast iron, before E.C. or one of the others could cook up some squirrel or catfish.

We made stew, on those trips. The shack was so small, odors of a stew could make the air in there seem as thick and rich as the Savannah River mud outside. Thick, rich, and delicious: an aroma that tantalized already eager appetites. When the meal was finally ready we would dig in like hogs. We probably sounded like hogs, too. We sucked the bones clean and we soaked up the last drops with hot biscuits. Then it was time to sit back and swap stories of fishing and hunting. Or my father and his friends did the swapping; I did the listening.

E.C., of course, would nearly always go first. He'd have some tale that was also a challenge: try and top this. Tilting back in his chair, the light

from the kerosene lamp dancing on his face, he'd begin with some atten-
tion-grabbing line that was, itself, a kind of challenge:

"The Savannah River bobwhite are the smartest quail in the world,"
he might say. Then he'd wait to make sure he had everyone listening,
sometimes a good twenty seconds or more, before he went on with his story.

"Those bobwhite'll either get up behind you when you think they are
in front," E.C. might say, "or they'll get a tree between them and you just
when you shoot. They've had me plugging more damn trees! Lemme tell
you, I can remember one time when I finally got a clean shot at one. I hit
that bird—killed him dead—but you know what he did? He grabbed a leaf
and he used it like a blanket. Covered himself up on the way down so I
couldn't find him. Now that is one smart bird."

As the night wore on, the others took their attempts at topping E.C.
Sometimes I tried too, in my own boy's way. On most weekends, however,
after a few hours of talk it was obvious that the rest of us were still
hopelessly outmatched. We'd arrange our blankets on the floor.

Then once the lamps were extinguished, the real action began. It was
as if you had given all the rats in the swamp the starter's flag. The roof of
the shack was made of tin, and their scrabbling back and forth across it
sounded like a bowling alley on Saturday night. They found their way
inside, too. The older men had long since grown accustomed to these
creatures, but a young boy like me, peering into those huge, glittering
rodent eyes inches away across the floor—I'll tell you, it made me shrink
up closer to Dad. Eventually, however, the day's exhaustion would take its
toll, conquering even my fear. I wouldn't know a thing until someone was
boiling a pot of coffee next morning.

A young boy learns respect for the swamp in a hurry, which was part
of the reason Dad took me. I don't recall being afraid of the place itself—
despite how I felt about some of the creatures in it. My main feeling was
fascination. The trees alone fascinated me: cone-shaped cypress protruding
from the murky water. On the one hand the swamp had quicksand, a quick
and merciless killer, and on the other it had such febrile profusion of life.
Gators, rattlers, and water moccasins were natives, here. I quickly learned
to respect their turf.

Those were great days, with freedom to experience something like
what the Georgia natives had. The ancient Creek and Cherokee had prayed
to the majesty of this swamp, these creatures, and in adventures like my

own had carved out their initiations as warrior braves. Thick above-ground roots and indomitable creepers challenged my every step, and the clean yet heavy smell of a still marsh exhilarated me. There was a sense of daring and mystery that, some days, kept me in a state of wonder from breakfast till stew-time. Memories include ducks stirring to sudden flight as a small boat encroached silently into their domain . . . the deep-throated bellows of hound dogs on the trail of a deer . . . the incessant chatter of the wily gray squirrel, which gave us many a good barbecue or brunswick stew.

With my Dad and I going back so often, I also learned to respect our companions in the cabin. Besides the famous E.C., there were loggers, mill workers, even moonshiners. Among Dad's favorites was a logger named Connie Lane, a sweet older hunter who arranged meals, sleeping accommodations, and many of our hunts. But all these widely various men were friends of my father, who I knew worked as an "executive" with a small lumber company named Georgia Hardwood. I wasn't really sure what an "executive" did, in those days, but I understood that his work was something not at all like these other men's. He wore a coat and tie, my Dad. He went to an office and nearly always returned with his hands clean, his clothes unmussed.

I could see the contrast between his place in life and that of these other men, even as a youngster. So, too, I could see that true equality reigned at our camp. Working in a corporate office didn't give a man any advantage over a timber faller in that clapboard cabin. Rather we were all measured by the number of fish we caught or birds we shot. That's one lesson I never forgot.

B ut while the social lessons of a swamp visit may have been subtle, the majority of my training as a young Southern gentleman was anything but subtle. Whatever I learned was emphasized by my mother's ever-ready switch—or once in a while my father's belt. The first words I learned to say after "Mama" and "Daddy" were "Yessir" and "Yes'm." If I didn't use these designations when talking to my elders, I could expect a swift and painful reminder.

A child in the South jumps through many hoops, intended to give a young person a solid foundation for determining right from wrong. Part of this comes via the church, beginning with Sunday School at a very early age. But the greatest source for basic values is, always, a child's family elders: parents and grandparents and, in a house like mine, loving servants.

My mother was the family disciplinarian, the one charged with "bringing me up." It was she who let me know when I did something wrong, and who corrected me. She was swift, fair, and unswerving in her justice. Generally she used the same sort of switch her father and my Dad's had used on them, a thin and whiplike shoot off a tree outside our apartment. You could say she was the "first sergeant" in my early life. Dad, on the other hand, more often let his natural sternness take care of the discipline. He didn't have to take up a switch. He carried himself with such implicit authority, I respected his least wish immediately and without question.

As I look back, I realize that instilling values was a crucial aspect of my relationship with my parents. Survival skills, the work ethic, respect for one's elders, right and wrong, a strong faith in God—these were all part of what was being imparted. Though at the time, well . . . it's more than a little difficult to appreciate the instillation of lifetime values when you've been sent out to cut a switch that will be applied to your own personal behind.

Now, it must be said, I was hardly a bad kid. Rather, corporal discipline of this kind was part of my environment, as the son of Southerners not long off the farm. Many a time my Mom and Dad let me know they'd had the same switchings or worse when they were young, and so—after the stinging had faded, at least—I didn't feel singled out or branded as a misfit. Just the opposite, I understood I was part of a long chain of family values, extending far back into the past. I was part of centuries of clarity between right and wrong, a clarity that had to be reaffirmed generation by generation.

During my preschool years I lived in an apartment complex in downtown Augusta, Georgia. My playmates were a rough-and-tumble bunch, and a pecking order was quickly established. Small for my age, I was a natural candidate for low man in that order. But that wasn't how I saw it, no sir. The same discipline that was teaching me right from wrong was also, from the first, teaching me to stick up for what I believed in. Soon enough, I was getting into fights.

Then again, with that group, a fight didn't always require something as grand as sticking up for what you believe in. It seems like we were always slugging it out. The Second World War was on then, or it had just ended, and a lot of boys were trying to prove themselves as tough as their G.I. older brothers and uncles. Also, myself, it just wasn't in me to back down from a challenge. I got a good share of lickings for that. It all evened out, though, because I gave some lickings in return.

But while my parents were all for their boy showing a little gumption, I believe I fought too much for their liking. One of those fights made my mother angrier than I'd ever seen her. It happened after I'd had an accident at school—practically tearing off my ear on a barbed-wire fence. A doctor had done a good job of stitching, then had wrapped a bandage around and around my head, almost like a turban. The doctor, who knew the nature of kids in that area, admonished me not to get in any fights and mess up his careful work.

When I went outside to play, Mother also was precise in her instructions. "Bobby," she said, "don't you dare get in a fight, or you'll get a real whipping when you get in!"

But less than five minutes after I'd gone outside, I was down on the ground and one of the bigger kids in the neighborhood was pounding on my head. I don't know how I forgot my mother's warning; I don't recall now what triggered such a thoughtless fight. But by the time I got free of the bully, the bandage was soaked with blood and Mom was "seeing red" in more ways than one. Fortunately, the damage to the ear was superficial. The doctor was able to re-bandage it, but he had a few choice words for me while he worked.

I don't think that kids fight as much today as we did back in Augusta. I doubt that it's because the human animal is any more civilized now; more likely it's that youngsters today have more organized activities and other distractions. For the kids in small Southern communities, especially those thrown together in somewhat crowded living conditions, fighting was second nature.

That, too, is part of a Southern heritage. The War Between the States, after all, went on long after the Southern forces had every reason to stop; that's no accident. Manpower, food, ammunition, and even the room to maneuver had dwindled terribly. But the will to continue fighting died a hard death—if it ever died at all.

Most Southern children learn about the Civil War at an early age, either in school or through family discussions. The Rebel Yell, "Dixie," and even recognition of the Stars and Bars most likely came before national traditions, for a young Georgian in the 1940s. There really are those in the South who have never accepted Lee's surrender. It is difficult to explain to a Northerner the intensity, the bitterness, that remains ingrained in the Southern fiber even more than a century after the war.

My own indoctrination to the Civil War came in a most graphic way. We would often spend summers and vacations at the old Virginia farm where my father was reared. The property was in Dinwiddie County, near Petersburg. That city had been the site of a long siege, and battles such as Five Forks had been fought only a stone's throw away. The land itself still yielded artifacts from the war, Minie balls and pitted bits of weaponry, even eighty years or so after the last Rebel had laid down his arms. More than once, my Dad told me about using the lead balls to make fishing-line sinkers.

Keeping the memories of those battles alive was a sacred trust for my grandmother, the former Pauline Beville. She liked to relate tales of the war passed down from her Beville and Boisseau ancestors. For her, as for my parents, steeping the younger generation in the cultural heritage of the South was a privilege and a duty. More than once she pointed out that my grandfather, John Robert Pamplin, had been born in 1861, the year the Civil War began.

I never knew this John Robert; he died before I was born. But I often heard how he and his three sons cultivated thirty of their 200 acres with mule and plow. The farm was the sole support for the family. It had been a hard life, but they hadn't thought of themselves as poor.

They'd raised a few cows for milk and cream, raised chickens and hogs too, the hogs being the main meat staple. The farm had no running water. Instead, it had an outhouse, complete with a mail-order catalog for reading and other duties. Grandmother cooked on a wood stove, and one of the chores of the boys was to see that the wood box was stocked. I had my share of chopping and splitting when I visited there, too. And I carried in water from the well.

Getting the pail to the house with water still in it could be a major problem. Big people could carry two pails at a time, and thus be balanced, but a youngster had all he could do to carry one in front of him with both hands—making the journey from the well was one of bumps, trips, sloshes, and spills.

Pork was still the primary meat source on the farm when I visited as a boy. My grandmother did have a refrigerator, but even so, some of the pork she kept in it aged well beyond the time when most people would have eaten it. Myself, I didn't know what was wrong with it. I just knew it smelled bad and tasted funny, but that you ate what you were served when you were at the farm. Grandmother also sold fryer chickens as well as eggs, and as a child I was fascinated with the ritual of slaughtering the chickens. Yes, it was a gory sight. As any farm kid knows, the saying "running around like a chicken with its head cut off" has a basis in fact. Decapitated chickens can go into an absolute frenzy. Grandmother Pamplin solved that indelicacy, however, by tying the birds' feet to a clothesline. While they hung helpless, she methodically cut off their heads with a large knife, cautioning me to stay clear of the spurting blood.

It was hardly a pretty sight, yet I don't remember it with anguish or disgust. I experienced it as a natural step that a farmer took to put food on the table.

Often when evening shadows crawled across the porch of the old Dinwiddie County farmhouse, Grandmother, quiet and motionless, would sit looking out over the freshly plowed sandy soil. Her weathered countenance held no mystery, for the farm itself revealed the long history that must have occupied her thoughts. The ancient house was deteriorating in the weather, and the outhouse leaned away from the wind. Chickens roamed freely through the yard, leaving their droppings at will. Since I never wore shoes during the summer, I was constantly scraping my feet on the grass—especially before I was allowed into the house.

The farm was fun for me as a youngster, but to the adults who depended on it for their food and shelter, it actually took the measure of their character, developing a stubborn dedication to work and a good measure of faith.

Grandmother was a peaceful lady except when her dander was up. When that happened, you ran for cover. She had a terrifying, unbending stare, and woe to the person who contradicted or crossed her during such a spell. I remember distinctly one occasion when I turned the butter churn over. It caused a terrible mess, with sour milk and butter filling the cracks between the floor boards. Grandmother would have whaled me good if my father had not spanked me first.

Other times she might sound all fired up, but as soon as I got to know her, those times didn't worry me. Her tone only reflected the combative determination characteristic of a farm-country Virginian. That happened most frequently during family discussions about almost anything from what the President had said to how to treat a neighbor's sick cow. When opinions differed, defense of a position would be something like the obdurate power of the dug-in Confederates at Cold Harbor. So-called "discussions" could get quite heated. I came to realize that a Virginian is a very opinionated individual.

Grandmother's opinions carried a lot of weight not only because they were practical, but also because they were usually right, to boot. More than that, though, she was the voice of the South: genuine, rooted, and full of feeling.

"It's a good land, Bobby," she would tell me. "It's raised your father and his father and other men like them. Whatever a man does, wherever he goes, when he has grown up here he'll always carry the rub of the Southern landscape. He can wash it off his face, but he won't flush it out of his soul."

Many youngsters today—even in grade school—have a chance to make a Dad proud through organized athletics. But in our neighborhood there was no such opportunity. Sand-lot and pick-up games were the extent of team sports, and rarely did any father come out to watch one of those sprawling melees.

But I had a better chance to win my father's approval. I could go hunting. To most Americans, baseball is the national sport, but not to the Southern male. Hunting is not only the number-one pastime, to men like my father; it shapes their entire way of life. My journey along that path began when Dad gave me my first BB gun at age five. That act signed the death warrant for many of the birds in our neighborhood. Big folks hunted birds, so I hunted birds. What I didn't know then is that there are such things as seasons and limits, and that some birds are game birds, while others are not to be hunted.

When I began hunting in earnest with my Dad's friends in the Savannah River swampland, my first job was to help clean the game the men had killed. From the very beginning, my instincts told me that if I made Dad proud, he in turn would look good in the eyes of his companions. Approval from my father thus meant approval for him, as well, and so it was doubly important to me. I strove to make him look like the best Dad in the world. He would inspect my work with a critical eye, since this part of the hunt had to be mastered before I could participate in the actual shooting.

After I'd passed that test, my first real hunting was for squirrels, the forest "varmints" that later wound up in our nightly stews. The swamp was heavily populated with these scampering creatures, and after giving me lessons in how to shoot them, Dad stationed me in an area where there were many nests and hickory nut cuttings. He put gunnysacks on the ground for me to sit on, to help keep off chiggers and other insects, and then he'd pretty much leave me on my own while he covered another location. I was under strict orders not to leave my stand, and by then I'd heard enough stories about cottonmouths and quicksand to keep me from questioning authority.

I quickly learned that the hunter didn't have to hunt squirrels—it was the other way around. Stalking a squirrel is, in fact, largely counter-productive. The frightened rodents will always keep their tree between themselves and a hunter on the move. Chattering and scolding, they will move around the tree just ahead of you, making it all but impossible to take aim. But the stationary hunter can silently wait them out, and often get clear shots. Indeed, if a hunter sits still, a squirrel's curiosity will always overcome his fear. Minutes after the gun report that fells one of their fellows, others will nose out onto the same branches. It wasn't unusual for Dad and me to sit at our stations and kill dozens of squirrels in an outing.

Those hunts represented some of the most wonderful times I spent with my father when I was young, times all the more precious because they were so rare. He was putting in long hours at Georgia Hardwood and had little time to share during the week. Some of the days he did spend at home, though, were very special. I doubt there are many fathers who read annual business reports or *Wall Street Journal* articles to their children at bedtime. That's what I grew up with, however. From very early on, Dad was making sure I received a proper business education. It was a gift that I still treasure, not only because it developed a special relationship between my father and me, but also because it's proven a major contributor to my work in business.

On top of that, getting this business education from my father helped make up for what little education I was getting from the public schools in Augusta. Born in 1941, I represented the leading edge of what would become known as the "baby boom." My first-grade class was so large it was held in an auditorium, where we sat in chairs rather than desks. We had to try to balance boards on our laps for writing surfaces, an exercise that probably was more useful later for buffet dinners and church socials than it was for learning. No, my schooling hardly began auspiciously.

The opposite is true of my early church experience. When one is reared in a particular environment, he always carries certain aspects of that environment. I was reared in a Christian church and indoctrinated with Bible stories. Sunday was church day. I began with Sunday School, then went to the morning church service, then returned at night for another service. I was allowed to play some between Sunday School and the service, since Dad was an usher. But when it came time for the sermon, I was expected to be at my seat beside my mother.

My mother was the parent responsible for creating a Christian environment. Each morning we would gather at the breakfast table for a devotional. And since my mother was a Sunday School teacher, the material was usually a preview of what was to happen Sunday. She had a way of casting the Biblical characters in the drama of their culture, bringing them to life according to the unique qualities of their time, making my nerves tingle at the reality of the story. She spent hours on her visual aids, creating scenery and a wide range of characters. We had our own dramatic production each Sunday. I must place squarely on my mother's shoulders a generous portion of credit for sealing me as one of Christ's own.

My most memorable childhood church experience came when I was seven or eight years old, and Billy Graham came to Augusta. The Reverend

Graham was just getting started at that time, and he stayed at our minister's house while he was in town. When I heard him at our church—Augusta's First Presbyterian—his zeal and enthusiasm for Christ were like nothing I had ever encountered. At Reverend Graham's invitation, I came to the altar and accepted Jesus Christ into my life.

Little did I know what a profound influence that acceptance would have on me from then on.

CHAPTER 15

Robert Pamplin, Junior
The Teen Years

N O DOUBT ABOUT IT, Billy Graham had given me a new window into my Christian beliefs. It wasn't until years later, however, that I began to see through it clearly.

My deeper Christian understanding came after Dad moved the family to the Northwest—after Georgia Hardwood became Georgia-Pacific and began expanding its holdings. By then I'd begun to come to grips with faith's lifeshaping paradox: with the way good emerges from adversity.

My first serious taste of adversity came while the family was still in Augusta. I had always been healthy and active, the sort of child who could scrap with the neighbor boy on Friday and shoot a dozen squirrels on Saturday. My parents were surprised and worried, then, when I suddenly began losing weight and energy shortly after beginning the sixth grade.

They took me to a doctor. I can remember that visit as if it were yesterday: the time of day, the sunny weather, and most of all the stark, white walls of his plain office. The physician took one look at me and said:

"You've got hepatitis."

He could tell from the yellow cast of my skin and my eyeballs. As it turned out, his diagnosis from that simple external observation was accurate, but to make matters worse, I also had a viral infection and intestinal flu.

The next few months were about as miserable as a kid can endure. Little Bobby Pamplin was known throughout the neighborhood as a kid who loved activity, all kinds of activity, not just fighting and hunting. But now I was forced to spend most of my time in bed. My parents didn't mind holding my schooling back a year, since my father had once lost a year after he'd broken his leg. They brought in a tutor for me, so that my education wouldn't lag too badly. But it was my body, not my mind, that worried me.

My energy had dropped away; I began to think of myself as a weakling. Worse still, after the disease had come and gone, my activities were

curtailed again by a trick right knee. During a grade-school football game
a year or so after the hepatitis cleared up, I'd evaded a tackle with a quick
down-field cut, and unexpectedly found myself on the ground, writhing
with pain. It was as if I'd been blind-sided. Yet this injury came from
within, from some wrenching I'd given my knee. It felt deformed, there on
the ground; the cap was twisted to the side of the joint.

The doctor unceremoniously reached up my pant leg and, in a moment of blinding pain, twisted the kneecap back in place. After that my
entire right leg went into a cast.

After the cast came off, however, I continued to suffer from that trick
knee. It plagued me badly throughout high-school freshman basketball.
That season, in fact, proved a time of reckoning, regarding my knee.
Afterwards I had an operation, moving the kneecap down to a less exposed
position. I never suffered another dislocation, but my leg never fully recovered either. I could no longer go out for any team or activity I wanted.

Things have a way of working out, however. I took inspiration, as
children will, from a very simple and highly popular movie of the time, *Wee
Gordie*. It was about a Scotsman determined to make his weak body into a
showcase of muscle and strength. This Gordie left the windows wide open
at night, letting the brisk Scottish air infuse him with vigor. He started a
weight program, and through hard work developed himself to become a
contender for the gold medal in the Olympics. What inspiration!

Now I should admit, while I'm confessing to these childish encour-
agements, that I've often been accused of playing the "Glad Game." This
was a game created by the author Eleanor Porter, for her heroine Pollyanna.
Pollyanna of course tried to find the good in everything; her name has by
now become synonymous with optimism. One year at Christmas, Porter's
heroine asked for a doll. When the presents got mixed up and she was
instead given a pair of crutches, she didn't complain. Instead, playing the
Glad Game, Pollyanna said, "Isn't it great that I don't have a broken leg
and don't have to use these?"

Like Pollyanna, I have irrepressible enthusiastic belief that everything
which happens in my life will be for the best. I have it as an adult as well,
though my source now isn't any children's novel, but rather Paul's Epistle
to the Romans: "All things work together for good, for them that love
God." And I had that same forward-looking quality in my early years—

even when, unlike Pollyanna, I had to use crutches. I believed I could be a Georgian Wee Gordie.

The Scotsman's story somewhat paralleled another one, a tale I'd read on the backs of comic books while I was laid low with hepatitis: that of Charles Atlas, the bodybuilder who had transformed himself from a "ninety-eight-pound weakling"—his ads never failed to mention that—to a mighty specimen of strength and energy.

The knee operation had caused permanent weakness in my leg, and, as I say, my hepatitis had left me badly concerned about my overall physical condition. But if Atlas and Gordie could change themselves, so could I! Sending away for the Charles Atlas Program is not something a kid tells his peers about. Nevertheless, secretly, I became a subscriber to the program.

It was a fairly simple regimen. Push-ups, sit-ups, chin-ups, and other good old-fashioned exercises were combined with weightlifting. And then, when I began to see results, I was taught a way of life as well. I understood that pride in your physical being, spurred by exercise and good eating habits, develops pride in other areas as well.

The Atlas program did something else important for me. It led me to Joe Loprinzi, trainer at Portland's Multnomah Athletic Club and a devotee of weightlifting. Joe is a man for whom fitness was a way of life, and he approached it with a fervor that was infectious. My immediate goal, when I went to him, was to overcome the atrophy in my weakened leg. But working with Joe quickly showed me that the Atlas program could be much improved upon, under the supervision of this master lifter. At first Joe's regimen called for me to be at the club each Tuesday and Thursday, but as my muscles began to toughen and bulge, I found myself adding days.

Still, I would probably have been content with basic body-building, except for what happened one day early in my sophomore year. I was working out with the school football team, who were in the Club weight room trying to build strength for the season. Being a competitive lot, these players began to challenge each other about how much they could military press. That is, they were bringing the barbell to their chests and then lifting it to arm's length overhead without jerking the body or bending the knees. And after every round, they'd increase the weight on the bar. Naturally, I couldn't resist the contest.

With all the cheering and laughter, Joe's attention was diverted our way. Now, these players were husky, weighing 180 pounds or more. Myself, I ran about 125, and the lifting started at seventy-five. But as the weight moved up, I surprised myself by staying with it. I didn't reach my limit till the bar weighed 130.

The football players went on from there, naturally, and I did feel a twinge at seeing how much some of them could lift. But after those husky teenagers had all left the room, Joe pulled me aside.

"Bob," he asked, "how much did you lift?" When I told him, he widened his eyes, impressed. "One hundred thirty pounds is exceptional for your weight, Bob," he said. "Do you realize that only about five percent of the people in the world can lift their body weight?" He nodded, letting the idea sink in, and then added: "I believe that you could become a weight lifter."

J oe explained that there were three Olympic lifts—that is, strength lifts used in the Olympics—and that there were regular AAU meets featuring those lifts throughout the United States. "I believe," he told me, "that with some training you could make the Club team and do well in these meets. There really aren't a lot of people who have natural strength and can lift their weight. You have that gift."

So I got my next example of what it meant to use my gifts to their fullest. I began to train as a lifter, working a tough daily regimen with Joe. We did splits for the clean and jerk, dead lifting for the snatch, pressing off a rack for the press, plus the usual all-around toning. After months of this, always under Joe's careful coaching, I was ready to enter the Oregon State Championships in Eugene.

My coach also laid out careful preparations for the event. "I don't want you to lift for two days beforehand," he said, "so your muscles will have a chance to rest. Eat only fruits, vegetables, and lean meat. No Coke, desserts, or sweets, and stay away from the starches." My weight, 123, was already at the upper border of the class in which I'd have the best chance for taking home a trophy.

"When you weigh in," Joe warned me, "we don't want you to have to sweat it off. You will lose too much strength. And Bob, get plenty of rest."

Such lectures had been going on for several months now, of course, and so I was ready for that momentous Saturday. That morning early, at the Club, my weight was right where it was supposed to be. Then we were off to Eugene, about a two-hour ride south of Portland. On the way down, Joe kept prepping me:

"Don't bend your back on the press, Bob, and keep your knees locked. Once you get the weight up, lock your elbows and don't drop the weight until the judge claps. You have to hold it two seconds. Two seconds, Bob! And whatever you do, don't start with too much weight. You have three chances at each lift, so don't get yourself in a position where you can't make one. It will destroy your total."

Familiar as my coach's warnings were, they helped pass the time. In Eugene I kept things simple, weighing in, chalking my hands, getting occasional swigs of fresh orange juice and honey to supercharge the adrenaline. Whenever the PA barked *"Pamplin,"* I was off the bench quickly and reporting my intended weight to the officials.

Eventually we came to my second lift in the press. Confidently I let the officials know I was going for 145 pounds. The attendants arranged the appropriate weight on the bar and then I was over it, concentrating on all the techniques which Joe had patiently taught me. Hands equal distance from the center, arms straight down from the shoulders. Back straight, knees bent. Pull up quickly and flip the wrist so that the bar will fall on the chest as you come to a standing position. Lock the knees, push the bar over your head, lock the elbows, hold for two seconds—two seconds, Bob!—and then listen for the clap. It went so smoothly, my mind was still going over the details as I was dropping the weight at the end of the lift.

As I returned to the bench, Joe greeted me with a grin I'd never seen before, a grin bigger than I'd ever known he was capable of. He held a paper with some figures on it, and when I approached he pushed it in front of my face.

"Bob," he exulted, "you've just broken the state record!"

I looked at him vacantly. I couldn't really comprehend what he was saying. He had to tell me a second time before I caught on, and then in another few seconds I was so excited, I thought that my last chance at the press I would jam the bar right through the ceiling. And I just about did; I lifted a greater weight than I'd ever managed before.

But, in one of those little humiliations life offers from time to time, I held the Oregon state record for only about fifteen minutes. Another competitor in my class put up a still heavier bar-full of weight, more even than I managed in my third lift.

That left me a bit disappointed, yes. But an inveterate Glad Game player like myself couldn't come away from that meet feeling anything less than exhilarated. I will always remember that I was a state record holder, even if it was for only a few minutes. And Joe, in keeping with all he did for me in those months, has never forgotten either. In the 1980s I saw him again on the street, on a day when I was out with my youngest daughter. No sooner had I introduced her than my old coach began to tell her about my "state weightlifting record." I didn't even feel too bad when he mentioned that it was only for those few minutes.

Competitive lifting is never easy, and especially not for a boy who's still growing, as I was. One thinks of weightlifters as linebacker-sized behemoths who constantly eat spaghetti to keep up their bulk. That may be true for the heavyweights, but for me it was just the opposite. My best competition weight was that same 123 pounds, and to keep from getting bumped up into the next class I was on a constant diet, right through high school. Every morning I had wheat germ oil and vitamins, and a month before a meet I had to particularly watch what I ate, usually sticking to just lean meat and vegetables. Two days prior to the competition, I'd even cut down on my water, and the day of the meet, before weigh-in I'd go to the steam room to try to shed the last few ounces.

A tiny difference in my personal weight could be costly, as I found at a Northwest Regional championship. That time, I just wasn't able to starve or sweat off a stubborn extra three pounds, and had to move up to the 132-pound class. As it turned out, in all three Olympic categories I lifted as much as I ever had, and I took third in that higher class. But down in my usual category, I would've had an easy win.

As an adult, I have few regrets about my childhood and youth. That's part of the Glad Game too—or rather, part of the teaching from Romans 8:28. But I can think of a few choices I might make differently, if I had to do them over again. And one of those involves weightlifting.

Because I'd placed second in the Pacific Coast championships, I was invited to participate in the Junior Nationals, held in California that year. I decided not to enter, however. Part of my reluctance was a concern that I might not earn one of the three places in my weight category, but there was more to it than that. Also I had a girlfriend who wanted me to take her to the big dance at school. Ah, priorities! But when I saw the scores published after the Juniors, I learned that my usual lifts, nothing more, would have placed me second. Who knows, I might have won first if I had pressed the leader.

That did happen once, in an especially exciting meet. The guy in the lead had me beat cold, but he got cocky and tried too much weight on the last lift, the Clean and Jerk. He couldn't handle it, and so ruined his total score. Not only did I win the meet, but also I learned something from his mistake. From that time on I was careful not to attempt a lift I didn't know I could handle.

While the regimen of weightlifting was hard, most of the rest of my time in high school was not. My best buddies were a bunch that enjoyed a good time, and my friends in school weren't limited to them or to any other single group. I can't help feeling, now, that my open-mindedness when it came to my Portland friends was a reflection of my early days in the Augusta apartment and the Georgia swamplands. There I'd become comfortable with all kinds of people, and years later, in the opposite corner of the country, the early training held true.

In high school, my ability to get along was particularly important at election time. I seemed to be able to pull together coalitions for class elections, and held several positions as a result, including Senior Class President.

With those positions came responsibilities. Most of those I handled well, but there are a couple of notable exceptions—a couple of other things I'd do differently, if I could. One of them nearly ended my high school career prematurely.

With a friend named Dick, I was planning a pledge party for the Deacons, a social club of which I was president. We'd lined up the cream of the freshman boys to attend, and it was important we give them a good time. As I recall, Dick was suggesting we have a dance. But then he added a dangerous twist:

"Most of the members," Dick said, "think we should have a beer party. They think it'd be cool to show the freshmen how the big boys do things."

No doubt I should have vetoed the idea then and there. A beer party was serious trouble; we'd risk expulsion. But I kept my mouth shut, taken by surprise more than anything else, and that was all the encouragement Dick needed. He went on as if the matter were settled, and the only question that remained was where we'd set up the kegs. None of the members' parents were going to be away Saturday, Dick said. We'd have to find another location. An illegal get-together needed privacy.

Finally I found my tongue. "I don't know," I said. "A pledge party is a school function. If we get caught with beer, we'll really be hung out to dry."

"But we've got to impress those pledges," returned Dick. "It's our best opportunity."

If only he hadn't done that: mentioned opportunity. I've rarely been able to refuse a good opportunity.

"Okay," I said. "Okay, let's do it."

I told Dick that he'd have to find the place. Myself, I put up the notice on the activities board. This would advertise a "pony ride" for the pledge party. Every boy in school, just about, would know what this meant: a party with a pony keg of beer. There'd been other such illicit events at Lincoln High, as in most schools in the 1950s. "Pony ride" was just one of the code expressions students used to keep the principal and the teachers in the dark.

So began the keg party that got me suspended. It was my senior year, too, supposedly the best year of my life. I'd jumped all the hurdles of being an underclassman, and I was looking forward to taking advantage of senior status. I was even ready to take a few chances.

For this was the era of be-bop-a-loo-la, whomp-bomp-a-loo-bomp and Elvis. We had our share of greasers, sporting the "duckbutt" hair style, black leather jackets, white tee shirts with cigarettes rolled up in the sleeve, and tight jeans tapered at the ankle. Tough guys. The more knife marks they could point to, the greater the respect they got. In particular I recall a giant who occasionally attended P.E., a boy just covered with scars. I remember the conversations about him, after that first day in the locker room.

"Did you see those *scars?* "

We all concluded that this big guy had to be tough as they come and mean to boot. He was tough all right, but later we found that he wasn't mean at all. He just lived in a rough neighborhood.

Other kids were the students. Many of these had horn-rimmed glasses—"four eyes," as the nastier kids among us would call them. Others had soft skin and a little baby fat cushion around the middle. And then a third group simply floated through the days. These were nondescript young people simply putting in their time, not really participating. It might have been their own choice, or it might have been because they just weren't accepted.

Finally, there were the "popular kids." These were the athletes and class officers, the members of social clubs and those who were bound to show up in the yearbook with captions like "student officer," "letterman," "best dressed" or "most likely to succeed."

You didn't just fall into a group. You had to earn your position. For instance, to be a real greaser took either a souped-up motorcycle or, like the giant from P.E., a mass of knife scars. And you wore the mark of your position with pride, as long-ago squires wore the colors of the knights they served.

The long and short of all this was that after three years of learning the ropes I believed I had a solid position in the school—a position that allowed me to take chances. I wanted, especially, to make the Deacons the best club. And there seemed, at that misguided moment, no better way to bring in the impressionable freshmen than to show them how worldly we were. So Dick and I planned our "pony ride."

We decided to deliver the keg in a hearse. After all, who would imagine that a group of teenage boys would be carrying around beer in a hearse? And Dick had arranged a good place, under a viaduct. There we'd have woods on either side, and the traffic noise from overhead would hide any laughter and shouting. Yes, we thought we were untouchable.

The hearse backed up to our hideaway. The party began, attended by all the best freshman prospects. Then when we were well into the swing of things, someone from the neighborhood came strolling down the trail.

"Oh no!" I exclaimed.

"Run!" Dick yelled.

Boys scattered left and right into the woods. Dick and I grabbed the keg and hustled up the bank to the waiting hearse. We stowed the incriminating evidence and I stomped on the gas. Laughing, thrilled, Dick and I both thought we had made a good get-away.

But the next Monday, in my third-period class, I received a summons from the vice principal. He needed to see me in his office immediately. As soon as I got there, I could tell I was in for trouble. Dick and some of the other Deacons were sitting around the vice principal's desk, deep in conversation, and they all had very long faces.

"Sit down," said the vice principal.

His voice was matter-of-fact, but carried a distinct angry edge. He didn't beat around the bush, either. "Did you and Dick here organize a beer party for new club pledges last Saturday?"

I was speechless.

"Well?" he pressed. "Did you?"

Just as when Dick had first brought up the beer party, I didn't know what to say. The vice principal didn't wait long for an answer, though. He spun around in his chair and picked up two quart jars sitting on his credenza. "These were brought in by someone strolling down by the viaduct out on Macadam Boulevard. They were used by boys having a beer party there."

His voice seemed to get sharper with every word.

"Is that right?" I said, or tried to say. Above all, I hoped he wouldn't ask again if it had been me.

"Was it you?" he asked.

And then, taking a breath, he answered his own question: "It was you and all these boys present. We know it."

I'd had time enough to get control of my fear, by then. As calmly as I could, I challenged the vice principal. How, I asked, could he be certain that it was us?

Was that ever a mistake. The man dismissed all the others and then, once the door was closed behind them, he let me have it.

"Bob, I've lost my patience!" he said. His voice was so shrill, so highpitched, it actually distracted me from the trouble I was in. For a moment there, desperate for relief, I almost laughed at him. But then the vice principal was spelling out my situation more clearly.

"You have two options," he said, "just two. Normally I would expel you. But since you've got such good grades and you haven't been in trouble before, I'm inclined to just give you a suspension. But you have to prove to me you're worth it. If you don't want to be expelled, you have to make a complete confession of the whole business right now."

My thoughts ran the gamut. I can't rat on the others, but, boy, am I in a pile of trouble. . . . "Can I think it over during the lunch hour?" I asked, with all the courage I could muster.

He scowled but nodded. "Get out and come back at one o'clock," he barked, shrill as before.

I made a beeline to the cafeteria. I found Dick, explained, and then asked: "What did you tell him?"

"We told him the whole story," my friend admitted. "Our backs were to the wall. We didn't want to get expelled."

So at one o'clock sharp, I was waiting at the vice principal's door. My confession was short and simple, and his reply was briefer still:

"You're suspended. And you'll have to resign as Senior Class President."

The suspension passed, of course, and I graduated Lincoln with honors, in 1960. Now, years later, memories of high school seem to run together, with neither outstanding highs nor depressing, irrevocable lows. All in all, my teenage years didn't have as much of an effect on my character as they do for some. Maybe this was because of my early experience—or, more likely, it was because my period of truly profound change came during my first two years of college. Yes, my high school years saw a few scrapes, a few infractions for which I was justly punished. Yet for the most part it was simply a fun four years, an era of wide horizons and untroubled waters.

There was another notable exception, however, on a certain Fourth of July.

For as long as we could remember, several of my friends and I had wanted to explode a fireworks bomb on the school grounds. And as it turned out, on this occasion a bomb is exactly what we got. I had a can of black powder that I'd used once to fire a Civil War cap-and-ball pistol, and I figured that if a little powder exploded enough to blow a ball out of the pistol, a lot of it should deliver flash and noise enough to satisfy even my most spectacle-hungry friends.

I'd seen many Saturday matinee western movies, in which the cowboy poured out a trail of powder on the ground, leading back to the powder keg. When the cowboy lit the powder, he always had time to get out of the way of the blast. So I followed the movie formula, pouring out a short trail between the fuse and the powder can.

I don't know if my powder was fast-burning, or if—more likely—the movies aren't to be trusted. In any case, no sooner had I touched a match to that powder than it flashed and exploded immediately, practically under my nose. I got my fireworks bomb, all right. But it got me, too.

The explosion burned all exposed skin on my head and hands, and the pain was as if my entire face was being held down on a red-hot burner. If Hell is supposed to be eternal fire, then pain such as I felt at that moment should cause everyone in the world to try to avoid it.

The most serious problem was my eyes. When I tried to open them, the pain was so bad I could barely squint. I could see nothing but the etched afterglow of the explosion. I was rushed to the hospital, where the facial burns were treated in the emergency room. The physicians kept shooting me up with pain killers, but these didn't seem to quell the intensity of the burning on my face and hands. Finally, a doctor said they could give me no more; more would be dangerous. I had to simply lie there in pain.

My terrified parents called in an eye specialist. Though I could still see some light and dark, the man couldn't be sure, just then, what the eventual damage might be. For myself, it felt as if a burning coal were embedded in the iris of each eye.

Finally they had me bandaged like a mummy. Rolling to my room on a gurney, I was beginning to feel better. I'd been told that my eyes, though singed on the lens, would probably be all right once healed. My skin had suffered mostly second-degree burns; only one small area had received a third-degree burn. And the pain, at long last, was beginning to subside.

It seems that my physical dilemmas have generally taken up a year at a time. Now it took a full twelve months to toughen my skin, so the red splotches would blend to an even white pigment. During most of that time, blood blisters always followed the slightest blow to my face. I was lucky, to be sure . . . if luck is what it was. The experience could have led to permanent blindness, but my eyes healed perfectly, and my sight was never endangered.

In the days that passed before those mummy's bandages came off, I had long thoughts about what it would be like to live a life of perpetual darkness. When the day came that I was able to use my eyes once again, I was so relieved I wanted to cry out in thanksgiving. From the bottom of my heart, I prayed that I'd never face such darkness again.

Yet this trial was only the beginning. I had a far worse challenge ahead.

CHAPTER 16

Robert Pamplin, Junior
Hard Work and Obedience

DURING THE SUMMERS of those high school years, I worked in lumber and plywood mills. Physical labor was nothing new to me. Dad had started me on summer jobs when I was in the eighth grade, and with the way he and Mother had overseen my chores, they'd instilled the work ethic even earlier. But still, now that I was a teenager, living away from home in a millworkers' boardinghouse was a new experience.

It was, as well, a considerable responsibility. On my own for the first time, making and spending my own money, I had to make good, make the right choices. I had to prove I could handle adult autonomy. And yet with all that weighing on me, I can't deny that another part of me—no small part—found this work an adventure.

The initial two weeks on my summer jobs were usually the most trying. At first, I'll never forget, my hands took an awful beating. The lowest millwork assignment is flipping the heavy sheets of plywood as they come out of the sander. The sheets have to be handled on the rough sides and edges, and they're too slick to pick up with gloves; I had no choice but to work with open sores until my hands healed and toughened. The foreman even complained that I was getting blood on the plywood, though he was unable to offer any suggestions as to how I could keep it from happening.

Older, more experienced mill workers just passed me by, attending to their own jobs and giving me no quarter. A few times I'd catch flashes of a smirk, since everybody knew this assignment was the worst in the plant—just the place to start a green kid. I hung in; I didn't cry "Uncle." After a week or so I could finally sense the acceptance of the foreman. The man had been literally breathing down my neck most of the time, after all; he'd stood a few feet behind me, like an executioner ready with the ax.

No matter how tough a task was, I knew I was expected to complete it as a man—and with a smile. I was the kid in the plant. The upshot, at the plants, was that the plywood-flipping job wasn't my only bad assignment.

I shoveled tar, cleaned the train tracks, swept, fed plywood into the dryer, off-beared the dryer (that is, I pulled the plywood panels off the conveyer belt and stacked them), and ran Gluepete Gloop, the glue-mixing machine. On a given day, any of these might be worse than plywood flipping. And then there was the dreaded chore of unloading the fifty-pound sacks of lime from the rail cars. Lime was used in making the glue, and some of the powder always collected on the outside of the bags. The rail cars were hot and the sweat on my bare arms activated this exposed powder. As a result, my first layer of skin would be burned off after unloading the lime by hand.

Yet even then, the best thing for it was to keep my mouth shut and work hard. I was likewise warned, whenever I started at a new mill, that I was to make no mention of unions. I was expected to do what I was told and ask no questions, and for that I would be paid the princely sum of $2.17 per hour. The job was no brain burner, either. The mill foremen just needed a body warm and flexible enough to do the work. At the end of each day I was exhausted. Returning to the boarding house, I could look forward to either a creative hot dog dish or hamburger fixed in some exotic down-home way—though, to be fair, sometimes the burger fixings were borderline tasty. But what could one expect, paying only twenty bucks per week? The breakfast was bacon and eggs, coffee and milk, the lunch a sandwich, fruit, dessert, and milk, and the dinner the hot dog or hamburger surprise, nearly always with potatoes and a vegetable, plus still more milk.

I boarded in the attic, that first summer. You could only stand up straight in the center of the room, at the peak of the roof. The bathroom, shared by all the men in the house, was on the main floor, and as might be expected, it was hardly a gem of modern plumbing. Many a time I found myself tiptoeing from the bathtub across a floor lathered with the refuse from an overflowing toilet.

Sharing these accommodations, one summer, was a drunk who died in an auto wreck during my time there. The man was a sad case, a former Marine who'd never recovered from the shell shock he'd suffered during the island campaign in the Pacific. Nor was his the only strange story from among that colorful assortment of laborers. Most of these tales I kept to myself, knowing better than to tell my parents. I didn't want to worry them.

Just the opposite, I wanted to come away from every summer job a success: a young hand esteemed for his willingness and cooperation. Every summer, I made it happen, working my way through these same demanding cycles. I took the worst the mill foremen could give me, and I slowly won their respect. I grew up a lot.

Yet my experience in the mills was nothing compared to my introduction to college and military life at Virginia Polytechnic Institute. The school was my Dad's alma mater, and that of both my uncles as well, so I thought I knew something about what to expect. But I was about to experience some of the greatest changes of my life.

From earliest days one dictum had been drilled into me again and again: once you start something, stick with it and see it through. That thought was certainly in my mind as I took on the drudge jobs in the mill, and again as I reported at VPI as a freshman.

The program I'd selected was intended to lead not only to a degree, but also to a commission as an Army officer. VPI in the early 1960s was a military school of about 4000 young officer candidates, in Army and Air Force programs. The campus, its buildings mostly imposing polished stone, at first glance suggested a bristling gray fortress. Yet the broad expanse of lawn was inviting. At the fortress's center were the drill field and lower quadrangle, two areas with which I was soon to become intimately acquainted.

As I say, Dad had told me about his experiences at Tech. We'd laughed about some of his times there as a cadet, and I knew that freshmen were called Rats and subject to some hazing. Those discussions, however, were finally no preparation.

I arrived two weeks ahead of the returning upperclassmen. This was an indoctrination period, designed to familiarize us with the military routine of the school. We were issued uniforms, an M-1 rifle, and assigned to dorms. And, within a very short time of our arrival, we were made to understand that a VPI Rat had less status than the dogs that wandered onto the campus from nearby Blacksburg.

At one of the first formations, an upperclass officer gave us a warning my father had told me to expect, an old line intended to help break us in—or break us down.

"Look at the man on your right," this cadet announced, "and the man on your left, because come spring they're not going to be here."

Tech had a famously high attrition rate, losing two out of three of its first-year men. The officer was simply reminding us of that, bluntly perhaps, but without in the least exaggerating.

My first roommate was a good example of the kind who couldn't cut it at Tech. Not long after school had started, he asked me, "Bob, do you think it will get worse?"

"We haven't seen anything yet," I replied. "From what my Dad told me, I'd say it's going to get ten times worse."

The next day, when I got back to my room after drill, he was gone. He'd left a note asking me to turn in his M-1 for him, and with that he'd simply walked off campus. Lots of others followed.

But now I was alone. The next day, our first Sunday, we were marched as a company into town for church. Friendless, wondering if I'd be the next to go, I tried to find inspiration in seeing the whole corps marching up the main street of Blacksburg to worship. That afternoon, we were given "privileges in the company"—meaning, mostly, a welcome break from the harassment of upperclassmen. I took time simply to sit. In my half-empty room, on my bed, I let my head hang a bit. But then, when my despair was at its lowest, I felt a hand on my shoulder.

I raised my head to see a tall, raw-boned boy with such a broad grin I knew at once he must have grown up on a farm. He stuck out his hand, and in a slow, Southern drawl said, "Hi, I'm Floyd. Floyd Aylor. I'm your new roommate."

He too had lost the closest thing to a buddy he'd had here at Tech. We commiserated for a few minutes, getting acquainted, and that alone seemed to be what I'd needed to get back the energy to go on. The experiences that followed at VPI made Floyd and me the best of friends. Indeed, even now we have breakfast every Friday, and we still count on each other's help. Floyd also works as my partner in many business ventures.

At the time you're going through military hazing, it's hard to see any justification for some of the treatment. The whole system can seem dehumanizing. For myself, just for starters, my treatment as a VPI freshman lowered my status startlingly. I went from a high-school senior class and social club president to a Tech Rat. Or RAATT, actually—these upperclassmen liked to put a lot of stress on the word. Whatever the pronunciation, however, it boiled down to being considered the lowest form of life.

As soon as VPI's fall term started, Rat routine became standard. We had to be up at 4:30 A.M. to begin preparations for the first formation and the PI—police inspection—of the room. Shoes had to be shined, brass buckles, buttons, and insignia "blitzed" even brighter than the shoes, and the entire uniform had to be brushed and then dabbed with masking tape to get rid of lint. Cap-visors were rubbed with Vasoline to shine like a mirror. In addition to the uniform, the room had to be in perfect order: the bedcovers tucked so tightly that they would bounce a coin, the clothes hung in the proper sequence and spaced the designated amount, each textbook placed where it belonged on the shelf, and any shoes not on our feet put away. And woe unto the Rat who allowed any sign of dust in even the most out-of-the-way places in the room.

Before breakfast we had formation and inspection, and then we were marched to the mess hall. There, Rats were required to eat a "square meal"—that is, the utensil carrying food had to be brought up from the plate in a direct perpendicular, then across at a ninety-degree angle to the mouth, all while sitting at attention on the front two inches of the chair. We could speak to upperclassmen only when spoken to. We could look nowhere but straight ahead; anything else was termed "cutting your eyes," and strictly forbidden.

Small wonder we Rats slugged down our food as quickly as we could, a "squaring meal" of ever-larger bites, in order to get out from under the watchful eyes of the upperclassmen. But as we passed from building to building on campus, we were allowed to walk only on the extreme right-hand six inches of the sidewalk, and there, too, we had to march at attention, without cutting our eyes. Anyone we met on campus had to be greeted with "Good morning," their rank, "Sir." Even stray dogs were met with "Good morning, Dog, Sir!"

The natural result was that we spent as much time as possible in our rooms. In the same way, classes were a welcome relief. Sometimes, at our desks, we could even relax our posture the least bit. In our dorm rooms, however, Rats remained fair game for any upperclassman. We could be quizzed about anything from the history of VPI to the middle names of the Cadet Corps officers. Mistakes subjected the freshman to "Rat demerits," which he worked off by cleaning an upperclassman's room.

Afternoons, we had lab classes, drill, and athletic participation. We were out of our rooms and unprotected, in other words, and thus easy prey for upperclassmen. And even when we had a free moment in our rooms, dog-tired though we might be, we didn't dare lie down. Didn't dare loosen the bedcovers. The room had to be ready for PI at all times. Myself, I soon decided never to sleep under the covers. All year long I spent my nights on top of a made bed, with only a blanket over me. It made my morning chores a lot easier.

This withering discipline, as I say, forced many a freshman out of school in the first few weeks. That freshman year proved, above all, that misery does indeed love company. Surviving Rats understood that, on campus, the only people they could trust were their fellow rodents. We were all individuals, unquestionably, from diverse socioeconomic backgrounds and with widely different interests. But we speedily developed a lasting camaraderie.

Monday nights, all in all, were the worst. Then the upperclassmen held Rat Meetings. We were assembled in a stuffy room, where we "braced." That is, we snapped into an almost painfully erect posture, in which according to regulations we could hold a matchstick between our shoulder blades and under our chins. After that came all kinds of verbal abuse. Upperclassmen handed out demerits freely. Sometimes the punishment meant studying braced, with the room door open and the room ready for inspection.

I got by, I must admit, in part because I was lucky enough to have a visit from my father. Dad had come to the area on business, and he arranged for me to get away for most of an evening, even though first-term freshmen were not usually permitted off campus after 7:30 P.M. Dad and I had dinner, went to a movie, and played a game of miniature golf. As we talked, I commented that the hazing was a lot tougher than I'd expected.

"I used to laugh when you told me what they did to you," I said. "But this isn't funny. I don't know whether I can take it for the rest of the year."

Dad's reply was just what I needed. "Son," he said, "if you go through this first year, I'll be proud of you."

A simple statement, yes. But my father's promise of respect proved powerful enough to carry me through the remainder of my Rat trials. I took whatever the upperclassmen dished out and kept up acceptable grades. I won a gold medal in rope climbing, an exercise that came easy to me thanks to my weight training. Indeed, though I didn't know this in my Tech days, I've learned that the sort of upper-body strength a man uses in rope climbing has been a family trait for almost a thousand years now. One of my earliest ancestors, the Crusader hero Sir Robert Lawrence, could climb so quickly and skillfully that he was the first soldier over the wall at the siege of Acre.

At VPI, my success that first year was affirmed on Rat Day. On that day I was selected to bid for Captain of K Company by my fellow freshman. I found this honor especially gratifying, since Rat Day was a time when roles were reversed—when we at last got to treat the upperclassmen to some of the guff they'd been handing us. Oh, it felt good to order them around for a change.

Many times, that first year at VPI, I asked myself "Why?" What were these upperclassmen trying to prove? But when a young man's undergoing hazing, as I say, he doesn't realize the values that are being imparted. It feels like Inquisition torture, and that's all a young cadet can handle, for the moment. Yet there are significant values infusing the torture, values such as humility, trust, belief in oneself and one's unit, and honor—above all, honor.

Virginia Polytechnic, like the U.S. Service Academies and other military schools, had a strict honor code. Violations of that code could lead to dismissal and a "drumming out" of the Cadet Corps.

The code had four basic violations: lying, stealing, cheating, and the failure to report another cadet for committing one of those offenses. A cadet who knew of an offender and didn't report him was considered as guilty as the original. Thus all of us were required to be both fully honest informers and upright individuals ourselves. When a cadet turned in a paper or exam, he had to first sign a statement that the work was his and his alone.

Honor code violators went before the Honor Court. At his hearing the accused had a chance to plead his case, usually with the help of an upperclassman "defense attorney." If the Committee found the cadet guilty of a serious code violation, dismissal was the ultimate punishment, and "drumming out" the most chilling and spectacular means of carrying out that punishment.

The ceremony always took place in the dead of night, before the entire cadet corps. No lights were allowed on campus. Even the lights along the roadways that bisected the school were shrouded with blankets. The campus was already quiet, since it was past call to quarters and lights out. Seniors would go to each room and wake the cadets, informing them that they were not to talk, but to get dressed in the uniform of the day and assemble for formation in fifteen minutes. Then, in formation, each company was marched to the lower quadrangle. In the eerie subdued light, with the drummers from the corps band rolling a beat like that for an execution, a cadet could feel as though he were living a nightmare. You had to dig your nails into the skin of your hands to know that this was no dream. As the sentence was read, the convicted violator was stripped of his buttons, stripes, and any symbol of the corps or the school. The corps then did an about face on the disgraced cadet, and were ordered by the chief officer on duty never to mention the offender's name again on campus. As far as VPI was concerned, he had not existed, and he would not be permitted ever to return.

All in all, the honor code was one of the most important ways that VPI kept us busy, obedient, and honest. The Rat system was intended to instill humility, on the one hand, and build character on the other. It taught you that you were subservient to a larger group, and at the same time it "made a man of you," demonstrating that you had greater personal resources than you'd ever known.

This character reinforcement combined with a deepened humility proved, in time, of inestimable value. Beyond that, I benefited simply from achieving what I had, as all successful students do, and building up special and lasting memories. Virginia Polytechnic helped make me a leader both in athletics and by means of my personality skills. Selected company captain by my peers on Rat Day, chosen by upperclassmen to be a member of the elite freshman drill team (which earned second place in the Cadet

Corps) and winning a medal in intramural athletics—these all bolstered my faith in myself as few other school experiences ever could.

I completed my sophomore year deeply grateful, and yet attracted now to an entirely different academic environment. I put in an application at Lewis & Clark College, a liberal arts college in Portland, and was accepted for the fall of 1962. Years later, on reflection, I realize that I thus gained the best of all worlds in my undergraduate education. I benefited from the character, discipline, and spiritual examples implanted at VPI, and from the more scholarly atmosphere of Lewis & Clark.

CHAPTER 17

Robert Pamplin, Junior
Living Out Dreams

M Y JUNIOR and senior years at Lewis & Clark College led to graduation with a B.S. degree in Business Administration in 1964. I didn't live on campus, making me the sort of student sometimes called a "daydodger," but I worked hard. Besides my studies, I had a part-time job keeping books for a downtown office building in Portland. I paid my own way, those two years at Lewis & Clark, as I've paid for all my college education since.

At Lewis & Clark, I saw academics from a new perspective. After the routine at VPI, where I'd had little sleep because of all the hours involved in military duties, I now had ample time to study and, on top of that, hours to spare for my job. I found time even for two correspondence courses. These were a New York Institute of Finance course on brokerage procedure and the University of Wisconsin's course in investment banking, both of which would prove, before long, more than worth the effort.

So my traditional four years of college went by—in a decidedly un-traditional split. After that I went to work for Blyth and Company in Portland, in their account executive training program. Yet, concurrent with my Blyth training, I stayed on as a full-time student at Lewis & Clark. I wanted degrees in accounting and economics, both of which I believed essential for the high-level business work I saw myself getting into eventually. And more than that, after those life-shaping two years at Virginia Tech, I just didn't feel comfortable if I wasn't busy every waking moment.

I was in my early twenties, a heady, energy-filled time for anyone. I would study in the morning before the market opened, study during every break, and study at lunch. Then after work I cracked the books once more before attending night classes. I completed my accounting degree in a year, and in the same period passed all the examinations required to become an account executive.

Driven though I was, however, some more sensible part of me did let me know, from time to time, that it was physically impossible to keep up this kind of pace. Eventually I recognized that I couldn't pursue my educational goals and maintain a full-time job. Thus I left Blyth to finish my B.S. in economics. I became a day student again.

And during that second sojourn at Lewis & Clark, I began to invest in the stock market. For years, after all, I had been steeped in the art and science of investing. Now it was time to apply this accumulated knowledge.

My training dated back, happily, to those preteen years when my father would come into my bedroom with *The Wall Street Journal* or Standard and Poor's *Stock Guide*. By the time I entered Lincoln High, he'd taught me about stocks and bonds and how to evaluate a company. Then too, there were my more recent investment and finance courses, which also helped buoy me. Everything fit, in other words. My investments reaped no small reward, with the profits allowing me not only to finish my education at Lewis & Clark, but also to see me through an M.B.A. degree at the University of Portland.

And I kept busy, as ever. In addition to attending classes and investing, I served as president of the Alpha Kappa Psi business fraternity, eventually winning the Distinguished Service Award from the national organization. Better still, in 1966 my long hours poring over the texts were honored with *The Wall Street Journal* Student Achievement Award in Economics.

Then, just before the market downturn in the late 1960s, I sold my holdings for investment in another venture. The timing couldn't have been better for getting out of stocks and bonds, and for seeking timberlands in the South. Indeed, these acquisitions were both an investment and an adventure. Outfitted with a high sense of purpose, and with my educational pursuits at bay—temporarily—I went to Georgia with the same optimism that many an immigrant Englishman had felt in the seventeenth and eighteenth centuries: I went to "ranch the colonies."

Sylvania, Georgia, a small town on the Savannah River midway between Augusta and Savannah, would hardly seem a mecca for real estate investment. But for a young man who'd hunted throughout the area as a child, an attentive son who knew from his father's recent successes at Georgia-Pacific what Southern pine could mean for an investor—well, for such a man, Sylvania was the logical place to go.

And I knew just the person to help me with this new venture. Jerry Manack.

Jerry, a solid and swarthy woodsman of Italian extraction, had been a friend and hunting companion for many years. He was the kind of hunter for whom a rifle or shotgun become almost an extension of his eyes and hands. Hunting, though, was not Jerry's only talent. He was a woodsman in the professional sense, as well as in the personal realm. Thanks to him, I was able to invest in Georgia timberlands.

As for Sylvania, the place was as solidly conservative and "down home" as Jerry Manack. Anyone who has traveled on the back roads of America has been in a Sylvania, whether it be in the South, the Midwest, or in the foothills of the Sierra Nevada. A town of 3300 Bible-Belt souls, Sylvania had a main street with a single signal light, a dry goods store, an old-fashioned soda fountain and drugstore, and the county courthouse— the place served as the seat of Screven County. The town's angled parking spaces were filled with pickup trucks interspersed with Cadillacs and Lincolns, the latter vehicles representing the more fortunate retired farmers, as well as an occasional moonshiner who'd "made it."

After I talked with Jerry Manack about my plans, suggesting that the pine stands outside his home town might be worth something, I discovered he had a unique way of gauging a timber tract's value. He would walk through different sections of the land and count each tree that, in his judgment, would be worth a twenty-dollar bill.

"See that tree?" he would say. "That's worth a twenty-dollar bill. All you have to do is look around you and count the twenty-dollar bills."

But that was just part of Jerry's hands-on technique. Also he jawed with the owners, usually local farmers, in their own language. With him I could go into any home in the backwoods of Georgia and talk with the folks—"talk country," as they say.

This was not a ploy, of course, not for either of us. Jerry was still a native, and I'd lived in Augusta long enough to know something of the land and its people. Besides, my days on Grandmother's farm and in the swampland hunting cabin had blessed me with the ability to be comfortable with persons of all walks of life. A Georgia sharecropper or swamp huntsman, a distinguished economics professor, a bigwig in the board room of a major corporation—all these were the same to me. It was a trait that proved its value again and again.

Still, while I'd done my share of swamp time, there's no denying that Jerry was more knowledgeable in the woods than I. More than once he kept me from stepping on a rattler. One day in particular, in the middle of summer, mosquitos were so thick they nearly blinded us. We had to keep our mouths closed to avoid an early lunch. That day Jerry saved me from rattler- or moccasin-bite no fewer than three times.

"Never give a moccasin a chance," he would tell me. "They have a nasty temperament—just love to bite you."

But then he'd add, "Now don't be afraid of 'em, either. Just hit 'em in the head with a good hickory stick."

I followed this advice as best I could. As for Jerry, he carried that hickory stick with him everywhere, and when the snake was longer than the stick, he would instruct me to keep the snake's attention while he snuck round behind it to "pop it one." Sometimes I felt like so much dangled bait.

And snakes, he warned me, might want to take a swim with us when we took our after-work bath in Briar Creek. He wasn't worried about that, either, though. He said all we'd have to do was duck under water. Jerry reasoned that a snake can't bite under water; it would drown.

Thankfully, I never had opportunity to test that theory.

Our Georgia investments paid off for a number of reasons. For one thing, like my father before me, I always made sure to give each timber owner a fair price. One old farmer, I remember, said he would sell only if we gave him cash and a new Lincoln. We gave him the cash, all right, but the man bought his own Lincoln.

But the foremost reason for our success was the simple system behind it. Jerry and I searched out lands that had been planted during the government pine-seeding program following the last war. We calculated that those trees were about five years away from maturing, in size, from pulpwood to saw timber .

Pulpwood value was about half that of saw timber's, so, in theory, only about five years was needed before the pines would double in value. In addition, we looked for property that had a good stand of mature timber. Usually the mature timber was deep in the swampy part of a property, and since those wetlands were as rife with snakes and other vermin as ever, such trees were in many cases overlooked by other potential buyers.

The way we did the numbers, then, was what my father would call "just common sense." Our purchase price on the timber was never more than what we felt we could get for a cutting contract on the mature timber, plus the value of the newly planted pines—though, remember, those pine values were at pulp prices, not saw timber prices. This formula meant we considered nothing additional for the land itself. As we looked at it, the land was free.

Then after we sold off the mature timber, we presented the property to investors priced according to the income-producing potential of the pine when it reached saw timber size. Also we reminded investors that, over those same five years while the pine was maturing, the land itself would more than likely increase in value.

A simple system, yes. Yet it was overwhelmingly effective. In most cases Jerry and I ended up with double our original outlay: 100 percent profit.

Myself, as those profits accumulated, I couldn't help seeing my father's training in my success. What has always impressed me about Mr. Bob Pamplin, Senior, is his unique combination of brilliance and—again—common sense. The innovative thinking behind the Southern-pine venture was my own, to be sure. I found the opportunity, and I came up with the process. Yet it was also the sort of canny stroke my father had brought off a dozen times while building up Georgia-Pacific. For those who know how stodgy and unimaginative businessmen can be, a freethinker like Bob Senior deserves the word "genius." And yet, even more impressive for anyone who refuses to play the money game conservatively, my father never fails to turn a profit. That's where common sense comes in. He can see opportunities that escape everyone else's attention, and yet he also keeps a sharp eye on the bottom line.

For my father as for me, our deepest satisfactions come out of an unusual definition of success. If you look up the word in a dictionary, you'll first discover something about "wealth" and "power." But true success—if

Mr. Webster will forgive my saying so—lies outside the relatively minor issue of worldly fortunes.

As I mentioned earlier, I sincerely feel that I was given my investment opportunities for a larger purpose, just as I feel my life-threatening accidents and illnesses have been for a reason. That purpose or reason doesn't have a dollar sign on it. It is measured rather by the abilities and affinities a person is born with, the traits and skills given one by God and by the dozens of generations that have come before. True success lies in pushing those skills to their fullest, and in knowing you've done so. True value lies in the self and in awareness of the self, allowing both to be lifted to greater and greater levels of development.

I first began to reach those wonderfully fulfilling new levels with Jerry Manack, in the Georgia backwoods.

I decided that same philosophy could work with farm lands in Oregon. When opportunities in Georgia timber began to dwindle in the late 1960s, I returned to the Northwest looking for farms that might be made profitable in a similar way. I searched the Willamette Valley especially, and between the Valley and the Pacific Coast.

With any venture involving substantial amounts of investment capital, timing can be crucial. As I began buying farms and acreages in Oregon, I realized that once again my fortunes were being guided by a greater purpose. Destiny could not have been kinder to me.

Oregon, when I was buying, had not experienced a land boom in some decades. I found willing sellers at fair prices, particularly with marginal properties that needed attention. On these properties, I was able to lease the cultivation rights while still holding title, making it profitable for the lessee and for my company. Field crops, row crops, and nut tree orchards were all part of the land purchases of that period.

And then Destiny took a hand. Oregon real-estate values rocketed in the mid-'70s. Everyone from rock'n'roll stars seeking a woods retreat to investment companies looking for new development properties came to the Northwest, buying up the open land. My speculation again paid off handsomely.

This was a period of adventure for me in the business world, then—and in my recreational life as well. I was on the verge of living an experience that had once been only a childhood daydream. It's common for a child to fantasize, of course. When I was little I would often dress in an outfit that I felt was appropriate for my chosen hero of the day. One time I might be a lone cowboy heading off a band of marauding Indians and, another day, an adventurer in the jungles of Africa, helping Tarzan save a defenseless safari from charging rhino or menacing natives. But during the summer months, when the moist Georgia air was nearly suffocating with heat, I would seek relief in dreams about my special exploit: big game hunting.

So fortunate have I been, in my life a good portion of this fantasy has come true. As a boy of twelve, I spent many wonderful days with Athabascan native guides in far northern Canada, hunting with my father. We were hundreds of miles from civilization, traveling on horseback most of the time, having a glorious adventure. We climbed mountains, tracked rare wilderness trophies, and lived off the land. Few youngsters can claim to have killed moose and other big game when they were twelve, as I got to that summer.

B ut the complete fulfillment of my childhood fantasies came later, in these same late 1960s, along the Mara River in Kenya. I went to Africa on a hunting safari, hoping above all that I'd bag at least a couple of the "big five" of big-game sportsmen: lion, elephant, buffalo, rhino, and leopard.

It seemed at first that my hopes would be frustrated. For days we tracked in the shadows of leopard and lion, but we could never place ourselves in a good position for a shot. We followed up on all the rumors from the Kenya natives, scouting the plains and the timbered areas, or sitting long hours by baited traps.

On one occasion we situated ourselves at the end of a dry wash, intending to head off three lions we'd heard were moving that way. We must have been desperate for action, because as I waited I realized that my guide and I had stationed ourselves dangerously. From where we were, we'd only have gotten off a quick running shot before the lions would have been on us. My .375 bolt-action rifle needed to be reloaded after each shot, and his . 470 Nitro Express double rifle could only be fired twice. That meant three shots for three confused, prowling, angry lions. The longer I sat there, the more I realized that this fantasy might turn into a disaster.

We stood our ground, but I let out a quiet sigh of relief when the lions didn't show.

The real test, and the complete fulfillment of my boyhood daydream, came two weeks into the safari. We were hunting the most ornery and deadly big game in Africa, the African buffalo.

The beast has more than earned this distinction. His explosive temper, and his ability to absorb a few high-powered slugs and still muster a deadly charge have won for the animal, among other tokens of respect, an honored place in the African writings of Ernest Hemingway. He is black, with almost hairless skin. He weighs about a ton, stands five feet high at the shoulder, and carries horns which can measure five feet from point to point—a terrifying arsenal. On top of that, the African buffalo's a highly intelligent animal. Endowed with acute perception in all five senses, he has the brains to use these senses to his advantage. When hurt, he won't simply retreat. Rather, circling skillfully, a wounded buffalo will often confuse a tracker and lie in hiding until the hunter approaches—and then charge without warning. Just such a deadly charge takes place at the climax of Hemingway's great story, "The Short Happy Life of Francis Macomber."

I was no Hemingway, but I wanted a trophy buffalo. For days my guide and I sought one. The region had been experiencing a drought, and grass was sparse, the game spread thin. Then at dawn one morning a group of Masai men wearing rough cotton togas and carrying spears appeared on the trail, telling us in their native tongue about a nearby herd of buffalo containing several large bulls.

We were skeptical. Too often these "leads" had resulted only in long, fruitless treks through jungles and over hot dusty plains. The area these Masai were talking about, however, did sound promising. It was thickly wooded and close to good grazing. The principal ingredients for a likely buffalo habitat seemed in place: lots of food and easy access to the woods in case the animals sensed danger.

After conferring with our trackers, we decided to scout the herd. As quietly and cautiously as possible we moved through the grass and toward the trees where the Masai had directed us. My senses had gone to Red Alert: my spine seeming to grow bristles, goosebumps rippling down my arm.

Rarely have I felt such excitement—or such fright. I knew, somehow, that the climactic moment was nearing. In a few minutes I would come face to face with something that would want to kill me and would have no trouble doing so if given the chance.

We emerged from the first clump of trees into an opening in thick brush. At last we could see our long-sought prey: two fine, wide-horned bulls trailing a herd of cows and calves. The bulls, their senses acute as ever, had stopped for a moment to look for what they'd scented behind them. The guide studied the animals through his binoculars, leaned over and whispered that I should try for the one in front, bigger of the two. Then his eyes hardened.

"Shoot him behind the foreleg, in the heart, and don't make a bad shot of it. If you wound him, we have to track him down."

I knew what he meant. If I only wounded the beast, we'd have to track him through his own home territory. And he'd be aching and furious, and nothing would satisfy his rage except destroying those who'd hurt him.

I took a deep breath, lined the cross hairs of the .375 in the right spot, and squeezed the trigger.

The report of the rifle, the shock of the recoil, and the smack of the bullet as it hit the animal's tough hide all came at once. Then, even while shaking off the recoil, I was ejecting the spent shell and ramming home another cartridge. I was ready for a second shot. The guide had his hands up, however, waving me off

"The other bull's moved in front!" he whispered, pointing. Indeed, I no longer had a clear shot at my target.

"Let's see what happens!" the guide added.

The bulls began to move off together, disappearing into the woods. I had missed the vital spot. The buffalo was only wounded. For the guide and me, sharing a glum look, there was nothing to say, no choice except to follow. My spine bristled again, my stomach fluttering for good measure. How could I not have put home that first shot? Now my trembling stomach sent bile up my gullet: the bitter taste of knowing that my life was on the line. One mistake, just one, and I was a dead man.

I followed in the footsteps of the guide, but it was like walking through a foggy kaleidoscope of colors. I longed for my old friend Jerry's confidence in the woods, and had the distinct sense that I was falling—so endlessly falling it was as if I'd stepped into an abyss. Was this "adventure"? The fulfillment of a childhood dream?

"There he is!"

The cry of the guide wrenched me back to reality. I too saw the bull, his magnificent head thrashing from side to side, brandishing a set of pointed and brutal horns.

The bull lowered his head and started to move through the thicket. I brought up my rifle, but all I could make out through the scope was a blur behind that thicket. I kept following the movement and finally got a fix on a black spot between two trees. It had to be the buffalo, though I had no idea just what part of the buffalo.

I fired, jammed in another cartridge, fired again. The black spot in my scope continued to move, then disappeared altogether. The animal and I were like boxers circling each other in the ring, and now another round had ended.

My guide and I followed the bull for quite some time, knowing the whole while that he was getting sicker and meaner by the minute. More than likely he was carrying three bullets by now, and we spotted occasional telltale smearings of gore. Then the woods began to open into small clearings dotted by thick clumps of brush: an excellent area for a wounded beast to hide and prepare himself for one last charge.

Our African trackers were with the guide and me again, helping spot the bull's trail. They led us round a thicket, and there the beast was, the closest I'd seen him yet.

He was staring back at me from the center of a tight clearing. He was waiting, I realized. He wasn't going to charge until all of us were out of the thicket, exposed to his horns.

The gun-bearer handed me the rifle. I raised it, took careful aim—and then heard nothing more than an impotent click when I squeezed the trigger. The gun had dry-fired. In all the excitement, neither the gun-bearer nor I had realized that I had a spent round in the chamber.

The guide threw up his rifle. But, going for the head, trying to stop the buffalo cold, the man only sank a bullet harmlessly into the thing's horns.

Stung, bewildered, the animal lowered his head.

"Look out!" the guide yelled, "He's going to charge!"

The guide and everyone else in the party hightailed it for cover; I reached for another cartridge. I wasn't ready to run, somehow. I'd come out of my earlier dizzy fright into a sudden vivifying clarity. I was alone against a wounded African buffalo. This was what I'd come so many thousands of miles for. This was what I'd wanted since I'd been a boy in Augusta. And I had time for one good shot.

As the buffalo stamped his hooves and readied his charge, I shoved the shell into the chamber and brought up the rifle. I dropped the beast where he stood.

That night we ate oxtail soup and boiled buffalo tongue. The guide and others in the party asked me why I had stood my ground, when the smart move at that point would have been to cut and run. To this day I'm not entirely sure why. I do remember the clarity of the moment. And I know I'd rehearsed just such a scene in my childhood bed in Georgia, many times. But there'd certainly been nothing that could be called a reasoning process, in that moment before the wounded bull. All I know is that some time before that moment, while my guide and I had still been tracking the beast, I'd made up my mind that I was going to stand my ground. It would either be me or the buffalo.

And afterward, when I came to understand how vulnerable I really was in the face of that sinewed fury, I too realized I'd been awfully cavalier in the face of Fate. Yet nonetheless, I'd been spared. Again I wondered why. I knew it was for some greater reason than fulfilling the daydream of a small Georgia boy. I knew, given how my family and I define "success," that I hadn't been given my abilities simply in order to enjoy good hunting on the Kenya plain.

Yes, my life was going wonderfully by then. I'd won recognition for community and academic service, including an honorary doctorate from the University of Portland and a Distinguished Alumnus award from Lewis & Clark. Appointments by the Governor of Oregon and the President of the United States to important commissions had marked high points in my civic stature. All that, however, paled in comparison to one very different high point: marrying Marilyn Hooper in the mid-1960s. For it was Marilyn—relaxed yet ever-perceptive Marilyn—who during those same good years noticed what looked like a speck of tar on my leg.

CHAPTER 18

Robert Pamplin, Junior
A Speck of Tar

B OB WHAT IS THAT on your leg? It looks like a bit of tar. What did you get on you?"

"Oh, it isn't anything, Marilyn. Just a mole. It's nothing to worry about."

Or was it? For years I had heard and read about the seven danger signals of cancer, and I knew one sign was a mole that changed color. I had one of those now: a spot on the front of my right leg—the leg I'd injured in eighth-grade football—just below the knee.

Even so, I told myself, surely a mole wasn't anything to worry about. If this one turned out to be malignant somehow, no doubt the problem would be gone as soon as it was cut out. After all, I had never heard of anyone dying from a mole. Leukemia and lung cancer, now, I knew those were dangerous. "Mole cancer," on the other hand, had to rank pretty low on the list. And yet, after Marilyn called the thing to my attention, it occurred to me that I might be rationalizing, whistling past the graveyard. Not long after she'd pointed it out, while driving home, I reached down and felt the mole through my pants leg. I realized I hadn't been aware of it for some hours, and I hoped it might have gone away.

It hadn't.

Marilyn, my Marilyn. Who else but she could ever have noticed so small but crucial a thing? It was 1973 and we'd just returned from Hawaii, a vacation for the two of us alone. No business pressures, no phone calls, and neither of our two darling girls, Amy and Anne. We'd missed the girls, naturally, but it had been nice to set aside some time for my wife and me to be a couple again.

A couple, yes: even my first encounters with the broadly smiling Marilyn Hooper, in the charged social atmosphere of the mid-1960s, made it clear that she and I shared a rare bond. Even then, eschewing the fevered and apocalyptic style of the time, Marilyn took care to show a tender understanding of very different people and the issues with which they wrestled. She had an inborn, gracious acceptance of daily challenges; I could tell at once that she was—only simple words can express it—a nice person, just plain a nice person, with a heart as generous and sun-warmed as old Georgia itself.

And after our first few dates I could see that Marilyn had something else as well, something that seems at first thought contradictory. She had drive, Marilyn. She respected achievement, and she wanted to get somewhere herself. Despite her innate kindness and restraint, a calm which has me confident that every day will be a success, Marilyn shares my sense of discipline, my determination.

Even now in the 1990s, many years since our wedding and nearly two decades since my bout with cancer, Marilyn's efforts still astound me. It's not just that she's been President of Portland's Junior League and then of the Parry Center (for emotionally disturbed children). It's how she's balanced that sort of community commitment with the far more demanding work of raising two girls. At first, like many businessmen's wives, Marilyn took care of most of the childrearing herself. It was she who made certain that little Amy and Anne learned the difference between a job half-done and a job well-done, just as my mother was the one who did that for me. Our gentle Marilyn can be a taskmaster, no question about it.

Yet after she began working in the League and for the Parry Center, Marilyn's family skills really blossomed. She taught me then how to take a greater part in the parenting—and, more's the miracle, how to feel good about it. My wife didn't merely order me to look over the girls' homework, for instance, but rather lovingly showed me how to make that kind of day-to-day attentiveness part of my routine. The challenge of raising kids in a two-career household, after all, is not simply sharing the workload. It's sharing without resentment, without feeling unfairly burdened. And when Marilyn's activities outside the home began to expand, the girls and I were so fortunate to have her guidance for our family's new configurations.

Till then our household strategy had been, in effect, Mom Rules. Now it became Mom and Dad: Yay, Team! And that team was stronger for the change, undoubtedly. Both girls received excellent grades right through high school, and outstanding scholarship offers afterwards. And those offers weren't purely academic. It helped, too, that they placed so highly in the U.S. Tennis Association rankings. Myself, I got a far greater kick out of their success, knowing that I'd had a substantial part in it. And for that, as I say, I have to give ultimate credit to my wife Marilyn.

Her personality combines unlikely elements, in other words—unlikely, and perfect for me. As the years go by, it seems more and more as though, like so many of the developments that have graced my life, Marilyn and I were placed in each other's care for a reason.

And on our return from Hawaii, she noticed that "speck of tar."

I wanted to get all the sun possible in Hawaii. Thoughtlessly, I tried to make up for Oregon's bleak winter skies in a single day. I tried—and I paid the price. Severely burned, my skin peeled in massive strips. I suffered the heat of a well-turned suckling pig just off the spit, and glowed with a color to match. By the time we headed back to Oregon, I thought my skin had caused me about as much trouble as it ever could.

Then once we returned home my blotchy epidermis returned to normal, and Marilyn noticed the mole.

In the weeks that followed, the mole remained, its basic ebony changing shades just slightly. And though it didn't hurt, it continued to grow irregularly. Marilyn, showing her taskmaster side, began to insist I see a doctor. I kept putting off making an appointment, hoping that the mole was not a serious problem. Deep down, though, I felt a hard-to-explain uneasiness. I didn't want to see any doctor. . . .

Finally, seeing that the mole was changing hues again, I yielded. In short order I found myself in a medical-facility cubicle, looking at a padded examination table covered with a long strip of paper. Some of the horror stories I had read as a child rushed through my mind, along with some of the horror movies I'd seen, like rain clouds kicked into high speed by a Pacific storm. The images were so vivid. I could hear the shrieks of pain from manacled prisoners on the rack. I could hear the skitter of rats across a stone floor—or were they the swamp rats of my childhood nights in that hunters' cabin? The dominant images in my head, however, were those chain-bound prisoners. The poor nameless men and women stared into space, their expressionless eyes fixed on some unknown tormentor in the darkness.

What the forgotten convict in my head saw, of course, was the torment of not knowing what would happen next or how severe the trouble might be. It was a long ten minutes in that sterile cubicle. At last Dr. Shields bustled in, a man I'd seen socially on several occasions. Here on his turf, however, in his white smock . . . he was another person. He could even have been my prison torturer.

"Hello, Bob," he said, nicely enough. "What seems to be the trouble?"

I told him about the mole. I minimized my concerns, of course, still whistling past those night-dark tombstones. I wouldn't have bothered, I assured him, except my wife had insisted.

"Good for her," he said. "Now, let's have a look."

Shields looked over the mole carefully, touched it several times, and then fired off a swift volley of questions. How long had I had it? When did I notice the changes? How much had it grown? Fruitlessly I sought behind these questions for some hint of his feelings or conclusions. He gave me none. He only told me, before stepping outside, that he wanted his partner to have a look at the mole too.

Alone again in that white room, I was forced to realize for the first time that "the speck of tar" might be more serious than I had allowed myself to believe. Still, though, it was hard for me to accept that something so tiny, growing or not, could be a critical threat. After all, I was in my early thirties, the fabled "prime of life," and exercising regularly at the Multnomah Athletic Club to boot.

Doc returned in a few minutes, and introduced me to his partner. Then they were both looking at the mole, fingering it, and throwing medical jargon back and forth. Really, they ignored me. For them, for those few moments, I was nothing but that cornflake-sized piece of discolored flesh. Yet it was me who was attached to that flesh—me, in a heavy sweat. I'd had a good deal of experience with doctors, beginning with my knee problems so many years before, and I knew that when they talked this way it was serious.

Finally, they dropped the jargon. Raising their eyes from the mole, they noticed the man again.

"Bob," Doc Shields told me, "this could be cancerous. We don't think so, but we're just not sure either way. What we have to do is excise it—cut it out—and send it into the pathology lab for a biopsy."

I nodded, mastering my nerves.

"We'll let the lab boys tell us what we're dealing with," Dr. Shields concluded. "And we can take it out right here."

I have to admit I was relieved. The prisoners in my head faded, replaced by the friendly bespectacled faces of the "lab boys." Dr. Shields cut out the mole, stitched up the incision, and I went on my way. I was scheduled to return in a week to have the stitches out and get the report from the pathology lab.

I passed the week without much worry. If the mole had been particularly threatening, after all, wouldn't they have told me? And yet there was that chance . . . that awful chance. I wouldn't let myself think about it, and Marilyn remained as smilingly focused on the present as ever. Together we waited for the lab report, neither of us suffering any concern that felt out of the usual.

In fact, I was confident when I returned to Shields' office. When I'd left home that morning I really didn't feel that this day would be different from any other; I believed the problem of the mole was behind me.

The routine at Doc's office was just as it had been the week before: the out-of-date *Time* magazines, the sterile walls, the stiff paper on the examination table. And with all that, I found myself tormented by a resurgent imagination. It wasn't long before the confidence I'd come in with had melted into something resembling anxiety. Oh, the waiting! Was this, I wondered, how it felt to have an audience with the Pope? Today though, I was waiting to hear from the Pope's boss. . . .

I fought down a shiver. Don't think about it.

Finally Doc Shields blew into the room as if he'd been shoved. He wasted no time on tact.

"Well, Bob, you've got a malignant melanoma."

"Malignant melanoma?" I frowned. "What's that?"

"A cancerous mole, Bob."

And then, briskly, offering no room for questions, he told me what he was going to do. "We're going to cut this wide area—" he penned a oval on my legflesh, around the incision where the mole had been— "about like so. If we're lucky, that will get it all."

The oval shape on the front of my leg looked about four inches across. Silently I studied it, a palmist trying to read the future. Shields meantime continued to describe the procedure: "We'll cut that out, and then we'll put in a patch off your leg up here"—he touched me on the thigh— "for a skin graft. What we take out, meantime, we'll send back to pathology, and they'll cut it into small sections and examine it all through a microscope. If there are any cancer cells, pathology will find them."

Melanoma . . . cancer . . . incision . . . pathology. I heard these words, I knew this man, and yet there remained something impossible about the whole experience, something I couldn't believe in. How his talk ran on. I had to struggle to keep up with it, across widening ripples of unreality. They were going to look for cancer cells. If they didn't get it all with the first operation, they were going to open me up again and remove my lymph glands. And then there was chemotherapy, tying off my leg and flushing it out with chemicals.

I thought, but it was just a *mole!* Could so much devastation spring from a single speck of tar!

Shields was still talking about lymph glands and procedures. Finally, one phrase skimmed across my rippling unreality, too fast and deeply plunging to strike so strangely as the rest. *Cure rate*, I heard the doctor say.

Cure rate. A businessman like myself, I knew the meaning of "rate." It meant that there were times when this disease wasn't curable.

Doc Shields finished explaining the surgical procedure. Still turning over that awful two-word phrase, I sat before him nodding in brainless agreement, like a child with blind trust in a parent. And I complied eagerly with the nurse, making an appointment to go to the hospital at the next available date. In fact, in my rattled state it came as something of a shock to me that I couldn't go get the skin cut out that very day. I'd never thought that hospitals have schedules and limits, and you can't just move someone out of a room—or off of an operating table—to suit your convenience.

I left the clinic in a blur. It seemed that all the joy of my recent life, the dreams come true and the boyish wishes granted, had been smashed. Among the mess of shards, too, lay the remnants of a child's fairy-tale hope for a happy ending. My movements were mechanical, without feeling. As I slipped into the seat of the car, tears welled up. I caught an underwater glimpse of myself in the mirror, and it was as if I was fading out of the picture. Was that what life and death meant? One minute everything is sharp and clear, and the next you fade from view as though you'd never been there in the first place?

Driving home, however, it was amazing how the simple mental demands of traffic signals and steering wheel pushed the blurring dread from my mind. Even though I wanted to think about my plight, my attention was constantly diverted by the traffic: where I was going, what I was doing. That's how I'll beat this, I told myself determinedly. I'll keep busy every moment, I won't give myself time to think. Malignant melanoma wouldn't stop an old Tech Rat!

But each time I found myself without action, at a red light say, my eyes would water again. Glimpses of the children, my wife, some happy moment together would seep up with the tears, pictures that would float briefly in my mind's eye. Then, one by one, they'd sink.

The day of the operation was September third—my birthday. Most people would have tried to make it another day, thinking, "What a birthday present!" But I didn't really care. Surgery was one step closer to putting cancer behind me. On the operating table, before the sodium pentothal put me to sleep, a last form of prayer took hold of me. With a groggy voice and thick tongue I murmured, "Doc, thanks for operating on me. Make me well."

That first word, "Doc," sounded just like "God."

My next conscious thought came in the recovery room. I was cold, then, cold as a drowned man washed up out of the cold Pacific. My body, from what I could tell, had been placed on a slab of marble. Slowly my mental faculties began to return, and I moved my hand down my hip to see if they had removed my leg. That had been a bad notion of mine, a paranoid fantasy I suppose. I'd thought that, if the cancer had spread, the doctors would remove my leg.

My thigh was still there, I was glad to discover. But I had to muster all my concentration to get my toes wiggling and make sure I felt them wiggling. Yes, I felt them; the lower leg was intact too.

This alone made me feel better. And when I was wheeled back into my bedroom, who was there but Marilyn, the woman who'd taken the crucial first steps towards finding out what ailed me. At once, bending close, she whispered that the doctor believed that all the cancer had been removed. Shields was, she told me too fast for me to get a word in edgewise, ninety-five percent certain that the excised area was clean. After that, the flow of her words, her sustaining love . . . after that, relief is far too weak a word for what I felt. I took Marilyn's hand, her warm hand.

The doctor's visit the next day was less heartening. He brought home more of the insidious nature of cancer. "The problem is," he said, "if we missed just one cell, if one got away and has reached the lymph glands, or another part of the body, then the whole chain could start over again." He told me he'd sent the excised section to pathology, as planned, and I'd need a few more days in the hospital.

"Before we release you," Doc Shields said, "we'll have a better sense of the results."

They say that medical students studying pathology begin to imagine symptom after symptom of the diseases being discussed. There in the hospital, I learned the power of this phenomenon. I felt a bulge in my esophagus and immediately worried if there were cancer in there. The staff quickly checked it out, rushing me into an upper body scan and a barium test. But this, of course, only made me worry all the more. Was my body infested? I remembered what my mother and father had told me about their own blood-type incompatibility, the reason they'd never been able to have other children. Did I have some threat like that lurking in me? Throughout the week my anxiety about the pathology report mounted, as did Marilyn's. We did our best to act brave in front of Amy and Anne.

The report came in the afternoon on the sixth day. Once more Dr. Shields was quick and matter of fact. No sooner was he in the door than he'd announced the area was clean. There were no rogue cells, nothing to worry about.

Again, my feelings far outstripped the words I might choose for them. Exhilaration, solace, renewal, comfort, joy . . . these merely touch the fringes of my thrill, my relief And had a boulder just been lifted from my chest? A boulder the size of Hawaii?

Once more Marilyn and I were clasping hands, smiling hugely.

Later I found out that the boulder hadn't been removed, exactly, but merely shifted. I was to be subjected to multiple examinations over the next five years, making sure that the cancer had really been removed. So, regardless of the lab report, for the next six months I spent an awful lot of time at Doc's. I went weekly. At each examination Shields would check my lymph glands, since swelling was a sign of cancer, and examine the incision for any lesions, which would also indicate that some murderous cell had escaped the scalpel.

To me, going in for those visits was almost like going before a judge for sentencing. If he found cancer, the man could even pronounce the sentence of death. Thus each day became enormously precious, and especially those immediately after an examination. I left the office thanking God for another week of grace. But as the next visit approached, I'd feel my week of life dwindling, and once more there'd surge up the fear that I wouldn't be given another reprieve.

After six months, I was able to extend the time between visits to two weeks. Then, gradually, it became a month between office calls, and finally a full six months. And my attitude changed once I was past the weekly visits. I saw the Doc and myself as working on a five-year game plan. Five years without the disease and I'd be considered cured.

A t age thirty-five, two years after the operation and with everything apparently going my way, I still couldn't escape the awareness that death might very well be lurking round the next corner. Yes, I was fulfilled and prosperous and about to begin working with my father, the job I'd wanted all my life—for 1976 was also the year the two of us got the R.B. Pamplin Corporation off the ground. But despite these happier thoughts, these intimations of dreams come true, I couldn't shake my mole's chilling reminder that all I had could be gone in a moment.

At first, it crushed me. Some people with cancer have been told they have only a specific, limited time left, that the disease has gone beyond the control of medicine. The initial shock must be devastating. Such cases are terrible tragedies, of course, tragedies I'm glad I never had to face. But at least for victims like those the question is over with then and there. In my case, however, the question remained open for months and months. With each visit to the doctor my anxiety rattled and sprung through me almost unmanageably. I was like a condemned man being brought to the electric chair over and over again, receiving each time some sort of maddening, temporary stay.

And these things prey on a man unrelentingly. The first year of my visits, just before Christmas, the pressure of visiting the doctor was heightened terribly when I had to have a suspicious lesion removed. Then I had to wait again, right through the celebrations of Christmas, for another pathology report. Yes, the lesion proved to be benign. But what a miserable Christmas! So my emotional roller coaster sent me up and down, up and down, for five years.

Standing up against the pressure, anxiety, and dread, however, was something better. I developed, also, the firm certainty that I had two mighty armies striving to help me, doing battle on my behalf. One army was earthly, the other one heavenly.

The earthly army, of course, was the hospital and the doctors. But the other army was even more important.

Many, many friends—brothers and sisters in Christ—were crying out to God for my recovery.

And since I did recover, I am confident of two things, as I look back on those days now. I do believe that God answered the earnest prayers of my friends and family. And I do believe that God spared me so that I might do good for His kingdom. He has a use for me, yes. He had a purpose for my awful luck with the fireworks bomb, and for my coolness before the African buffalo so many years later. In these moments and so many others God impressed upon me the importance of keeping myself right with Him—for after death it is too late.

But I guess there will always be questions.

Why me? Why was I saved? Questions like these are inescapable. For what purpose has God spared me from this test, and from the others that have come in my life?

One thing is clear, however, whenever I think back on that "speck of tar." It is clear that God has loved me enough to apply shock treatment to my soul. His direction for my life has come in jolts, always forcing me out of naked dependence on self and back into a humble trust in Him. Not long after my bout with cancer, I went back to college—to Western Conservative Baptist Seminary, studying for the ministry this time. I earned my

Masters and Doctorate there in the late 1970s and early 1980s. But I got a lot more than a piece of heavyweight paper out of my years in that lovely seminary up on Portland's Mt. Tabor. There I came to grips with last questions, with issues of mortality and purpose. Thanks in part to my quiet years of study, in part to my anxious months of trial, I now serve this same shocking, loving God as best I can as founder and pastor of the Christ Community Church south of Portland.

All things, Paul reminds us in Romans 8:28, work together for the good. And Billy Graham, similarly, says that anyone among us can stand up for Christ. I myself, by means of pain and pressure and fear, have been brought once again to faith. By means of darkness, I have been made to see an unfailing light.

Why spared? Why blessed?

He knows the reason, and He loves me. That is enough.

CHAPTER 19

Robert Pamplin, Junior
Twelve Oaks Farm

LIKE FATHER, LIKE SON.

Sure, it's a cliche. But a "trite phrase or expression," as Webster's defines "cliche," only got that way because a lot of people were repeating it. And those people were repeating it, after all, because there was a lot of truth in it. The saying applies, indeed, across genders. As Dad to two high-powered daughters, I'd better not neglect the cliche's corollary: *like father, like daughter.*

Children take after their parents, no question about it. But there's a deeper truth beneath the trite, namely, that children also want to match their fathers. Sons and daughters want to make their mark in the world, since (in most cases) few things in their own personal world made so striking a mark as their fathers. The younger generation wants, even, to do something a little bit better than the older. They have that challenge, flung down at too young an age to forget. But to outdo your predecessor in the area where he excelled is a tough row to hoe indeed, one measured by impossible standards.

And so, in part simply to protect themselves, children often choose an entirely different line of work from the one which has worked for previous generations. If the mother is a crack corporate lawyer, for instance, then the daughter settles happily into life as an author of children's books. Also some offspring differentiate themselves from their parents in a more specialized way. Some go after success within roughly the same vocation, but in an unexpected arena. If the father's a successful classical pianist, say, the son starts a rock'n'roll band. Both use the same inborn gift for music, but the son seeks rewards (worldly and otherwise) that he can truly call his own.

I've encountered a number of people who believe such a wildly different approach will never work. It's too hard, they say, to begin with an entirely new and naked idea and see it grow into an indisputable success.

Myself, however, I've never doubted that possibility. Never for a moment! Yes, it takes imagination and—yes, beyond a doubt—lots of old-fashioned, sleeves-up hard work. But achievement can come out of nowhere, from a totally unforeseen direction. And believe me, that kind of success is worth more than the conventional sort. It has your own stamp on it, only, not your father's or anyone else's.

My own father started in business with a small lumber wholesaler; he was the fifth employee in the office. He spent his entire career with the same company, rising to President and Chairman of the Board. When he retired, Georgia-Pacific Corporation had profits that made it a leader in the forest products industry, and stock that was among the very strongest on the New York exchange. A couple of chapters back I used the word "genius" to describe what he's done in finance and management, and I must add now that I'm not the only one to have said so. Into his eighties, Robert Pamplin, Senior, continues to be lauded across the business world as head and shoulders above nearly any other top executive.

Now, that is a hard act to follow. I'd be crazy if I thought otherwise. But it was never my intention to pile a few additional rocks on top of Everest, just so I could claim to have climbed a little higher. Certainly I didn't feel that I should avoid a career in business just because my father's record was so outstanding. That would have been self-destructive. Yet while I'm proud of the man, even a bit of a braggart about his achievement, nonetheless I've itched to be accepted as a successful entrepreneur in my own right. By my mid-thirties I'd had success in the stock market, and with timber and farmlands and real estate investments. But I still wanted to do something that was entirely my own. I wanted to begin with some venture at its very inception, and nurture it into a roaring success.

Like any son faced with an extraordinary father, I understood in my heart that there could be only one way, namely, finding something new. Creativity, innovation, freethinking—these were my keys to making a mark for Robert Pamplin, Junior.

That quest led me to Twelve Oaks Farm.

E stablishing my own success involved some luck with timing, some good horse sense—that's a pun, as you'll soon see—and no little faith in others. On top of that, it entailed encountering a legend.

For several years Marilyn and I had owned a farm near Newberg, Oregon, down the lush Willamette Valley about forty-five minutes from Portland. The place was both a family retreat and a working filbert farm. Some time after buying the place, I decided I wanted a riding horse at the farm. This was at about the time of my struggle with that insidious malignant melanoma, and my family and I could use the extra enjoyment that horse rides can provide.

A friend suggested I ought to look into cutting horses. These are highly trained, highly skilled animals, used to isolate a single cow or calf from a herd. While cutting horses were developed to work on ranch stock, nowadays many are used strictly in competition. The purses in these contests are large, similar to those of horse races. My friend's logic, in suggesting such a specialized animal, was that it didn't cost any more to keep a cutter than to maintain a decent riding horse. More than that, there was the chance the investment might pay off. Besides, a properly trained cutter is a marvel to ride.

The search for the right horse took me to Pleasant Hill, Oregon, and a stable managed by Carmen and Norm Bryant. The Bryants were established cutting horse trainers. In competitions throughout the Northwest and up and down the Pacific Coast, they regularly took home blue ribbons and modest cash prizes. At Carmen and Norm's I found a horse I liked, and they agreed to teach me to ride. Then as I got to know the Bryants, over the next months, they shared with me their dream of someday breeding and training truly superior cutting horses.

After one of my lessons, Norm asked me to visit with them over some hot tea.

"Bob," he began, "people have made it big in raising and showing cutting horses." Norm looked down at his cup, like an old tealeaf reader trying to divine the future. "Purses at the big shows are very high, you know. Why, at the National Futurity a breeder can share a purse of over a million dollars. That's not going to happen to everyone, of course, but let me tell you something that might be every bit as exciting."

I figured it was time to put in my two cents worth.

"Norm, riding horses is fun, but I don't want to get involved any deeper unless there's a profit to be made."

The rancher's eyes narrowed slightly in thought.

"A hobby," I went on, "should also make money, Norm. That's just the way I feel about it."

Norm had impressed me as a quiet man with an easy smile and a ranch drawl. He was personable, and had never shown the kind of suppressed excitement I saw in him today. I was encountering a new side of the man, in other words, as he shifted his talk about cutting horses to the question of making money in the business. His eyes were bright, his drawl had picked up speed, and he was gesturing so enthusiastically that anyone watching him would have gotten interested. I must admit that by the time the discussion ended, I was caught up in the idea.

When it came time for me to go, he pressed a magazine on me. "Take this with you," Norm said. "It's got an article about the greatest sire of cutting horses that ever lived, Doc Bar. A dentist bought Doc Bar for little or nothing. Then some of his offspring went on to become national champions. That dentist gets a fancy price for breeding, I'll tell you. The horse is worth a fortune now."

That night, as I read the article, I became a believer. There was gold in "them thar hills"—but could Norm and I find it?

Over the next few months we put together the ingredients of a different future for Twelve Oaks Farm. We put up barns and stables; we strung fence and poured concrete. Working from scratch, putting in one sunup-to-sundown day after another, we sweated in the summer sun and grunted through the fall's wind and rain. That first winter, still hard at our preparations, Norm and I often came in from our labors blue from cold, shivering as we waited for tea and cocoa. But in time Twelve Oaks Farm was made over. It became an operating horse farm.

The stallion we selected for breeding purposes was a son of Doc Bar. And the stallion's dam was special too; she was Annie Glo, a mare highly respected for her consistent wins, no matter who was riding her. We started, in other words, with two champions.

Better than that, our new three-year-old stallion—his full name was Docs Superstar Bar—became the family's pride and joy. He was a handsome, glossy bay with a deep chest and a refined head: short ears and clean, graceful throat-latch. And at a little more than fourteen hands and 1100 pounds, Superstar was a balanced, tightly structured athlete, with lots of muscle definition in the shoulders and hindquarters. On top of that, he showed agility, quickness, and lots of "cow sense"—an intelligence about how to guide a chosen cow. Finally, he had charisma, a rare pride in himself.

Without question, on paper we'd picked up one of the outstanding young cutting-horse stallions in the nation. Yet Docs Superstar Bar, at $30,000, was still a gamble. At three, he hadn't yet proven his ability as a sire, and hadn't been truly tested in the cutting arena. The youngster was also behind in his training, due to an earlier injury. I suppose, looking back, that this stallion was an acquisition rather like many of the companies my father bought for Georgia-Pacific over the years. My "new holding" had assets that others hadn't noticed, or hadn't believed in.

At Twelve Oaks, protecting our investment, the Bryants and I developed a breeding farm providing the very best of care for both resident broodmares and mares brought in for stud service. Norm and Carmen took a course in breeding at Colorado State, and after Docs Superstar Bar had spent a few weeks getting used to his new home, our program was launched.

Superstar's first foals were born in 1979, and almost immediately they began proving what the Bryants had always felt about the stallion. Norm told me that the people who'd bred those colts were simply delighted. They called Superstar's children "the most sensible, trainable colts they'd ever had," Norm said.

The colts all proved uniformly first-rate athletes. Even when they came out of different kinds of mares, our stallion's colts were easy to spot. They were good-headed, strong-legged and stout in the hips, with nice necks and good muscle definition: in short, as handsome and powerful as their daddy.

"And the best thing," Norm enthused, "is that every one of those colts, as soon as I've started them on cattle, they've just been real 'cowy.' They've all really got that cow sense." Norm told me that, as a man who'd broken colts all his life, he'd have to place Superstar's offspring "in the top five percent" of cutting horse trainees.

"Cow sense," of course, is what establishes an outstanding breeding operation. Cutting horses need more than superb athletic ability. Also they have to out-think the cow. This mental capacity isn't something a trainer can teach; it can only be inherited. Our Superstar, now, was proving that if a horse owner wanted his foals to have cow sense, Twelve Oaks was the place to go.

Meanwhile, although the emphasis at the farm remained on breeding, Superstar's own training continued. We restricted him to limited "showings," beginning in 1978, but right away he proved as good in the arena as he was back on the ranch. Superstar lived up to his name—at his first show he walked away with the Reserve Junior Cutting Championship.

In ten shows that year he won six firsts and three seconds. He ended 1978 as the Oregon Quarter Horse Association Champion Junior Cutting Horse. In '79 he placed well in several senior registered cutting classes, and earned the prestigious Certificate of Ability from the National Cutting Horse Association.

And in that same year Superstar's progeny began to shine as well. One of his first foals, Candee's Hot Sox, was Champion Weanling Filly in three Oregon shows. Another jewel in Superstar's crown also appeared in '79, when his dam, Annie Glo, became NCHA World Champion Mare. Although she was sixteen years old and pregnant, she qualified for her induction into the NCHA Hall of Fame.

All this good news hardly went unnoticed in the cutting horse world. Twelve Oaks Farm began to get bookings from as far away as Canada, Minnesota, and Nevada. Before Superstar's colts were even old enough to start on cattle, they were selling for up to ten times the breeding fee.

So this was my way of making my own mark, my own success separate from my father's. Or this was, at least, the personal success I found the most surprising, and therefore the most satisfying. I had helped build a great horse farm. I'd helped in the planning, and in the sloshing through mud during the winter when the buildings went up—sometimes it seemed like we were treating the animals better than we were treating ourselves. I pitched in digging fence-post holes, stretching wire, buying broodmares, delivering offspring. I'd traveled across the country and back. Most importantly, given how much of this enterprise was in the hands of Destiny, I'd prayed fervently on its behalf.

In 1982 we sold Superstar for more than $800,000 cash. After five short years, in other words, we earned back more than twenty-six times our original investment—on the sale of the horse alone. The breeding fees and the payments for offspring out of the Twelve Oaks broodmares had been, along the way, many times more than the initial $30,000 outlay. Then there'd been Superstar's show earnings, the sales of his offspring, and his breeding fees, all like whipped cream on top of the rest.

Today when Norm and I put up our heels and gab, inevitably our conversation comes around to Superstar and Twelve Oaks. Yes, it's easy to sit there and pat ourselves on the back—but that's not the direction our thoughts usually run, in the end. For Norm and Carmen and I share an unshakable conviction that what happened was the work of God.

"Too many things have gone right," Norm will say, "things out of our control. The way this operation shot down the road, well, luck only goes so far!"

Of course, I realize that Norm and I were good businessmen too, honest and fair. We tried always to give horse owners the best deal we could.

"But," Norm says, "we just never ran into the problems that usually go along with a developing operation. I just can't help but feel in my bones that Someone was up there looking out for us."

For their commission in promoting the sale of Docs Superstar Bar, I wrote the Bryants a check for more than $200,000 and gave them some offspring to boot. Norm was startled by the gesture, genuinely, but I wouldn't have had it any other way. Twelve Oaks began with a shared commitment, a shared dream. And, like father, like son: Bob Senior and I have always felt that if someone works hard to help you achieve success, you should share that success with him. Had it not been for Carmen and Norm, the Twelve Oaks breeding operation and Docs Superstar Bar might well have never happened.

Yes, as Norm says, too many things went right along the way for this success—special and personal though it was for me—to have been an accident. So the Bryants and I remember and honor God's role in the venture. Without His grace and blessing, worldly achievement is nothing.

CHAPTER 20

Robert Pamplin, Junior
The Gift

N OT LONG AGO, a friend told me of an experience he'd had while flying back to Portland from Washington, D.C. In many ways his story reveals the essence of my personal philosophy.

My friend, John, was seated next to a young man dressed in an expensive suit. During the flight it quickly became obvious that this man was frightened almost to death at the whole idea of traveling by plane. When the aircraft encountered turbulence over the Rockies, his anxiety grew to a near frenzy. Pale and wild eyed, he gripped the armrests of his seat as though he expected to drop out of the skies at any moment.

John, who'd been reading, thought perhaps he could ease his companion's mind. He initiated a conversation, and the two of them roved over a variety of subjects. When they got to their respective professions, the nervous passenger startled my friend by explaining that he was a civilian inspector with the U. S. Air Force. He traveled to different air bases all over the world, the jittery young man said, nearly always going by plane. And, he confessed, he was deathly afraid of flying!

Naturally curious, John asked: "Can't you change jobs?"

"Oh," the younger man replied, "this job pays very well and has lots of security".

Security—that was his word. Security, meaning in the financial sense. He certainly felt no personal security going back up into the air over and over again.

"Isn't there anything that helps?" John asked.

"Not really," the man admitted. "I've tried both prayer and booze, but neither gives me much comfort. I guess I'm just doomed to tough it out."

My friend, you should understand, isn't one to pry into another's affairs. But by now he'd become genuinely concerned about this fellow. He asked one question more.

"If you don't mind my asking," he began, "when you pray, do you mean it? Do you really feel it, or are you just doing an exercise that you feel you ought to go through?"

His companion was thoughtful for a moment, plainly unoffended. Finally he said, "I guess I've asked myself that same thing. What troubles me is, I really don't know. I haven't come up with a satisfactory answer myself."

The two sat silent for some time. The uneasy younger man began glancing wide-eyed out the window from time to time, again, and he'd never entirely relaxed his grip on the armrests. John started to think, with a sinking feeling of his own, that he'd actually made the situation worse. But then the young man turned back to him.

"Listen," he asked, "do you pray when you fly?"

"You bet," my friend replied. "But let me tell you something. I started praying a long time before I started flying. And if there's a difference between your prayer and mine, I guess it must be that I believe in prayer." John, you see, is one who believes—that's part of why we're friends, I guess. Still, he was a bit unprepared for the well-dressed passenger's next question.

"Why do you believe as you do?"

A single simple word, *why*. Yet so often the answer it demands is far from simple. Sometimes we can only stammer as we try to bring our thoughts together—thoughts shaded by pent-up emotions and experiences. In the introduction to my section of this book I pointed out that, while I'm pleased my Beville ancestors have their own marble bas-relief back in England, I myself am no marble sculpture, no flawless finished stone. In this, I'm like the rest of the imperfect world, including my reverent friend John. I have no immutable edifice labeled "Personal Faith."

On the contrary, personal faith is something that erupts out of our hearts in spite of our efforts to control it and to make it perfect. It is in fact the story of our lives, for those of us who believe. Faith shapes us, weaves its colors through us, working as great a meaning into our failures and moments of stupidity as into our successes and days of clear thinking. It's the opposite, ultimately, of a church carving, cold and isolated. True faith can't be separated from who we are.

Why do we believe?

Myself, I'd put the question another way. Why, I'd ask, do we exist?

W henever I struggle with that question, the recesses of my mind bring forth those parts of my life that seem most vividly alive: those moments when I was jolted by the distinct and unforgettable touch of the living God.

Those jolts, I must repeat, have little to do with the sort of worldly fortune that has so graced my life. Just the opposite, they can involve as little as a penny. Indeed a single penny, incredible as it may sound, was practically a life and death matter once when my wife and I visited Communist China.

Marilyn and I were there in the early 1970s, while the revolutionary leader Mao Tse Tung still ruled the Asian mainland with an iron fist. Everywhere, soldiers armed to the teeth stood on guard. Few things attracted their attention as much as a pair of blond Americans. It was summer where we were—Canton, mostly—and the soldiers' bayonets glittered menacingly in the sun. If we needed any proof that they meant business, we got it a day or so later when we heard what they'd done with a local purse-snatcher. Mao's police had stood the man against the nearest wall and shot him: a summary execution in broad daylight.

Integral to this martial law was a strict accounting of every last cent of Chinese currency spent while in the country. Marilyn and I had to declare precisely how much money we had when we entered the country, and then on the way out we had to declare whatever was left, and at the same time show receipts verifying every expenditure. Posted signs made clear that harsh penalties could be imposed for so much as a single unaccounted-for penny.

We kept careful records, my wife and I, and at our visit's end we filled out the declaration forms dutifully. Yet as we packed, the night before we were to leave, I discovered a few forgotten coins in one of my pockets. Of course, in most countries a person would simply change the form accordingly. Not in China, though. Entries had to be made in ink, without strikeouts or erasures. And even if Marilyn and I had been inclined to hide this tiny bit of currency (surely the Lord would understand, we thought) our forms would still have shown that we'd changed some money for which we had no receipts. Unnerved, my wife and I couldn't help but recall the petty thief who paid for his transgression with his life.

Our only way out seemed to be to purchase something of equal value to these few coins. Yet it was awfully late by now, only a few minutes before the stores closed. At last, I came up with the idea of buying stamps. These were issued in many denominations, and always came with a receipt. Still, even after I was lucky enough to find a place open and to get a few stamps, I had a penny left. A single Chinese penny.

Marilyn and I slept holding hands that night. We prayed a little longer than usual before going to bed, as well. It was another of those moments when one gives oneself over to faith—when one has to trust that the idiocy of the so-called civilized world will be overcome by the goodwill of God. That happened, happily. Even in Mao's China, they weren't going to shoot someone over a penny.

Yes, the influence of the Divine can be felt in unlikely places. Nothing human, to borrow an appropriate phrase, is foreign to Him.

The incident with the Chinese coin, indeed, exemplifies much about the Savior's effect in our daily turmoil. It suggests the two different aspects of His loving attentions.

In the first place, many a human sorrow is, after all, nothing but a penny. It's some small thing made large in our imaginations by fear and ignorance, appearing finally as some outsized, grandiose horror. Wasn't that the case with the Augusta bullies who used to pick on me? Weren't they, in the end, nothing worth getting my nose bloodied for?

Then too, on the other hand, God's mighty power is at times most deeply felt in something as tiny as a penny. A child's glance, a whispered word, an extended hand—things as seemingly inconsequential as these can at times make all the difference in the world. Many a life has been changed forever by less. My own life, certainly, was changed by a speck of tar.

My Chinese penny, then, calls to mind both kinds of Divine presence. At times Christ relieves us from fretting unnecessarily over some mundane jot or tittle, some problem exaggerated by human misunderstanding; at other times, He pokes His fingertip through the skin of our lives, nudging us deliberately towards awareness of a greater cause. In both these cases, however, the true value doesn't reside in the penny. It doesn't reside in the ephemera we call "security" in this world.

No. In either case, true value is in the Coin of Faith.

W hy do I believe, when I pray? Why am I able to allay my fears, while that poor young man on the plane couldn't seem to master his?

I suppose I can see how my belief sounds like Pollyanna's Glad Game, like I'm giddily turning everything into a Christmas present from a roly-poly, white-haired Father above. But I repeat, my source these days is no children's book, but rather Scripture itself: *And we know that all things work together for good to them that love God, to them who are called according to His purpose.* St. Paul here isn't saying that all things are good. Rather, he too is calling attention to the more profound security, the more precious coin.

And is the idea of being "called according to His purpose" really so distant from our commonplace affairs? Is it really such a giddy fantasy? When my fourteenth century ancestor Lora de Waldeschef Beville found herself untouched by the Black Plague, though all around her were dying, she certainly doubted and feared her Lord's plan. She wondered if she had the stuff to withstand the horrors He seemed to be visiting on the world. And yet it turned out Lora had been spared in order, quite literally, *to serve His purpose.* She became His lay minister, helping lead the decimated population of Warwick back to belief and assurance.

The Robert B. Pamplin, Jr. family (left to right) Anne, Robert, Marilyn, Amy Pamplin North and Walter Arthur North, Jr.

Lora's hard-won renewal hardly seems like the Glad Game. There's nothing Pollyannaish about rediscovering, in the face of death, the grace and power that ordinary flesh, blood, and brains can rise to.

Thus when I think of the unknown ways in which things are working towards the Lord's purpose, I often think of my daughters. They are, like Lora, the purpose in the flesh: faith in a mustard seed, which when it grows is the greatest among herbs.

Amy was born in 1967, Anne in 1970. I know them so well, down to the roots of their hair. Yes, their hair: the year Marilyn became President of Portland's Junior League, I had to take over the combing and braiding. I began making dinners two or three times a week, too. And after I made sure the girls cleaned their plates, I cleaned them myself—washing dishes was my job, every night. Yet even standing over the sink, with my back to the kitchen, if one of the girls came into the kitchen I knew whether it was Amy or Anne. They were that much a part of me, linked to the pattern Christ is weaving around my life.

And the laughter they gave me, that too is part of the Divine pattern. Should I try to recall the many teddy-bear designs we sewed into little Anne's clothing? Should I describe the time I was vacuuming and discovered, under the sofa, a heap of Amy's rejected fluoride tablets? The very *tappeta-tap* of my girls on the stairs could make me chuckle.

Yes, they've got a light step, a fine limber American athleticism. Both Amy and Anne were superb athletes, winning sports letters all four years in high school. More than that, throughout their teens Amy and Anne won high rankings in the United States Tennis Association, capturing many tournament trophies. I was a part of these triumphs as well. Often I took one or both girls out onto the court before a match, to warm them up. Often, too, I was their transportation. The hours I spent on the road with those two calls to mind a line from the sportswriter Julie Vader: "Behind every great athlete is a parent with a reliable car."

Nor was sports their whole life. Not with Marilyn and me looking over their homework night after night, their math in particular. Both proved excellent students, and Anne won two college scholarships, one in sports and the other in academics. But under the circumstances, tellingly, my younger daughter thought it best to return one of these awards. Anne believed that, since one of the scholarships came from the state, it would better serve a youth from a less privileged home.

That last detail, that generous spirit as alive in my youngsters as it is in myself—I'd say that's a concrete, entirely un-dreamy instance of God's goodness at work in my life. That's the sort of thing which makes it possible, when I pray, to believe.

A lot is riding on my daughters, after all. Once again, as so often in the past, it will be the women of the family who must carry on its story. The thousand-year anniversary of our earliest recorded ancestor will come up during the lifetimes of Amy's and Anne's children, if not during the lifetimes of my girls themselves. Live long, my Amy, my Anne; live and grow in Christ.

Without our first Savior, I firmly believe, no family could ever itself have been saved, so many times over the past thousand years. And without Him, too, my own paltry few dozen years would have amounted to nothing. A fortune never sprouts by itself, after all. A surgeon's scalpel alone can never get out all the melanoma.

And why has this Savior saved my family? Why has he so blessed me, and spared me?

In the next chapters, I'll try to tell you why.

CHAPTER 21

Robert Pamplin, Junior
The Source of Good Things—The Spring

THE SPRING on the old Thaxted Farm of my Pamplin forebears, in the ancient agricultural lands of England, burbles out of the earth clean and pure. Surrounded by ferns and trees, attended by birds and deer, it's a place where something flows out of nothing: a sanctuary to the mysterious act of creation itself.

Now, creation takes some wildly diverse forms. My very name, for instance, was once sometimes Paunfiliun, sometimes Pamphiloun. In the days of near-total illiteracy, when that seagoing ancestor first emigrated from Pamplona, spelling was more laissez-faire (though back in this book's second chapter, out of consideration for contemporary readers, I used the contemporary transliteration). Similarly, the Beville name was at first de Beville, at the beginning of this thousand-year story. Briefly, later, it was de Welles-Beville. And the Lawrence, Boisseau, and Flournoy genealogical trees all likewise sprouted some startlingly various foliage.

Every family begins in mystery, and every family comes often into new mystery thereafter. Yet I believe that the same single nourishment flows through all these roots and branches, all these re-configurations and unpronounceable spellings. The same miracle is at work in every one of them.

Generation after generation, this protean force has climbed the centuries. Injustice, war, murder—none of these has stopped it. Nor have self-doubts, psychological failings, or troubles in the home put an end to the ascent. Generation after generation, some invisible spring has renewed and sustained an astonishingly broad spectrum of humanity.

So, now, I take the turn of a new millennium as a rare opportunity to look back and understand. I lean out from my present rung.

As best a climber can, I peer down at that distant spring. I look away across low medieval churches, and over toward far-off Viking ships. Then slowly I draw my gaze back up the ladder towards where I'm now at rest; I look over revolution and plantation and sawmill. I examine again corporate board rooms and hospital recovery rooms.

I try to see what has made the climbing possible.

And here, in these closing chapters, I try to share what I've seen.

My list of the different family names, a moment ago, I hope makes clear how this sort of historical progress is hardly limited to this one unusual group. "Family," indeed, can seem like much too exclusive a word for the many divergent peoples covered in this book.

But then, the philosophy that I want to express in the next chapters isn't intended for any one family alone. It's philosophy that provides a means for anyone to triumph over history. It's intended for the Family of Man.

Such a triumph, of course, derives in part from principles anyone in our greater Family could think of. The Pamplin successes are a matter of hard work, discipline, and integrity; of loyalty, generosity, and kindness; of caring for others and maintaining a strong faith. Such virtues aren't secrets, to be sure. Anyone in the greater Family of Peoples could put together the list, if they took the time.

But now I need to do more than make a list. I need to embody those virtues, somehow. By the medium of this book, I have tried to make the Saviour's working through these last thousand years come alive. I've tried to flesh out how others have nourished themselves at His ever-flowing spring, and have come to see His shaping in their own lives. Thus I can't abandon these many generations that have gone before without a direct statement of the principles by which they came to that sense of God in the self.

We have visited, in this book, with men and women who strove to resemble their souls' highest dreams. Now I must explicate those dreams—becoming a millennial psychiatrist, as it were. I must state in no uncertain terms what the greater Family has been trying to achieve. I must provide a warning, also, about what it has been struggling against.

Imagine the scene. There stood Geoffrey Pamplin (or Paunfiliun or Pamphiloun), seeing the spring at Thaxted for the first time. Though his old friend de Berlada had told him about the place, the Spaniard's reaction was probably much the same as ours would be today: amazement and delight. Why had God provided him with this extraordinary gift?

Now, seeing this book of mine, this spring-fed family tree, we ask the same question. Why do certain remarkable qualities seem to keep flowing out of the same oddly interrelated people?

Even so simple a gift as rope climbing, for instance, appears to have enriched all the generations from Sir Robert Lawrence on. I've got the gold medal from Virginia Tech to prove it. And generosity within the community has been a part of our makeup at least since the tiny Lora de Waldeschef Beville began feeding the Warwickshire poor.

As for my father's extraordinary rise from barefoot Virginia farm boy to one of the wealthiest and most respected men in the business world, that too reiterates the accomplishment of many a forebear—though at a far higher level of success. My father's something like a twentieth century version of the colonial Amy Beville, tenaciously holding on through all setbacks, and steadily augmenting every piece of good fortune God sent his way.

Myself, I see the seeds of my philanthropy in old Lora, and in Robert Beville Armiger's annual gift of a milk cow for the Cambridge poor. I see my ability to adapt and come up with new solutions in Athaliah Boisseau's survival strategies for the siege of Petersburg, and in the open-minded thinking of the "sot-weed factors" John and Essex Beville. And I see my lifelong commitment to education and Christianity in the philosophical Thomas Flournoy.

We sometimes call people who have extraordinary talents "blessed"— or, more cynically, "lucky." Yet there is, as anyone who's been through this book's earlier chapters can see, a certain relentlessness about this so-called luck. Not even Geoffrey Pamplin's unjust execution could stop his family's nourishment at his spring, and no denial of God's will in one's life can put an end to His calling, His shaping. Didn't the jealous Pharisees attempt to end Christ's own flow of wisdom and miracles? Yet even their efforts worked to the good. God used the horror of the crucifixion for the betterment of all humanity.

As you do not know the path of the wind, wrote King Solomon, or how the body is formed in a mother's womb, so you cannot understand the work of God, the Maker of all things. Likewise, when my father and I give of ourselves—sometimes of our money, but also of our imagination, our problem-solving, and our time—what we give is merely the shadow of the path of God's great wind. We only ride on that wind, as we are nourished by the waters of His spring. We aren't the elemental source ourselves. We can't give the ability to make money, we can't give good judgment, we can't give compassion. Only God can do that. Rather, my father and I, along with the ancestors featured in this book, strive to serve as examples, embodiments, witnesses to the true Source.

Yes, I am only a witness, finally. I hang here humbly on my rung, after fifty-some years of my own personal climbing. And I say what I have seen. I say, with my horse-breeding friend Norm Bryant, that no one could be simply "smart" and "lucky" enough for everything to have worked out as well as they have for me. Too much of my life has been for the best, even my bout with a malignant melanoma, for it to be less than the hand of God directing my efforts.

This is, after all, the power of positive thinking. Not that it merely makes us happy, turns us all into Pollyannas. Rather, it's the conduit by which the Savior's refreshing life-force flows into us, and feeds us for our climb.

Humbly I ask: let me now witness further. Let me tell you how you too may tap into those living waters. Let me make this book not merely your pastime, but your tool.

CHAPTER 22

Robert Pamplin, Junior
The Source of Good Things—Dreaming, Loving, and Doing

I F MY TALE'S going to serve as a tool, you as readers need to know what it's made of. You need to know whether you've gotten reliable goods; you need to know about the tool's *metal*, and the man's *mettle*.

Forgive the pun. It's apropos, here. Wordplay is to the point, oh yes, because anyone seeking to understand how Christ has worked through me and my ancestors is going to find some surprising answers, containing surprising meaning.

As I pointed out a couple of pages back, the success of the extended Pamplin family derived in part from virtues anyone could think of. My forebears observed the Commandments and showed common sense (or most of them did, anyway), and out of these traditional values came success. But I must point out again, patient preacher that I am, that *success* itself is a word which contains some surprising meanings. *Success* has been very much a relative condition down the generations. Geoffrey Pamplin, for example, who saw three of his sons hanged and then went to the gallows himself, was hardly a success in the same sense as my father and I.

Now, that difference is precisely the issue, when it comes to judging mettle—both my own and that of this handmade tool. For just as success has proven relative, over the last thousand years, so has adversity. My ancestors faced some of the worst trials history offers, no question about it. They faced loss, hardship, and the awful impact of war. But a few of my family's steepest obstacles, a telling few, were in fact brought on by wealth and influence. The most blatant case was the tormented Sir Robert Beville, Junior, the friend of Cromwell who let the family's ancient Cambridge lands slip away. And a number of others, among them young Robert Lawrence and old Athaliah Boisseau, learned that their good money and high position didn't mean they were spared the necessity of forging better selves.

The point is, Christian guidance is just as vital in a life that seems superficially full of abundance and free from care as in a life with the wolf at the door. That's one of the principal surprises in what our Savior has to say to us. "The rich," wrote the English theologian and poet George Herbert, "knows not who is his friend." The rich, I would add, too often doesn't realize how Christ Himself can be his friend.

Herbert's countryman John Wesley, the eighteenth-century founder of Methodism, noted disappointedly that many a man who'd benefited from faith—who'd increased his fortune thanks to faith—ended up letting those same benefits lead him from faith's path. That is, the theologian again and again saw proof that solid Christian living leads naturally to prosperity. As I keep saying, anyone can understand how perennial qualities like integrity and diligence and so forth will help a person succeed. But Wesley saw, further, that dangers lurk in the success which Christ helps create. Rising fortunes, unfortunately, soon seduce more than a few believers into abandoning the very values which have brought them worldly success.

John Wesley wasn't alone in recognizing the problem, of course. Ever since Homer lamented the pride of Achilles, deep thinkers have pointed out that whatever makes a person great can also be his or her downfall.

Thus I want to emphasize, here, what's needed in addition to fundamental virtues. For Christ our Savior went beyond the ten rules of good living handed down by His prophet Moses. Christ added the startling, vivifying assurance that miracles are waiting just around the next corner.

Our Savior is an *innovator*. That's my point. Those genuinely guided by Him will find themselves constantly shaken free of old perceptions, old limitations, and the pitfalls that have yawned under the prideful since the dawn of time.

Myself, I've faced no Infidel horde, endured no end-of-the-world bombardments. Nonetheless my life too has been shaped by serious challenge. I was born at a time of worldwide destruction, when war-smoke smudged the skies over Russia, over Manchuria—as well as over Auschwitz and Dachau. In a sense, the whole world was locked in a struggle to maintain the fragile and hard-to-define Godliness the Bevilles and Pamplins had exemplified down through the centuries. And as I grew to maturity, fittingly, I came to adopt that struggle, that task, myself. I strove to use my gifts (including the basic gift of being born in a place untouched by Holocaust) for the good. In contrast to the nouveau-riche Christians who disappointed John Wesley, I strove to convert the virtues which had benefited me into an active force that would benefit the whole of society. Like the Savior who inspired me, I tried to leave my mark in the ever-expanding outward ripples of a reinvented world.

Indeed, I believe I've been moving towards such invention all my life. Even as a child, I remember, I couldn't help imagining better for myself and my loved ones. I remember. . . .

. . . I could clearly see the drops of water in a slow bead along a rust-spotted crack in the well bucket. My grandmother always set her bucket on top of her well wall, after she'd drawn up what she needed, and for long minutes afterwards the leftover spill would dribble gradually down the outside of the wet metal. When each drop reached the bottom, it gathered weight for a second or two, then fell to the parched ground. I liked to sit watching, that summer, while drop after drop fell and sizzled. What small moistening it provided evaporated at once in the Virginia heat.

This was about the hottest summer I had ever experienced. And though I was only ten, I knew that, were I a farmer, I'd have reason to worry. The soil was hard, riven with cracks. The June and July rains had been skimpy.

For me, summertime was a lazy time anyway. The oppressive heat kept even my knockabout activity to a minimum. My body wilted under the stifling blanket of humidity. Like many another boy or girl, I tried to wait out the worst in the coolest place possible: in my case, beside my Virginia Grandma's well in Dinwiddie County.

There was virtually no sound, except for the occasional chirp of a robin or the badgering of a blue jay. I was motionless except for my eyes, following the drip of the bucket's condensation.

One might consider such moments lost or useless, but to me they were, in fact, precious. In them, I had a chance to let my mind wander into daydreams: across far peaks and chasms and onto spectacular movie sound stages.

Sometimes I would be one of Robin Hood's swashbuckling Merry Men, sometimes a Rebel soldier charging up Little Round Top. This day, however, I was a great detective, on the model of London's Sherlock Holmes. I was being called upon to solve a most unusual and baffling case. And as my mind drifted from the parched reality around me to the fog-bound city nights of my imagination, I found myself refreshed as if by actual cooling water. The creative corners of my mind worked their miracle of renewal again.

In the years since that quiet moment by the well, my dreamy ways have never really left me. I still take such mental expeditions away from the heat and pressure of the day. The difference is, as an adult I've progressed from the ethereal to the achievable. I suppose I dream at night like everyone else, but the dreams I remember come during the day, when I take odd moments now and then in order to visualize what ought to be.

As a child I entered a make-believe world because I needed to restore myself—to get back, if I may be allowed another pun, my personal "well-being." As an adult, I strive instead to improve the world around me.

I've learned to channel my dreams according to the realities of a given need. I have seen poverty, I have seen hopelessness, I have seen human beings failing to live up to their potential—and it's that towards which my imagination is directed. My source may be a kind of make-believe, but the innovations I've come up with are practical. And in that same surprising practicality, my innovations prove how satisfaction and a better way can still be found beyond our quotidian limitations.

Those limitations, after all, are the only thing a non-dreamer can see. By being a dreamer, I see the world's walls and fences better than non-dreamers do. I can see over the walls, to the workable benefits beyond.

Thus just as my wealth isn't solely about me, so this book isn't intended solely for me and mine. Some pages back I argued that *Heritage* reaches beyond my family. Instead it embraces the greater family—the Family of Man. Considering the many different branches of ancestry this book explored, the different spellings my very name went through, I'd have to be blind to believe this story is for the glorification of two contemporary American Pamplins alone.

So too, the glue that has bound my family and helped it prevail against history's long odds is hardly the wealth and power that happen to be my lot at the moment. It's not those conventional and misleading definitions of success. Rather, just as glue itself is something that comes between jagged broken parts and softens the edges in order to bind up a new whole, so my greater family's most durable element has been its skill at solving, facilitating, and overcoming differences. It's as if, at moments of crisis, humankind can count on a few saving drops of such stuff. It's as if we had a guardian angel who came not with a sword or a harp, but with a tube of glue and a few good ideas.

Such ideas are part innovation, part organization. They require both the drip, drip, drip of letting one's dreams flow, the way I did by my grandmother's well, and then the shaping of dreams into practical and beneficial solutions.

Yet I must emphasize that it's an angel who brings us these solvents, this ability to compromise and fix. The true toolmaker, I believe unalterably, is Christ our Savior. My forebears didn't surmount the hardships they faced simply in order to make a handful of recent Pamplins rich. They experienced God's justice, rather, because they kept in mind the greater betterment of all God's family. Given a firm allegiance to the Divine, and an unyielding awareness that Christian meaning pervades every action, they couldn't help but prevail.

If God is with us, Scripture asks, who can be against us? And should we doubt whether God is with us, we in the greater family, we need only look to see if there is love. In the pages that remain, here, that love is the story: His love, His doing, with me as his instrument.

Can we define God's love?

It isn't, to begin with, that warm flush of feeling they sing about in pop songs. And it's more, too, than the mature and subtle forms of private communication that truly connected people can share. Rather, love is a privilege given by God, as a defining aspect of our humanity. Because we are of God, we can love; because we love, we know we are of God.

Thus love also carries considerable responsibility.

Love indeed generates no small emotional power, even for those past the age of a first crush and its hormonal surges. But to have real substance, the emotion must be grounded in principle. For any love to have the glue I mentioned above, the enmeshing and unbreakable quality which enables the greater family to endure—for that, principles of trust, fidelity, and patience need to have a place within the hot sweeps of high feeling. And yet too, while principle gives love continuity and meaning, simple human emotionality remains essential to its power nonetheless. Emotion provides love with its fire, the spark that sets off sudden, unbidden dreams of better.

Without the emotion, love would never produce the visions necessary for new solutions. Without the principle, love could never be harnessed to any solution more lasting and practical.

When I love someone, whether family or friend, I want the feeling to have a tangible effect in both our lives. I want it to be so solid as to remain true whether we're facing sorrow or triumph, whether we're seeing eye to eye or having differences. Then too, I want there to be serendipity in its solidity. I want flexibility enough for spontaneous thrills. And I never want my love to sour into jealousy and selfishness, into the low urge to exclude all others from the happiness I enjoy. Yes, look how much God gives us to expect from love! We seek a vindicator and protector, a source of tenderness and delight, and ever-flowing restorative waters impossible to pollute.

Small wonder, then, that love insists on a high degree of responsibility. Like the skin of a frog, love has both a warty side and one that is silky smooth. Our boundless expectations regarding this greatest of God's gifts have to do entirely with the silk side, with the frolicsome serenity love creates, and the exultation of somehow sharing that laugh-filled peaceableness with the world at large. Nonetheless, love has its warts, very real warts. Of course, these are the hard times: the times when our life's climbing becomes a trial.

Like everyone, I relish love's high points. But I know full well that God has given me that feeling, that power, precisely so that I can prove its mettle when I stumble across the warts of difficulty. The troubled periods are when the principle must take hold, and love must forge itself into something better. It's when the glue must seep in and hold, when character must shine through.

Reared in the southern United States, in mid-century, I share with most others of my time and place a traditional understanding of

Biblical principles. In the same way, a close relationship with my father was more or less bred in the bone.

Indeed, my Scripture-enriched closeness with my father puzzles those of other backgrounds. They can't understand how two generations can so smoothly mix business and friendship. Bob Senior and Bob Junior have been a thriving business partnership for years, since 1976 with the R.B. Pamplin Corporation and before that in many less formal arrangements. Yet throughout that time we've remained the closest of friends, sharing precisely the sort of love I described earlier. It's a love full of emotion—at risk of hyperbole, let me say I'd die for the man—yet grounded in trust and mutual respect. We have not tried to separate those feelings, assigning some to family, some to work. Instead, we have allowed all the elements of friendship and love to saturate both.

I can understand that this kind of relationship might be perplexing to a person who's never experienced it. Far more familiar, after all, are those family business situations beset by communication breakdowns and other failures. How often have we heard a father complain, "I made my son the president, and now he's *kicked me out*!" Jealousy and avariciousness, I say again, can spoil even God's unparalleled generosity. Sometimes, too, there's a more subtle spoiling. Out of desire not to hurt or not to quarrel, sometimes honest differences go unspoken and, over time, begin to fester. Friendship and respect slip away.

Just as we expect a lot from love, in other words, it demands a lot from us. *Responsibility*, I say again, is its price: God requires a constant vigilance towards the demands of His love, in order to prove we are worthy of it.

Of course, there are many types of love and friendship besides that shared by my father and me. All are important; all provide some measure of God's gift. In a healthy relationship between parent and child, indeed, love will evolve through many stages. The jocular respect shown by the young adult differs enormously from the open-armed affection of the preschooler. Yet love exists in all of these, infinite, ever-adaptable, and at any point along the way it can feel as intense as it was in the first moment of infant bonding. Maybe the appearance of the love has changed, but never its root character.

All love matters, yes. All partakes, to some degree at least, of its renewing and nourishing force. Thus it's a betrayal of love's essence to separate it into isolated compartments: love for parents in one slot, love for a spouse in another, and love for friends in still a third. When it comes to love, you can mix apples and oranges.

Not surprisingly, then, love leaves many confused. They suffer, for instance, from the notion that when a spouse comes into a life, parents must make a neglected exit. Not so! God doesn't measure our stewardship of love by our ability to slot it away into separate cubbyholes, but by our ability to recognize His multifarious and yet unified Will in its many, many forms. We have within us the capacity for all types of love, each with its own defining marks and its moment of advent, each interwoven with the others to create the human tapestry that is a fully developed being.

The Bible outlines that tapestry. It teaches readers to honor their fathers and mothers, yet teaches them too that a man should leave his father and mother and join with his wife to become one person. How reconcile such contrary dictates? For a believer like myself, the process is simple—as easy as applying glue to a broken coffee cup. Scriptures require that a husband leave his parents for his wife, yes, but they say nothing about then forgetting the love and honor still due those parents. In a marriage between two who are called to Christ, the in-laws don't simply fade into the wallpaper. They are still very much present, as living examples of love's divine changes.

Neither the accepted mores of society at large, nor even the rule of law, is the prime mover of human endeavor. Rather, what most unmistakably defines us and our actions must come from the heart. And it's God's love that rules the heart, yes, and I would add now that this love is best recognized by its principal aspect, compassion.

Sometimes we just don't know if it's right to care for a particular person, but we experience the uncontrollable urge to love anyway. That's compassion: our Heaven-given ability to identify with another, and to empathize. Such empathy, indeed, recognizes that the Savior shares His love with every soul on earth. By following the impulses of that compassion, then, quandaries about who to love are quickly resolved. We don't have to worry about the response our love inspires in us. We need only act, because the Divine refreshment flows through us all.

A s for my love towards my parents, that has of course been a part of me since I came into this world. Not that I always understood the many parts of this extraordinary, expansive emotion. When I was still a boy, taking their punishments as well as enjoying their affection, I couldn't always reconcile the wartier side of love with its silky-smooth opposing face. "We are doing this for your good," they would say, "because we love you"—but I just couldn't understand what a switching would have to do with love! For some of my readers, still, such an upbringing might seem harsh. Today, however, I look back and see a good reason for every whipping my parents gave me.

They understood that growing pains were the warts of love, the essential rough ground over which everyone has to work his way. The struggle towards love's happier, silkier side carries every child, more than likely, into an occasional spanking. Thus in their punishments as in their moments of support, my mother and father were always there when I needed them. Just as they said, they were doing what was best for me. By means of pain as well as pleasure, they were showing me love.

And again, God's many-faceted gift worked its magic. I grew up independent, self-reliant. I was able to stand on my own two feet, to think for myself. When I was six or seven or eight I would never admit that I deserved my whippings, naturally, but my movement toward integrity proved so true, so inexorable, that in my heart I always knew what each was for. In the same way, by taking some lickings on the playground, I learned to get along with people. And because I didn't get any help in doing my homework, I learned to think and analyze.

Of course, my formative years also involved simpler elements. My father wasn't thinking of the divine cosmos, most of the time, but rather merely passing along what he himself had learned. Likewise my mother was teaching me what her parents had taught her.

They'd both been raised in times more trying than my own, times when sooner or later they'd had to tackle every problem on their own. My mother and father had never been poor, exactly, but they'd certainly needed to count their pennies. This long-standing need for humble practicality, throughout their upbringing, taught both of them the "common sense" which my father still claims is the basis of his business success. They knew from experience that only by facing life on its own terms, without silly self-delusion but without the crippling fear of failure either, could one

develop such common sense. And in order to make me likewise self-suffi-
cient and confident, they sometimes reduced matters to the same stark
simplicity they'd known in childhood.

Then too, while much of this learning took place in the home, I
received many an important lesson on the playground or in the classroom
as well. Public school too was part of my parents' plan. For though my
mother and father themselves had once grumbled about their studies, since
they'd had no choice in the matter, in time they'd come to realize that such
schooling offers value far beyond what a boy or girl can pick up from
textbooks and lessons. Public school, my parents realized, also offers a
unique amalgamation of personalities; it offers widely different levels of
social status—*instructively* different levels, all mixed in a single classroom
or assembly hall. This breadth of exposure helps hatch the worth of the
human soul. So my mother and father, wanting me to be similarly exposed,
always saw to it that I attended public school. After my elementary years
they could have afforded a private education, but they didn't want to raise
me with the sparkle of a silver spoon. Rather, they wanted me to know the
special qualities that live in each of us. They wanted me to understand that
a famous artist's talent is no more or less valuable than that of a humble
carpenter. We are all children of God, my mother and father wanted me to
learn, and worthy of Him simply as members of His race.

Of course, the public-school approach sometimes forced me over life's
rough edges. I didn't always appreciate that. Indeed, there were days when
conflicts over my behavior ended up in my backside feeling a bit "warty"!
But I'm eternally grateful for the way my parents' teaching brought me at
last to the lovely silken side of experience. Because of that teaching, I
learned to invest in stocks before I was a teenager. I became acquainted with
moonshiners, millworkers, and dirt farmers and so could ever afterwards
pass for "one of the boys." In the same way, I was left unshakably confident
in my basic abilities. I knew I could get things done.

Best of all, my parents' direction enabled me to face the challenges of
wealth. Thanks to them, I could avoid the pitfalls that lurk in a life of
relative privilege—the unexpected trials with which I began this chapter.
I suffered no laziness, no lack of direction. Indeed, my first sizable financial
reward didn't come as "free money," but rather as a nest egg to be guarded
and properly incubated.

When my Virginia grandmother (the one with the well) passed away, I inherited only a limited amount. My father had planned it that way, wanting to see if I could employ what I had been taught and somehow make the money grow. Rising to the dare, as it were, I took this bequest and worked it through the stock market carefully. With it, I made my first million while an undergraduate in college.

My father wanted to give me time before I would receive my legacy. He wanted me to make my own way, be my own man, just as he'd had to be. He didn't want me to miss out on the satisfaction of creating an estate on my own, or on the pride of seeing my own innovations bear fruit. In short, I got a greater gift than anything a well-off executive like my Dad might have picked up at the shopping center: I got my dignity. I got the backbone a person needs to make his or her wealth work for the good.

Yes, good parents can make gifts as impressive, as sustaining, as affecting as our Savior's. By recognizing that both they and their children are nourished by the same Divine Love, they can instill not only faith in that Love, but also faith in self and skill. Myself, every day I get down on my knees in thanksgiving for the bountiful blessings of my mother and my father—and of Our Father.

How then do we put together these many diverse elements in order to do something for the greater good?

The issues I've been talking about so far have been related, to be sure. But they haven't exactly cohered. I've been speaking of the need for faith whether one is rich or poor; of the loving balance between dreams and responsibility, as well as between responsibility and compassion; and of linking up parental guidance and Biblical wisdom. I've covered a great deal, no question.

But do you see how I've tried to ground all of it in my own story? In my spiritual growth since those dreamy moments beside my grandmother's well? For the problem-solver juggles just such multiple components not merely with the intellect, but with the entire history-enriched tapestry of "well-being." Yes, once more the pun's appropriate, since humor is a part of that tapestry.

The problem-solver confronts each new difficulty not merely as a thinking creature who knows the water cycle and the nature of plants, but also as a spiritual being who can hover dreamily over whole centuries and continents, awaiting the sudden sweet updraft of inspiration. The problem-solver is, all in all, very much like our innovative Savior: a combination of the wildly creative and the soberly rational.

Now, chief among the skills needed, to make a previously unforeseen solution a working part of daily life, are organization and communication. Organization comes first. Though it seems like an obvious thing to say, sometimes half the battle is simply recognizing the problem: clarifying where it lies, and isolating it from confusing related issues. That alone can require seeing things in a new way. My success with Jerry Manack, in our Georgia pine ventures, derived largely from just such a fresh understanding of both needs and resources. Next, once the problem has been clearly outlined, the necessary innovations must be developed. This step is, as I say, the dreaming part of the process: one sits and watches the drip from God's spring, trying to imagine a way that water can irrigate so parched a land.

But the working out of that solution can't be like a dream. Its benefits must be, again, practical. If the problem calls for resolving a dispute between people, for instance, the end result can't be unilateral, dictatorial. The compromise, as St. Paul reminds the Romans, must work to the good of all concerned. From the outset, the problem-solver must let the parties involved know that no one will be totally satisfied, but all will benefit.

But . . . *problems?* The word bothers me. I try not to think of problems, myself, but rather of opportunities. The more vexing the question, the greater the opportunity for salvation through innovative thought and application, and the more valuable the resolution for everyone concerned.

When I bring a dream to reality, I arrange the details so as to create a number of general benefits:

1. Each solution must be in some way innovative.
2. Each must have practical consequences.
3. Each must work to the good of everyone involved.
4. Each must be properly timed to bring together as many positive elements as possible.

I approach each decision—virtually each action—with this philosophy in mind. Such an approach may seem to demand too much of the world, which doesn't usually yield so many happy endings. But I can't help returning to my faith: to a covenant as old as the rainbow. If a person can truly believe that our Savior is working through us towards the salvation of all, the natural result is a similar flexible effort for the good of all. A believer just naturally comes up with ideas which bridge the gap between creative brainstorming and businesslike efficacy.

The examples that follow will, I hope, free up others' thinking, so that they too may enter the spring-fed stream of both personal redemption and public amelioration. One of the greatest joys I have found in life is in helping others, and that joy is compounded when I am able to achieve it by breaking new ground, inventing new answers to thorny and long-standing riddles. My hope is that others now can share in the invention—and in the fun.

I NNOVATION CAN BE AS SIMPLE AS HARD WORK.
At the University of Portland, I've worked as a member of the Board of Regents, as an adjunct professor, and, originally, as a graduate student. There I earned two Masters degrees, an M.B.A. and an M.Ed. A private school with a long-standing Catholic affiliation, by the late 1960s the University had maintained a top-notch academic quality for some seventy years. And it was a lovely place to work, with a North Portland bluff-top campus that commanded a spectacular view of the city port. Its looks recall the sort of sedate Southern grove of academe that my ancestor Thomas Flournoy helped support.

By the end of the 1960s, however, the society-wide uproar of that decade (a turmoil that in part reflected changes in the Church) had caused slack enrollment. The college, in fact, was on the brink of a yawning gap in finances, dangerously overextended.

U of P had borrowed money to operate, and tuition, auxiliary fees, and gifts would no longer cover its costs. Soon its debt ran close to a million. By 1971 the University was dipping into its endowment. In response, the banks sent a clear signal that the school's credit was in jeopardy.

The crisis came to the surface not long after I'd joined the Board of Regents. Though just thirty at the time, I'd built up a strong attachment to the school. Only three years before, after all, I'd been a U of P student myself. The last thing I wanted was to see the school shrink—or severely reduce quality.

More than that, I believe I saw the Savior's age-old challenge in the unhappy figures spelled out by the University Board. The predicament, precisely because it was so widespread and had infected the morale of nearly everyone involved, required truly new thinking, genuinely innovative Christianity. Solving this problem would take me far beyond the *personal* challenges I'd faced a number of times already, challenges regarding my own growth and resources. The University's dilemma was outside of me, a difficulty in the larger world, by means of which I might discover anew how Christ worked to the larger good.

At the heart of the trouble, I saw, lay the school's commitment to an unnecessarily wide range of academic programs. U of P simply had more going on than it could afford, such as doctoral programs in education and psychology. If enrollment built back up, then the University could expand accordingly. But as always, growth would cost.

Increased enrollment would require a number of expenses. Better advertising and public relations were called for, of course, but perhaps even more important was the sort of person-to-person advertising generated by having a happy and dedicated faculty and staff. And so long as salaries remained endangered, or uncompetitively low, the quality of teaching and services would lag.

In the short term, then, the University had to liquidate its most oppressive debt. At the same time it had to win back bank confidence by issuing firm administration level guarantees to balance its budget.

People who truly cared about the University of Portland needed to put their money where their hearts were. We needed to prime the credit pump. At an emotion-charged meeting of the Board of Regents in the fall of 1971, I asked for the opportunity to begin that priming. I announced that my father and I would personally cover half the University's debt— half of close to a million. And then I told the Board that I expected them together to contribute a matching amount.

Several of those around the table could hardly believe their ears. Those few argued that any investment in the school at this point was throwing good money after bad; they all but suggested the place was beyond saving. My reaction, rather than digging in my heels and creating conflict, was to try to develop a sense of larger purpose in these reluctant partners. I understood their hesitance, I said. I was a businessman myself, I assured them, and I knew a bad investment when I saw one. But I appealed to their own private definitions of "working to the good."

An *institution* was at stake, I pointed out, not just an investment. Moreover, this institution carried the name of a city we all lived in and loved. Turning to each member of the Board, I labored to make them see the broader impact of the University of Portland. I spoke of the difference a place like this made in the local culture, in the very fabric of society. I reminded them that troubled times were rocking the country as a whole, and that learning and tradition took on extra importance in such times. In other words, I told the Board, the University was a place of principle.

One by one, these men came around to my notion of the greater good. Of course, that notion wasn't mine to begin with, but rather Christ's and his apostle Paul's. In that tempestuous Board meeting, the true healing presence was, as ever, our Savior's. I was only too happy to act as His agent, persuading my fellow Regents to join in a personal sacrifice for the benefit of the college and the city.

So the plan was taken to the administration. Father Paul Waldschmidt, President of the University, seemed nothing short of stunned as he heard the Board's pledges—stunned and overjoyed. Yet the news that followed was even better. When we took the plan to the college's lenders, we could present those same financial pledges along with administration guarantees that U of P would operate within a balanced budget from then on. We had what it takes to make a tight-fisted banker relent: a unified Board and a firmly committed administration, led by Father Waldschmidt and the Vice President of Finance, Dr. Arthur Schulte (my old Dean at the Business School, as it happened). The loan officers opened their purses again. The University was given more time to pay off its debt, and greater leeway for future financing as well.

Make no mistake, what we did in those first years of the 1970s was a terrific sacrifice—a sacrifice shared by the Board, the administration, and many others throughout the University community. But because of those efforts, we were able to make a fine school flourish again. Not only did U of P retire its debt and balance its budget, but also, over time, it reinstated salary increases for the faculty and even invested a budget surplus. With that investment, new projects could be financed without having to borrow from banks. Twenty years after the crisis, the University has booming enrollments, a growing endowment, a range of curricula unmatched in the city, and impressive levels of endeavor in all fields.

And myself, what did I learn? I saw that sometimes the new solutions Christ calls us to are nothing more than old-fashioned hard work and shared sacrifice. Sometimes innovation is nothing more than getting a little intimate with people: reminding them of what they once believed in, and selling them anew on the value of those beliefs.

T EACHING TOO NEEDS THE CREATIVE TOUCH. Shortly after I and others turned things around at the University of Portland, in the early 1970s, I became chairman of the Board of Regents. Thus the Dean of the Business School was perhaps being a bit innovative himself when, in 1973, he asked me to join his faculty as an adjunct professor. He was shaking off the destructive old notion of closeting talent away in cubbyholes: Regents in one, and faculty in another.

The Dean wanted me to teach a two-semester course called Small Business Problems. This course had been part of the School's curriculum for some time. It was sponsored by the Small Business Institute of the Small Business Administration. I could see right away how doing as the Dean asked might lead to extraordinary rewards.

Few experiences can match the fulfillment of passing along not only what one has learned in the classroom, but also what one has picked up in the hard-knocks school of the American marketplace. For my lessons, I could refer to something more substantial than a textbook. Then too, I've always had a special affinity for academics. Even as a working adult, I've kept on furthering my education. Altogether I've earned some eight degrees, including two doctorates. What's more, as I explored my family history in order to pull together this book, I discovered that the joy of learning is as much a part of my makeup as a strong upper body or pale blue eyes. I see that joy in a man like Robert Seville Armiger, for instance, reading the first English Bible printed with moveable type. I see it, too, in Amy Butler's shelves full of books, and in the two doctor sons of Athaliah Boisseau.

So I told the Dean I'd join his faculty, starting in the fall of 1973. I then teamed up with an excellent colleague named Roger Crabbs, and together he and I put the course through a gimlet-eyed analysis. Where was it weak? How could we do better?

The principal problem seemed to be that the Small Business class, as part of the standard business curriculum, didn't rise above ordinary academic challenges. It didn't set itself apart, and so didn't inspire maximum performance from the students. In other words, Crabbs and I had to raise the perceived value of the course. So, to begin with, we made our class a tough one to attend—or to miss. Both semesters, Small Business Problems met once a week only, at 6:30 AM.

In most courses, after all, students assume they can slough off at least two or three class meetings a semester. In mine, however, anyone signing up at once understood that every single meeting was critical, and that only the discipline of a Virginia Tech "Rat" would allow them to make that 6:30 time slot. In short, students were pumped up before they reached the classroom. They knew they faced the no-nonsense demands of the world beyond college. Really, in that class Crabbs and I put into practice the dictum that my farmer grandfather John Robert Pamplin lived by: *Work that should be done is done now.*

At the same time, we increased the coursework. During the first of the two semesters we assigned the students to investigate the problems of selected small businesses. This entailed hours of preparation and classroom time, for Crabbs and me as well as for the students. We professors had to pore over every business, one by one.

Now, these businesses had all agreed beforehand to take part in the program. They'd been selected, in part, because they'd had a loan guaranteed by the SBA. Thus in one way or another they all suffered, as the course title suggested, "Small Business Problems." So at the end of the first semester Crabbs and I required our students to submit position reports: statements which detailed whatever weaknesses they'd found in their assigned businesses and which recommended ways to correct those weaknesses. The second semester, my students—college kids though they were—had to actually implement their recommendations.

The course presented extraordinary challenges, in other words. Conventional wisdom would argue, indeed, that no one would sign up at all.

But in my life I've generally found that, if a man tries to fall back on unconventional wisdom, he'll swiftly find himself flat on the floor, surrounded by rubble. Year after year "SBP" filled to capacity.

Part of the reason for this success, unquestionably, is that the course asked so much of students and teachers alike. Working alongside our U of P scholars in their investigations, Roger Crabbs and I discovered again and again that every venture has its own unique problems, problems that textbooks don't always cover, and so our own real-world seasoning proved invaluable. Crabbs and I never simply whisked students out the door with orders to solve some head-spinning melange of financial difficulties. Rather, we used our experience to guide them toward understanding and practicality. Crabbs and I realized that the best measure of SBP's success wasn't merely in the classroom, but in the credit and debit columns of the business-owner's books.

In the same way, my co-professor and I could mix up teachings intriguingly. We kept mostly to fundamental business tenets, of course, but I never neglected to throw in the occasional dose of my father's "common sense." Organizational skills, too, received special attention. I drilled it into the students that, the better their organization, the better their ability to motivate people further down the lines of that organization. The better the plan at the top, the better the success overall.

Naturally, I had students who worried that they weren't equal to the task. They were, among other things, apprehensive about delving into local company records. Nine out of ten of them had only known businesses from library books, not flesh-and-blood entities. But soon, with my help and Roger's, these apprentices were examining accounts like professionals. They determined strengths and weaknesses and devised many a workable plan. The program worked so well that my classes actually saved a number of businesses throughout Portland and Vancouver, Washington (just across the Columbia River). And after the first year, the course had a lengthy waiting list; it may have been the most popular in the program. Crabbs and I were even selected national finalists in a teaching competition sponsored by the SBA, a competition in which we went up against professors from some of the most prestigious business programs across the U.S. For two years straight (until my malignant melanoma inspired me to become a student again myself, at Western Seminary) the SBA rated Crabbs and me among the ten best nationally.

Impressive though it was, the success of my course may seem at first glance to have little to do with faith in Christ. It may seem more an affirmation of pedagogical freethinking, rather than of any profound spirituality. But I see the Master's hand in my work for Small Business Problems, unmistakably. This class too, after all, worked to the greater good—as I say, my students saved many a nearby business. More than that, however, my teaching demonstrated what I believe is the true Christian notion of "success."

As I've mentioned elsewhere in my chapters, the dictionary definition of "success" seems to me misleading. Webster's is too quick to relate success to wealth and power. What a genuine Christian would call success, on the other hand, has no dollar sign on it, no weighty title on the door. To me and to my fellow believers, success means working out whatever God has given us *to its fullest possible expression.*

Success means pushing one's gifts: getting into class by 6:30 in the morning, for instance, or overcoming inappropriate shyness about examining someone else's finances. In my own case, yes, using my gifts to the utmost does include making money. God the Father has given me and my father that skill, and we try to take it to the limit, day by day. But just as I have other skills as well, a student of mine needn't go on to become a tycoon—whatever that is—in order for me to consider him a success. He or she need only, as the Savior asks, take up his or her own personal abilities and follow. For the path of the Savior, after all, leads to the ultimate. The path of the Savior allows no cup to pass.

C REATIVITY'S HIGHER CALLING: TO HELP A FRIEND.
My innovations have been successful, I believe, because I always allow for God's innovations. That is, I always allow timing to play its role. If I sense the timing is not right for action, I back off. On the other hand, when the timing is right, I'm Johnny on the spot. My recent purchase of a small company provides a telling example.

Oregon Wilbert Vault manufactures burial vaults, caskets, and other funeral-related items for the mortuary industry. I learned that this firm had a good reputation in its industry, and many substantial assets. In the late 1970s, in fact, I approached the owners with an offer to buy. But we couldn't work out a satisfactory agreement. The timing—God's hand in these affairs—just wasn't right.

Not too much later, though, I received a call from a good friend and neighbor, Bob Cena. Bob had just left a high level management position, and he wanted advice about his next career move. But once I realized that such an honest and superb businessman as Bob was free, I came up with something much better for him than a mere referral. I decided, instead, that God's timing had come around again: that here was another opportunity to work for the greater good.

Bob Cena and I looked into a number of business opportunities. We examined several companies, talking several times a week, and yet none seemed promising until the possibility of taking on Oregon Wilbert Vault resurfaced. The company had strayed into problems, but it still had a lot of solid potential. Like me, Bob saw that potential. And like me, he was an evenhanded and skillful negotiator, willing to craft and re-craft a deal until it was attractive for everyone on both sides of the table.

Our challenge, in this case, was to create a leveraged buy-out that looked nothing like a leveraged buy-out. The LBO's of the 1980s were notorious for their shady trappings—their junk bonds, especially, were hardly worth the paper they were printed on. I didn't want to debilitate the company by selling off assets to pay for such high-interest bonds. Nor did I want to lay off workers to reduce cost. I intended to improve Oregon Wilbert and make it last, not tear it apart for a quick profit. And, most important, I neither wanted to buy the company outright for Bob—which would have left him with no vested interest in its success—nor wanted to leave him dangerously out of pocket. In short, in this venture as in all my ventures, I knew that success would follow from working for the betterment of everyone, not just for my own self-enhancement.

In the case of OWV, I first went after the company's expenses. With Bob's help I negotiated new, lower-cost insurance coverage and bank loans. Then we arranged a non-competition agreement that would pay the former owners over twenty years, but which accelerated depreciation to a mere five years, thereby improving the cash flow considerably. And for ownership purposes Bob and I purchased only a small amount of the outstanding stock ourselves; the balance was bought by OWV. Finally, my friend and I bought the real estate and buildings and leased them back to the company.

The upshot was, the company paid for its own property out of its own cash flow, and saved taxes in the process. All told, the buy-out cost to Bob and me was an amount equal to one-tenth of Oregon Wilbert's net assets.

In the few years since, OWV has easily paid off the leftover costs. Bob Cena is now running his own company, and his family remains just down the road from my own.

If a man can recognize the moment when the Divine Hand is ready to convert loss and need to gain and fulfillment, he can't help but prosper. In this case I expressed that recognition by the simple act of loving my neighbor, following our Savior's ancient commandment. Yet in my submission to His will I was myself rewarded—in a deepening friendship as well as in more worldly terms. God's grace is with us every minute, to be sure. But during those moments when He can make a difference in our lives, if we seize His almighty hand, the subsequent reward is His witness to us.

NEW THINKING BRINGS NEW EXCITEMENT: WE ALL OWN HISTORY.

Lewis & Clark College is another significant institution to me. There I worked as a student, faculty member, president of the Alumni Association, received the Distinguished Alumni Award, and finally, like my father, I was Chairman of the Board of Trustees. Elsewhere in this book you've come across stories of my family's commitment to the college. In the 1960s and 1970s my father gave freely of his time and his good judgment, while writing out more than a few checks as well, and once my own ventures met with success I began to do likewise.

After some years of providing such support, however, I came to understand that at Lewis & Clark, too, innovation was needed. Here, too, there was a danger of getting stodgy. Yes, the school's financial health remained basically sound. Lewis & Clark never endured the sort of dire straits faced by the University of Portland. Nonetheless, for the school to grow, it would require the occasional special uplift such as only Christ-inspired fundraising can bring.

Fundraising, I've learned, means so much more than writing checks. Few people realize it, but "resource development" of this kind requires constant education and refinement, constant polishing of technique. Myself, over the years, I've tried to elevate philanthropy to something of an art form. I've tried to come up with ever more exciting devices—innovations, —in order to seize the imagination of administrators, alumni, and even the public at large.

So, when Lewis & Clark needed a boost in the early 1990s, I dreamed up the Chairman's Challenge.

As always, I began by aiming high. My dream for the school remains about as ambitious as they come. By the turn of the millennium I'd like my first Portland alma mater, though already highly regarded as a liberal arts institution, to rank with the very best private colleges in the country. As the 1990s began, my objective became to unite the entire Lewis & Clark community behind that inspiration—to make their institution the "miracle college" of the decade.

The key concept, as I saw it, was that notion of unity: I had to pull together a highly diverse population, a population at times only tangentially connected. After all, my father and I had been among those who helped bring new colors into the college's human spectrum. Mr. Pamplin, Senior, and I had helped boost both Lewis & Clark's minority enrollment and its international stature. Now I needed to pull together those many diverse constituencies, to make them all players in my dream, to raise perceptions of the college's quality across a widespread public base.

In short, we needed a quantum leap in awareness. Lewis & Clark had to make a sudden splash, some spectacular display proving its special caliber. We needed a media event.

Now, one of the central defining aspects of a college is its library. Divergent groups of all kinds use the library, and unite in their identification with its worth. Those from a college with a poor library shake their heads and make excuses, while those from a college with an exceptional one boast about it for years to come—even to their grandchildren. The reputation of Harvard, for instance, rests in large part on its legendary book collections, which include original papers of John Keats, Lewis Carroll, T. S. Eliot, and many others.

Of course, in order to better Lewis & Clark, there was no point searching round for a new manuscript of Keats' "Ode on a Grecian Urn." But if the college's library could be in some way dramatically improved, it would spur an overall upgrade in stature. Yet if the Chairman of the Board of Trustees (my position at the time) merely donated a healthy sum, that wouldn't by itself do the trick. I had an eye-catching amount in mind to start the ball rolling, a million dollars. But simply writing the check wouldn't create the essential combination of campus unity and national excitement; a check wouldn't generate a common interest that was at once broadly based and deeply felt.

Rather, I needed something that was both highly visible and open to participation. If others could share in the event, they'd establish a personal stake in the project, an individual as well as group ownership, and this would insure lasting interest.

So, the 1992 Chairman's Challenge. I devised a family-friendly spectacular, one that would take place on a single day, and that would be open to anyone who felt up to a little exercise. At its core, it was a phys-ed fair. A number of physical challenges were set up on the Lewis & Clark campus, among them less-taxing competitions such as relay races, walks, and fun runs for children and parents. But the so-called Main Event was in the gym: an open invitation for anyone to match the standards I'd set earlier that year in certain core calisthenics.

I'd ground out 116 pushups without stopping, twenty-four pull-ups at the chinning bar, some 625 uninterrupted sit-ups in 15 minutes, and a sixteen-foot rope climb (my old Tech standby) in just under eight seconds from a seated position and without the use of my legs.

Pretty good for a fifty-year-old man? Pretty good for a "cancer victim"? Yes, the figures are impressive, and of course I'm proud of them—but I must repeat that my point isn't to boast, here in these closing chapters. Nor was it back during the Challenge. In the first place, I set high standards because of my special understanding of success. I've spelled out that Pamplin's Dictionary entry a couple of times already, and as regards the Chairman's Challenge, since for me success is such a private matter, a self-determined measure, doing less than my best in the Lewis & Clark gym would have been a betrayal of that same hard-earned sense of who I am and what I'm about. Doing less than my best would've meant I wasn't committed to my dreams after all. Besides that, it would've been an insult to all the ancestors who came before me, to the men and women who gave me my muscle, my wind, my stamina.

And I had a more practical concern, when it came to the event at Lewis & Clark. The more remarkable the challenge I set, after all, the greater its public impact. The higher the standard, the greater the interest.

If the point of the event was to make the college more outstanding, then the numbers alone had to rate a second and third look.

As for the rules of the Challenge, those were simple. I didn't want anything too complicated for a thirty-second TV sound bite. Anyone who could exceed my exercise standards, in any one event, would earn $25,000 for the college library. More than that, their name would appear on the new library addition. If just forty toned-up men or women could "Beat Bob"— the catch-phrase invented for the newspapers—the facility would have its additional million.

On the day of the competition, the crowd included some 2500 students, alumni, staff, faculty, parents, and others. It was, to choose a phrase from my 1960s days at the college, "a happening." And before the games got under way, I took a moment to make sure everyone's eyes were focused squarely on the prize. I reminded them that today's excitement provided a challenge in more ways than one. It provided everyone who participated with a chance to help a college and its campus in a way that had *never been done before*. Thus everyone on the scene was in fact making history, a piece of history they could call their own forever.

I asked the people there to cast their minds forward some twenty years or so into the future. I asked them to imagine bringing their children or grandchildren to Lewis & Clark, on that distant day. When they came, I said, they could point to the library. They could say, "See that building? I helped build it."

All this, of course, made for great media exposure. Doing something that's never been done before always does. The publicity alone was worth many, many millions more for the school. The Chairman's Challenge, colorful and exciting and unique, received television coverage throughout the Northwest and in more than a few national and even international markets. For the next two months it was featured on the in-flight movies of American Airlines. Write-ups appeared in a wide variety of publications, not just the local papers but *USA Today* as well, and were part of a lengthy article for *Forbes* magazine. Less than a year after the event, Lewis & Clark appeared to have been "discovered" by the national press. Journalists in all media regularly contacted the school for stories.

N EW THINKING BRINGS NEW HOPE: WE ALL OWN THE CITY.

Portland, Oregon, has its ghetto area, like every other major city. This is the neighborhood called North-Northeast—not far, as it happens, from the University of Portland. Here lives the so-called African-American "underclass," plus recent Southeast Asian and Latin American immigrants and a smattering of white urban poor. North-Northeast carries the all-too-familiar scars of urban blight. There are boarded-up houses and storefronts, burnt-out abandoned cars, weed-choked vacant lots littered with broken malt liquor bottles, rusty syringes, stolen tires, and shopping carts. Trash lies heaped at the curbs. Gang-inspired graffiti decorate the walls. Portland's versions of the Crips and Bloods operate here, and many a summer night is torn apart by automatic-weapons fire.

These outward signs are, to be sure, only the symptoms of the true problems. Such problems won't yield easily, not even to a tireless optimist like myself, because they're so basic, so simple. The poor, Christ says, are always with us. Prominent among the ills of North-Northeast, for instance, is simple fear.

Most residents are decent law-abiding families who'd like nothing better than to live untroubled and productive lives. They'd be more than happy to clean up their mean streets and rid them of crime.

But fear paralyzes these citizens, the sort of fear a person suffers when a teenager with a gun seems more powerful than police or politicians—more powerful, for that matter, than a rich white businessman with a lot of talk about Jesus and a soft Georgia accent.

Such fear leads soon to hopelessness. And hopelessness, in turn, deepens into an utter apathy towards learning how to fix what's broken. And all of this, of course, is exacerbated by a grinding lack of money.

North-Northeast has seen occasional efforts to help, granted. But these have been, for the most part, one-shot efforts from outside the neighborhood. Such programs may make these blocks look more promising for a few brief months, like slapping a quick coat of paint on a decaying house. Just as such houses quickly reveal their sagging foundation and lack of decent drainage, however, so the touched-up neighborhood soon makes clear that this help was only skin deep. Such outside programs, well-intended as they might be, fail to involve the residents on a long-term basis. They don't empower the people who live in the neighborhood to take control of it.

Like any true Christian, any right-thinking Portlander, I'd like to see my neighbors living decently and safely. And given the family I come from—a father who used his resources to help make integration work in the South—I felt a special motivation to do what I could. But I also had enough education, and enough of my Dad's "common sense," to know the dangers of simply blundering in and treating the neighborhood as if it were my own.

Before I could do anything for the North-Northeast, then, I had to arrange meetings with residents. I needed to learn not only what held the neighborhood back (I'd gotten some idea of that just from reading the papers), but also what plans and programs of their own they already had in place. Easier than setting up something entirely new, certainly, would be working with groups and systems already in place. Christ's model, after all, is to get everyone contributing—even the least of these, He says.

In these meetings with local leaders it quickly became obvious that, first off, everyone wanted their neighborhood to start looking like a neighborhood. That is, they wanted it to look less like a garbage dump. Growing up surrounded by rubbish, naturally enough, produces a rubbishy self-image. I don't have to cite national statistics to make the point. It's a simple matter of logic. In a trashy neighborhood, everything turns to trash—including the people who live there. Aspirations to better seem ludicrously out of place, and with that starts the vicious cycle of fear, hopelessness, and ignorance.

In short, the area first had to be cleaned up. In a well-kept neighborhood, garbage gets noticed: people can see who is making the mess. Those who refuse to change their ways, more often than not, will soon choose to leave. They don't want everyone watching. But in North-Northeast, as in distressed neighborhoods across the nation, the challenge was to establish an ongoing and internally rooted program, as opposed to another one-shot outsider effort.

In part because of my meetings with local residents, a consortium of church groups, neighborhood organizations, and government agencies came together. This was, for the time being, a single-issue outfit. We were only concerned, for the moment, with the dirty streets. My own contributions were money and a unique youth-improvement plan.

I put up enough for the consortium to hire young people to work in pairs throughout the neighborhood, two youths per street and each one from some different agency or organization. I suggested that each pair include one young man or woman who had been in trouble with the law and one who hadn't, so sometimes a street kid was working with a church-goer. And I saw to it that the youths were well paid for their efforts. It was important that they want to hold on to the job, and that they get a feeling for how the world should work—for how hard work and tangible results bring a reward. So these North-Northeast boys and girls went out, two by two, just as Christ instructed His disciples to go.

As I've said, the problems of North-Northeast are the most complex I've faced, the most deeply and dishearteningly ingrained. Thus they demand the greatest range of Christian guidance. My cleanup project, though at first glance it appears to address only one area of the neighborhood breakdown, in fact reaches far beyond well-swept sidewalks and curbs— and in the process embodies many of the Savior's precepts and parables. The project provides a living example for just about every one of the Gospel metaphors I've used in this entire thousand-year history. It is the mustard seed; it is the master's talents wisely invested; it is the lowly Samaritan stooping to aid the bloodied traveler; it is the prodigal son come home to salvation.

Around North-Northeast Portland, the teams of young street cleaners were told to introduce themselves to everyone on their assigned blocks. In the process the teenagers made sure to get permission for any extra work that might be needed on the residents' private property. Most importantly, the cleanup crews took time to arrange the support of the locals.

No outstretched helping hand can do much unless it's met by the upraised hand of the one who's *being* helped. By this time I'd seen it again and again: the need for shared struggle between the Samaritan and the man who'd fallen among thieves. I'd seen it in every kind of philanthropic effort, from the Lewis & Clark Chairman's Challenge to the various charities I've worked with as pastor of Christ Community Church. And in Portland's North-Northeast, anyone who lent his sweat and muscle to the street cleaning couldn't help but take more pride in the neighborhood, and couldn't help but resist any backsliding into disrepair.

The local leaders and I are trying to use these young men and women as an inspiration for others. We're trying to start ripples of good works moving ever outward.

Lately, the two-man crews have become a fixture on their assigned blocks. They don't just pick up litter, they repair run-down houses and do odd yard work. In the process they help address a related cleanup issue, namely, the difficulty low-income individuals have in affording basic home-and-garden tools. As an additional element of this program, each street gets the equipment it needs for maintenance. Thus the youngsters, employed year-round, keep their area clean until the homeowners there can take over the work themselves. By means of their humble brooms and rakes, the crews move the North-Northeast locals towards an esteem for their homes and, concomitantly, towards esteem for themselves—all thanks to this one limited but critical campaign.

Stronger self-esteem is something this program intends to accomplish for the youths in the crews as well. Getting the streets clean means little if, in the process, we don't also straighten out at least a few troubled youths. It does no good for the community if the kids learn nothing more than how to push a broom. Rather, their new responsibilities should help the total person. Once these youngsters are trained, they themselves should become teachers, leaders—the innovators who themselves will come up with the next set of necessary solutions.

This personal transformation is at the heart of the novel approach I and others are trying in North-Northeast. The program begins with appearances and then works inward to the content of character. These teenage crew members get additional payments not merely for sweeping an extra street or two. Instead, the program has extra funding set aside for whenever a young man or woman can prove he or she has developed a new athletic skill. In the same way, there's payment for some concrete evidence of increased spiritual awareness, or for earning better grades in an academic area of their choice. The program rewards kids for development in all areas—for improving the total person.

Thus far, everyone touched by the work of the young street cleaners has absorbed an essential lesson. They've come to understand that this was a long-term commitment, no tawdry coat of paint. And they've come to realize, as well, that in me they've got one soft-spoken Georgian who's going to stick with them and their community.

Chapter 23

Robert Pamplin, Junior
The Source of Good Things—Lessons Learned the Hard Way

OVER THE YEARS, I have been fortunate enough to win public recognition. Among the honors I am most glad to have are the Distinguished Leadership Medal from the Freedoms Foundation, the National Caring Award from the Caring Institute, and honorary degrees from some of the country's finest institutions of higher learning. Besides that, there's been the especially gratifying appreciation for my books. Anyone who's gotten this far into *Heritage* must realize by now that I am a bibliophile—a book-lover. The tome in your hands is my tenth, and some of my previous publications have seen printings of 20,000, 30,000, even 50,000 copies.

Yet this public acclaim has left me humbled as much as happy. Book sales and awards don't simply recognize my achievement and my service, after all. They make a statement about my character as well. Without character, the merit of any honorary plum shrivels like a prune; without character, I'd never have won anything.

Thus I've been humbled by these prizes. Character is something I can't claim to have forged all by myself, something I owe in large part to the generations of hardworking men and women before me, and to the God they worshipped. Indeed, my grandfather—my father's father, John Robert—always held fast to the axiom that "the most important asset anyone has is character."

For John Robert Pamplin, character was made up of integrity, trust, and keeping your word. That word, he believed, was given in order to be kept; it wasn't to be altered or abridged to suit the changes of the moment. For your word represents what you are. Simply put, counting on a person's word means counting on their character. Reinforcing that commitment is consistency—that is, a person either proves consistently good, or consistently bad. And if a person proves consistently good, he or she breeds confidence in his or her character. Such a person can be counted on.

This is another invaluable initial step in problem-solving. You need only face the difficulty with a commitment to what's right. If you have it in your mind and heart to do what's right, you can depend on all things working to the good, as St. Paul says, in the long run. For in reality, life is not complicated. We just make it complicated. Generally, this is because we try to force a rationale on why something improper may be acceptable.

In the same way, problem-solving isn't complicated either. My efforts may have won awards, but the essential undertaking doesn't require award-winning levels of cogitation. This has been impressed upon me whenever I've tried to help young people struggle to prevail despite the hard knocks of their lives. I could see at once that these teenage men and women all had brains and talent enough to succeed. What they needed, however, was something simpler. They were timid. They lacked resolve, lacked confidence. What they needed was character.

And since they needed something simple, I gave these Portland youngsters a simple task. A simple task, I say—but one that demanded a lot of work. I have always believed in hard work. Precisely because it produces sweat, causes blisters, and tires muscles, hard manual labor provides an excellent home remedy for anxiety and disquiet. I knew it would do the job for these teenagers too.

So, I put them to work on one of my farms.

The youngsters' first job was the essence of simplicity. They had to move a pile of rocks from one corner of a field to another by hand. In fact I'd had this pile of rocks put out in that field myself, just so these kids could move it—but of course I didn't tell them that. Also I'd seen to it that the rocks were large enough to require, in most cases, more than one pair of hands. That is, getting the rocks into and out of the wheelbarrow would take teamwork.

The job took several days. By the end, not only the youngsters' hands had been toughened. Also their spirits had been stiffened; they'd gained that all-important belief in self which comes from having met a hard challenge. They'd developed the elemental building blocks of character. The simple demands of work had done this for these kids, though their personal problems had seemed complicated, even insurmountable. Physical exertion, and overcoming the aches and pains that go along with it, had once more reduced problems in the mind to manageable levels.

Again and again, I've found it amazing how God has given this power to the labor of our hands. When a physical challenge is overcome, a person feels good, no matter what the spiritual or psychological quandaries he or she brought to the task. And by letting us feel good, God sends a clear message. Similar diligence in all our tasks, He is saying, will guarantee success.

The young people I'd brought out to my farm graduated eventually to other jobs. Eight or ten days of moving rocks was enough to set up those first building blocks of character. The youngsters' subsequent assignments also required manual labor, but now they began working with a wider variety of people. Now they had to fend for themselves among year-round farm hands, migrant laborers, and the ranch managers. They worked side by side with men and women from all walks of life. Such an exposure helped to make the youngsters' own personal problems seem smaller and more manageable still. The kids were forced to realize that others too had a hard time of things, indeed sometimes a much harder time of things than they themselves. My formerly troubled kids came to appreciate their many advantages.

This was all most of them needed—the second major building block of character. My youngsters had to realize that God had given them advantages, too, advantages and opportunities. They had to combine this new, happier understanding of their place in life with the new self-worth provided by the earlier physical labor. After that, I must say, in every case these young men and women have gone on to use the talent and advantages that God gave them. Once more, things have worked to the good; these youngsters have become successful, even enormously successful.

And it all started with a rock pile.

At times, in jest, I've been asked—why the rock pile? My answer is simple. As I've explained earlier, I myself was consigned to hard physical labor while still a freshman in high school. I was sent to work in a plywood mill. And I'd no sooner punched the time clock than I found myself facing a pile of hardened tar and unfinished boards. A foreman explained that I had to haul the entire pile to the bed of a truck parked some distance away. This selection of mill debris—just like my later selection of farmland rocks—contained nothing but pieces large enough to require moving individually, by hand. As for the truck bed, that was shoulder high. In other words, every piece of rubble had to be hefted overhead ("pressed," as we say in weight-lifting), thrown into the truck bed, and then moved up to the cab-end of the bed.

I learned in a hurry what real work was all about. But after that awful job was done, believe me, I didn't fear working beside any man. I felt as if in a single aching and sweaty day I'd moved from puberty to manhood; I felt character burgeoning within me. And this passage meant, as well, that from now on I had to act like the man I was expected to be—the man I knew I could be. So I realized what it meant to be squeezed to do your best. Like anyone who dedicates an all-consuming resolve to creating a master-piece, I learned to concentrate every fiber of my being on achievement. It was an unforgettable schooling, granted me by men whittled from wood hard as iron. It taught me that I could put in the work to fulfill any task.

And it all started with a pile of debris.

B ut age brings with it reflection, and deeper levels of realization. Youthful enthusiasm is at once tempered and strengthened, as a broader understanding of reality seeps in. With age, I realized that my young man's willingness to work, and even my learning the meaning of work, was only part of the wisdom that constitutes character. Unquestionably, the labor proved worth it. My spirit was toughened, for good. But as the years went on I came to understand that sometimes the human body and mind, however eager and disciplined, are tools insufficient to the task. I came to see that humanity alone, confined to its own powers, always had to struggle within those limits.

All this I perceived in time, and the single essential aid to my widening perception was faith—my deepening faith in God and His working to the good. With God's help, I came to comprehend human limits. And then came my last, furthest insight, namely, that only with this same divine help could humanity transcend its limits. Man molds the sand, but God inspires the design.

The Pamplin family from the beginning has adhered to the richly rewarding traits of discipline, moral rectitude, and social responsibility. These are fine qualities, of course, and I've tried to underscore their value in the dramatic re-creations presented here. But the family's underlying sweetness and trustworthiness was a matter of character, ultimately, and character derives in the end from faith. My ancestors professed the strength of their faith in thought, word, and deed. Many died with a vision of God in their minds and a whisper of His name on their lips.

Better still, theirs was a *working* faith. My forebears didn't closet their belief away in ritual and mystery. They acted out God's laws day by day. In their every least dealing they demonstrated that the human mind is a gift from God, and thus to be used for His greater glory, rather than for rationalizing some way round His canon.

Thus for my ancestors love was important, but disciplined love was indispensable. They loved their children, their neighbors, their country—but they always adhered strictly to the greater discipline required by God's Love and Word whenever a child or neighbor or country behaved contrary to His teachings. Their faith never deluded them into a madness based on mystic mumbo-jumbo rather than on the honest labor of hands.

Through the centuries generations of Pamplins have become a repository for the miraculous. That they survived at all, and especially that they survived with caring and integrity, provides irrefutable testimony to the strength of their faith and the spring-fed force of the Divine moving through their lives. God has been an integral part of this family, and his blessing warmed and increased in keeping with their obedience to His law.

There is much in life that is a mystery. But with faith, the unexplainable loses its worrisome nature. The power of faith was best explained by my wife's English-born grandfather, who saw a vision of a deceased school chum, a boy he'd known in his teenage years across the Atlantic. A very religious person, my old in-law's response to this supernatural event was: "There are some things one can't explain—only God knows." And as for the bountiful blessings that have come to my father and me, there remain many mysterious elements about those as well. But the mystery, as I say, doesn't worry us. Since he and I realize that those blessings are from God, we too say: Only He knows.

CHAPTER 24

Robert Pamplin, Junior
The Source of Good Things—Loving, Caring, and Giving

B Y NOW I HOPE I've hammered out an answer to the question raised at the beginning of these philosophical passages. I hope you have some grasp of why so many previous Pamplins survived and prevailed, and why so much of what I've put my own hand to has worked out for the best. I can put my argument in a nutshell, of course. I can say, like some witty phrase maker, that dreaming leads to loving and loving to doing, if all are suffused with God's grace.

But I want to be more than a phrase maker, at the end of this long climb up the centuries. I want to inspire further climbing, and better; I want to bring on, not just self-examination, but success.

And in order to truly represent that success, I need to look first at a man who seemed, for much of his life, a failure.

C ut in front of him!" the boys screamed at the driver. "Force him into the ditch!"

"We've got to show that *white* trash he can't make eyes at one of our kind."

And in another few minutes, the angry foursome had forced poor Ron off the road, hauled him from his own car, and worked him over from belly to head. Not that Ron appeared at all to deserve the beating, to anyone with an open mind. A big rawboned kid, he stood well over six feet tall, with a winning smile and handsome black curls. His eyes seemed to forever sparkle with a hint of mischief. It was easy to see why a girl might take a liking to him—even one with a little more money and a slightly finer house.

So the better-off boys had gone after Ron, that night in the early 1950s. And as he lay by the side of the road after his "whupping," bruised and aching and furious, the stubborn young Southerner vowed that he'd make something of himself. He'd get his revenge not in some dark alley, but rather where it counted: in the world of work, home, and rewards that last.

Unfortunately, there are things almost impossible to overcome, no matter how hard you try. Ron just couldn't seem to get that one life-squaring break.

After graduating from high school, the handsome young man worked the oil fields in the Southwest. He made good enough money, and saved what he could. Then he moved still farther west, determined to make a success at farming.

But as it was for generations of my forbearers, for Ron too farm life proved one tough way to make a living. Thirty years he worked, applying himself to the tractor, the hoe, the baler, but it seemed that for every season he got ahead there'd be two when he fell behind. Ron seemed doomed to remain "white trash" forever. Creditors circled like vultures and gossip-hungry neighbors could hardly talk about anything else.

Most people would have crumbled under such hardship. But not Ron. He was just amazing, really; he never got bitter and he never gave up.

During his last couple of decades as a farmer, I got to know Ron. I saw his integrity, his strength, and soon I was proud to call him a friend. I found, indeed, that in his own simple and down-to-earth way he epitomized friendship. He maintained a Christian standard of neighborliness, never complaining even about the local gossips. He steered clear of discord or contention. And during those rare winters when his barns had enough to spare, Ron was immensely generous.

For God's love is exemplified in those as unlucky as Ron every bit as much as in the more fortunate. God's love reveals its markings especially when a hardscrabble farmer does his best to help those even less well off. For true giving is giving from the widow's mite: offering what little you have. Ron practices the principle every day of his life.

Once when my equipment was down, he came over and worked a combine all night to get my wheat in on time. For all my wealth, to Ron I was only a neighbor in need. And like the Samaritan in the parable, he truly loved his neighbor. He made his own harvest more difficult, in order to help. He didn't say, "I'll be there in a few days." He just geared up his combine and drove over to my farm.

Every Christmas season, Ron works a highway stand selling trees. There's notoriously little profit in the Christmas-tree business, particularly out in farm country, where people won't pay more that eight or ten dollars for something they could just as easily go out and cut down themselves. And the weather can make the work miserable. Most people, forced to open a stand in order to bring in a few extra bucks at the end of the year, can't help but grumble blackly about how little their efforts are bringing in. They can't help but squeeze every last penny from the venture. Ron, for his part, does need the money, certainly. But he's also sensitive to families who just don't have enough to buy that special tree. He sees the wanting in children's eyes; he reduces prices for some, makes an outright gift for others.

The man is, in short, one of the finest people I know. He puts Christian love into practice, by means of heartfelt friendship and giving until it hurts. I've learned a great deal from this neighbor. Most of all, I've seen proof of the rewards that follow when a person refuses to fall into bitterness and self-interest.

In turn, trying to follow the man's example, I've done what I can for Ron. He leases acreage on my farm, which helps both of us in small ways. In Ron's case, happily, the arrangement means that this former "no-account boy" has found economic security at last. It's the least I can do. For thanks to this good neighbor, I learned what it really means to *care enough to give.*

In the last chapter I provided a variety of examples from my long experience in giving. In every case, as we saw, I didn't merely write a check. Rather, since from the first I've helped support only those ventures and organizations in which I genuinely believed, I've striven to express that belief by giving more than money alone. In this way, again and again I've brought in far more funding (as well as other kinds of help) than I could ever have donated on my own.

Just now, at the end of the century, American colleges, community organizations, and other deserving projects depend more than ever on fundraising to insure growth and a balanced budget. Greater demand for services, higher costs across the board, and ever scarcer government support have combined to drive the demand for more and more private donors—

and to require that those donors really dig deep, making their gifts more of a sacrifice. It became essential, then, that I learn what made people feel that they should give.

It wasn't important that I felt they should give. That much was basic; I wouldn't have become involved if I didn't feel others should give. But I had to learn how to make my enthusiasm contagious. I had to stir others' hearts, change others' minds, and make them give because *they* wanted to.

Quickly I discovered that one of the worst stumbling blocks, in bringing anyone else around to my way of seeing things, was that giving had become synonymous with material goods and money. In most people's minds, giving wasn't giving unless it was solid as hard currency.

This seemed to me to be as bad a misconception as the general manhandling of the concept "success." In Webster's the verb "give" is allied with "sacrifice," "produce," and "bear fruit," among other synonyms. It is in no way limited to tangible, measurable quantities. A person can give from his bank vault or his orchard, yes, but also from his store of time and talents.

The key, I came to believe, was that underlying any kind of treasure passed along there had to be something entirely *intangible*—an emotion. If that emotion were there, then the notion of giving in more than the financial sense would be there. If that emotion were there, in fact, it would be the true gift. And what emotion am I talking about? What could serve so many purposes at once?

A simple thing, really: caring.

A number of years ago I wrote a book entitled *The Gift* which dealt with the why of giving, the lessons I learned about why we give. In it I presented five basic reasons for giving. Briefly, they are:

1. Some contributions are made in order to build up a person's standing in the community: with a friend or with a superior. In this case a person gives to their boss's "pet cause" because it will help insure a solid position with him.

The problem with this kind of giving is that it is selfish. The gift is made with the giver's benefit in mind, rather than anyone else's. A gift that carries the fingerprints of selfishness is a gift devoid of humility.

2. Many gifts are made because we like to see things flourish and grow. We take pride in the beauty and success we help build. The same applies to our wealth. Once a person's fortune grows, and he or she has more

than enough to cover the necessities of life, some of the excess should be committed to others. It is at this stage that one should consider, first, sharing God's good bounty with the neighbor in need.

3. As a gift becomes less practical and more from the heart, heartfelt emotion kicks in naturally. A person begins to feel the need to give, and to empathize with the hardship of those who get the gift.

In other words, God's love is felt where it always is, in the heart—and there it defines the true gift.

4. Probably the best way to visualize this next stage is to think of a king. A king has everything money can buy, and no great incentive to gather more possessions. What he wants most, instead, is to satisfy less easily gratified desires, in particular the longing for fame. He wants his name to pass down through posterity, so that the generations coming after him will have a testament to his importance. He wants his name spoken with reverence, forever and ever, amen. So he endows a temple, a library, an academy—some place in which future generations will be hearing of his generosity long after he's gone.

5. Such a desire for fame can motivate terrific largesse, of course, as it has for the rich and powerful from the kings of the Old Testament right down to contemporary high-rollers. But giving of this kind is again stained with the fingerprints of self-interest. It's by no means reprehensible, and certainly never unwelcome. But the true gift springs out of pure caring; whatever fame follows must be, at first, beside the point.

Thus at every turn, God's love remains demanding. Our Savior doesn't require us to be famous, or to be rich; His commandment, rather, is that we love our neighbor as ourselves. Giving must be at its core a reflection of that love, that caring.

These definitions of giving didn't begin with me. I've mentioned already the kings of the Old Testament, with their temples and their programs to feed the poor. But our present notions of giving derive more directly from the ancient democracy of Greece, in which the wealthiest citizens were expected to enhance the quality of public life by providing funds for public amenities such as baths and meeting places. In fact, the word "philanthropy" is derived from the Greek *philo*, for loving or dear (the root also of "Philadelphia," named for brotherly love), and *anthropos*, man (the root of "anthropology").

That tradition of aristocratic giving was then adopted during the Roman Empire. Hundreds of years later, during the Middle Ages, the Catholic Church was added to kings and noblemen as a source of true giving. The clergy helped establish poorhouses, homes for orphans, centers for study, and hospitals. With the discovery of America, settlers then brought these traditions overseas. Benjamin Franklin, for instance, organized a number of public programs in Philadelphia. And Franklin, like all great community-minded thinkers, changed the rules somewhat. He urged that each citizen, not just the wealthy, aid his fellow man. He argued that everyone had some sort of resource to contribute, some sort of talent or energy that could make the city a better place. And the end of the nineteenth century saw the heyday of American beneficence, when millionaires like Carnegie and Rockerfeller endowed colleges and parks and public facilities across the nation.

In other words, philanthropy has been climbing the centuries. The history that this book has tried to dramatize has provided an ever-expanding definition of human sharing. What my ancestor Lora did for the poor of Warwick during the Black Plague, for example, was improved on by her descendant Robert Beville Armiger. And both their good deeds were topped by the new thinking of the teenaged Ella Boisseau, who freely sacrificed her youthful energies to aid suffering former slaves and Rebel soldiers alike. As for my father, he found at least a dozen previously unthought-of ways of lending support, with his use of Georgia-Pacific stock especially.

Now, in these closing pages, I sound a call for yet another redefinition of giving—yet another improvement in the historical process of brothers and sisters lending one another a hand. The novelist Leo Tolstoy, at the end of his masterpiece *War and Peace*, spent forty pages or so outlining his theory of history and human meaning. Now, if I may, I want to take just another page or so to do the same.

Today, with increasing demands on decreasing resources, it is imperative that we reach another plateau in the value of what we have to offer. Whether we give time, talents, or money, we must raise the stakes. We can no longer afford to say, passively, "Give me a dollar and I will purchase a dollar worth of value." Instead, we have to declare, "Give me a dollar, and I will make it into more than a dollar of value."

There's simply no choice. We must learn to help each other differently and better, if we are to bridge the ever-more-dangerous gap between needs and resources.

L et me offer one final example of what I mean.

In the early 1980s I started a church, the Christ Community Church of Lake Oswego, Oregon. One of its principal functions is to distribute food to relief agencies and children's homes. But I saw a need for more than another reiteration of what was already being done—for more than food drives to collect canned goods and appeals from the pulpit to fill the offertory envelopes. Those in need would derive so much greater benefit, I could see, if they could obtain the same food at a lower cost.

And I raise food myself, down on my Newberg ranch. Indeed, I raise especially *good* food. My beef feed on a blend of grass and alfalfa hay, plus a carefully figured dose of a grain supplement. This program fattens the cattle, but without empty calories; it doesn't add marbling to the meat. And my lower cost allowed me to grind up the whole cow for hamburger. I didn't need to sell separately the higher-priced steaks and rib cuts to reduce costs. So I realized, once I'd begun my church-affiliated food programs, that if the people who Christ Community served needed hamburger, they would have the highest quality money could buy—a hamburger that included all the top cuts.

My meat, in other words, sent a message. It signaled those in need that, just as Christ never gave the poor less than his best, neither would Christ Community Church. The poor, to us as to Him, were never worth less than our utmost. They deserved the highest quality. And, miraculous to speak, my new church was able to do this at well below what other agencies were currently paying for a considerably lower grade of hamburger.

In a similar way, Christ Community worked closely with farmers outside Portland to establish a ready supply of fresh fruits, vegetables, and eggs. Likewise we lined up the services of a bakery. We also approached local canneries, arranging low-cost purchases of dented or mislabeled prod-

Dr. Robert B. Pamplin, Jr., Pastor of Christ Community Church.

ucts. Knowing that relief agencies are always operating on a bare-bones budget themselves, we worked hard to provide as many products as we could at cost of production.

Along with roughly 30,000 pounds of ground beef, each year the church donates dozens of eggs, thousands of jars of peanut butter, tons of potatoes, and thousands of cans of fruit juices and vegetables. Christ Community provides this food absolutely free to some forty Northwest area service agencies, enough to feed 500 people every day. All we ask in return is that the agencies provide counseling to help their clients become independent, productive members of society.

This program has worked so well that, to those working in community service in the Portland area, it even has its own name: "innovative economics." Agencies that in the past had to spend hours and hours simply driving round hunting for food bargains can now devote that time to improving lives by other means.

One last time, then, I repeat my call for a fresh definition of giving. In the shrinking world of the new millennium, humanity must work together as never before, combining old systems and unheard-of innovations, simple flow charts and startling technology. The gap between resource and need, comfortable and needy, haves and have-nots is more threatening than ever, on the brimful planet we share these days. Indeed, these days, almost any working towards the good is a working towards the greater good.

We are all climbing the centuries, all going hand over hand towards the unimaginable future. And we must never forget: out of conflict can come opportunity, and out of concern, creation.

In my book *The Gift*, a man finds life-saving advice in a mysterious way. It comes as a small but beautifully wrapped present. Upon removing the bow and paper, the man finds a wooden box, with a lovely patina that bespeaks both great age and much handling. On its cover are carved several lines of poetry:

> *Man without character*
> *Is lost to the wind,*
> *And without a soul*
> *Only the Devil wears a grin.*
> *Money offers no reprieve,*
> *But the advice found herein*
> *Provides a secret for wealth*
> *And a guard against sin.*

Opening the box, the man finds a frayed and yellowed piece of parchment. Yes, parchment: the ancient rag-based stationery which can last for centuries. The writing on it is likewise very old, a fine, calligraphic script obviously scratched with a quill pen. The message, like the box and the parchment, bears a well-worn smoothness that makes plain it has been offered many times before:

> *My friend, happiness precedes wealth. It will be more important for you to find peace within yourself than to gain all the wealth in the world. You cannot spend peace and happiness. But if you have compassion for the needs of others, your Christian faith will grow and you will build great riches.*

BIBLIOGRAPHY

PART 1

CHAPTER 1:

Fowler, Kenneth. *The Age of Plantagenet and Valois*. Exeter Books, 1980.

Freemantle, Anne. *Age of Faith*. Time, Inc. 1965.

Grousset, Rene. *The Epic of the Crusades*. Orion Press, 1970.

Hallam, Elizabeth. *The Plantagenet Chronicles*. Weidenfeld & Nicholson, 1986.

Howarth, David. *1066—the Year of the Conquest*. Dorset Press, 1977.

Lichliter, Asselia Strobhar. *700 Years of the Beville Family*. McGregor & Werner, 1976.

Runciman, Steve. *A History of the Crusades. Vol. III, the Kingdom of Acre*. Cambridge University Press, 1966.

Strayer, Joseph R., and Munroe, Dana C. *The Middle Ages, 395-1500*. Appleton Century-Crofts, Inc., 1959.

Treece, Henry. *The Crusades*. Random House, 1962.

CHAPTER 2:

Coyne, Michael. *Pamphilon—An Essex Family*. Vine Press, 1992.

Freemantle, Anne. *Age of Faith*. Time, Inc., 1965.

Pamplin, William E. *The Pamplin Family and Connections*. Gateway Press, 1984.

Smith, Frank. *The Lives and Times of Our English Ancestors*. The Everton Publishers, 1974.

Tuchman, Barbara. *A Distant Mirror: The Calamitous 14th Century*. Alfred A. Knopf, 1978.

CHAPTER 3:

Cohen, Daniel. *The Black Death—1347-1351.* F. Watts, 1974.

Day, James. *The Black Death.* Bookwright Press, 1989.

Gottfried, Robert S. *The Black Death: Natural and Human Disaster in Medieval Europe.* Collier Macmillan, 1983.

Lichliter, Asselia Strobhar. *700 Years of the Beville Family.* McGregor & Werner, 1976.

Olesky, Walter F. *The Black Plague.* F. Watts, 1982.

Saul, Nigel. *The Batsford Companion to Medieval England.* Barnes & Noble Books, 1982.

Tuchman, Barbara. *A Distant Mirror: The Calamitous 14th Century.* Alfred A. Knopf, 1978.

CHAPTER 4:

Braudel, Fernand. *The Mediterranean and the Mediterranean World in the Age of Philip II.* 2 vols. Harper & Row, 1977.

Chute, Marchette. *Shakespeare of London.* Dutton, 1949.

Elton, G.R., *Reform & Reformation England, 1509-1558.* Harvard University Press, 1977.

Lichliter, Asselia Strobhar. *700 Years of the Beville Family.* McGregor & Werner, 1976.

Morgan, Kenneth O., *The Oxford Illustrated History of Britian.* Oxford University Press, 1964.

Plowden, Alison. *Elizabeth Regina—the Age of Triumph, 1588-1603.* Times Books, 1980.

Williams, Jay and Baldwin, Lacey. *The Spanish Armada.* American Heritage Publishing, 1966.

CHAPTER 5:

Ashley, Maurice. *Oliver Cromwell.* G.P. Putnam's Sons, 1972.

Barbary, James. *Puritan and Cavalier—the English Civil War.* Thomas Nelson, Inc., 1977.

Braudel, Fernand. *The Mediterranean and the Mediterranean World in the Age of Philip II.* 2 vols. Harper & Row, 1977.

Burne, Alfred H. and Young, Peter. *The Great Civil War—A Military History of the First Civil War, 1642-1646.* Eyre & Spottiswood, 1959.

Hill, Christopher. *Puritans and Revolution.* Secker & Warburg, 1958.

Howell, Roger, Jr. *Cromwell.* Little, Brown, 1977.

Kenyon, J.P. *The Civil Wars of England.* Alfred A. Knopf, 1988.

Lichliter, Asselia Strobhar. *700 Years of the Beville Family.* McGregor & Werner, 1976.

Ollard, Richard. *This War Without an Enemy: A History of the English Civil Wars.* Athenaeum, 1976.

Wedgewood, C.V. *Oliver Cromwell.* Duckworth, 1973.

CHAPTER 6:

Behrens, June and Brower, Pauline. *Colonial Farm.* Regensteiner, 1976.

Fradin, Dennis. *The Virginia Colony.* Regensteiner, 1986.

Gill, Harold B. and Finlayson, Ann. *Colonial Virginia.* Thames Nelson, Inc., 1973.

Jacobsen, Tim. *The Heritage of the South.* Crescent Books, 1992.

Lichliter, Asselia Strobhar. *700 Years of the Beville Family.* McGregor & Werner, 1976.

Randolph, Edmund. *History of Virginia.* University Press of Virginia, 1970 (originally, 1810).

Rubin, Louis D. Jr. *Virginia—A History.* W.W. Norton, 1984.

CHAPTER 7:

Basset, John, ed. *Correspondence of Andrew Jackson.* Carnegie Institution, 1933.

Beirne, Francis F. *The War of 1812.* Archon Books, 1965.

Brooks, Charles B. *The Siege of New Orleans.* University of Washington Press, 1961.

Burke, James. *David Crockett: The Man Behind the Myth.* Eakin Press, 1984.

Cashin, Edward, J. *The Story of Augusta*. Richmond County Historical Society, 1980.

Chidsey, Donald. *The Louisiana Purchase*. Crown, 1972.

Flournoy, Thomas. Papers, U. S. Library of Congress.

Flournoy, Thomas. Papers, 1799-1827, University of Michigan Library.

Garrett, Elizabeth Donaghey. *At Home: The American Family 1750-1870*. Harry N. Abrams, 1990.

Gilbert, Bil. *God Gave Us This Country: Tekamthi and the First American Civil War*. Anchor Books, 1989.

Green, Michael D. *The Politics of Indian Removal: Creek Government and Society in Crisis*. University of Nebraska Press, 1982.

Jacobsen, Tim. *The Heritage of the South*. Crescent Books, 1992.

Lyons, Grant. *The Creek Indians*. Julian Messner, 1978.

Martin, Harold H. *Georgia: A History*. W.W. Norton, 1977.

Northen, William, J. *Men of Mark in Georgia, Vol. VII*. The Reprint Co., 1974 (originally, 1875).

Owsley, Frank, Jr. *Struggle for the Gulf Borderlands: The Creek War and the Battle of New Orleans, 1812-1815*. University of Florida Press, 1981.

Parton, James. *Life of Andrew Jackson*. Mason Brothers, 1860.

Peters, Virginia Bergman. *The Florida Wars*. Archon Books, 1979.

Reilly, Robin. *The British at the Gates: The New Orleans Campaign in the War of 1812*. G.P. Putnam's Sons, 1974.

Rowland, Erin. *Andrew Jackson's Campaign Against the British*. Macmillan & Co., 1926.

Smith, George Gillman. *The Story of Georgia and the Georgia People*. Genealogical Publishing,1968.

Tucker, Glenn. *Poltroons and Patriots: A Popular Account of the War of 1812*. Bobbs-Merrill, 1954.

CHAPTER 8:

Cash, W.J. *The Mind of the South*. Vintage Books, 1941.

Catton, Bruce. *The American Heritage Picture History of the Civil War.* Doubleday, 1960.

Comager, Henry Steele, ed. *The American Destiny: The War Within.* Grollier Enterprises, 1986.

Davis, William C. *The Civil War: Death in the Trenches.* Time-Life Books, 1986.

Diehl, Lilla Gerow. *Tudor Hall and the Boisseau Family.* Privately published, Portland, OR, 1980.

Humphreys, A.A. *The Virginia Campaigns of 1864 and 1865.* Charles Scribner's Sons, 1883.

Jacobsen, Tim. *The Heritage of the South.* Crescent Books, 1992.

Jordan, Robert Paul. *The Civil War.* National Geographic Society, 1969.

Korn, Jerry. *The Civil War: Pursuit to Appomattox.* Time-Life Books, 1987.

McPherson, James M. *Battle Chronicles of the Civil War: 1865.* Macmillan & Co., 1989.

Rubin, Louis D. Jr. *Virginia—A History.* W.W. Norton, 1984.

Ward, Geoffrey C. *The Civil War: An Illustrated History.* Alfred A. Knopf, Inc., 1990.

PART 1, THROUGHOUT:

The Holy Bible, King James Edition, 1611.

Braudel, Fernand. *Civilization and Capitalism.* Harper & Row, 1981.

Lichliter, Asselia Strobhar. *700 Years of the Beville Family.* McGregor & Werner, 1976.

Encyclopedia Brittanica.

PARTS 2 AND 3:

The Holy Bible, American Standard Edition, 1901.

Cash, W.J. *The Mind of the South.* Vintage Books, 1941.

Grund, Francis, J. *Aristocracy in America.* Harper & Brother, 1959.

Pamplin, Robert B. Jr. *Another Virginian: A Study of the Life and Beliefs of Robert Boisseau Pamplin.* R.B. Pamplin Corporation, 1986.

- *Everything is Just Great.* Multnomah Press, 1985
- *The Gift,* Christ Community Church, 1986.
- Papers, R.B. Pamplin Corporation, 1976-1993.

Pamplin, Robert B. Sr. Papers, R.B. Pamplin Corporation, 1976-1993.

Peale, Norman Vincent. *The Power of Positive Thinking.* Prentice-Hall, 1955.

Ross, John, J. *Maverick: The Story of Georgia-Pacfic.* Georgia-Pacific, 1978.

AUTHORS

DR. ROBERT B. PAMPLIN, JR.

Dr. Robert B. Pamplin, Jr. is a businessman, farmer, minister and author of ten books. He has earned eight degrees, including two doctorates, in business, economics, accounting, education and theology. He has served on Presidential and State commissions and as chairman of two colleges. Dr. Pamplin has been awarded several honorary degrees, received the Distinguished Leadership Medal from Freedoms Foundation at Valley Forge, and the National Caring Award from the Caring Institute.

GARY K. EISLER

Gary Eisler is an award-winning writer whose works have appeared in *Forbes* magazine, *The Wall Street Journal* and elsewhere. A former newspaper editor, publisher and media consultant, he is also currently involved in forestry and springwater production.

JEFF SENGSTACK

Jeff Sengstack is a writer and video producer who recently concluded an 11-year career as an Emmy Award-winning television news reporter and anchorman. He also helped start and taught at a high school for dropouts, and served as marketing director for an educational music publisher.

JOHN DOMINI

John Domini is the author of *Bedlam*, short stories, and coauthor of *The Encyclopedic Dictionary of English Usage*, a textbook. His fiction and non-fiction has appeared in *The New York Times*, *Paris Review*, and elsewhere. He has taught at Harvard and Lewis & Clark College and is currently at Linfield College.

PHOTOGRAPHY

Pages 81 and 107
Terry Glover

Pages 334, 350, and 510
Bob Veltri, Virginia Tech.

Page 453
Creative Photography

Additional copies of *Heritage* may be ordered by sending a check for $24.95 (please add the following for postage and handling: $2.00 for the first copy, $1.00 for each additional copy) to:

MasterMedia Limited
17 East 89th Street
New York, NY 10128
(212) 260-5600
(800) 334-8232 *please use Mastercard or Visa on 1-800 orders*

OTHER MASTERMEDIA BOOKS

THE PREGNANCY AND MOTHERHOOD DIARY: Planning the First Year of Your Second Career, by Susan Schiffer Stautberg, is the first and only undated appointment diary that shows how to manage pregnancy and career. ($12.95 spiralbound)

CITIES OF OPPORTUNITY: Finding the Best Place to Work, Live and Prosper in the 1990's and Beyond, by Dr. John Tepper Marlin, explores the job and living options for the next decade and into the next century. This consumer guide and handbook, written by one of the world's experts on cities, selects and features forty-six American cities and metropolitan areas. ($13.95 paper, $24.95 cloth)

THE DOLLARS AND SENSE OF DIVORCE, by Dr. Judith Briles, is the first book to combine practical tips on overcoming the legal hurdles by planning finances before, during, and after divorce. ($10.95 paper)

OUT THE ORGANIZATION: New Career Opportunities for the 1990's, by Robert and Madeleine Swain, is written for the millions of Americans whose jobs are no longer safe, whose companies are not loyal, and who face futures of uncertainty. It gives advice on finding a new job or starting your own business. ($12.95 paper)

AGING PARENTS AND YOU: A Complete Handbook to Help You Help Your Elders Maintain a Healthy, Productive and Independent Life, by Eugenia Anderson-Ellis, is a complete guide to providing care to aging relatives. It gives practical advice and resources to the adults who are helping their elders lead productive and independent lives. Revised and updated. ($9.95 paper)

CRITICISM IN YOUR LIFE: How to Give It, How to Take It, How to Make It Work for You, by Dr. Deborah Bright, offers practical advice, in an upbeat, readable, and realistic fashion, for turning criticism into control.

Charts and diagrams guide the reader into managing criticism from bosses, spouses, children, friends, neighbors, in-laws, and business relations. ($17.95 cloth)

BEYOND SUCCESS: How Volunteer Service Can Help You Begin Making a Life Instead of Just a Living, by John F. Raynolds III and Eleanor Raynolds, C.B.E., is a unique how-to book targeted at business and professional people considering volunteer work, senior citizens who wish to fill leisure time meaningfully, and students trying out various career options. The book is filled with interviews with celebrities, CEOs, and average citizens who talk about the benefits of service work. ($19.95 cloth)

MANAGING IT ALL: Time-Saving Ideas for Career, Family, Relationships, and Self, by Beverly Benz Treuille and Susan Schiffer Stautberg, is written for women who are juggling careers and families. Over two hundred career women (ranging from a TV anchorwoman to an investment banker) were interviewed. The book contains many humorous anecdotes on saving time and improving the quality of life for self and family. ($9.95 paper)

YOUR HEALTHY BODY, YOUR HEALTHY LIFE: How to Take Control of Your Medical Destiny, by Donald B. Louria, M.D., provides precise advice and strategies that will help you to live a long and healthy life. Learn also about nutrition, exercise, vitamins, and medication, as well as how to control risk factors for major diseases. Revised and updated. ($12.95 paper)

THE CONFIDENCE FACTOR: How Self-Esteem Can Change Your Life, by Dr. Judith Briles, is based on a nationwide survey of six thousand men and women. Briles explores why women so often feel a lack of self-confidence and have a poor opinion of themselves. She offers step-by-step advice on becoming the person you want to be. ($9.95 paper, $18.95 cloth)

THE SOLUTION TO POLLUTION: 101 Things You Can Do to Clean Up Your Environment, by Laurence Sombke, offers step-by-step techniques on how to conserve more energy, start a recycling center, choose biodegradable products, and even proceed with individual environmental cleanup projects. ($7.95 paper)

Other MasterMedia Books

TAKING CONTROL OF YOUR LIFE: The Secrets of Successful Enterprising Women, by Gail Blanke and Kathleen Walas, is based on the authors' professional experience with Avon Products' Women of Enterprise Awards, given each year to outstanding women entrepreneurs. The authors offer a specific plan to help you gain control over your life, and include business tips and quizzes as well as beauty and lifestyle information. ($17.95 cloth)

SIDE-BY-SIDE STRATEGIES: How Two-Career Couples Can Thrive in the Nineties, by Jane Hershey Cuozzo and S. Diane Graham, describes how two-career couples can learn the difference between competing with a spouse and becoming a supportive power partner. Published in hardcover as *Power Partners.* ($10.95 paper, $19.95 cloth)

DARE TO CONFRONT! How to Intervene When Someone You Care About Has an Alcohol or Drug Problem, by Bob Wright and Deborah George Wright, shows the reader how to use the step-by-step methods of professional interventionists to motivate drug-dependent people to accept the help they need. ($17.95 cloth)

WORK WITH ME! How to Make the Most of Office Support Staff, by Betsy Lazary, shows you how to find, train, and nurture the "perfect" assistant and how to best utilize your support staff professionals. ($9.95 paper)

MANN FOR ALL SEASONS: Wit and Wisdom from The Washington Post's *Judy Mann,* by Judy Mann, shows the columnist at her best as she writes about women, families, and the impact and politics of the women's revolution. ($9.95 paper, $19.95 cloth)

THE SOLUTION TO POLLUTION IN THE WORKPLACE, by Laurence Sombke, Terry M. Robertson and Elliot M. Kaplan, supplies employees with everything they need to know about cleaning up their workspace, including recycling, using energy efficiently, conserving water and buying recycled products and nontoxic supplies. ($9.95 paper)

THE ENVIRONMENTAL GARDENER: The Solution to Pollution for Lawns and Gardens, by Laurence Sombke, focuses on what each of us can do to protect our endangered plant life. A practical sourcebook and shopping guide. ($8.95 paper)

THE LOYALTY FACTOR: Building Trust in Today's Workplace, by Carol Kinsey Goman, Ph.D., offers techniques for restoring commitment and loyalty in the workplace. ($9.95 paper)

DARE TO CHANGE YOUR JOB—AND YOUR LIFE, by Carole Kanchier, Ph.D., provides a look at career growth and development throughout the life cycle. ($9.95 paper)

MISS AMERICA: In Pursuit of the Crown, by Ann-Marie Bivans, is an authorized guidebook to the Pageant, containing eyewitness accounts, complete historical data, and a realistic look at the trials and triumphs of the potential Miss Americas. ($19.95 paper, $27.50 cloth)

POSITIVELY OUTRAGEOUS SERVICE: New and Easy Ways to Win Customers for Life, by T. Scott Gross, identifies what the consumers of the nineties really want and how businesses can develop effective marketing strategies to answer those needs. ($14.95 paper)

BREATHING SPACE: Living and Working at a Comfortable Pace in a Sped-Up Society, by Jeff Davidson, helps readers to handle information and activity overload, and gain greater control over their lives. ($10.95 paper)

TWENTYSOMETHING: Managing and Motivating Today's New Work Force, by Lawrence J. Bradford, Ph.D., and Claire Raines, M.A., examines the work orientation of the younger generation, offering managers in businesses of all kinds a practical guide to better understand and supervise their young employees. ($22.95 cloth)

REAL LIFE 101: The Graduate's Guide to Survival, by Susan Kleinman, supplies welcome advice to those facing "real life" for the first time, focusing on work, money, health, and how to deal with freedom and responsibility. ($9.95 paper)

Other MasterMedia Books

BALANCING ACTS! Juggling Love, Work, Family, and Recreation, by Susan Schiffer Stautberg and Marcia L. Worthing, provides strategies to achieve a balanced life by reordering priorities and setting realistic goals. ($12.95 paper)

REAL BEAUTY . . . REAL WOMEN: A Handbook for Making the Best of Your Own Good Looks, by Kathleen Walas, International Beauty and Fashion Director of Avon Products, offers expert advice on beauty and fashion to women of all ages and ethnic backgrounds. ($19.50 paper)

THE LIVING HEART BRAND NAME SHOPPER'S GUIDE, by Michael E. DeBakey, M.D., Antonio M. Gotto, Jr., M.D., D.Phil., Lynne W. Scott, M.A., R.D./L.D., and John P. Foreyt, Ph.D., lists brand-name supermarket products that are low in fat, saturated fatty acids, and cholesterol. ($12.50 paper)

MANAGING YOUR CHILD'S DIABETES, by Robert Wood Johnson IV, Sale Johnson, Casey Johnson, and Susan Kleinman, brings help to families trying to understand diabetes and control its effects. ($10.95 paper)

STEP FORWARD: Sexual Harassment in the Workplace, What You Need to Know, by Susan L. Webb, presents the facts for identifying the tell-tale signs of sexual harassment on the job, and how to deal with it. ($9.95 paper)

A TEEN'S GUIDE TO BUSINESS: The Secrets to a Successful Enterprise, by Linda Menzies, Oren S. Jenkins, and Rickell R. Fisher, provides solid information about starting your own business or working for one. ($7.95 paper)

GLORIOUS ROOTS: Recipes for Healthy, Tasty Vegetables, by Laurence Sombke, celebrates the taste, texture, and versatility of root vegetables. Contains recipes for appetizers, soups, stews, and baked, boiled, and stir-fried dishes—even desserts. ($12.95 paper)

THE OUTDOOR WOMAN: A Handbook to Adventure, by Patricia Hubbard and Stan Wass, details the lives of adventurous outdoor women and offers their ideas on how you can incorporate exciting outdoor experiences into your life. ($14.95 paper)

FLIGHT PLAN FOR LIVING: The Art of Self-Encouragement, by Patrick O'Dooley, is a life guide organized like a pilot's flight checklist, which ensures you'll be flying "clear on top" throughout your life. ($17.95 cloth)

HOW TO GET WHAT YOU WANT FROM ALMOST ANYBODY, by T. Scott Gross, shows how to get great service, negotiate better prices, and always get what you pay for. ($9.95 paper)

TEAMBUILT: Making Teamwork Work, by Mark Sanborn, teaches business how to improve productivity, without increasing resources or expenses, by building teamwork among employers. ($19.95 cloth)

THE BIG APPLE BUSINESS AND PLEASURE GUIDE: 501 Ways to Work Smarter, Play Harder, and Live Better in New York City, by Muriel Siebert and Susan Kleinman, offers visitors and New Yorkers alike advice on how to do business in the city as well as how to enjoy its attractions. ($9.95 paper)